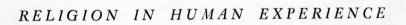

RELIGION IN HUMAN EXPERIENCE

JOHN R. EVERETT

Columbia University

RELIGION

IN HUMAN

EXPERIENCE

AN INTRODUCTION

New York

HENRY HOLT AND COMPANY

Copyright 1950 by Henry Holt and Company, Inc.

Designed by Maurice Serle Kaplan

Printed in the United States of America

For
BETTY *and* PEGGY
with affection and thanks

PREFACE

Anyone familiar with the field of religion is well aware of the trepidation an author feels when a book on the subject goes to press. Religion means so many things to so many people; and when religious convictions are held, they are usually extremely private. For anyone on the outside to presume to describe them often seems the height of blasphemy. And, for the most part, it is.

Yet books on religion are necessary. Whether we know it or not, we live in a religious world, and we are charged to deal with the facts of our world. This book is written for those who wish at least an introduction into the hopes, fears, aspirations, joys and ideals which go to make up religion.

There are many types of books on religion. Some have as their avowed purpose the creation and fortification of pious conviction. These books are written sermons and form an important part of the traditions they represent. Other books, and this is one, try to increase the reader's knowledge of the world in which he lives. Such a book is not a sermon and will not serve any devotional purpose. It will, or so the author hopes, make it possible better to understand fellow human beings and the cultures they create. It is further hoped that it will lead to a deeper self-understanding through affording a means by which the reader may examine his own religious feelings and ideas.

Any book on religion must necessarily leave out a great

[vii]

deal of important material. All the facts of human experience are meaningful, and conscientious interpreters feel duty-bound to gather and understand as many as possible. But space requirements impose limitations. Further, too much detail about too many religions tends to confuse and bewilder those who seek an introduction to such a vast and complicated field.

The material included in this book has been selected with an eye to the variety of religious life and to the insistent problems which constantly arise in the minds of interpreters. Four major traditions are considered in some detail: Hinduism, Buddhism, Judaism and Christianity. Two of these, Hinduism and Judaism, are parent religions from which two great world-conquering religions, Buddhism and Christianity, are born. The parent religions have had a history quite different from that of their issue. Hinduism and Judaism spring from a very dim past; their earliest records give little indication of their actual historic origins. On the other hand, Buddhism and Christianity are comparatively late, and our knowledge of them is correspondingly less clouded.

Some religions belong to a specific geographic area and to particular national groups. Such traditions do not seek new converts through missionary activity; they are usually content with an internal growth. In general, Hinduism and Judaism are religions of this type. Neither has ever tried to conquer the world, and only for short periods has any significant number of their adherents been concerned to convert peoples of other faiths and national origins. Buddhism and Christianity, on the other hand, have made their respective ways in the world by invasion and conversion. Today the centers of strength for both lie far from the countries of their birth. Thus, in a study of these four religions, we find a good comparison of national and universal religions, and are able to discern in clearer outline their differences and similarities.

A further consideration which influenced this selection is the fact that neither Hinduism nor Judaism has founders who were or are considered divine beings, whereas both Buddhism and Christianity do. This difference creates a second interesting comparative study of religious consciousness and experience.

It is, of course, quite impossible to consider any of these traditions as an unrelated phenomenon. As Buddhism expanded throughout Asia, it was constantly battling and then absorbing such indigenous religions as Confucianism, Tibetan Pön, Taoism and Shinto. Hinduism broke up into many groups and produced heretical new religions such as Jainism. Judaism was part parent of Islam, which for a time threatened the very existence of the Judeo-Christian tradition. And Christianity was profoundly influenced by Greek mystery cults, Manicheism, and Nordic and Slavic mythology. All these influences and offshoots are considered, but they are not given positions of special importance. The necessity of limiting the discussion has here had to take precedence over the intrinsic power and interest of these slighted traditions.

The most notable omission of this kind is the small space accorded Islam. Mohammed and his followers come into the story at two points—in the discussions of Judaism and Christianity—but Islam is considered only as it is related to the developments of these traditions. However, the reader can be consoled by the knowledge that most of the major religious ideas to be found in Islam are treated in the specific traditions of our study. The same can be said for the non-Hindu and non-Buddhist faiths of the East.

Primitive religions as such have also been excluded from systematic treatment, although the essential material of this anthropological research is incorporated in the first section and in the discussion of the major traditions. It is hoped that this means of using these highly technical researches will be a considerable aid in gaining a comprehensive understanding of religion.

A word should be said about the glossary and bibliography which appear at the end of the book. Both are highly selective. The glossary includes terms and concepts which teaching experience has shown to be the most easily confused and forgotten. It is offered as a convenient aid in reading the book, but not as a comprehensive dictionary of religious terms. The bibliography is a layman's guide to authoritative literature which is readily available in American libraries. It is not intended to be of much service to the research scholar.

What errors there are are wholly mine, although I have done all I know to avoid them. I wish to thank particularly Professors Herbert W. Schneider and Horace Friess of Columbia for reading parts of the manuscript. Their advice was invaluable. Most especially I wish to express my debt to the students of Wesleyan University, Middletown, Connecticut, for submitting to innumerable questions and to the course from which this book grew. Without their help I would never have known what to include. To the others with whom I have talked and from whom I have received so much aid, my most heartfelt thanks.

My greatest debt is to my wife, Elizabeth Sloan Everett. She made English out of my sentences and required me to clear up my confusions. By rights she should be listed as co-author.

J. R. E.

Columbia University
March 24, 1950

TABLE OF CONTENTS

I. NATURE OF RELIGION

II. HINDUISM

INTRODUCTION

[xi]

CONTENTS

III. THE EXPANSION OF BUDDHISM

CONTENTS

IV. THE HEBREW TRADITION

CONTENTS

[xv]

CONTENTS

LIST OF ILLUSTRATIONS

[xvii]

I

NATURE OF RELIGION

1

WHAT IS RELIGION?

RELIGION has been defined in so many different ways and for so many different purposes that even the most conscientious student feels confused. Our newspapers often refer to religion as "the true basis for morality"; many psychologists call it the "mythical complex surrounding a projected super-ego"; Marxian communists refer to religion as "the opiate of the people"; philosophers sometimes call it "a superstitious structure of incoherent metaphysical notions"; pulpit orators call it "man's search for the highest life"; some sociologists call it the "collective expression of human values"—and so the definitions go in endless procession. Each generation seems to define it in its own way, and each investigator is inclined to see it solely through the frame of his own limited investigation.

Confusing as these multifarious definitions are, they serve at least one excellent purpose. Their very existence points to the extremely complex nature of that phenomenon commonly called Religion. No single scholar has ever been able to encompass its entirety, and no single student has ever been able to exhaust the field. As soon as a definition is reached, some new fact intrudes which forces its revision. This is certainly one good reason for the perennial interest in the problems of religion.

The term *religion*, like *science*, *culture* and *history*, designates an area of human concern which has vague and constantly changing boundaries. Yet, for the most part, we know what we mean when the word is used. We know, for example, that religious services usually take place in a church or temple and not in a physics laboratory or an art studio. We know further that certain things are considered sacred, and others profane. During the last war, for example, the bombing of a business building did not seem as wrong, somehow, as the bombing of a church. And most people, even though they did not belong to the particular faith involved, would be quite shocked to see a young man and his girl sitting on an altar drinking cocktails and crushing their cigarettes on the head of a statue of the Virgin Mary. In a general sense, there exists a common knowledge about the things and activities belonging to religion. In the particulars, there is a stupendous ignorance.

RELIGION AND PHILOSOPHY

ONE of the most common confusions of this enlightened age pertains to the relation between religion and philosophy. Religion is not philosophy any more than politics is political science. There is such an enterprise as the philosophy *of* religion, and there are religious philosophies. The latter are technically *theologies*, but the term *religious philosophy* is now so widely used as to be almost a synonym. Before embarking upon a detailed study of religion, we should have clearly in mind that we are not pursuing a course in philosophy.

Philosophy can be very generally defined as the attempt rationally to understand the universe and man's relation to it. The key word in this definition is "rationally." By the use of reason, unaided by revelation or authority other than itself, philosophy tries to make sense out of experience. The philosopher is concerned to analyze and speculate. He tries to mold man's chaotic, jumbled and disparate experiences into a comprehensive whole which will satisfy the tests set up by a rigorous logic. If the philosopher is to build a real system, he must take account of all experience, even though he himself might consider one aspect of life to be normative. His basic duty is to solve in a rational fashion the problems posed by existence.

The religious man, on the other hand, is not trying to solve problems, he is not even trying to bring the chaos of life into an orderly whole; he is reacting to what he feels to be ultimate in the universe. He is worshiping, feeling and experiencing that which he will later call divine. But at the point of religious experience his attitude is not one of reflection, and his purpose is not theoretical construction. These, perhaps, will come eventually, but at the moment of religiosity he is totally involved in a direct experience which is unmediated by his intellect. Philosophy, then, is a theory about experience, while religion is itself a particular type of experience.

The philosophy of religion attempts to make a rational connection between the primary religious experience and an understanding of all experience. Many philosophers have been so impressed with the overpowering nature of religious experience that in their systems they have made it normative for everything else. These philosophies, which are usually called *theisms*, view all of life as a divinely ordered sequence. Their god or gods control the destinies of all living things as well as the various elements which comprise the inanimate world. To other philosophers, the religious experience is a psychological phenomenon which can be explained in purely natural terms. In such systems the reported experiences of the divine tell us something about the nature of the human animal, but nothing about the ultimate nature of the cosmos. There is no denial that religious experiences occur, but at the same time the interpretation given them leads to no conclusion regarding the ontological existence of god or gods. Religious experience is to be explained by psychology in concert with sociology. These philosophies are usually non-theistic naturalisms.

No matter what kind of philosophical interpretation one gives to religious experience, the fact of religion cannot be denied. There is no culture known to man in which there is not some form of religion. Its origin, like the origin of so many things, is lost in man's unrecorded past. However it is explained or understood, it has a past, it has a present, and it undoubtedly has a future.

RELIGION AND THEOLOGY

Just as religion and philosophy must be separated, so must religion and theology. Theology utilizes the tools of philosophy, especially reason and logic, to extend and work out the implications of a particular religious experience. Philosophies which consider religious experience normative never limit themselves to one special religious tradition. Rather, they search out the essence of religion from all of its various manifestations, the most primitive, as well as, the most civilized. If, however, one particular religious experience is made normative, the result is theology and not philosophy.

Theology and religion work closely together, and some commentators maintain that they are mutually dependent. It is certainly true that there could be no theology without religious experience. The whole theological structure comes out of the primary experience which is defined as religious. But it is also true that theologies perpetuate particular religious experiences by crystallizing them into special word formations which can be passed down from generation to generation. As a result, people who are taught certain specific theological propositions tend to identify their own religious experiences with those which have been given verbal formulation by the theologians. The result is so continuous an interplay between theology and religion that often the two become synonymous. When it is recognized, however, that religious experience exists prior to theological interpretation, it becomes clear that theology is secondary rather than primary.

Within theological systems there is no argument about the actual religious experience. All disagreement is centered in logical problems of extension and practical problems of application. Christian theologies, for example, are not concerned to prove the primacy of the experience of God through Christ; rather, they direct their energies toward an attempt to show how this experience means salvation, or how it gives a special knowledge of God, or how it requires man to engage in certain very specific worship practices, or a variety of like subjects. When the Bible is considered to be the revelation of God to man, then all theological statements must be in essential accord with it. And each of the different theologies will claim that it is more nearly in accord with the Biblical revelation than any of the others. Ultimately the disputes within any given tradition are settled by proof-texts and the usual philosophic canons of logical consistency. As we shall see, many difficulties arise when the meaning of the revelation is unclear; and since most revelations in the various religious traditions are ambiguous, there is limitless opportunity for theological construction.

The main task of any given theology is to link the religious experience of the adherents of one particular tradition with the other aspects of their lives. For the Buddhist, theology must explain why material desire is evil and why prayer before the Buddha statue is good. Christian theology must point out to Christians the nature of their social responsibilities and the necessity for a pure heart. The theologians in these two different traditions have no reason to be in agreement, nor should they be worried about disagreement. Each is performing a necessary service for his own tradition, not for another. To be asocial and withdraw from society is a prerequisite for salvation in some Buddhist theologies; such withdrawal is a passport to hell in many Christian systems. Theology's job is particular and definite. It can lay no claim to universality.

This does not mean that the theologian is unconcerned with building universal systems. Most usually he maintains that the religious experience and revelation which undergirds his thought is universally valid and that it should be the norm for all thought and speculation. On the basis of his authoritative documents he explains how the entire world was created, why other religions are superstitious mythologies, what the end of the world will be like for all mankind, and how all men should act while they are transient guests in this world. This claim of universality is sometimes due to sheer provincialism, sometimes to a confusion between philosophy and theology, and sometimes to the overpowering conviction that a particular revelation and a specific religious experience are the last and final word from the Absolute Creator of the Universe. In the latter case the theologian usually denies that there is any possibility of an independent philosophy; all thinking and speculation, he maintains, must be grounded in his particular faith. For those, however, who would make an unrestricted study of religion, such a position is untenable.

The history of philosophy is full of philosophers who claim to have arrived at the conclusions of a particular theology by the use of unaided reason. Wherever such philosophies occur, and we will see many, they must be judged by philosophical rather than religious standards. Western scholasticism and Indian Upanishadic philosophy are the two most outstanding examples. All of the thinkers who fall within these rubrics feel that religiously motivated theology and rationally motivated philosophy can and will come to the same truths if each rigorously follows its own particular method. For these and many other thinkers there is no ultimate conflict between reason and religion.

RELIGION AND ETHICS

ONE of the most insistent confusions of the modern mind is between religion and ethics. Matthew Arnold was guilty of this common misconception, and reveals it when he defines religion as "morality touched with emotion." Such a definition is possible only within the context of an advanced religion, and even then it is inaccurate. If we are to consider the entire range and variety of religious forms, his statement becomes doubly implausible.

Ethics concerns itself with man's moral relations and his specific definitions of right and wrong. In very primitive cultures such a concern is more often than not completely divorced from what we would commonly call religion. The religious practices of the primitive are devoted to an expression of dependence upon a power or powers lying beyond human control. Such dependence may be associated with fear, or it may be the fruit of a gripping experience of nonnatural power. In any case the impression upon the soul of the primitive is not one of superior goodness, but simply one of overwhelmingly superior power. This superior power of the nonnatural beings affects all of life, and therefore it must be dealt with in the proper fashion. Since these controlling spirits have many human characteristics, they can often be cheated, lied to, and surreptitiously disobeyed.

Primitive religious ceremonies are often devised to beg, cajole and deceive the nonnatural power or powers. A common ceremony is a sacred dance which figures prominently in preparations for war. It entails no humble prayer requesting supernatural aid because the cause is just and right. Rather, the dances are usually designed to whip the warriors into a fury of excitement with the conviction that certain stylized actions have a sacred and mysterious potency. In this instance the nonnatural powers are being bought with a ceremonial price. Sacred objects such as stones, trees, and even the cooking utensils of chiefs and medicine men are often thought to possess religious meaning and divine potency. If the *taboos* regarding these objects are recognized and respected, the person concerned will avoid misfortune and reprisal. If proper respect is not forthcoming, punishment will be meted out by the inexorable law of the sacred. The respect is not accorded because the nonnatural powers or even the resulting actions are good, but simply because powerful spirits are present. Most of the appeals made to these spirits have nothing to do with offerings of goodness, charity, justice and love; they are more commonly made through flatteries and bribes.

In a religious tradition of this kind, ethical concerns are conspicuous by their absence. But this does not mean that primitive communities have no ethical rules or moral standards. There are innumerable customary procedures which define right and wrong and which carry with them established punishments and rewards. Some of the most important regulations have nonnatural sanctions, but by far the larger number are enforceable only through the natural channels of communal authority. If one is to take the study of primitive cultures seriously, it is clear that ethics and religion have two different sources. One is born out of a feeling of dependence upon nonnatural power, while the other results from a response to natural social situations.

As cultures advance beyond their primitive beginnings, religion and ethics tend to coalesce. From the outset both areas are concerned with matters of conduct, although in separate spheres. As the nonnatural powers become intimates of the community, the chief of the tribe becomes divine, and the line between ritualistic practice and ethical conduct blurs. The chief becomes responsible for enforcing the rules pertaining to both. Soon the current laws regarding the protection of life, property and the family are considered sacred. Truthfulness, fidelity, kindliness, love, justice and mercy, all of which are necessary for the successful operation of a community, are first approved and then demanded by the particular deity or deities. As the society matures, its ethical ideals change in detail. Advanced religions usually content themselves with an insistence upon the divine authority of certain principles regardless of innovations in application. At one time both slavery and polygamy were sanctioned by religions which now condemn them. Social development produced new and different conceptions of justice and fidelity; and religion changed not its emphasis upon justice and fidelity, but its appraisal of particular institutional embodiments.

Ethical religion is largely the result of a tendency to interpret all of life as being fraught with ritualistic meaning. God or the gods extend their influence from a few localized objects or situations to the whole range of human activity and concern. The world comes to be understood as the result of some divine cause, and its history as a pattern of divine purpose. When this stage is reached, all of man's activities have cosmic meaning, and the fusion of ethics and religion is complete. As we will see, however, this sort of religion derives from a long process of development and cultural growth.

From the most rudimentary to the most advanced association of ethics and religion, religious conviction furnishes an earnestness and an intensity not found in ethics alone. The martyr who allows himself to be burned at the stake because he recognizes his duty to God expresses a depth of conviction that is rare among the nonreligious. The saint attains a height of moral excellence not because society requests observance of certain rules and regulations, but because his commitment to God makes life impossible if divorced from the holy will. Although neither the martyr nor the saint adds any new detail to the ethical code, they both embody the force and power of religious commitment. Religion and ethics must never be considered as one; but at the same time we should realize how immeasurably they gain by fusion.

RELIGION AND CULTURE

Just as religion must be carefully distinguished from philosophy, theology and ethics, so it must be recognized as a part, but not the totality of culture. In many cases, as we shall see, religion provides the particular and peculiar characteristic which distinguishes one culture from another; nevertheless it always remains a segment of the much larger total culture. E. B. Tyler, an eminent anthropologist, once designated culture as "that complex whole which includes knowledge, belief, art, morals, law, custom and any other capabilities and habits acquired by man as a member of a society." The extremely varied phenomena which constitute religion are simply a part of the complex which constitutes culture.

Any given culture is divided into two general parts—the physical and the spiritual. The physical aspect of culture includes all the tools and equipment which the people of a society use to achieve their goals. Artistic creations such as buildings, paintings, musical scores and the like are physical monuments in a particular culture. Books, clothing, means of transportation, machines for manufacture, agricultural implements are even more clearly classified in the purely physical category. All these are in some sense an expression of the knowledge and belief which a given society possesses. The ability to manufacture articles is first of all an ability to understand the laws and probabilities by which nature operates; the creation of cathedrals and temples results from a particular kind of religious belief; and the existence of books testifies to an intelligence operating prior to the printed page. The same, of course, can be said for all artistic productions.

The greatest part by far of any cultural tradition receives no direct physical embodiment. Its moral customs, legal codes and religious beliefs may be the inspiration for churches, halls of justice and books; but certainly only a fragment of their reality and power can be crystallized in physical form. The ceaseless activity of the human mind and the never-ending quest of the human spirit constantly produce attitudes and understandings which must live in the hearts and minds of men. When they are generally accepted, such attitudes and understandings become social institutions. Just as a college, a church or a state is far greater than the buildings which house it, so all institutions are spiritual rather than physical constructs. It is in the institutions of a culture that one discovers the fundamental realities upon which that culture's physical creations are built.

The basic institutions of society grow out of four fundamental experiences. The experience of blood relations living together produces the institution of the *family*; the experience of a larger group working for common ends which require common rules and enforceable regulations issues in that institution known as the *state*; the *economy*, the third major institution, results from the corporate social experience of getting and spending; and the *church* is the institutional embodiment of common religious experience. These are obviously not all of the cultural institutions man has created, but they do seem to be the most durable. As far as one can judge from the evidence at hand, no culture exists without them. The peripheral institutions which attach themselves to these fundamental four come and go with varying degrees of permanence. Consequently, if we are to define culture in its essence, we must look to the persistent spiritual structures.

Each of these four institutions is in some sense imperialistic. The histories of culture are full of serious and often bloody attempts on the part of the family to control all economic, political and religious life. In certain matriarchal and patriarchal societies, the head of the family or clan defines not only the proper political and economic relationships, but religious belief and practice as well. Very often a state has tried to break the hold of the family, church and economy in its effort to gain absolute control over the welfare and destinies of its citizens. Certainly no one familiar with modern totalitarian regimes can doubt the imperialistic fervor of power-minded states. In various instances the economy also has tried to control the total life of man. At many periods of history, the church, state and family have all been mere handmaidens in the effort to get and spend. And finally, the church, like the rest, has tried to exercise complete and final control over the lives of its people.

If we look back in history we can discover with little difficulty outstanding examples of cultural control by any one of these institutions. The most all-pervasive early institution is usually found to be religion. Probably the oldest tribunal for settling disputes was the church. As the representative of the local deity, the priest was considered to be on more intimate terms than anyone else with all nonnatural powers. The superior force of these powers gave corresponding weight to the priest's authority. As the ritualistic and ethical phases of conduct became fused, the administration of justice together with all its prerogatives of reward and punishment fell to the religious organization. Thus the laws of the state became sacred laws, and the state itself became an instrument of the divine will.

Religion took control not only of the state but also of the family. In predominantly religious cultures, the family came to be a sacred institution regulated by the church and its priests. Sexual ethics were established as divine rules, and deviations from the norm became sins. Religion sanctioned certain types of marriage relations with regulations governing the union with relatives and members of other tribes. The responsibility for children was assigned to either the wife or the husband, and in some cases to both. In religious marriage ceremonies, parents were made responsible for bringing up their children with definite instruction in orthodox religious beliefs. In all of the complex sexual and familial relationships, religion established the rules and the church and state enforced them. Specific sins were identified, catalogued and labeled with appropriate punishments for this life and the life hereafter. Throughout, the primary concern of the family was creating and maintaining a favorable relationship with whatever nonnatural powers the priests declared to be important. In such a situation the family obviously lost its independent institutional existence and became a segment of the everwidening province of religion. In effect the family became a religious organization with a concrete religious foundation and definite religious goals.

Within cultures of this kind, art, literature, science and philosophy all tended to become the servants of religion. Astronomy, one of the oldest of sciences, was long utilized by religion as a means for determining divine will and therefore as part of the basis for theological dogmatizing. The currently important literature consisted of hymns, prayers, stories about the god or gods—in short, instruments for worship. Decorative art and architecture gave their greatest talent to the interests of religion. Philosophy and theology were identical, and like all the rest, completely in the service of religion. Since disease was looked upon as punishment for sin, medicine was largely a matter of expelling evil spirits from the body, and doctors and priests were often indistinguishable. In all the activities of life, religion was the dominant factor. The institution of religion determined the content and direction of every human concern.

Naturally the getting and spending of wealth was also under the thumb of religion. Priests often decided upon the "just price" for an article, either manufactured or produced out of the land. Regulations concerning the use of property, the rights of ownership, the ability to transfer ownership from one generation to the next and a host of other economic questions were promulgated and enforced by religion. Laws of charity and philanthropic obligations were taught as being the direct commandments of the nonnatural powers. Just as happened with regard to the other basic institutions of life, economic activity was directed toward religious ends and given religious meaning.

When religion becomes as all-pervasive as this, it is possible to speak of a distinctly religious culture. Historically, such a situation has proved unstable, and religious cultures have given way to realignment. Sometimes it has been the state which tried to break loose first; other times either the family or the economy has supplied the revolutionary power. In any case religion, no different from other institutions, has fought valiantly and violently to preserve its hegemony. Religious wars have studded all cultures, and various means short of war are constantly being used to mediate this problem of power. But in spite of such tenacious resistance, culture is dynamic, and differentiation and reunification seem always to be the natural process.

The very presence of religion as a persistent cultural institution indicates its social nature. Religious ideas, like ideas in other areas, are transmitted from generation to generation by both the oral and written word. Certain experiences which members of a new generation undergo are interpreted for them by their elders. The structure of interpretation for religious experience is thus transferred from one generation to the next relatively intact. But such transference could not be made lacking a group or cult with a sufficient number of members to control a fairly large segment of the formal and informal educational program. In effect, the cult answers questions before they arise and gives the child a foundation upon which he can base his reaction to the persistent human problems he will inevitably encounter. In this fashion, within any given culture, the institution of religion perpetuates itself.

The efficacy of this perpetuation is largely dependent upon the continuing ability of the past tradition to give meaningful answers to the problems of the present. The history of religions is filled with the wrecks of discarded ideas and systems of interpretation. A religion which is born and receives its essential character structure from a pastoral people who live in relative peace finds it difficult to reorient itself in an industrial society. When a number of tribes organize themselves into a nation, this new political formation often changes the religious understanding of god or the gods, and consequently produces a different ritual and a different system of religious belief. New scientific discoveries sometimes render the old religious answers to problems obsolete and force either an extensive reinterpretation or a completely new doctrine. In any event, religious institutions are constantly changing as man's total experience changes. The vitality of a specific tradition is measured by the number of people who take its answers seriously and are willing to take its attitudes and its ideas of the divine as the final word. The missionary enterprise, which sends religious representatives from one group to another, is financed and staffed out of just such a commitment. For the missionary, the particular tradition which he teaches and preaches is not only the best but the truest apprehension of the divine. His success or failure will depend upon how well his case is presented and upon the strength and vitality of the tradition he is invading.

But it should always be remembered that religion is but one part of the total culture complex. The other institutions of the culture affect religion just as it affects them. No religion, whether it is confining its activities to its own culture or whether it is working a foreign mission field, is ever without the ideas and values generated by the other elements of its home culture. When Chinese Buddhism was exported to Japan, whole systems of law, ethics, family relationships and the like went with it. Christianity took over much from Stoicism, Greek philosophy and Roman law. In these and other instances that we will study, the intermingling of religion with the rest of culture makes it impossible to define "pure religion." There are, however, certain defining characteristics which will aid us in establishing the general boundaries of religion as distinguished from the other aspects of culture.

DEFINING CHARACTERISTICS: THE SACRED

THE earliest forms of religious life concern themselves not with gods, but with mysterious potencies which are designated by the term *mana. Mana* live in objects of the sensory world; they are also the animating principles which give power to spirits and disembodied souls. On the most primitive level, *mana* exist in everything and must therefore be reckoned with as extra-human influences on all things in the normal course of everyday life. There is a religious attitude toward these mysterious powers, all ritualistic and ceremonial practices being designed to propitiate and achieve proper relations with them. For the powers themselves are thought to be inhabitants of that vague area known as "the sacred."

Their sacredness lies in the fact that they exist outside and beyond the normal methods by which man controls his environment. They act in ways that are incomprehensible and mysterious, and they are possessed of a power far greater than that found in ordinary objects. The ceremonial observances which they inspire act as agencies of control and guarantee against the possibility that in given instances the sacred powers will show their displeasure and inflict punishment. After all the precautions of a natural kind have been taken, for example in the building of a canoe, it is still possible that forces beyond human control will swamp it and drown the occupants. When the seed is planted which some months later should produce necessary food, fences can be built and the fields properly cultivated, but still the chance remains that the crop will be ruined. These and a host of other activities in the daily life of the savage are subject to the whims and caprice of *mana* in their various manifestations. If the stipulated ceremonial precautions are not taken, the savage does not have far to look for the cause of disaster. If disaster occurs even after the proper ceremony, this only proves the incomprehensible and mysterious ways of *mana*.

As one might expect, the sacred comprises different things in different societies. In the ancient Hebrew Temple at Jerusalem, all the vessels used in the sacrifices were kept in a particular room and were possessed of special power. Priests were required to engage in prescribed purification rites before entering the room and touching the powerful objects. The Ark which the Israelites carried into battle had a similar but even greater potency. In other tribes certain rocks, possibly places where misfortune once befell someone, are considered sacred and possessed of power. Among some Christian communities the bread and the wine of the Eucharist have holy power and mysterious force. Throughout all the various religious traditions there are sacred objects which range from ideas and altars to sticks and stones. No one principle for determination of the sacred can be found since each group selects its own out of its particular and peculiar experience. As the experience changes, often as the result of increasing scientific knowledge, sacred objects become profane, and what was previously profane might become sacred. Over the long span of history such substitutions are the rule rather than the exception.

One of the defining characteristics of all religion, primitive or advanced, is recognition of the sacred. In primitive societies, where religious institutions are powerful and pervasive, the sacred permeates all of life's activities. In more advanced cultures, the sacred is often limited to things and ideas which are directly associated with the gods or god. These traditions not only have sacred scriptures which tell of deity and make divine will explicit, but they also have sacred places set aside for worship. The sacred in all traditions is linked with mysterious, nonprofane power.

DEFINING CHARACTERISTICS: GODS AND GOD

ALTHOUGH religions require the recognition of nonhuman power, the idea of god is not necessary. The vague spirits and ghosts who people the world of the savage are not, strictly speaking, gods. These ghosts and spirits are credited with all the power and many of the activities which are attributed to the later gods, but they have neither the personality nor the definiteness of character possessed by true gods. A true god possesses a supernatural existence, a proper name or distinguishing title, the power of thought as well as action, and, actually or possibly, a friendly attitude toward man. Ghosts and spirits may have some of these qualities; they certainly do not have them all. The distinction between gods and ghosts is sometimes blurred, especially when the ghosts are those of departed ancestors. In these cases the ancestor's character is remembered and his name is used when he is called upon. Moreover, this type of ghost is usually presumed to be friendly and helpful to those of his relatives who are still alive. Here, the ancestral ghost is almost, if not actually, a god.

For the most part, however, the concept of god has its origin in experiences quite different from those which give rise to ideas of ghosts and spirits. Ghosts appear to people in dreams and apparitions at virtually any time and under any conditions. Spirits wave the branches of trees, send water coursing down the hill, produce rain from the sky, and manifest themselves in a host of other ways. They may be animals, plants or inanimate objects. The concept of god, on the other hand, results from a higher degree of intellectualization and a more refined experience of the nonnatural. Although gods may become incarnate in animals or have residence in objects, they always maintain their own separate and supernatural existence. They are experienced in moments of religious ecstasy rather than in dreams or apparitions. The concept of god must be looked upon as a relatively advanced religious idea which springs from the necessity for explanation and cosmic friendship to a far greater degree than does the experience of ghosts and spirits.

It should be borne in mind that in any given culture all of these distinctions blur into one another. The classifications are useful only for purposes of analysis and should not be construed too rigidly. The Indian monkey-god Hanuman is certainly an instance in which the god and the animal are identical and indistinguishable. We will see as we go along how many men in different traditions have risen from their original human estate to eternal divinity. The history of religions is full of partial data, so that much of the reconstruction of origins must necessarily be considered provisional. The folk-tales and mythologies which comprise our original sources were never intended as study books for a systematic treatment of religion. Rather, they are the records of past religious experience designed to promote piety.

The earliest conceptions of deity are associated with local clan patrons. In many parts of the world these very simple clan gods are the heroes of the past whose exploits are recorded in the form of legends and myths. Often they are the part-mythical characters who are credited with founding the clan and entrusted with responsibility for its strength and well-being. In such cases the gods are commonly referred to as "father," "grandfather," "old one," "mother," or "grandmother." They are responsible for the welfare of a total social organization. They fight the deities of other clans when war is in progress; they give guidance and advice on the best methods of agriculture; and they protect against human enemies as well as against natural disasters such as floods, disease, famine and the like. The worship of such gods is a matter of public concern since they function for the benefit and protection of all members of the clan. What private religion exists is usually concerned with a number of specific departmental deities and the various ghosts and spirits.

As societies become more complex and as intellectualization advances, the division of labor for both man and gods increases. No longer is it necessary for one individual to be skilled in all the arts of protection and production. In the more complex societies some people specialize in warfare, others in agriculture, and still others build houses and manufacture clothing and equipment. This departmentalization of life on earth is reflected in the life of divine beings. Deities, just like men, have specialized fields of activity and power. The Masai tribe of eastern Africa, for example, has a chief god, the sky; but it also has gods of the market place, disease, war, the sea, sensual desire and many other activities and things. The Aztec civilization which the Spaniards found in Mexico had a highly complicated pantheon which included deities of nature on the one side and deities of society on the other. Investigation shows a wide variety of types: some gods are helpful and can always be called upon for aid in their specific fields, while others are capricious and wrathful and seem to demand more than they give.

The wrathful gods must be propitiated by the performance of sacred rites and the offering of proper sacrifices. The most violent of the deities often demand human sacrifice as evidence of man's absolute and utter dependence upon them. But agricultural deities, who are usually benevolent, require sacrifices in the form of grain or some other product of the land. There is no general principle regarding either the genesis of specific deities or the type of worship and sacrifice they require. Each culture sets its own pattern, and each cult has its own understanding of the function, origin and requirements of its gods. In general the deities belonging to this level of civilization are exclusive only in their special departments. Specific deities are not jealous of the others so long as they remain supreme in their own fields. It is the responsibility of the social group to find out how best to deal with the supernatural powers, and then to pass on this information from generation to generation. There is, however, a constantly shifting catalogue of gods. As man's activities become more specialized, the tendency is to increase the number of gods; on the other hand, the advance of man's own power over nature and society causes the death of some gods who were important to the past. In like manner changes are made in ritualistic practices as the gods themselves change from being benevolent to wrathful, from wrathful to benevolent. Thus, departmental deities have no stable existence over a long period of time. They change with the changing conditions of man.

The most constant of the specialized deities are those who have power over the world man enters after death. When man arrives at some specific understanding of death, these gods are endowed with fully defined characters. Many of the earliest deities of this kind have no relationship at all with the world of the living; their dominion over man's soul begins only with death. In more advanced cultures, however, the gods of the dead decide on the basis of the kind of life a person lived whether the newly deceased soul will be admitted to a realm of glory or whether he will be subject to torment and suffering. Wherever gods have such a power of judgment, they exert tremendous influence upon the whole conduct of life. In many cases every detail is regulated in accordance with their dictates since all major rewards and punishments will come after this temporary earthly existence runs its course. Obviously, in the monotheistic traditions, the universal deity who controls the earth also has charge of heaven and hell.

When the differences between good and evil become clearly manifest in a given culture, there is a tendency toward the coexistence of two gods, one good and the other bad. The good god is a friend of man and the guarantor of all human values; the evil god, always on the offensive, claims credit for all suffering both in this life and the life to come. One of the strongest dualisms of this kind is found in the ancient Persian religion which worshiped Ahura Mazda, the good "god of light," while concurrently fearing Ahura Mazda's archenemy, Angra Mainyu, the "god of darkness." A similar dualism occurs in parts of the Old Testament where Satan is called the "king of moral evil." In II Corinthians St. Paul calls Satan the "god of the present age." Such dualism always comes relatively late in the history of a religion; it indicates a deepening ethical sense and a firm conviction regarding the positive power of evil. Within dualistic systems of this kind, the god of darkness controls hell while the god of light is responsible for heaven. Of his own free will, man elects which supernatural power he will follow, thereby assuming responsibility for his ultimate destination.

In general, the representatives and controllers of the realm of evil are better called demons than gods. Although they are supernatural beings with definite characters and proper names, they are rarely if ever accorded worship. They are respected and feared, they demand and require placation; but they are never honored with devotion and trust. Even among the Mesopotamian Yezidis, who have been called "devil-worshipers," the real worship of the community is directed toward those gods who either are or can become the friends of man. In India, as we will see, the worship of Kali, Siva's violent and unpredictable consort, is directed toward her good nature and her often unused but nevertheless real ability to aid man in his struggle for the good life. The morally bad is therefore thought to have a nonnatural source and champion, but worship is reserved for evil's nonnatural counterpart—the good god. A part of the definition of a true god, as distinguished from a demon or devil, is that he be at least a possible friend of man. *Bona fide* demons can never be made into friends; they must always be treated as beings intrinsically hostile to man's highest values and ultimate hopes.

As the intellect is brought to bear upon religious experience, the concept of deity becomes more refined and increasingly sophisticated. Philosophical and scientific investigations take their challenge from the contradictions which appear in human experience. For these contradictions they attempt to find explanations which will be rationally consistent and intellectually coercive. The existence and character of the universal deities who are worshiped in the great monotheistic traditions of the world are proved and defined by rational argument. These deities are for the most part abstractions, considered to be far above the daily activities of man. Although they still possess personality and a warm friendship for man, they are nevertheless called upon to create and sustain the entire world. They are never localized to any one place, nor are they given a temporal existence. Man sees the handiwork of the one true god in nature, he recognizes the universal god's design in human history, and he finds friendship and communion through prayer. It is clear that the universal god is not concrete in the same sense that clan and departmental deities are. He is rather the complete master and king of the world.

As the supreme power, the universal god is the object of intellectual inquiry as well as worship. The scientist who investigates nature is gaining knowledge of god; the philosopher who seeks the absolute and final ground of all certainty is searching for god; and those who attempt to differentiate right from wrong are also in search of god through his will. Such a conception of universal deity requires that god be the source of all being, the end of all life, and the meaning of all existence. God, when considered in these terms, may be the result of philosophical inquiry without reference to a specific religious tradition, or he may be the product of theology. When the concept of god belongs to a philosophical system, it has been arrived at by purely rational speculation. On the other hand, the theologians' concept of universal deity is founded upon revelation and is a refined extension of a traditional religious experience. The philosopher's god is not a true religious god, although many theologians would claim that the philosopher had discovered a facet of the deity who could be known completely through the revelation they accept. Religion, however, is concerned only with conceptions of deity which include the necessity for worship. The ideas of god which find their expression in philosophical systems give rise to no cults, have no altars, utilize no priests and provide for no ritual.

Although the most important contemporary forms of religious life include ideas of god or gods, such conceptions are not absolutely necessary for religion. Religions have existed without deities. More than that, the founder of one of the great universal religions, Gotama Buddha, claimed to be an agnostic. If history is any guide, however, religion without deity is extremely unstable and seems inevitably to grow into some form of polytheism, monotheism or pantheism. In so far as this is true, the belief in gods and god constitutes one of the defining characteristics of religion.

DEFINING CHARACTERISTICS: WORSHIP

INVESTIGATORS into the nature and conduct of man can point to no time when man was not social; he has always lived with his fellows. Indeed, most definitions of man include some such phrase as "social animal." This does not mean, however, that social institutions have not grown out of individual responses to stimuli which have their origins in the external world. Religion, like all other societal phenomena, begins with individuals and their experiences. It is theoretically possible for a lone individual to be aware of the nonnatural and to worship it without direct association with any other human beings. In practice, however, his religious life is socially oriented and his worship practices are primarily conducted in concert with his fellows.

The nonnatural powers, whatever they might be—spirits, ghosts or gods—have some kind of relationship to those who recognize them. Although it is impossible to determine what the original avenues of approach to these powers were, the earliest methods known were through word and act. Ceremonies replete with dances, processions and verbal incantations abound in the most primitive of societies. In some instances the ceremonies are a mingling of magic and devotion, charm and prayer. The magical side assumes that the nonnatural powers operate under clearly defined laws which are known to the medicine-men and soothsayers. Here there is no attempt to ask the gods to intervene on behalf of man; rather, the magical acts and charms are instruments of force or control. As such they are technically not a part of religion. Religious activity is directed toward establishing friendly relations with the nonnatural powers one does not propose to control. In any given primitive ceremony the two are inextricably bound together, but it should be recognized that magic and religion have separate theoretical bases.

Religious worship is that activity which results from a recognition of dependence upon powers beyond man's control. As in the case of most gods, these powers may be friendly and benevolent; but, there is a price to be paid for their continued good will. Through long experience a community learns just what the gods require, and public ceremonies and prayers fulfilling these requirements are handed down from generation to generation. Each new generation is introduced to a particular form of worship as being the tried and tested means of propitiating the nonnatural powers and requesting their aid. As conceptions of these powers change, so do the mechanisms by which they are approached. As a result there is a constant growth in the worship tradition, with each generation adding little or much to the general body of practice. As civilizations develop, magical practices are gradually discarded and their functions are taken over by science. Religious practices, on the other hand, become more elaborate and more firmly embedded in the cultural tradition. Religious worship which does not claim to control the nonnatural powers can exist without difficulty side by side with advanced science, whereas magic is always doomed.

In general the methods of religious worship follow patterns similar to those devised for approaching temporal rulers. Expensive gifts of rare quality are offered as an indication of esteem and as a token of dependence. Agricultural deities responsible for harvests receive gifts of food and drink as grateful offerings from the people. In addition, prayers of thanksgiving are said, glorifying the particular god for his excellent treatment of his mortal dependents. In time of war, sacrifices are made and petitionary prayers are said to attain the help and guarantee of victory which only the god can give. The language employed in all these prayers is characterized by the same stilted formality as that used in addressing kings and princes. The courtly customs of bowing and kneeling, used to indicate deference to all-powerful temporal rulers, are also part of the ritual when deity is approached. It is natural that both religious worship and respect for temporal rulers should follow the same pattern of word and gift, since both are recognitions of power beyond control—expressions of dependence and declarations of devoted loyalty.

The practice of worship, like the other special activities of life, tends to be centered within a specific geographic area. In the very earliest times these places of worship were probably rocks, caves, rivers or hills where some special event of supernatural significance had taken place. The sacredness of these spots marked them off as the proper places for divine worship and necessitated their being protected from profane influences. With the continued elaboration of worship techniques, the constructoin of divine images and symbols and the development of ritualistic apparatus, it was increasingly necessary to build houses of worship and ultimately temples. The very building of these edifices came to be looked upon as a sacrifice to deity and a monument to his glory and grandeur. In some present-day religions and in almost all of the great ancient cults, the temple was considered the dwelling place of the god, and as such it required a greater magnificence of construction than any other building in the community. It was here, in the house of god, that man could best approach the all-powerful supernatural.

With the growth of temples and shrines and the increasingly elaborate ritual, certain people came to be charged with responsibility for the buildings and the services. These men, called priests, were sacred people, versed in the myths and stories relating to the deity and well trained in the proper performance of the ritual. Their lives were lived in an aura of sanctity and their activities were defined by their sacred duties. The worshipers, naturally enough, came to be dependent upon the priests as guides through the maze of inherited ritual and as messengers who would place their petitions before deity and perhaps intercede in their behalf. In some cults the power of priests and priestesses was greater than the power of ordinary temporal rulers. Since they possessed a high degree of sacredness in their own right and were the visible agents of the supernatural, they became the final arbiters of action and thought. As time went by, they perpetuated themselves by admitting only those of their own choosing to the sacred office. In some places, such as present-day Tibet and medieval Europe, the priests became the chief powers in the state and in practically all the other institutions of life. Since the perpetuation of the religious tradition was in their hands, the priests assumed responsibility for teaching and preaching in addition to their duties as ritualistic officials. In such circumstances, temples, shrines and church buildings were not only centers of worship activity, but centers of virtually the entire life of the community as well.

Although there has always been this external social worship of a more or less formal nature, its organizational development has led to an increase of private worship. In many cultures each home possesses images of its patron gods. For the most part these gods are departmental deities who benevolently oversee particular aspects of life. Special prayers are offered them, privately and without the aid of priests. There is no real cult for these gods; they are rather family deities who can be called upon to understand purely personal problems. In some traditions, notably the Hebrew and Mohammedan, such family deities are considered idols in the sight of the jealous cultic god who rules the total community. Priests warn against depending upon them, and their worshipers have often been subject to various kinds of persecution. By and large, however, private devotion to family patrons has not interfered with the public worship of the cultic god or gods. In some cases, especially where the priestly tradition is not too powerful, the divine images of the home are identical with those of the temple. And it is left to the particular individual to decide which type of worship he finds most meaningful and helpful.

Although religion, to be religion, does not necessarily have to employ any particular one of the great variety of worship practices, it is impossible to conceive of a religion which did not include some devotional form. The solitary individual who approaches the nonnatural without the aid of ritual, temples or priests is, if he recognizes his dependence, engaging in worship. No definition of religion could possibly exclude this fundamental form of religious activity.

DEFINING CHARACTERISTICS: MYTH AND REVELATION

MAN's understanding of the nonnatural which he approaches in worship cannot, by the very nature of the case, be achieved in the same terms as his understanding of the natural. The ordinary world of common experience teaches man certain regularities and "facts" which he cannot with impunity deny. The rudest savage knows that in order to reap a corn crop he must till the soil and plant the proper seed. He knows that fences must be built around the field to keep animals and human beings from crushing the young plants. In other words, he knows a great many facts of corn raising which have been taught him through direct experience. The natural world of the savage, as well as that of all people, is a world naturally understood. The experience of the nonnatural world is neither as definite nor as specific as that of the natural. Nonnatural beings are, for the most part, beyond the reach of the senses, and the ideas men have of them are the result of either religious imagination or revelation.

The religious imagination produces religious myths. In general these myths describe the character of the gods, what they have done for man, what they require of him, and what they promise for the future. In almost all early and late religious traditions there are myths which tell of the origin of the world and the process by which it is kept moving. Some savage tribes ascribe origination to a special animal which for that tribe has divine characteristics. In more advanced communities, the world is thought to have been created by a high god of the pantheon or the one supreme god. In any event, virtually all traditions have minutely detailed myths which outline for the worshiper exactly how, under what conditions and for what purpose the world of sense came into being. Sometimes the god created it out of nothing, sometimes it was hatched from an egg, sometimes the god slew a giant beast which he dismembered to form the various parts of the world, and sometimes the god fashioned the universe from a vast pool of motionless water. Most of these cosmogonies are highly elaborate and, as the tradition grows, become increasingly intricate.

Oftentimes, cosmogonic myths are ways of explaining not only the origin of the world, but also the reason for the existence of evil. In Manichaeanism the world of sense came into being because at one time Satan (darkness) got the better of God (light). Thus the Manichaeans looked upon the material world and all things connected with it as evil. When light finally triumphs over darkness, all materiality will vanish. In the Old Testament, God creates the world good, man falls from grace, and even nature becomes niggardly and refuses to supply food except as man labors and sweats to produce it. Many traditions speak of floods which covered the earth and killed all living things because man refused to abide by the ethical and ritualistic demands of god. Such myths afford an

[3 2]

explanation of evil and at the same time issue a threatening warning that the cosmic creator of good may once again strike down evil man. As the moral sense of the society is sharpened, myths are created to show how the new requirements are related to the old, and how they operate under the same divine authorization. Here again the religious imagination constantly expands and elaborates the inherited structure of myths.

The religious imagination is not only concerned with the causes of the natural world and their ethical implications, it also devises origins and explanations for human society and its institutions. For the primitive as well as the civilized, the origins of human history and societal organization are lost. This loss of factual data allows each group to trace its ancestry back in time to some powerful being who can be looked upon as a common parent and a high authority for feelings of exclusiveness. Many primitive societies trace their origin to an heroic person who was half man and half god. Often tribes with animal totems claim to be the offspring of a divine animal. Others, who recognize a nonnatural power in rocks or mountains, trace their ancestry to such inanimate objects. If the whole range of anthropological data is considered, there is no special pattern in these myths. The only thing that can be said with confidence is that all early tribes and many later nations consider themselves to be special creations of the nonnatural with a direct and continuous genealogical line connecting them with the divine.

The customs and institutions which originated prior to recorded history are usually regarded as the special inventions of divine personages. This is especially true of the all-important initiation ceremonies, family organization, governmental authority, and the external religious institutions found in primitive communities. The common arts of civilization—metalwork, woodwork, agriculture, weaving, building construction and the like—all have similar divine origins. In Greek mythology, writing was given to man by the mythical character Cadmus; among the Algonquins a gigantic rabbit, Michabo, is credited with teaching man how to fish and hunt; in India fire is the gift of the god Agni; and in Greece fire was stolen from Zeus and given to man by Prometheus. Among very early peoples virtually all the customs and arts of civilization which form the basic structure of the society had their origins in a mythical past under the guidance of a mythical founder.

Many of the religious myths which deal with the origin of particular social groups and institutions are a combination of myths and legends. Legends are historical facts which, either purposely or unconsciously, have been distorted in the process of transmission from age to age. This is especially true when the story concerns the biography of some great cultural hero who actually existed. Around the fact of his existence and his major exploit is woven a pattern of explanatory myth. From the very little that is usually known of such people a tale is spun which demonstrates his divine character as well as the majesty and power of his acts. These biographies, which are compounded of historical fact, legend and myth, serve as documents of religious authority for later generations and as the basis upon which those who follow build new understandings. It is often difficult, if not impossible, for late scholars to separate the history and legend from the myth. In so far as the religious functions of the three are concerned, such differentiation is unnecessary.

When the various kinds of religious myth are first propounded, the faithful within a particular tradition consider them to be accurately historical. Their accounts of the origins of the world, human society, customs, institutions, and the arts of civilization give a sense of continuity with the past and an authority for the present and future. It is not long, however, before some minds discover inconsistencies and, in comparison with other documents, inaccuracies. It therefore becomes necessary to interpret the myths in such a way as to preserve their authority and endow them with rational justification. One of the most usual ways of doing this is to interpret them allegorically. Allegorical interpretation flatly states that the myths are not what they seem to be; rather, the divine power has chosen this esoteric means of communicating deep and profound truths. The profundities are embedded in what appear to be folk-tales, mundane history and riotous imaginings. It is the task of the theologian to discover the various levels of meaning in the revelation and to make sure that those who practice the cult understand their import.

To one who does not belong to the particular tradition and who examines the sacred mythology from the outside, it appears not as divine revelation, but as primitive science and a collection of imaginative conceptions of life. The orthodox Christian looks upon the sacred scriptures of the Buddhists and Hindus as myths which reveal nothing about the character of the divine or his works; such revelation is restricted to the Christian scriptures and the institutions which flow from them. The same exclusiveness is felt to a greater or less degree by the orthodox of all traditions. When myths are considered to be revelation, they are treated as the creations of divine inspiration, not as products of imagination. Religious traditions are dependent upon myths, no matter how they are interpreted, for the propagation of the faith and a dramatic representation of divine attributes and demands.

DEFINING CHARACTERISTICS: THE SOUL

VIRTUALLY all the religions of mankind have had and do have a belief in something called a *soul*. In primitive religions the soul is a kind of insubstantial entity which maintains an independent existence within the body. It leaves the body during trances, in moments of unconsciousness, and during deep sleep. At death the soul is liberated from the body and continues its career in a disembodied form.

Belief in this vague something which carries life, thinks, and is endowed with personality provides a foundation for speculation about heaven, hell and immortality. Obviously the body of man disintegrates after death, but no such disintegration is apparent with regard to the soul. Visions of people long dead are often seen by those still living; and the souls of the dead sometimes appear in dreams and hallucinations. These and other experiences tend to confirm the notion that the world is peopled with disembodied souls who have a permanent nonphysical existence. When they are no longer limited by the physical world, their power becomes proportionately greater than that of souls who are still hampered by bodies. There are very few traditions which entertain no idea of the continued existence of the soul. Some of these few believe in a god who has the power to destroy souls, but even then it is possible through combat and bribery to stay execution and achieve eternal life. Wherever the death of the soul is possible, the tradition gives no indication of how it happens or why. By all odds the greater number of traditions have at least some rudimentary notion of immortality.

Ideas concerning the destiny of the soul after the death of the body vary from culture to culture. One of the commonest early conceptions is that the soul is reborn. Its new form may be similar to the old, or it may be on a lower level. In many ancient traditions, such rebirth furnishes the basis for the worship of animals and even plants. As religions in which rebirth is an article of faith become more complex and more concerned with morality, the particular reincarnation depends upon the moral character of the soul in the preceding life. These traditions, including Hinduism, Jainism and later Buddhism, place the gods within this cycle of birth and rebirth and establish a complete hierarchy extending from the lowest animal to the highest god. With the growing importance of the idea that life is ethically determined, hells of one kind or another are considered the necessary destiny of those who deserve extreme punishment for their sins. The traditions in which there is no conception of reincarnation usually assign departed souls a residence in either heaven or hell. Advanced traditions make no provision for disembodied souls to operate on earth or to have any real relationship with the living.

Virtually all religions give primary importance to their conceptions of the soul. It is the soul rather than the body which must be saved. Within the soul are all the things of real value, all the attributes we call human. The life of man is often looked upon as a struggle of the soul to free itself from bodily limitations and passions. Final salvation is achieved when this world is renounced in favor of the soul's search for rest in god. From this conception of an imprisoned soul many of the characteristic ascetic practices of religion take their cue. The world is evil, bodily desires are evil, matter is evil; only the pure immaterial soul acting with god is good. True happiness can be attained only when the pains and frustrations of physical existence are finally overcome. Religions following this tradition tend to be other-worldly, to point toward a salvation beyond the grave where transient materiality does not exist. With very few exceptions, the idea of a soul constitutes one of the most pervasive religious conceptions. Some commentators have maintained that it is the most important single defining characteristic of religion.

DEFINING CHARACTERISTICS: SALVATION

IT SHOULD be clear from our discussion so far that religions exist for a purpose. And it would be impossible to define the term *religion* without reference to the goals toward which it strives and the motives which underlie its efforts. In general the goals of religion are all concerned with one thing—salvation. And it is the desire for salvation which provides the motive power for religious activity.

An analysis of the history of religions indicates that people have struggled to be saved either *from* something or *for* something. In the most primitive traditions, salvation from the terrors of physical existence demands most of man's religious energy. The hazards of storms, floods, crop failures, preying animals and the like are so real and ever-present that divine help is constantly required in dealing with them successfully. Such ideas of salvation are distinctly this-worldly and concern themselves entirely with protection and escape. The divine forces are thought to be the controllers of the physical universe and consequently the most sure and efficient guardians against its adversities. Salvation of this type is, of course, not limited to primitive traditions. The most advanced religions have forms of intercessory prayer which ask deity for protection in war, safety during travel, escape from trying and difficult situations, and a host of other things. To seek the friendly cooperation of the nonnatural when facing the unexpected and unknown seems to be a most normal part of all religion.

However, salvation is not by any means wholly concerned with protection and escape. Many traditions, especially those in fairly advanced civilizations, are much less intent upon being saved from earthly peril than they are with being saved for a future heavenly existence. Whatever tortures and frustrations this life holds are more than compensated for by the promised happiness and bliss which will attend each saved soul in the life to come. In such traditions the unsaved or damned souls are consigned to hell and eternal torment.

These two forms of salvation in a sense constitute the positive and the negative emphases of the same thing. Even those who wish to be saved for heaven are at the same time being saved from hell. Salvation from the difficulties of life is obviously correlated with salvation for earthly happiness and peace. Except in analysis the two cannot be separated; in actual religious life they are inseparably mingled. However, emphasis upon one or the other aspect does give a definite character to a particular tradition. Wherever salvation is promised for another world, the significance of this life is restricted to those elements which serve as vehicles of salvation. Thus in some traditions science, philosophy, government, the family and economic activity lack any independent meaning. Those who devote their lives to such activities seriously diverge from the pursuit of man's true goal, which is the achievement of salvation. The long course of history has only one meaningful drama—the drama of salvation; all else is valueless and futile. Where traditions of this kind are strong, the cultures of which they are a part tend to be unconcerned with economic and social organization; instead, they place their emphasis upon ascetic contemplation and mystical absorption.

On the other hand, the this-worldly emphasis tends less toward contemplation and mysticism and more toward moralism and ritual. Whenever the fulfillment of life is thought to exist in this world, very particular attention is paid to the immediate requirements of deity. Since retribution is not far off, there is usually a greater sense of urgency, a more pronounced determination to discover the proper relation to deity and follow his will. As a consequence, most of the great ethical religions assume (in part, at least) that salvation is to be achieved within the limits of earthly existence. Often this salvation is considered to be the peace of mind, the nearness to deity, which come from correct action and proper thought. To people of such beliefs, a pious life means more than spiritual contemplation; it means active participation in whatever plan or design god has for this world. Ultimate reward or punishment may be meted out in some future life, but such judgment is incidental to the more important activities of earthly existence. The unknown future has only a tenuous meaning, whereas the actual present possesses an undisputed and insistent reality.

Often all these tendencies are found within the same general tradition, with one or another being dominant at any given time. Many of the other-worldly religions of the East, which for centuries had no concern for man's physical existence, have, within the recent past, reoriented much of their doctrine toward an interest in the affairs of men this side of the grave. As we will see, the various epochs of Christian history demonstrate a constantly changing emphasis, but nevertheless with both tendencies existing side by side at all times. The coexistence of these two tendencies in any given religious tradition serves to explain some of the most heated intramural controversies and schisms. It is part of the explanation for the multiplicity of Protestant Christian sects, for the break between Roman Catholicism and Protestantism, and for the split between Hinayana and Mahayana Buddhism. Few religious issues are more explosive.

The meanings given the term *salvation* are no less varied than the means by which salvation is to be achieved. Here again there are two extreme views between which most actual religious practice falls. At the one extreme are those who contend that man has absolutely no power over his own destiny. Salvation is entirely dependent upon god, and man can do nothing but wait upon the deity's pleasure. If any particular man should be chosen, it is through no merit of his own, but through the grace of god. The choice god makes is not the result of prayers, good works, or any other human activity; it is rather his free and unsolicited gift. The other extreme considers salvation exclusively and solely dependent upon the man's own abilities. The Buddhist *Dhammapada* puts it this way: "A man is his own helper; there is no one else to help." Usually this extreme of the religious spectrum has no conception of any kind of personal deity. There may be, as in some forms of Indian Upanishadic religion, an impersonal absolute into which the soul of man is absorbed; but the absorption takes place only through the self-effort of man. Again, as in Western Humanism, salvation is sometimes achieved through the concerted action of all men working together in the cooperative quest for earthly peace and happiness. In any event, salvation is the result of human and not divine effort.

Between these extremes lies the greatest body of religious thinking and practice. To be saved means to have cooperated with whatever nonnatural powers there are. Man must worship, he must abide by god's rules, and he must live his life in terms of divine commands if he is to receive nonnatural support in his quest. Sometimes belief in a particular set of dogmas is required, with no prescription regarding special rules of conduct; other traditions disregard belief in favor of a standardized ritualistic practice; while still others place primary emphasis upon rules of conduct in day-to-day affairs. Unless man upholds his side of the bargain, the fruit of the contract will never be realized. Whatever the details of the cooperative enterprise might be, the important thing, the common denominator, is that neither god nor man can do the job entirely by himself.

In religions which have personal gods, it is usually assumed that the deity could, if he so desired, grant salvation without man's help, since the gods are always possessed of greater than human power. But man must win deity's favor. The presumption seems to be that purely natural man has no claim on god except as he earns it through the fulfillment of special divine commandments. In some traditions man is such a poor, weak sinner and god is so majestic and powerful that an intermediary is required to pay man's debt to god and thus make salvation possible. The intermediary is then looked upon as the savior and is accorded worship as testimony to his goodness and power. In Christianity, faith in the savior Jesus Christ is considered the first step for all who would travel the road to ultimate salvation. However variously they are described, most salvation doctrines are indicative of man's sense of dependence and his great need for help and guidance.

To be saved from something and for something is a universal characteristic of religion. And it is through their individual doctrines of salvation that the different traditions achieve distinctive meaning.

WHAT IS RELIGION?

IT SHOULD be clear that there is no single definition of religion. All the phenomena which are usually classified as religions have theories of salvation, attitudes of worship, and some form of social organization. Not all traditions have conceptions of deity or the soul. Behind each of these characteristics lies the sense of dependence from which all religion seems to spring. This dependence, however, is an extremely complex and difficult thing which defies any single comprehensive definition. People have made religions of practically every form of human endeavor. In some cultures and in some periods of history, the state or the family or the economy has claimed the complete and subservient loyalty of vast groups. In such cases there is no question that the individual's religious energy is being directed toward objects which are not usually considered sacred or holy. Nevertheless, any general definition would have to include these instances as manifestations of religious life.

However man is conceived, he is clearly a being of many dependencies. He is dependent upon physical nature for his food, drink and shelter; and he is dependent upon other men for friendship, understanding and physical safety. In other words there is no such thing as man except as he is caught up in a network of dependencies. Religion must therefore be considered one restricted area of dependence among many. And as we shall use the term in this study, it is limited to those aspects of culture in which we find great numbers of men expressing their ultimate and final dependence. As we shall see, the major traditions of the world interpret this dependence in terms of a god or gods. Our working definition of religion is, therefore, the activity of man resulting from the recognition of nonnatural powers upon which he feels ultimately dependent.

II

HINDUISM

INTRODUCTION

TO MOST Western minds India presents both an enigma and a challenge. The greatest religion of India, which embraces two-thirds of its people, is usually known as Hinduism, yet this term indicates such a wide variety of religious beliefs, rites and practices that it becomes impossible to speak of it as a unity. The variety of belief, language, racial stock and custom forms one of the difficult barriers to the Western mind. Beyond this is the fact that the peninsula of India has cradled an essentially different culture with different problems, solutions and attitudes.

Although the enigma is great, the challenge to understand is also strong. India has been, and seems destined to remain, a source of inspiration and beauty for the world traveler. The historian finds in this relatively small area much that aids him in the understanding of man's progress and retrogression on this earth. But to the student of religion, India presents the greatest challenge. Here we can see the most primitive anthropomorphic faith existing side by side with the most complex and sophisticated philosophical speculation. In India can be found nature worship, magic, polytheism, monotheism, religiously organized societies, and mystical anarchy. It is perhaps true to say that India is the mother of more different religious ideas than any other section of the globe.

It is usual to divide Hindu religion into five general periods: (1) The Vedic stage. The Vedas, for which this stage is named, is the oldest body of Indian religious literature. It dates from about the time of the Aryan invasion to around

1000 B.C. The Aryan tribes began to enter India, through the northwest, sometime between 3000 and 2000 B.C. The dating here is extremely uncertain. (2) The Brahmanic stage. This stage takes its name from the Brāhmanas, which is the name given to a great mass of priestly (or ritualistic) works. The works themselves are detailed explanations of the origin and function of certain rites and ceremonies. This stage marks a tremendous growth in the power and authority of the priest. (3) The philosophic stage. In this period many of the best Indian minds turned to speculation on the nature of reality and on man's relation to it. The major writings of the period, the Upanishads, were largely the work of individuals who based their ultimate faith in the Vedas. In effect, the Upanishads attempt to systematize the revelation found in the Vedas, while at the same time translating and extending the Vedic ideas into philosophic discourse. (4) During much of the period in which the Upanishads were being written, India produced its great heretical sects. Two of these sects achieved tremendous historical importance—the Jains and the Buddhists. Jainism is still strong in India; Buddhism, although extinct in the country of its origin, has spread throughout the whole of Asia. Although both have their origins in Vedic religion, they were destined to become religions in their own right. (5) The final stage, for our purposes, can perhaps be called the theistic-devotional period. In this period the two great modern branches of Hinduism developed—Vishnuism and Sivaism. Here is the consolidation after the attacks of heresy and the fusion of devotional and philosophic interests.

2

VEDIC INSPIRATION

THE hymns of the Vedas are not the product of one age or of one hand. It may very well be that many of them were composed before the Aryans actually arrived on the peninsula of India. We do know, however, that they were not written down until well after the Aryans had made India their home.

The Vedas reflect a society that made its living chiefly from the soil. Although the major part of the society worked with cattle, hoes, plows and axes, there were a number who worked as builders and artisans. The woodworkers built locks for the irrigation canals as well as wagons and war-chariots. However, the division of labor was not great and the economy was fairly homogeneous. The artistic productions were limited, but probably highly refined. Archeologists have found intricately carved cups and other works dating from this period. From evidence supplied in the hymns it is known that the women were adept at weaving and mat-making. In all, one can picture the economic situation as being of a primitive pastoral character, much like that found in other areas of the world.

The political structure rested on the family and its extension into the tribe. The position of chief was often hereditary, but there is also evidence that in some cases the chief was elected. The king or chief was not an absolute ruler; rather, his judgments and actions were often limited by a poorly articulated, but nevertheless definite, sense of community justice. Theoretically, at least, no earthly ruler was beyond the sovereignty of moral law. In practice, the Vedic peoples probably lived amid a mixture of tyranny and political freedom.

However much we might speculate on the nature and character of the politico-economic organization, it still remains speculation. The only data scholars have to use is offered by the Vedas, and they deal almost exclusively with religion. The secular elements are at best secondary and are most sketchy and incomplete.

There are four collections of Veda that are usually called Rig-Veda, Sāma-Veda, Yajur-Veda and Atharva-Veda. These collections are known as Samhitās and form the substance of the Vedic religion and literature. Of them all, the Rig-Veda is the most important. Although parts of this collection were probably composed before the Aryan invasion, it is impossible at this date to distinguish them from the rest. The Sāma-Veda has no real value of its own. For the most part it consists of selections from the Rig-Veda placed in a different order. It is, by and large, a liturgical collection which was arranged for use at the sacrifice. The Sāma-Veda was probably collected to meet the needs of a developing ceremonial religion. Beyond this it adds little to our understanding of Indian religion.

The Yajur-Veda is of quite a different nature. Although it too borrows a great deal from the Rig-Veda, it adds a number of original prose sections. The Yajur, like the Sāma, serves a liturgical function, but it deals primarily with the order and arrangement of sacrifice. Both the Sāma and the Yajur indicate a well-established ritualistic religion.

The Atharva-Veda represents a later period in the Indian development. Whereas the Rig-Veda gives its attention to so-called "high" gods, the Atharva deals with magical spells, demons and formulae-incantations. The Atharva was long without the status of a Veda, but, for our purposes, it is necessary to consider it second only to the Rig. The Rig is more the expression of a thoughtful upper-class, while the Atharva indicates the popular lower-level interests of the larger number of Indians.

THE RIG-VEDA

IN THE Rig-Veda is found the impassioned poetic expression of human souls seeking a refuge from the complexities of life. The physical forces and changes of nature present to the primitive, as well as the modern, a flux and confusion that must somehow be conquered. The powers of nature seen in storms, sunshine, rain and wind must be dealt with because of their beauty and terror. There were some poets who were content to contemplate the beauty and forget the terror, and these unburdened their souls with hymns to gods such as Varuna and Mitra. Others wanted success in battle and guides for an active, direct life. These sang and wrote hymns to one of India's most famous deities, Indra.

It is undoubtedly true that the early Vedic gods were identified with some aspect or force in nature. In the earliest stages there was a god, named and definite, for each one of the aspects or forces. For example, one hymn is addressed to Vāta, the wind, in the following terms: [1]

Travelling on the paths of air's mid-region, no single day doth he take rest or slumber.
Holy and earliest-born, Friend of the waters, where did he spring and from what region came he?

Germ of the world, the Deities' vital spirit, this God moves ever as his will inclines him.

[1] All quotations from the Rig-Veda from the translation by Ralph T. H. Griffith (Benares: E. J. Lazarus and Co., 1897).

His voice is heard, his shape is ever viewless. Let us adore this
 Wind with our oblation.

(Rig-Veda X.168.3,4)

Or the setting of the sun in the West:

How is it that, unbound and not supported, he falleth not although directed downward?

By what self-power moves he? Who hath seen it? He guards the
 vault of heaven, a close-set pillar.

(Rig-Veda IV.13.5)

It is interesting to notice the awe and wonder expressed in
the above lines—the questioning spirit that seeks not so much
to know an answer as to express the question correctly. There
is no terror in these poets, rather a delight in the recognition
of a mystery they are powerless to penetrate. Again, there is
no attempt to control the god or force of nature; rather, the
poet is content to give words to his devotion and love. This
acceptance of mystery and contentedness with worshipful devotion can be found in certain types of religious life in all
cultures.

All the Vedic gods are not of the atmosphere and sky.
Many live and work on earth and form an important part of
daily life. Agni, for example, is fire. He lies concealed in wood
and other combustible substances. If two sticks are rubbed together Agni comes forth in all his glory and dances before the
eye. He is beautiful in his multicolored robes as well as useful
for his heat. More often than not the beauty of Agni is the
subject of such a hymn as this:

His flames that wax not old, beams fair to look upon of him
 whose face is lovely, shine with beauteous sheen.

[52]

The rays of Agni, him whose active force is light, through the
nights glimmer sleepless, ageless, like the floods.

(Rig-Veda I.143.3)

Although most of the hymns in the Rig-Veda are worshipful and express little fear, there are some, addressed to the god
Rudra, that speak of the wrath and anger of a god. Surpris-
ingly, there is very little attention paid Rudra, but when it is,
the poet seems to express doubts and fears of a high order. In
the hymns to Rudra the Vedic Indian comes face to face with
that irrational, fateful, incomprehensible force which strikes
down children for no crime and makes the good suffer for no
reason. One Rudra hymn is as follows:

O Rudra, harm not either great or small of us, harm not the growing boy, harm not the full-grown man.
Slay not a sire among us, slay no mother here, and to our own
dear bodies, Rudra, do no harm.

Harm us not, Rudra, in our seed and progeny, harm us not in the
living, nor in cows or steeds.
Slay not our heroes in the fury of thy wrath. Bringing oblations
evermore we call to thee.

(Rig-Veda I.114.7,8)

It has often been pointed out that one of the prime reasons
for the few references to Rudra and the consequent expression
of fear lies in the fact that the hymns were composed by poets
who sang for the kings and the wealthy. By virtue of their station they had fewer political, economic or social fears and
were thus relatively safe from the sufferings which beset common men. They had physicians to care for their sick, many
horses (so that the death of one made little material difference), and many comforts. Much of the ugliness and brutality
of nature and man escaped them, but is to be found constantly

[53]

in the experience of the lower ranks. Thus the dread of the unexpected and the frantic attempts to control the unfriendly find their greatest expression in the Atharva-Veda and not in the Rig.

LAW AND THE GODS

As THE Vedic religion develops further, moral aspects are added to the gods of physical origin. The figure of Varuna, the god of the sky, is progressively transformed and idealized into the moral overseer of the world. It becomes Varuna's function to punish evildoers and reward the good. The good things of this life come from him, and other gods and men obey his commands. In some hymns he is the cause of the regularity in the sky, keeping the moon and stars in their courses; he causes rivers to flow in the proper direction and the wind becomes his breath. Thus the laws of nature and the laws of morality are established and maintained by this god of gods, the supreme ruler of heaven and earth. It is to the supreme god, Varuna, that some of the most magnificent Vedic hymns are sung.

The mighty Lord on high, our deeds, as if at hand, espies:
The gods know all men do, though men would fain their deeds
   disguise.
Whoever stands, whoever moves, or steals from place to place,
Or hides him in his secret cell—the gods his movements trace.
Wherever two together plot, and deem they are alone,
King Varuna is there, a third, and all their schemes are known.
This earth is his, to him belong those vast and boundless skies;
Both seas within him rest, and yet in that small pool he lies.
Whoever far beyond the sky should think his way to wing,
He could not there elude the grasp of Varuna the king.
His spies descending from the skies glide all this world around,
Their thousand eyes all-scanning sweep to earth's remotest bound.

Whate'er exists in heaven and earth, whate'er beyond the skies,
Before the eyes of Varuna, the king, unfolded lies.
The ceaseless winkings all he counts of every mortal's eyes:
He wields this universal frame, as gamester throws his dice.
Those knotted nooses which thou fling'st, O God, the bad to
  snare,
All liars let them overtake, but all the truthful spare.[2]

The identification of natural and moral law in Varuna is
one of the most important stages in the development of Indian
religion. In a sense it is an example of the way in which the
human mind always seems to strive for a unity amid the diversity of life. Many interpreters of religion point to the fact that
almost all religious traditions begin with a large number of
scattered nature deities with little or no moral flavor. After a
time there is a recognition of the social or moral life of man
which seems to obey certain laws of cause and effect. It is not
long after this recognition that the order of nature and the
order of life are fused under one god or principle.

Closely associated with this movement toward moral and
physical unification is the tendency to reduce the number of
gods. In primitive groups there are, as we have seen, virtually
as many gods as there are recognizable forces in nature. In the
Vedic hymns we see the original polytheism being slowly but
surely reduced until Varuna is found to be the controller of
all nature. This does not mean that the hymns ultimately arrive
at monotheism. Rather they seem to conclude in an area between polytheism and monotheism called henotheism. *Heno-*
theism has been defined as "a belief in single gods, each in
turn standing out as the highest." This would seem to indicate
the dominance of one god or another in the mind of a sup-

[2] Although this hymn is from the Atharva-Veda (IV.16.1-5) it is more
akin to the spirit of the late Rig-Veda. It has been translated into verse
by Professor Muir and is printed in Vol. V of *Original Sanskrit Texts*, p. 64.
(London, Trübner & Co., 1870.)

pliant at any given moment. In the moment of worship, the god addressed stands out as the greatest and highest, with all other gods receding to the periphery of interest. Thus henotheism is a rather chaotic state between avowed polytheism, with each god important and supreme in his own sphere, and monotheism, in which only one god is recognized as having existence.

The law which Varuna established and by which he rules the world is called *Rita*. The word literally means "the course of things" and was probably first suggested by the regularities of nature. The seasons that invariably follow each other, the course of the stars, the sun, and the moon, the movement from night to day, and seemingly inevitable consequences of certain types of action all point to the existence of an "order." It seemed to the Vedic Indian that there must be something behind the visible world of flux and change. There must be something to cause a kernel of corn to produce a cornstalk and not a lotus blossom, some pattern of orderliness that "measured out the air's extended spaces" and made the "earth enduring" throughout the march of time.

It is not long after such speculation begins that the world of sense becomes an unstable parade to be heavily discounted in favor of the eternal and uninterrupted order itself, which thus becomes the final will of Varuna and the law of justice and nature. The trust that is placed in Rita changes the nature of both the religious practice and the beliefs regarding the gods. As nature becomes more orderly, so does society and so does the act of worship. The early Vedic nature worship was chaotic to the extent of being unpatterned and incapable of systematic understanding. With the introduction of Rita it becomes possible to establish and delineate the gods and their functions.

The hymns of the later period usually invoke both Varuna and Mitra. Mitra and Varuna are the keepers of Rita and in many hymns they are both endowed with the ability to for-give sins and punish wrong. Both maintain the character of sky-gods, Varuna being associated with the night and Mitra with the day. In any event, Varuna and Mitra are inseparable, and are often spoken of as the sons of Aditi, or the Adityas.

THE SUN GODS

IN ADDITION to Varuna and Mitra, the Vedic hymns also deify the sun. The solar deities go under various names such as Sūrya, Savitir, Vishnu and Pūshan. Vishnu, when considered as a solar deity, is held by the Rig-Veda in a relatively un-important position. He (sometimes under the name of Sūrya) is the god who covers the earth and is so vast that no mere mortal can ever reach or touch him. When the sun is called by the name of Savitir, there is more of a moral function attached to his works, He is often prayed to by the sinner seeking forgiveness, or for enlightenment in time of moral confusion. He therefore acts both as guide and forgiver. Pūshan, on the other hand, is a solar deity, but he does not forgive sins nor is he the object of wonder and awe. Rather, the hymns addressed to Pūshan indicate his function as a friend. In effect he is a protector, a cosmic friend, who can be counted on to guard over the traveler and assure crops and cattle against destruction. He is much more of a pastoral or agricultural god than any of the other solar deities. He is not so august that man cannot approach him, and he is sufficiently flexible for man to direct a variety of requests to him. The following selection from a Pūshan hymn gives an indication of the way he is addressed:

O Pūshan, bring us to the man who knows, who shall direct us straight,
And say unto us, It is here.

May we go forth with Pūshan who shall point the houses out to us,
And say to us, These same are they.

May Pūshan follow near our kine; may Pūshan keep our horses
safe:
May Pūshan gather gear for us.

(Rig-Veda VI.54.1,2,5)

By way of contrast it is interesting to note the difference
in form and tone when the Vedic poet approaches Sūrya.
Sūrya's augustness and distance from the worshiper are seen
in the following:

His bright rays bear him up aloft, the God who knoweth all that
lives,
Sūrya, that all may look on him.

The constellations pass away, like thieves, together with their
beams,
Before the all-beholding Sun.

His herald rays are seen afar refulgent o'er the world of men,
Like flames of fire that burn and blaze.

Swift and all beautiful art thou, O Sūrya, maker of the light,
Illuming all the radiant realm.

Traversing sky and wide mid-air, thou metest with thy beams
our days,
Sun, seeing all things that have birth.

(Rig-Veda I.50.1,2,3,4,7)

INDRA THE MIGHTY

In all the Rig-Veda, the most prominent of the gods is Indra.
Of the total number of hymns we have, he is mentioned in at
least one-fourth. Indra is the most anthropomorphic god in the

[58]

Vedic pantheon. His very human qualities cause him to be jealous, to overeat, to brag about his exploits, and to be given to lust and drunkenness. He is in effect a human hero-god who performs all the actions of man, but who does so against a cosmic backdrop. He is able to kill monsters and protect his worshipers from any and all dangers. With his great strength he supports the earth and sky while at the same time controlling the spread of the earth. All the superlatives in the Sanskrit language are applied to him, yet his heroic proportions are always incapable of description.

It is usual to think of Indra as the national hero-god of the Aryan invaders. As they came into the Indian peninsula they had constantly to battle the dark-skinned Dasyus who already were settled in the land. If the Aryans were to win the land they had first to crush the native Dasyus population. It is Indra who serves as the great vital god who leads in the blood-thirsty battle and who lives the life of excess and exploitation. In many ways Indra is the deification of the jingoistic elements in a nation that was destined to conquer a weak enemy.

It would be improper to think, however, that this was all that Indra represented. In the history of almost any national god can be found periods of war which require him to be a bloodthirsty fighter. Although Indra came to have a definite character of this kind, his origin is undoubtedly found in visible nature. The difficulty lies in determining what aspect of nature. The general Hindu tradition calls Indra a storm-god who uses thunder and lightning to accomplish his purposes. But just when the conception takes shape is lost in prehistoric time. Moreover, there is another Vedic god, Parjanya, who is usually referred to as a storm and rain deity. The hymns addressed to Parjanya are undeniably associated with the storm and could mean nothing else, while the Indra passages seem capable of various interpretations. Although there have been many interesting theories advanced regarding Indra's origin, there can, at present, be no final word. The following selection, which describes Indra's most important deed, will at least show how Indra's worshipers conceived of him.

I will declare the manly deeds of Indra, the first that he achieved, the Thunder-wielder.
He slew the Dragon, then disclosed the waters, and cleft the channels of the mountain torrents.

He slew the Dragon lying on the mountain: his heavenly bolt of thunder Tvashtar fashioned.
Like lowing kine in rapid flow descending, the waters glided downward to the ocean.

Impetuous as a bull, he chose the Soma, and in three sacred beakers drank the juices.
Maghavan grasped the thunder for his weapon, and smote to death this firstborn of the dragons.

When, Indra, thou hadst slain the dragons' firstborn, and overcome the charms of the enchanters,
Then, giving life to Sun and Dawn and Heaven, thou foundest not one foe to stand against thee.

Indra with his own great and deadly thunder smote into pieces Vritra, worst of Vritras.
As trunks of trees, what time the axe hath felled them, low on the earth so lies the prostrate Dragon.

He, like a mad weak warrior, challenged Indra, the great impetuous many-slaying Hero.
He, brooking not the clashing of the weapons, crushed—Indra's foe—the shattered forts in falling.

Footless and handless still he challenged Indra, who smote him with his bolt between the shoulders.
Emasculate yet claiming manly vigour, thus Vritra lay with scattered limbs dissevered.

[6 0]

There as he lies like a bank-bursting river, the waters taking courage flow above him.
The Dragon lies beneath the feet of torrents which Vritra with
his greatness had encompassed.

Then humbled was the strength of Vritra's mother: Indra hath
cast his deadly bolt against her.
The mother was above, the son was under, and like a cow beside
her calf lay Danu.

Rolled in the midst of never-ceasing currents flowing without a
rest for ever onward,
The waters bear off Vritra's nameless body: the foe of Indra sank
to during darkness.

Guarded by Ahi stood the thralls of Dasas, the waters stayed like
kine held by the robber.
But he, when he had smitten Vritra, opened the cave wherein the
floods had been imprisoned.

A horse's tail wast thou when he, O Indra, smote on thy bolt;
thou, God without a second,
Thou hast won back the kine, hast won the Soma; thou hast let
loose to flow the Seven Rivers.

Nothing availed him lightning, nothing thunder, hailstorm or
mist which he had spread around him:
When Indra and the Dragon strove in battle, Maghavan gained the
victory for ever.

Whom sawest thou to avenge the Dragon, Indra, that fear possessed thy heart when thou hadst slain him;
That, like a hawk affrighted through the regions, thou crossedst
nine-and-ninety flowing rivers?

Indra is King of all that moves and moves not, of creatures tame
and horned, the Thunder-wielder.

Over all living men he rules as Sovran, containing all as spokes
within the felly.

(Rig-Veda I.32)

Indra will have nothing to do with the alien people who
worship other gods. His jealous nature and his actual triumphs
on the field of battle tend to make him the supreme god of the
Vedic pantheon. As he takes over more and more of the functions of nature and society, he displaces the majestic and essentially serene Varuna. Varuna is not a fit god for an active,
fighting and conquering people. The early hymns of wonder,
glory and worshipful mystery give way to the harsh, powerful
and in many ways destructive hymns to Indra. The mysterious delicate beauty of the dawn and the wise moral blessedness
of Varuna are lost in the unrestrained and unconquered ex-
hilaration of Indra. Often Varuna and Indra are confused and
spoken of as two names of the same deity.

I am the royal Ruler, mine is empire, as mine who sway all life
are all Immortals.
Varuna's will the Gods obey and follow. I am the King of men's
most lofty cover.

I am King Varuna. To me were given these first existing high
celestial powers.
Varuna's will the Gods obey and follow. I am the King of men's
most lofty cover.

I Varuna am Indra: in their greatness, these the two wide deep
fairly-fashioned regions,
These the two world-halves have I, even as Tvashtar knowing
all beings, joined and held together.

I made to flow the moisture-shedding waters, and set the heaven
firm in the seat of Order.

By Law the Son of Aditi, Law Observer, hath spread abroad the world in threefold measure.

Heroes with noble horses, fain for battle, selected warriors, call on me in combat.
I Indra Maghavan, excite the conflict; I stir the dust, Lord of surpassing vigour.

All this I did. The Gods' own conquering power never impedeth me whom none opposeth.
When lauds and Soma juice have made me joyful, both the unbounded regions are affrighted.

All beings know these deeds of thine: thou tellest this unto Varuna, thou great Disposer!
Thou art renowned as having slain the Vritras. Thou madest flow the floods that were obstructed.

Our fathers then were these, the Seven Rishis, what time the son of Durgaha was captive.
For her they gained by sacrifice Trasadasyu, a demi-god, like Indra, conquering foemen.

The spouse of Purukutsa gave oblations to you, O Indra-Varuna, with homage.
Then unto her ye gave King Trasadasyu, the demi-god, the slayer of the foeman.

May we, possessing much, delight in riches, Gods in oblations and the kine in pasture;
And that Milch-cow who shrinks not from the milking, O Indra-Varuna, give to us daily.

(Rig-Veda IV.42)

POETRY, UTILITY AND INSPIRATION

THE religion of the Rig-Veda is compounded of two quite different elements. In the first instance it is possible to see the usual form of primitive religion in the deification of natural forces and the development of certain formulae designed to propitiate and attain the "good graces" of the personalized gods. In this aspect, Vedic religion acts out of utilitarian motives and gains an effective control over the powers that lie outside the normal rational will. Here the recognized forces of the external world are put in anthropomorphic form and brought under control. The second aspect of the Rig-Veda is not so crass and certainly not so utilitarian. In many of the hymns there is no attempt to control, but rather an attempt to express the highest mysteries of life and nature. They sing of the glorious beauty of the world and the radiant goodness of man as he lives under the benevolent guidance of Varuna. In the one element we find the satisfaction of the human need for coming to terms with those aspects of reality that can hurt and be generally harmful, while in the other, the Vedic Indian recognizes the awesomeness of beauty and the holiness of mystery.

Because of this mixture of sublime poetic flights with materialistic satisfaction, the Vedic poems are often misunderstood. The tendency is to try to make them fit into a neat scheme of some preconceived classification of religions. In general the Rig-Veda denies such systematization. They are at once the unfettered poet's dream and the activist's tools of conquest.

Even this division between poetic inspiration and utilitarian activity cannot be made too absolute. The god Soma, who is responsible for inspiration, soon becomes the god of intoxication, for even poets who try to ascend the heavens require some surcease of sorrow. Life may have its moments of divine illumination and poetic inspiration, but those moments last for only a short period and cannot be induced at will. What is called spiritual illumination or deeper vision comes to man when his soul is somehow elevated. It is little wonder that the drink that causes elevation should become divine. Such

[64]

statements as, "We have drunk the Soma, we have become immortal, we have entered into light, we have known the gods," are not uncommon in Vedic worship. Indeed, the idea that physical intoxication is the same as divine inspiration can be found in many religious traditions.

Not only is the idea of inspiration a confusion of the so-called spiritual with the physical, but the same confusion is also found in the Vedic treatment of faith. Faith for the Vedic Indian was undoubtedly equated with a belief in the existence and activity of the gods. Many early hymns indicate this conception in such words as:

Indra, what mortal will attack the man who hath his wealth in thee?
The strong will win the spoil on the decisive day through faith in thee, O Maghavan.

(Rig-Veda VII.32.14)

This early idea of utilitarian faith slowly gives way to faith as truth and wisdom. In the Yajur-Veda faith is seen as truth:

The Creator having beheld two qualities separated truth and lie from one another.
He put unfaith into lie, faith he placed into truth.

(Vajasaneyi Samhitā 19.77)

The idea of faith being synonymous with truth is replaced in the Atharva-Veda by the idea of faith as synonymous with wisdom.

Daughter of Faith, born of zeal, sister was she of the seers that did create the beings.
Do thou, O Girdle, assign to us thought and wisdom; also assign to us zeal and strength.

Throughout these writings, and in spite of the changing conception, faith seems to become more and more a matter of spiritual insight. In effect, faith at the early stage is for certain people a means of gaining the gods' favor; then it moves on to become the truth and wisdom of the world. It then goes even higher to become a goddess, an object of worship.

> Faith, the goddess, is the firstborn of divine order,
> Upholder of all, foundation of the world.
> That Faith do we revere with our oblations;
> May she create for us an immortal world.
>
> (Taittirīya Brāhmana, 3.12.3.1,2)

This is certainly the highest rank to which faith is raised.

At the same time faith becomes the means by which the Brahmanic priest controls his people. It is put to the use of ritual, and results as the object gained when a sacrifice is properly performed. Faith thus becomes something that the priest can dispense at will, and his will is usually dependent upon the nature and extent of the sacrifice. What had previously been a high form of religious consciousness degenerates into a useful device for priestly control. It is possible to find such mixtures as this in virtually all the Vedic religious notions.

Whatever else can be said of the hymns, they form the basis for later Indian thought. The Brāhmanas, to which we now turn, extend and emphasize the sacrificial and liturgical aspects of the hymns, while the Upanishads work out the various philosophical implications found in the hymns. It must always be remembered that the Rig-Veda forms much of the primary datum for Indian philosophy and religion.

3

BRAHMANIC FORMALISM

IT IS just as impossible to date the period of the Brāhmanas as to date the earlier hymns of the Veda. It is known that the Aryans continued their conquering march, but generally the Brahmanic period is one of consolidation and social crystallization. It was, for example, in this phase of Indian history that the caste system was defined, implemented and extended to many other groups. The Brahmans brought the aboriginal tribes under an ecclesiastical rule that assigned each tribe a specific place and each occupation a specific function. But it was primarily a priestly and not a secular rule.

From the evidences found in the literature of the period it is known that the conquered lands were divided into small kingdoms. Active trade relationships were established by the use of both overland and water routes. There is some evidence to indicate that trade was maintained by the Aryan Indians with such countries as Babylonia and possibly Greece. In any event the period was one of growing wealth, social solidification and expansion.

The religion of the period takes its essential character from an extension and elaboration of the sacrificial elements found in the early Vedic literature. As we have seen, the Rig-Veda was characterized by a spontaneous worship of the forces of nature. The religious spirit was free and relatively untroubled and unhampered by formalism. The Vedic poets sang and composed their hymns as they felt the inspiration. There was little orthodoxy to prescribe the mode of expression. Indeed, it was so free that one god after another was elevated to the highest position without any direct conflict with an established theological structure. This immediate, vital and spontaneous religious reaction was destined for death at the hands of institutionalization. It is for the establishment of orthodoxy that the Brahmanic period is important in Indian religion. It added little to the religious insights expressed in the Vedas.

PRIESTLY POWER

THE Brāhmanas, which form the basic literature of the period, were constructed as guide-texts to the increasingly complicated ritual practices. The sacrificial rites, which are really of secondary importance in the hymns, are placed in the highest possible position. With this increased importance of sacrifice and liturgy went an overwhelming exaltation of the priest. Whereas the early Vedic singer (the *risi*) had been honored as an inspired worshiper, the Brahmanic priest became the keeper and owner of revealed truth. Whereas once the Vedas had been considered for what they were, beautiful expressions of a singer's religious experience, they now became the repository of eternal truth. Thus the inspiration of one age becomes the formulae of the next.

Since the Vedic hymns are now to be considered as revealed truth and the sacrificial rites as absolute prescriptions for correct religious practice, the priest's duty becomes an enormous one. He must be well educated in the sacred scriptures and well trained in the conduct of the holy rites. No simple worshiper can approach the seat of the divine in a sudden burst of religious ecstasy. The head of the family can no longer find his way through the complicated maze of ritualistic prohibitions and sanctions. The priesthood thus becomes a profession. And the duty of this profession is to mediate between the gods and men. Here we see one of the most important stages in the development of religion. The individual worshiper stands in a passive role while the grace of god is dispensed by the priest.

It is not unusual, therefore, that the form should become more important than the spirit. The priests became virtual dictators of the people, for they had the power to give or withhold the beneficences of the deity. In the eyes of the believing people the priest became, if not a god himself, at least the only person who could speak for the gods. As in all professions, those doing the work must somehow be paid. Thus the priest could and did declare that fees paid to him had the efficacy of a sacrifice. It would be strange indeed if such authority were not abused and used for exploitative purposes.

The Brahmanic priests were neither stupid nor necessarily conscious exploiters. They naturally had their own ideas of their worth, and consciously or not they did place themselves on the highest possible social and economic level. In their many codes and social laws they took the attitude of benevolent dictators. They knew what was best for the people and saw to it that their wills were imposed. Often, however, these legal codes exhibited an intense regard and love for the people. Whatever their delusions of grandeur, they cannot be called insincere. It is perhaps fairest to say that they were victims of their own tradition quite as much as the people were victims of Brahmanic power.

MONOTHEISTIC TENDENCIES

IN THIS period theological ideas also undergo a change. The tendency toward monotheism which we noted in the early Vedic hymns becomes more and more pronounced. The conception of Brahman can be seen only indirectly in the Rig-Veda, but it becomes of great importance in the Brāhmanas.

In effect, it is the single principle that lies behind the universe. It is behind all gods and all men; it is impersonal, and it is finally looked to as the creator of all things. In the Satapatha Brāhmana, Brahman is described as follows: "Verily in the beginning this universe was the Brahman. It created the gods; and, having created the gods made them ascend these worlds: Agni this (temporal) world, Vāyu the air, and Sūrya the sky." After this creation, Brahman itself went up to "the beyond." Then Brahman is pictured as having worried about how it was going to descend again to the world of its creation. Brahman finally decided to accomplish this feat by the use of two principles, form and name. Whatever has a name and has form thus belongs to the universe and, in fact, establishes its limits. ". . . As far as form and name, so far, indeed, extends this universe." He who possesses knowledge of these two becomes imbued with the power of Brahman.

Here is certainly justification of a rather high order for the education and knowledge necessary for the Brahman class. The exactness and extent of the knowledge of all things that have a name and have form is so tremendous that few people are capable of its achievement. As a consequence, it was not unusual to believe that the ability for such high achievement could be gained only by birth into the particular caste of Brahman. The hereditary caste is thus given a strict theological undergirding.

Certainly Brahman, as impersonal force, does not take over the whole of Brahmanic theology. In some places the older creator deity, Prajāpati of the Rig-Veda, is raised to the level of the highest god. He is personal and is thought of in almost purely monotheistic terms. He creates Agni, who is identified with this world, and Brahmanaspati, who becomes the lord of the cultus, the leader of prayer and the organizer of worship. But even in those aspects of the religion which elevate Prajāpati, Brahman is important. Since most of the Brahmanic worship leads toward a conception of the sacrificial nature of the universe, sacrifice is conceived as embodying the principle of creativity. And in this idea there is an identification of Brahman with the single creative principle of the world. Here again the Brahman caste is elevated to a position of supreme importance. It is only by proper birth and rigorous education that one can be possessed of Brahman and capable of understanding the mysteries of sacrifice.

In the popular religion of the day these monotheistic tendencies were probably unimportant. The masses of the people continued to worship the chaotic polytheistic pantheon found most especially in the Atharva-Veda. For the most part this popular religion was magical and full of charms and superstition. In the period of Brahmanic formalization of the so-called purer Vedic religion, the witchcraft and magical practices of the Atharva-Veda offered an outlet for the mass of the people. On the popular level the medicine man took the place of the priest. It was his duty to scatter the spirits and effect an easier and less fear-filled life for the lower castes. The Brahmanic priests had placed themselves so far above any true understanding of the religious needs of the masses that these needs were bound to find expression in folklore and superstition.

The meaning of the highly refined ritual and obtuse metaphysical doctrine was reserved, it would seem, for those who could study. This study required a certain amount of leisure and protection from the unpredictable, but such a fortunate state was granted only to the few; the rest were required to work long and hard in a world that could always be counted on to produce the unexpected. The prayers of the masses were prayers of necessity with the definite purpose of gaining a right relationship with the forces beyond technical mastery. The prayers of the Brahmans, on the other hand, were said for the sake of saying them. We might say that the prayers of the people were *prayed*, while the prayers of the priests were *said*.

The religion of the period can be characterized as priestly on the upper levels and superstitious on the lower. The tendency toward philosophic monism and religious monotheism is pronounced, yet polytheistic worship is not given up. There are many examples of high philosophic speculation mixed with the most animistic types of worship practice. Such abstract concepts as time, love and the first principle are deified and worshiped as personal gods. Time becomes Kāla, love is Kāma, and the first principle goes under the several names of Purusa, Prajāpati and Brahman. Rudra, the wrathful and fateful god of earlier times, becomes the lord and guardian of animals and is called by the name, Paśupati.

ETHICS AND IMMORTALITY

IN THE Brāhmanas can be found an explicit ethical system mixed with a vague conception of after-life. It would be expected that the formalism of the period would produce a very specific and definite attitude toward right and wrong. The highest good is thought of in terms of duty. Life is one vast system of moral duties—duties to gods, to priests, to men and finally to animals. In some portions of the Brāhmanas all creation is included in the duty structure. If any man was to be considered good, he would of necessity have fulfilled all the requirements. To question or trespass a duty was to transgress the divine will and consequently to disturb the eternal harmony established in the world. One of the most outstanding duties placed upon man was the requirement that he tell the truth. To trespass and speak falsely was an affront in the eyes of Agni, the lord of vows, and Vāk, the lord of speech. One could never expect to conceal this sin simply because it was hidden from the eyes of men: Agni and Vāk would always know.

It was within the power of the gods to give immortality. Its promise is held out in the literature to those who rightly understand and rightly act. Since most all the actions of life are conceived as within the province of duty, a deficiency of action results in the displeasure of the gods. Often an early death is promised those who transgress the law. In other places the sinner is promised complete annihilation, while the virtuous are to be rewarded with immortality. It is interesting to note that the conception of rebirth is here introduced as a reward and not a punishment. We will see later thought making the wheel of birth and rebirth into an agony from which man seeks escape. The Brāhmanas are by no means consistent regarding this problem. There are some passages that speak of all men being born again to receive their reward or punishment; other sections speak of the dead being placed on the stars of the night-sky; still others appear to offer rewards only in this life. However much confusion there may be, it should be recognized that immortality becomes, at this point, an important part of Indian religion. In the Rig-Veda there is only the slightest mention of the virtuous being reborn, and little is said regarding his future condition.

In the Brāhmanas the question arises as to the length of time man must suffer or be rewarded. Since life is so short, it hardly seems just that its sins or virtues should have everlasting rewards or punishments. Although it is impossible to say with any finality, it does appear that in the Brāhmanas the idea of rebirth includes a suggestion that when one life shall be amply rewarded or atoned for, a new life will begin with the account clear. However this may be, it is only suggested and cannot be stated as a well-developed belief.

Toward the end of this period we find a definite class of ascetics developing. In the period of the hymns, self-denial was practiced to a certain degree, always with the belief that the gods would be more pleased and that the ascetic would gain in spiritual riches. Near the conclusion of the Brahmanic period, bands of ascetics moved to the woods and hills where they wore clothes of skins and lived entirely on the edibles of the forest. For the most part they continued to observe the caste lines of their village brothers and generally followed the ritualistic worship of their ancestors. In addition to their rude living and traditional worship, they developed methods of flagellation and austerity. They would sit in uncomfortable postures by the day and week, eating just enough to stay alive. They often went high into the hills with little clothing to endure the coldest nights; at other times they would sit with warm clothing in the hottest sun.

The purpose of these endurance feats was usually twofold: first, they hoped to attain the highest favor of the gods; and second, they hoped to be rewarded with miraculous powers. As time went on there developed a kind of admixture of high moral purity and mysticism; no longer were there merely the earlier utilitarian motives. A special aspect of the hermit's life was his frequent union with the Brahman or one of the gods. In any event, his was a council of perfection that offered an example to all lesser men who could not endure such mortification of the flesh. The hermits were a constant reminder to the people that what was done for the gods was less important than what man was able to give up for them. This is probably a logical extension of any sacrificial religious system.

4

PHILOSOPHIC RELIGION

IN MOST classifications of Indian religious history the Upanishads are known as the Veda-anta, or the last chapters in the Vedas. This signification is to indicate that the Upanishads contain the essential elements of Vedic teaching. The form, however, is quite different from the previous Vedas. The early Vedas were composed of hymns, rites, charms and incantations in a rather unsystematic grouping; the Brāhmanas contain the structure of a legalistic ritual system; while the Upanishads deal with a more intellectual and philosophical approach to the problems of life. It is in the Upanishads that we get a clear picture of an attempt to see behind poetic symbol and worship to the absolute reality upon which life rests.

The religion of this period of philosophic speculation remained much as it was, with the general mass of Indians continuing to offer innumerable sacrifices to the older gods. The Atharva-Veda was still in popular use, and the Brahmanic priests continued in their roles of god-men. However, there was a decided revolution taking place among the school-men and the thinkers of India. These it was who began expressing dissatisfaction with what seemed to them to be the rather childish, if quaint, poetic expressions of the early period. Moreover, there was a general feeling that the forms of Brahmanic worship were empty, or at least in need of clearer understanding. The vague pantheism and polytheism of the

popular religion fairly cried aloud for clarification and comprehension. It was from this general intellectual unrest that the
greatest philosophic documents of India were generated. It is
also true that these documents form the essential basis of all
subsequent Indian philosophy and speculation.

CREATION AND ONENESS

IT IS probable that men in all stations and conditions have
wondered about the nature of reality. In a sense the Vedic
hymns are expressions of this wonder. In them the external
elements of physical nature are made final and absolute when
they are deified. The search continues, however, since the inevitable question regarding the reality behind the gods is
raised. There seems to be within the human mind a drive
toward unity, a search for the one reality that explains all the
multiplicities and confusions of our world of appearance. We
have seen how this tendency was given early expression in the
Indian literature. As the questioning spirit again arose after
the rather sterile ritualism of the Brāhmanas, it began to look
behind the gods of the earlier tradition. It not only investi-
gated the gods, but also the various theories of creation that
had been established. The writers of the Upanishads could not
rest amidst diversity. The ultimate ground of all being is what
they sought—the ground of both human and divine events and
objects.

In one of the early Upanishads creation is described as follows:

> In the beginning this world was just Water. That Water emit-
> ted the Real—Brahma [being] the Real—; Brahma, Prajāpati;
> Prajāpati, the gods.
>
> (Brihad-Aranyaka Upanishad 5.5.1)[1]

[1] Unless otherwise indicated, all quotations from the Upanishads are from
R. E. Hume, *The Thirteen Principal Upanishads* (London, Oxford Press,
1921. By permission).

In this theory of creation the eternal substance out of which all things come is described as water. *Being* as such, or that aspect of things which causes them to be called *real*, is Brahma. But even Brahma is a derivative from water. In another early speculation the source of all being is defined as space.

"To what does this world go back?"

"To space," said he. "Verily, all things here arise out of space. They disappear back into space, for space alone is greater than these; space is the final goal.

"This is the most excellent Udgītha. This is endless. The most excellent is his, the most excellent worlds does he win, who, knowing it thus, reverences the most excellent Udgītha."

(Chāndogya Upanishad 1.9.1,2)

The idea that there is some one essence or substance from which all things proceed is described differently. Sometimes it is described as space, sometimes as water, atmosphere or a giant egg. But it is always some one essence.

As time went on, a further refinement was introduced. It was concluded that the primal element was not anything so concrete as water or anything so definite as space. Rather, behind even these seemingly universal factors was the true reality. And this ultimate of ultimates was taken to be Brahma. Such phrases as "Verily, in the beginning this world was Brahma" appear over and over again. The objective universe could be traced through its many appearances to its final ground—Brahma. When not speaking simply of creation, but of life itself, the author of the Chāndogya Upanishad says: "Brahma is life. Brahma is joy. Brahma is the void." Brahma thus becomes the ground of all being, that from which all things come and toward which all things go.

It is obvious that Brahma must be recognizable in two forms. There are the things of this world: objects which seem to be complete in themselves and separated from each other by space are certainly describable in phenomenological terms. The senses bring us reports of objects, and their reality cannot be denied. Yet if this world of sense is to be described as real, it must also participate in or be a part of Brahma. The world of appearance and differentiation must also be in some fashion linked to Brahma.

THE TEMPORAL AND ETERNAL

ONE of man's most amazing experiences is the recognition of eternal motion and change linked with a constant regularity. Men come into existence, grow to old age and die. Yet this is not the end of man. The structure that we call *man* seems to be different from the particular men that are born and die. A seed is planted in the spring, it grows into a beautiful flower and finally dies. Yet this is not the end of floral beauty, for next spring a new flower is formed and it is much the same as the flower of the previous year. The recognition of this unification of the eternal constant with the temporal manifestation leads the writers of the Upanishads to conclude that there are two forms of Brahma, the timeless and the temporal.

There are, assuredly, two forms of Brahma: Time and the Timeless. That which is prior to the sun is the Timeless, without parts. But that which begins with the sun is Time, which has parts. Verily the form of that which has parts is the year. From the year, in truth, are these creatures produced. Through the year, verily, after having been produced, do they grow. In the year they disappear.

(Maitri Upanishad 6.15)

Although we may admit that there are two forms of Brahma, it is not proper to ascribe equal importance to both. The world of the senses is filled with error and confusion. Man is often incapable of telling truth from falsity and good

Siva and Durgā. Siva is pictured as the walking ascetic. (*Coomaraswamy Collection, Boston.*)

Siva and Parvati encamped for the night. (*Coomaraswamy Collection, Boston.*)

Siva under Kali, the Terrible. (*India Museum, London.*)

Krishna, an incarnation of Vishnu, giving instructions to Arjuna before the great battle which is described in the early sections of the Bhagavad-Gita. (*Prussian Museum of Ethnography, Berlin.*)

Left, Standing Vishnu. *Above*, Vishnu on Garuda.

from bad. This is particularly true when he concentrates his attention on the moving stage of temporal actions and things. But the only true reality is one and indivisible. Thus, if man is to recognize the high light of truth and if he is to distinguish truth from error, he must go through the particular manifestations of Brahma to the undifferentiated universal Brahma. It is here and only here that he will find the truth, clarity and simplicity which he seeks.

The tradition of the earlier Vedas and the Brāhmanas held to the efficacy of sacrificial acts performed in the cult worship-exercises. With the introduction of such a philosophic idea as the Upanishadic Brahma, there is serious question raised as to the importance of the normal sacrificial acts. The Vedic poets had been able to give a definite content to the objects of their worship. The worshiper knew what kind of thing the god wished sacrificed, and the Brahmanic priest understood the necessity and intricacy of a set worship formula. In other words, the religious practices were built upon deities who possessed visible and knowable manifestations.

The Upanishadic Brahma, however, was more of a philosophic abstraction than a knowable deity. There was no way of really comprehending the ultimate reality (Brahma). Every attempt to give definite content to the conception proved a failure. It was only possible to speak of Brahma in a negative fashion. Any attempt actually to describe Brahma usually went something like this:

Verily, in the beginning this world was Brahma, the limitless One—limitless to the east, limitless to the south, limitless to the west, limitless to the north, and above and below, limitless in every direction. Truly, for him east and the other directions exist not, nor across, nor below, nor above.

(Maitri Upanishad 6.17)

Brahma thus becomes inconceivable, limitless, unchangeable, untouchable, and entirely aloof from the ordinary life of man.

. . . It is unseizable, for it can not be seized; indestructible, for it can not be destroyed; unattached, for it does not attach itself; is unbound, does not tremble, is not injured.

(Brihad-Āranyaka Upanishad 4.5.15)

The religious needs of the mass of Indian worshipers could hardly be met by such a conception of the absolute. Brahma, as god, was in all things, yet outside all things; he was the ground of the world and yet the world of experience was outside him. Whatever we can experience was outside him. Whatever we can experience and express must of necessity be limited, and if it is limited we should not worship it as Brahma, for Brahma is unlimited. There is ultimately no way of describing it by positive content in either words or actions. Cultic practices became severely limited, if not entirely superfluous. It is little wonder that the Atharva-Veda and the Brahmanic priests continued to flourish in spite of this later development.

The problem raised by the Upanishad writers is a universal one. When the spontaneous worship practices of the cult are subject to rigorous reflection, the results are, more often than not, devastating to certain forms of the worship. Religious exercises in their purest form are immediate reactions of a sensitive soul to the mystery of existence. The object of the worship varies with the individual worshiper, but whatever the object, it is usually personalized and given a definite character. The god, in effect, becomes a being among other beings. The philosopher in his reflection elevates something beyond any object and speaks of an absolute, or the unconditioned, or as in India, Brahma. In so doing he invariably depersonalizes god and makes him more an object of intellectual contemplation than of fervent worship. Whether or not this can be said of all religious traditions is a matter for further investigation. It certainly seems true for this period of Indian development.

THE SOUL AND THE COSMOS

IF BRAHMA is conceived as the infinite and ultimate essence of the universe, the next question arises with regard to the relationship between this ultimate ground and the finite ego. The objects and things of this visible world are manifestations of Brahma. Is the human soul also to be lumped in the same category with sticks and stones? The Upanishad writers think not. The individual self was for them the ranking reality. The soul (Ātman) is thought of as the innermost essence of man.

Yet we are still left wondering what the self really is. Man certainly consists of the food he eats; that is, he has a body. Behind this outer shell there is another self. This other self the Indian calls "vital breath" (Prānamya Ātman). The breath is as necessary to life as the physical body, and in addition the breath produces speech. Even this, however, is not the essential soul or self, for behind the vital breath lies another self called "will" or "mind" (Manomaya Ātman). The will seems to be more firmly embedded than either breath or the physical shell. By will deeds are performed, food is taken and breath is drawn and expelled. Before the actions of the outer selves can be performed, the will must be present. The will is in turn dependent upon consciousness, so a further self (Vijnānamaya Ātman) is found consisting of consciousness. Thus the individual is thought of as a composite of at least four different selves.

There is, however, a final absolute essence which lies in back of all of these selves. This is "the self as pure bliss" (Ānandamya Ātman) and is called the "true essence of existence." In the Taittirīya Upanishad the philosopher speaks of those who understand the essential unity of the human person. After death they go through the following stages:

> . . . He who knows this, on departing from this world, proceeds on to that self which consists of food, proceeds on to that self which consists of breath, proceeds on to that self which consists of mind [or will], proceeds on to that self which consists of understanding [or consciousness], proceeds on to that self which consists of bliss.
>
> (Taittirīya Upanishad 2.8)

Thus the soul (Ātman) is thought of as consisting of various selves with one self (bliss) as the highest. This innermost self is constant and beyond the limits of any change. It can never be subject to the inroads of time but is eternal in its own form. "The self (Ātman) is free from evil, ageless, deathless, sorrowless, hungerless, thirstless. . . ." Ātman in its highest sense is the purest reality. In each individual there is Ātman, something infinite that is seemingly encased in the finite. The human soul is therefore looked upon as the highest limitless reality. It is, in the words of one of the Upanishads, "the Real."

It is now possible to see how the thinkers of the Upanishads arrived at their famous equation: Brahma = Ātman. When the investigation leads through the physical universe, the essential unity of all things is called Brahma. Brahma becomes the cosmic principle that pervades all things and supports all things. When the investigation is conducted by introspection, the ultimate unity and ground of being is found to be Ātman. The objective and subjective here become one all-pervading unity. The two names, Brahma and Ātman, are simply two names for the same reality, arrived at from different directions. It is the identification of the soul with god. The universal principle of the objective world is identical with that of the human being. "Verily, that great unborn soul (Ātman), undecaying, undying, immortal, fearless, is Brahma." "The soul (Ātman), which pervades all things, this is Brahma."

The unity of all being which the hymn writers of the early Vedas sought is finally reached by these philosophers of the Upanishads.

> . . . As all the spokes are held together in the hub and felly of a wheel, just so in this Soul all things, all gods, all worlds, all breathing things, all selves are held together.
>
> (Brihad-Āranyaka Upanishad 2.5.15)

Here the problems involved in polytheism, henotheism and monotheism are left far behind. If there is any theism that can be ascribed to this type of belief, it is a rough form of pantheism. All the world is god, and god is all the world. The earlier gods represent mere aspects of the great all-inclusive totality. Nothing positive can be said of this Real except by cataloguing all superlatives. In the final analysis such statements as the following are the only ones possible.

> Unmoving, the One is swifter than the mind.
> The sense-powers reached not It, speeding on before.
> Past others running, This goes standing.
> In It Mātariśvan places action.

> It moves. It moves not.
> It is far, and It is near.
> It is within all this,
> And It is outside of all this.

> (Iśā Upanishad 4-5)

There is no way for the truth in this religious mysticism to be confined in the normal categories of knowledge. It stands so far outside the usual conceptual apparatus of the mind as to degenerate into nonsense when put into words. The mystic insight can only be experienced; it cannot be adequately told.

Man's puny powers of communication can point to the reality, but his symbols can never capture it.

UPANISHADIC ETHICS

THE ethical ideal of this religion is self-realization through oneness with God. The soul is never content with the satisfactions of finite achievement. Wealth, fame and the material goods of this world count for nothing when compared with the inestimable riches of unity with God. It is up to man to free himself from the trammels of this world. He must renounce the satisfactions of material desires and worldly ambitions in order to find his pathway to salvation. It is through the renunciation of the empirical self that the eternal soul is released to find its home with god. To seek the gratification of the flesh is to court frustration and misery. The life of the spirit is man's perfect freedom; his bondage is the illusion of temporal success.

All desire is not evil; it depends upon the object desired. He who desires the things of this world becomes a sensuous beast. He who desires to be with god becomes a saint. The "true" desire is the mystic's quest; the "false" desire is the worldly man's misery.

Such doctrine is bound to lead to a disregard for the condition of man's earthly existence. The problems of social justice, economic equality, political rights are all essentially unimportant. It is true, however, that the Upanishadic emphasis upon the inner nature of goodness tended to soften the caste lines which the Brahmanic priests had so harshly delineated. Those who could find their release from the tension of existence through mystical union with Brahma-Ātman could achieve the highest salvation regardless of caste. It was more a matter of inner worth than of accidental birth. The secret knowledge of the universe was available to all who could reach it, and no priest could stand in the way.

However this might be, there was a general diversion of interest from the conditions of this life. Such an attitude hardly provided a dynamic for the development of a practical science or for the overthrow of economic or political tyranny. The production of gadgets to make life more comfortable, the invention of new tools for more efficient manufacturing and farming, or the development of political and economic structures for greater liberty and greater consumption fell outside the interest of this religion. Its votaries clung to virtues such as mercy, restraint and charity, but these were passive, certainly not part of what the Western mind calls a progressive faith. The result was a seemingly prosperous but actually static social state. All interest lay in the eternal, thus making things temporal sublimely unimportant.

It is not surprising that this mystical ethic of renunciation should lead to asceticism. As we have seen, asceticism was already an important part of the Indian religious expression. In a sense the renunciation found in this period is an extension of the sacrificial idea found in the earlier Vedas and the Brāhmanas. In the earlier period the sacrifice is made as a barter with a deity. If an individual gives up what he wants, if he gives up his chance for worldly satisfaction, the deity will in return grant him salvation. In the religion of the Upanishads the renunciation of worldly pleasures is not really a sacrifice but comes because the individual recognizes that temporal concerns are incapable of quenching the thirst of the soul. To turn to the things of this world is to deny the possibility of bliss which can only come when man releases his hold and allows himself to find eternal peace with god. The doctrine of the Upanishads is consequently a reinforcement of the asceticism already prevalent in India.

It would be incorrect, however, to characterize the religion

of the Upanishads as being purely ascetic and concerned solely
with individual salvation. One of the most important concepts
of subsequent Indian religion and ethics was formulated during this period under the name of Karma. The law of Karma
is to the moral sphere what physical law is to nature, a basis
of predictability and uniformity. The early beginnings of this
conception are seen in the idea of Rita found in the Rig-Veda.
However, the Rig-Veda does little to elaborate on it and it is
left to the Upanishad writers to construct a definite idea of the
uniformity found in moral life.

The doctrine of Karma (the word literally means *action*)
is generally defined as the theory that a man's future reincarnation is determined by his actions in this life. In essence the
doctrine is one of continuing reward or punishment for past
deeds that will be meted out on this earth rather than in some
heaven or hell. After death a person does not find his final
refuge with god or satan as in some other religions; rather
he is sent back into this life in the form of a higher or lower
animal. If he has been generally good, he will come back in a
higher form, and if evil, he will come back as a lower animal.

According unto his deeds the embodied one successively
Assumes forms in various conditions.

Coarse and fine, many in number,
The embodied one chooses forms according to his own qualities.
[Each] subsequent cause of his union with them is seen to be
Because of the quality of his acts and of himself.
(Svetāśvatara Upanishad 5.11-12)

It is not a question of some superhuman power determining
the fate of an individual. His fate or his rebirth is entirely in
his own hands. It is his own character that makes the next life
higher or lower. Hence Karma is to be viewed as a law of life
just as gravitation is a law of the physical universe. Man will

reap precisely what he sows. There is no chance of placing the blame on the capricious will of a deity. "A man becomes good by his deeds and he becomes bad by his deeds." His destiny is in his own hands and his future upon his own shoulders. Throughout, a strong emphasis is placed upon individual responsibility.

What social ethic there is in the Upanishadic philosophy enters at this point. The good deeds by which a person reaches true freedom are defined as "disinterested work." If actions are performed from selfish motives they contribute to the weight of Karma. The only thing that binds a person to the chain of birth and death is his expression of egoism and his propensity to fulfill his material desires. It must be remembered that in India the people lived in a constant condition of scarcity. What one person had another could not have. If a given individual was in bondage to material pleasures, he tried to gain goods for himself rather than to serve others. This selfishness loaded him with Karma. The teachings of the Upanishads warn men that they must control their natural impulses, which are egoistic. They must control them if they expect ever to escape the round of births and deaths, but more importantly, if they are to achieve the perfect freedom which is oneness with god. Karma is thus the punishment for self-regard, and perfect freedom is the reward for selflessness.

Those who go hence without here having found the Soul (Ātman) and those real desires (satya kāma)—for them in all the worlds there is no freedom. But those who go hence having found here the Soul and those real desires—for them in all worlds there is freedom.

(Chāndogya Upanishad 8.1.6)

The doctrine of Karma is not mechanical. It is always possible through correct self-discipline to rise above the necessity for rebirth and to stretch life out to meet the infinite. Man is not necessarily selfish, for his acts are never wholly determined. At each moment he is always free to assert the freedom that is the core of his existence. Freedom is not granted by god; freedom in man is god. Man's affirmation, in terms of belief and deeds, is his to make. He must conquer himself, and by so doing he attains oneness with god. It is important to remember that Karma is not a doctrine of determination but a statement of punishment for acts committed in freedom. An individual's station or situation in this life is due to his Karma, but the future is left open. If he knows himself for what he really is, if he has seen into the depths of his own soul, and if he learns the truth that speaks to him, his future will be ever higher than his past.

It is obvious that the Karma theory offers an explanation for the conditions of this life and a hope for the future. It tends to make the believer content with his present physical status (whatever might be his caste), but leaves a chance for future glory. The necessity for doing good is strongly felt, but this goodness should not be thought of in material terms. Man's highest aim is not material wealth, fame or victory in war; it is still union with the absolute. Good deeds must therefore be thought of in spiritual rather than physical terms. The believer sacrifices for another's spiritual welfare; the sacrifice would not be good if it contributed to the satisfaction of another's carnal desires. With this the idea of goodness is transformed. To be truly good is to be selfless in such a way as to cause others also to be selfless. The possibility of rising in spirituality at the expense of another person's fall is not a part of the system.

SALVATION BY PHILOSOPHY

THE way of salvation offered by the Upanishads finally reduces itself to knowledge. It is by knowledge of the self

(Ātman) that the individual discovers all his small, ignoble and selfish desires to be false. Knowledge of Ātman releases the self from its worldly chains, makes for virtue and finally causes the round of rebirth to stop. In the Katha Upanishad appears the following statement of this doctrine:

> He, however, who has not understanding,
> Who is unmindful and ever impure,
> Reaches not the goal,
> But goes on to transmigration.
>
> He, however, who has understanding,
> Who is mindful and ever pure,
> Reaches the goal
> From which he is born no more.
>
> (Katha Upanishad 3.7-8)

In another place a Upanishad writer goes so far as to say that "by knowing it one is not stained by evil action." Here it would seem that a person with self-knowledge, a person who supposedly has been saved, can perform evil but remains un-defiled and is thereby not loaded with Karma. What this evil could be, the writer does not say. In any event, the usual con-ception is of the identification of knowledge with virtue. The existence of other conceptions simply points up the fact that the Upanishads were written over a long period by many writers. It would be impossible to construct a unified, con-sistent system from the many fragments we now possess.

If a pantheistic interpretation were given to this problem it would seem likely that true knowledge would raise the indi-vidual above the area within which moral distinctions operate. Such distinctions are for the level of the material every-day world. God is above them. And thus the individual who rec-ognizes himself as part and parcel of god would also be above moral goodness and evil. In fact, the Brahma-world into which the knower is released is beyond all temporal distinctions. In the Real there is no space, no time, no true, no false, no black, no white, and no good or evil. It is the world in which no speech is known and in which there is no distinction between subject and object. Speech, indeed, is often thought of as the prime characteristic of man's temporal existence.

. . . Verily, if there were no speech, neither right nor wrong would be known, neither true nor false, neither good nor bad, neither pleasant nor unpleasant. Speech, indeed, makes all this known.

(Chāndogya Upanishad 7.2.1)

The world might call an action evil, but if a man has the supreme knowledge he is beyond worldly scorn or punishment. "As a man when in the embrace of a beloved wife knows nothing within or without, so this person when in the embrace of the Soul knows nothing within or without. Verily, that is his true form."

One of the difficulties with such a doctrine of salvation is the hard fact of day-to-day experience. In a theoretical sense one might well assent to this form of philosophic religion, but what of the constant requirements of mere living? A living must be earned, work must be performed, and human contacts must be kept relatively constant. An isolated mystic, one out of many thousands, might be able to follow this path of absolute renunciation, but the large majority of people could never achieve it. The demands of ordinary life are too great.

In the course of common existence the so-called worldly desires were constantly demanding satisfaction. To meet this very practical problem, certain thinkers of the Upanishads developed Yoga practices. The word itself means yoke or harness, and it was an attempt to harness the mind and senses. The practice of Yoga includes such things as controlled breathing, concentration on a single object or the sky and the repetition of mystic words. All of these are designed to bring the individual to a comatose state which will reveal the world of the senses as shadowy illusion. The experience of Yoga is to show the person, if only for a short time, the wonders and mystery of Brahma. By rigorous self-discipline an individual can be renewed and revitalized almost at will. He need never succumb entirely to the things of this world for he is always free to stop whatever he is doing and go into the mystical trance. The proper words, such as Om, taj-ja-lān and Tad-vana, are often used as names of Brahma, and they therefore serve to fix attention upon the One.

These practices, which became so characteristic of later Indian religion, are here merely suggested. In a sense they are artificial means for gaining the insight so sought after by the mystic. However, they are perfectly consistent with the Upanishadic conception of the self. In order to be at one with Ātman, man must first slough off the fetters of this world and become indifferent to and undistracted by the flux and flow of objects and all things bearing distinguishing marks. To attain the desired unity it would seem to be efficacious to concentrate on some single thing to the end of final absorption. Controlled breathing recognizes that there is a close correlation between sleep and regular breathing. This physiological fact was as well known to the ancients as to the moderns. In any event, such practices offered a solution to the practical problem posed by the theory of the Upanishads.

The movement from the religion of the Vedas to that of the Upanishads represents a change from the physical to the immaterial. The Vedic gods were nature deities and little was done to get behind them. In a sense, the goal of life for the Vedic worshiper was physical fulfillment, a happy earthly existence. His hymns were spontaneous and full of awe and praise. Although the writers of the Upanishads accepted the divine authority of the Vedas, they penetrated to the ultimate unity behind the gods. Gods as well as men, they believed, exist in a totality. The totality found by the Indian was not the monism developed out of natural science, but the spiritual essence of all things. Rather than monism it was pantheism. The Real is god; the Real is eternal; the Real is Brahma-Ātman; and the Real is inexpressible in the language and mental constructs of man. It surpasses all intellect, yet it is understood. Here was seen the end of all misery, the end of all evil, the end of suffering and the end of struggle. In it the philosopher's prayer is answered.

> From the unreal lead me to the real.
> From darkness lead me to light.
> From death lead me to immortality.

5

THE GREAT HERESIES

THE lofty speculations and the highly disciplined practices found in the Upanishads did not belong to the religion of the average Indian. For the ordinary Indian, religious thought and practice were on a much more naïve level. The popular religion can be characterized as a heterogeneous mass of polytheistic, monotheistic and pantheistic belief. The Brahmanic priests continued to hold to the efficacy of a highly formalized religious worship, but even here there was nothing that could be called a universal church. The people worshiped much as they always had. There was widespread belief in magical formulae and superstitious incantations. The Western notion of a well-organized hierarchy with a central body of codified orthodoxy was almost completely lacking. The people worshiped in the tradition of their family, tribe, and village. Out of the confusion created by independent speculations and the necessary privacy of mystical union came the development of more specific religions and more generalized popular philosophies. It must be remembered, however, that the Vedic hymns and the Upanishadic philosophizing formed the substructure from which the new religious movements sprang.

In the sixth century before the birth of Christ, India was in an intellectual, political and religious turmoil. The time was ripe for some kind of solidification that would bring order out of confusion. Large numbers of men were leaving their homes,

breaking with their traditional social ties and becoming wanderers in search of salvation. The world of literate schoolmen
was split among a variety of philosophies and ways of life; the
world of the nonliterate was just as chaotic. Many gods and
many systems of salvation competed for supremacy. Politically, it was a time of aggressive warfare among the established dynasties. Each dynastic family was striving to extend
its control over wider and wider areas.

Coupled with this religious, intellectual and social unrest
was a development toward a more rigid caste system. The
Upanishadic speculation had tended to soften the caste lines.
To this tendency the Brahmanic priest responded with stricter
differentiation. Castes were being multiplied rather than
merged. The towns were divided into definite sections within
which the various castes lived. Those belonging to the priestly
(Brāhman) caste were rigorously segregated from the warrior
(Ksatriya) caste. These in turn were segregated from the
commercial (Baniyā) caste. The untouchables were forced
outside the city gates. These caste divisions established separate communities which were socially complete units. They
never mixed except under the most scrupulous rules. Friendships were generally confined to the caste of birth, but services
of one kind or another could be performed across caste lines.
Government was usually in the hands of the Ksatriya, while
trade and manufacture were carried on by the Baniyā caste.
The collection of refuse and the "dirty work" in general was
conducted by the untouchables. In a sense, the Brāhmans exercised spiritual, yet unorganized, authority over the entire
community. Their major interest, however, was in personal
salvation and they had little time for missionary work among
the other castes.

It was out of the Ksatriya caste that the two great leaders
of Indian heresy came. Gotama Buddha and Mahavira established sects which attained a high degree of historical impor-

tance and effectively challenged the Brāhmanic rule. Both these reformers were rooted deep in the Indian tradition, yet both rejected the authority of the Vedas and the priests. In a sense they are outgrowths of the inquiring spirit found in the philosophers of the Upanishads. The two sects, Buddhism and Jainism, arose under similar conditions in the same age and section of India. One, Buddhism, was destined to spread throughout Asia, while Jainism was to become an important part of the distinctly Indian culture.

MAHAVIRA THE JINA

VARDHAMĀNA, who is usually called by his more popular name, Mahavira, was the son of a wealthy member of the feudal aristocracy. His father, Siddhārtha, was chief of one of the most powerful Ksatriya clans, which went under the name of Nāya. Mahavira's mother, Trisālā, was the daughter of the king of the Magadha clan, another of the prominent Ksatriya families. Mahavira's early childhood was thus spent amidst luxury and political power. His friends were of his own class, and his original religious message was directed toward those of the Ksatriya and Brāhman castes.

The tradition of the Jains states that Mahavira was born in 599 B.C. and that he died in 527 B.C. He lived with his parents until they died and his eldest brother, Nandivardhana, took over the control of the family domain. Mahavira then left his home to become a member of a group of monks which the Nāya clan supported. In this Mahavira was following a tradition very similar to that found in the Catholic countries of the West. The eldest son succeeds to possession of the estate and the younger sons of ambition are sent into the Church. Mahavira was twenty-eight or thirty when he joined these monks, who followed the Rule of Pārsvanātha, an ascetic who had lived some two hundred and fifty years earlier. In general, the austerities of the Rule were those familiar to Indian ascetic practice. The initiate was to give up all worldly desire in an attempt to free himself from Karma and the cycle of rebirth.

Mahavira was a diligent novice. He was first required to fast for two and a half days without allowing himself to think of food and drink. After this initial act, he was required to give away all his worldly possessions. Since Mahavira was a younger son they could not have been very extensive, but his later followers wrote as if he had the wealth of a great temporal lord. When the fasting and the renunciation of wealth were over, he was then required to strip off his clothes and pull out his hair by the roots. This last act was to indicate his absolute abandonment of care for his body and his final willingness to harbor only the desires of the spirit. After pulling out his hair, Mahavira left his house and "entered the state of houselessness." He became a wandering mendicant.

The Venerable Ascetic Mahavira for a year and a month wore clothes; after that time he walked about naked, and accepted the alms in the hollow of his hand. For more than twelve years the Venerable Ascetic Mahavira neglected his body and abandoned the care of it; with equanimity he bore, underwent, and suffered all pleasant or unpleasant occurrences arising from divine powers, men, or animals.[1]

For Mahavira, as for later Jains, the question of clothing was of great importance. One of the manifestations of worldly knowledge of good and evil is found in the feeling of shame. If man feels shameful, he is in some sense aware of the fact that he is being something he should not be. To feel shame at being naked is to say that one is aware that he should be clothed. The true ascetic must rise above such distinctions. He must achieve the kind of blissful purity that is described

---

[1] The Kalpa Sûtra. Translated by Hermann Jacobi in *The Sacred Books of the East*, Vol. XXII, pp. 259-260. (London, Oxford Press, 1884.)

in the opening chapters of Genesis in the Jewish-Christian scriptures. Adam and Eve felt no shame and were at one with God until they ate of the forbidden tree. Originally they were above the knowledge of good and evil. After doing what God had forbidden, their first reaction is shame at their nakedness. In the life of the Indian ascetic we find the same kind of analysis. Salvation is withheld from us by our involvement in a world in which such distinctions are possible. To feel shame is to know sin; therefore to rise above shame is to conquer sin.

For a period of twelve years Mahavira wandered from town to village, "indifferent alike to the smell of ordure and of sandal, to straw and jewels, dirt and gold, pleasure and pain, attached neither to this world nor to that beyond, desiring neither life nor death." The picture we get from the tradition is that of a silent, wandering mendicant who spent his time begging and meditating upon himself. It was self-knowledge that he sought, and "he exerted himself for the suppression of the defilement of Karma."

In the thirteenth year of Mahavira's ascetic life he attained the supreme knowledge. His period of preparation was over and he became Jina, the conqueror of Karma. The final illumination came at the conclusion of a second two-and-a-half-day fast. From this time forward he had "complete and full, the unobstructed, unimpeded, infinite and supreme, best knowledge and intuition" called Kevalajnāna. Armed with this powerful insight, Mahavira set out to make known his message for mankind. He began to preach and teach his way of salvation to all. His own life became his doctrine's greatest example.

Mahavira's sermons were directly anti-Brahmanic. The Brahmans were teaching that birth was in the last analysis more important than deeds or knowledge. The members of the Brahman caste were automatically secure in their salvation, while those of the lower castes could count little on righteousness or ascetic practice for theirs. At the very best they would have to be reborn Brahmans before salvation from the eternal birth and rebirth could be attained. Mahavira preached that birth was unimportant and that the entire future was dependent upon the destruction of Karma. For him caste had no ultimate significance.

Mahavira spent the next thirty years expounding his doctrine. As time went on he connected himself with a legendary succession of twenty-three earlier seers, therefore considering himself a reformer rather than the founder of a new faith. Pārsvanātha, the founder of the Rule which Mahavira entered at the beginning of his career, was also thought to be in this line of Jina. The Jain tradition places its beginnings with a person called Rsabha many centuries earlier. There is little question that the doctrines taught by Mahavira were much older than he or even Pārsvanātha. It is impossible at this date to tell how much Jain history prior to Mahavira is legend and how much is fact. We do know, however, that Mahavira was the genius who made it into an important religious group.

Mahavira's great contribution was in organization. During his thirty years of preaching he gathered together large numbers of men and women from the Ksatriya aristocracy. In order to avoid the temptations inherent in the ascetic's wandering life, he organized four classes or orders—monks, nuns, laywomen and laymen—into academies or schools. Over each academy he placed one of his chief disciples, and over the entire system Mahavira himself maintained tight control. It was the function of the community to offer peace and a chance for meditation under the most favorable circumstances. No work was done by the monks or nuns; the laymen and laywomen served to support them. The lay members of the community could keep the Rule in only a limited fashion, but this limited renunciation was efficacious for their salvation and aided the more devout monks and nuns.

Much of the strength of the Jain movement can be found in the fact that it filled the need for a socially organized religious expression. Caste lines were still maintained, but those who were members of the community had a sense of belonging to and with others. Jainism, along with Buddhism, grew and prospered because it met the religious needs of large groups of Indians who were left out of the Brahmanic scheme and who were floundering in the confusion of the period. Jainism introduced not only a restatement of old doctrine, but also order for the laymen as well as the monks. Those who had to do the work of the world were no longer left out of religious consideration.

Although the practices and ethical injunctions of Jainism are numerous and complex, their philosophical basis is simple. Ultimately it ends in a very different system than the one found in the Upanishads, but there are also many marked similarities. It should be remembered that Jainism was a popular movement and therefore had to develop a position that was readily comprehensible.

THE "NINE TRUTHS"

THERE are nine so-called "fundamental truths" of Jainism. Underlying most of them are the ideas that man must somehow escape the cycle of birth and death and that his soul will find peace only when it is totally unconditioned by the material world. The world of our sense experience is filled with Jiva and Ajiva. Jiva is often translated as life, vitality, soul or consciousness. Ajiva is the opposite of Jiva, and is recognized as the inanimate. These two are not to be confused with spirit (Ātman) and matter, but rather they represent gradations of being. In this world there is no such thing as pure matter; there is nothing that does not in some way participate in spirit. The same can be said of pure spirit. The phenomenal world recognizes only gradations that move toward purity of spirit and away from involvement in matter. The true desire of man should be the release of his soul from the world. Essentially this means the final liberation of Ātman in such a way as to make it totally unconditioned.

The gods are to be thought of as souls which have attained a higher degree of purity than the soul of man. In Jainism there is no creator god, and the ultimate release of the soul is not conceived of in the pantheistic sense found in the Upanishads. Once all Karma is destroyed, the individual soul gains complete deliverance, or Moksa. A person who attains Moksa remains an entity but he becomes boundless. His entrance into Nirvana is not absorption into Being, but the maintenance of the self at its highest and purest level. This is a level even beyond the gods. Both gods and men are striving for Moksa and boundless residence in the eternal Nirvana. The ultimate and final reality is this released, ideal soul.

With this as a base, the Jains established a well-articulated system of salvation. In order to gain the final liberation it is necessary to know the ways in which Karma is acquired (Āsrava), the ways of stopping the acquisition of Karma (Samvara), and finally the way in which Karma can be destroyed (Nirjarā).

Karma enters the Jiva through the senses and through thought. If a person concentrates on the things of the senses, on worldly objects whether they are beautiful or ugly, he opens a "channel" through which matter becomes a part of his soul. He marries himself to this world instead of renouncing it for the higher life. The natural consequence of such a marriage is a spirit of possessiveness, a desire to own objects. By so desiring, he raises the objects of sense to a high level of importance and thus weights himself down. In this sense Karma is thought of as being material. It adds weight to the soul and therefore forces a rebirth on a lower rather than a higher level.

However, it is not only through the senses that Karma enters; it also comes by way of evil thoughts. Man can be degraded as easily by thinking as by acting. To be dishonest or untruthful in thought is just as much a sin (Pāpa) as to be dishonest or untruthful in action. "As a man is in his heart, so is he" is a phrase well constructed for Jainism. The thought of lust and the desire to be deceitful open a further channel for Karma. In this the Jain is emphasizing the importance of man's motivations as well as his actions. To be really pure, there must be neither thought nor action of an evil character.

In order to block the channels by which Karma enters (Samvara), it is necessary to achieve a correctness in both action and thought. Here the Jain enumerates the requirements for holiness. The holy man will never kill any living thing. All animals possess Jivas which are trying to achieve Moksa. It is therefore necessary to avoid walking on flies, worms or any insect. The dutiful Jain will walk for miles along a road, where it is easy to see and avoid creeping insects, in order to avoid walking across a grassy plot where it is impossible to see what hides underfoot. Such elaborate rules for the protection of life are particularly binding upon the monks and nuns. But even the lay members of the sect are told to be especially cautious in this regard. To destroy life is a cardinal sin (Pāpa); to avoid such destruction closes one of the widest channels through which Karma can enter the Jiva. Interestingly enough, this does not mean saving life. There is no injunction which requires man to act in such a way as to restrain others from the taking of life. The rule has a purely negative function in that it only prohibits killing.

The Jain is further prohibited from harsh speaking, from uncleanliness and from lustful practice. If he speaks kindly, endures the pain of illness with a tranquil spirit, practices chastity, and remains indifferent to praise, he effectively blocks the entrance of further Karma into his soul. By this process the Karma that he has already acquired will be used up and no further Karma added.

As a large tank, when its supply of water has been stopped, gradually dries up by the consumption of the water and by evaporation, so the Karman of a monk, which he acquired in millions of births, is annihilated by austerities, if there is no influx of bad Karman.[2]

There is therefore a close connection between the stopping of Karma (Samvara) and the destruction of Karma (Nirjarā). To destroy existing Karma, or to "consume" it, it is necessary to go beyond the blocking of channels to active reverence and intense spiritual exercises. Here the kind of austere life lived by Mahavira serves as an example. Concentration on the soul, the study of doctrines, intense meditation and bodily asceticism all contribute to Karma's destruction. The true saint recognizes the necessity for both Samvara and Nirjarā. The result of these austere practices is to loosen the bondage of the soul (Bandha) to Karma and permit the ultimate deliverance in Moksa. There is a softer side to this concept of salvation, however. The good actions (Punya) which lead to peace of mind are just as necessary as the more negative proscriptions found in Samvara. The nine basic truths of Jain teaching can be summarized as follows:

Jiva—The principle of life or consciousness.

Ajiva—The inanimate objects on the other end of the scale of being from Jiva.

Āśrava—The ways of acquiring Karma: channels such as evil thoughts, conceit, senses, and deceit.

[2] Jaina Sûtras, translated by Hermann Jacobi in *The Sacred Books of the East*, Vol. XLV, p. 174. (London, Oxford Press, 1900.)

Pāpa—The idea of sin, which includes such things as ..ypocrisy in meditation, dishonesty, destruction of life and unchastity.

Samvara—The ways of blocking Karma. This includes such things as patient endurance of pain as punishment for past sins, not speaking harshly, indifference to pain and abhorrence of the unclean.

Nirjarā—The destruction of Karma. These are positive practices such as reverence, meditation, study of doctrine and bodily asceticism.

Punya—The performance of actions which lead to peace of mind. These are actions of merit.

Bandha—The bondage of the soul to Karma. This expresses the extent of the connection between the Jiva and Karma. If by accident a life is taken, the repentant soul is less bound to the Karma than one who does not repent.

Moksa—Final and complete deliverance from the round of births. A person who attains this state is called Siddha, a boundless one. The soul remains an entity, but takes residence in Nirvana.

ORGANIZATIONAL EXPANSION

As MIGHT be expected, the Jain community was not composed of a multitude of totally convinced ascetics living in perfect harmony. The structure as it was established by Mahavira grew and expanded, but with its growth there developed two very distinct parties. There were those who longed for the austerity and purity of the founding Mahavira and his disciples. They felt that the Jains were becoming too lax in their ascetism and that their path of salvation was much too easy.

There was conflict over the position of women and the wearing of clothes. The old question of whether or not women could gain Moksa without first being reborn as men became particularly acute as more women came into the cult. This Digambara group, which was committed to the stricter asceticism, maintained that women must be born men before Moksa could be possible and that no clothes should be worn by the ascetics. To this they added the belief that once a saint had obtained a high degree of self-renunciation, he would no longer require food to stay alive. Finally, they insisted that the Jain idol, Tīrthankara, should always be represented as nude and with downcast eyes.

The Digambara was a reforming group within the general community. After a time, about 79 or 82 A.D., the Digambara broke away from the main body and set up a cult of its own along what it conceived to be the pure lines of Jain belief as enunciated by Mahavira. This schism weakened the Jain church and made it less of a power. Constant and countless dissensions followed. Sects began to split off for what now seem to be relatively minor reasons. The rigorous asceticism of the original community was hardly spiritual food for mass consumption. Few of Mahavira's direct followers wished to see the austerities relaxed to a popular level. In addition to this internal difficulty Jainism was in constant conflict with the Brahmans and the Buddhists. The Brahmans claimed to speak with religious authority for all Indians and they considered the Jain communities a direct challenge to that authority. The Buddhists, on the other hand, were a young reforming sect much like the Jains. Their doctrine was considerably less ascetic, however, and in many ways represented a greater mass appeal. In a country where all these conflicting elements were constantly joined in battle, it is no wonder that schisms multiplied the sects.

Almost all sects of Jainism are agreed that they do not worship their gods but use them as helps in getting rid of Karma. The gods are not thought of, then, in the usual religious sense. In fact, some sections of the Jain scriptures speak of the gods as being inferior to men since they cannot attain Moksa until they are born as men and go through the trials of a material existence. Nor are the gods in the Jain pantheon all good. Some live in hell, where they do their work of torturing the Jiva. These (Rudra, Ambarasa, Kāla, Dhanu, Kumbha and ten others) busy themselves with acts of torture and attempt to hurt man in every way possible. Many of these Jain devil-gods can be identified as the demons of the Atharva-Veda. They represent the causes of mysterious happenings that men fear. When they catch a man, the possibility of his ever regaining a chance at Moksa is very remote.

GODS AND SALVATION

THE gods in heaven generally represent the helpers of men, in the Jain system. Sūrya inhabits the sun, Candra the moon, Graha the planets, Tārā the stars and Naksatra the constellations. These and all the other gods of heaven are ruled over by the one supreme Lord, Indra, to whose commands they are subject. By virtue of his position, Indra is also man's greatest help. There is a story told of Mahavira's life which illustrates Indra's character. At one point in his travels, before his illumination, Mahavira was sitting under a tree by the side of a road. He was deep in contemplation. A farmer came down the road driving a herd of cattle and asked Mahavira to look after the cattle while he went on an errand into the village. Mahavira did not hear or see the farmer. When the farmer came back, the cattle had strayed away and Mahavira was still deep in meditation. Since the farmer could get no reply from Mahavira, he spent the whole of the night looking for his herd. As he went off in the wrong direction the cattle came back and settled alongside Mahavira. In the early dawn the farmer returned. Upon seeing his cattle he started to beat Mahavira. Indra was watching the saint and intervened by driving the farmer away. Indra then asked Mahavira for permission to guard over him so that no such incident could recur. Mahavira refused protection and insisted that he wished to find Moksa alone. However, the god was still worried lest Mahavira be accidentally killed, so he established Siddhārtha, a brother of Mahavira's who had become a god, as his protector. All this was unknown to Mahavira.

This story illustrates the provisional character of the gods and their relations with men. The gods could aid man, but they were in no way responsible for salvation. In fact they lived in a world much like India. They were divided into separate castes and the members of each caste lived together. Some of the gods, ninety-nine of them, were classed as outcaste or untouchable, and these were the servants of the higher gods. Each god had his function, and Indra ruled all with absolute authority.

What worship the Jain engages in is directed toward the twenty-four Tirthankara. These are the half-legendary and half-historical prophets of Jainism. Mahavira was the last of the original twenty-four. All the Jain temples contain statues of the Tirthankara before which rites of one kind or another are performed. Even here, however, it is hard to tell whether the Tirthankara are worshiped or simply venerated. It is probably most accurate to say that the Tirthankara are venerated and that the real object of Jain worship is the individual's own eternal soul. Indeed, some commentators hold that the religion of Jaina is a religion without worship.

The most distinctive element in Jainism is not its belief either in asceticism or in Karma, but its means of gaining ultimate salvation. The gods of Jainism are a part of the general Indian culture and are not to be considered in any way the exclusive property of the sect. Jainism's scheme of salvation, however, includes the so-called three Jewels which sum up the peculiar nature of the movement. The first Jewel is right faith —the belief that Jina (conqueror) has been able to overcome the world; the second Jewel is right knowledge—knowledge of the Jain explanation of the world and the nature of the soul; and the third Jewel is right action—the methods for stopping and destroying Karma and obtaining the final release. In all these, Jainism is much closer to the Brahmanic religion than to Buddhism. In fact, it has always remained distinctively Indian while Buddhism, which arose out of the same conditions, has become an international religion.

GOTAMA THE BUDDHA

THE founder of Buddhism, Siddhartha Gotama, came from the same caste as Mahavira, the Ksatriya. Although his birth and early years are obscured by mythical and miraculous stories told by his followers, it is known that he was born about 560 B.C. to a wealthy land-holding family belonging to the Çakya clan. At an early age he was married to his cousin, who was the daughter of the king of Kali. In so far as we are able to determine, Gotama lived the normal life of a scion of the wealthy ruling group, learning to fish, hunt and in general to participate with proficiency in the sports of the aristocracy. There is little more than this that can be called historical in the record of his first twenty-nine years.

In his twenty-ninth year he renounced his family and left his wife and child to go into the world as an ascetic in search of salvation. In this action he was no different from a large number of Indians of the period. The legend states that on the night of his son's birth, he sent for his driver, Channa, and ordered him to make his horse ready for a long trip. As Gotama left his house he went to the door of his wife's cham-

ber for one last look at his sleeping child. Although he wished
to take the child Rahula in his arms, he dared not for fear of
waking his wife. After leaving the house he rode away to become a mendicant monk, wandering in search of salvation.

On the road he took that night to Kapilavastu, Gotama en-
countered four signs which seemed to point to the misery and
mysterious blackness of the condition of men. The first was
an aged man who pulled himself along with no apparent purpose in a life with no apparent reason. The next was a sick
man whose body was wracked by fever, an instance of suffering that seemed meaningless and absurd. The third was a
corpse being drawn along by mourners who were tearing their
hair and crying at the loss of their friend and kinsman. The
fourth was a mendicant monk who was enduring the most
profound suffering for the good of his soul. For Gotama these
were examples of the great enigma of life. What is life's meaning? And how can the various degrees of suffering and death
be comprehended in terms which do not make life an absurd-
ity? There is little doubt that it was this problem which sent
Gotama in search of the key to life's tragedy and mystery.

After riding some distance, he gave his possessions to his
servant Channa and sent him back to announce his departure
to his family. Gotama proceeded on foot to Rājagaha, the capital of Magadha, where he associated himself with a Brahman
teacher named Ālāra. In his study with Ālāra he found little to
satisfy him, so he went from one Brahman teacher to another.
In each instance he asked the same question: For what reasons
do men suffer? Each time he got the same answers which were
based largely on the so-called orthodox systems of philosophy
that found their roots in the Upanishads. Again and again was
expressed the belief that by doing penance and practicing austerity a mortal can gain the insight he seeks. The simple statement of the doctrine was unsatisfying, and Gotama resolved
to try the method for himself.

Together with five disciples, Gotama set out for the heavily wooded area of Uruvela, where for the next six years he engaged in the most profound penance and rigorous austerity. The extent of his self-mortification spread his fame for miles around, and new disciples were added to his group. One day, after a long fast, he fell to the ground, and his disciples thought he was dead. But when he arose he was both alive and completely disillusioned about the method of salvation he was attempting. He became convinced that his suffering was due to mental rather than physical causes. The result was that he gave up his self-mortification and began to take food. To his disciples this appeared to be an act of great impiety and they promptly lost their faith in him. According to their doctrine, no man could achieve salvation without completely suppressing the body, and this tenet Gotama was now denying. They rejected him as a spiritual failure, and he was forced to continue his search alone.

After giving up the Brahmanic path to salvation, Gotama continued to wander and meditate. Soon after his disciples left him, Gotama came to the banks of the Nairanjarā and sat in the shade of a Bo tree. As he sat, he pondered the various phases of his life and the content of the philosophies he had been taught. Nowhere was he able to find an answer to his problem. The Brahmanic teachers had taught him to be ascetic and to renounce his body, yet such a renunciation had proved of no avail. He knew that to go back and live the life of a prince would furnish no ultimate solution. Where was the answer to the riddle of misery and suffering? Was he, as well as the rest of mankind, destined to die without knowledge and without understanding?

As the day wore on, his doubts and fears became stronger and his knowledge became less. No matter where he turned the result was the same—a black, impenetrable wall of mystery. By sunset he had come to a resolution of his problem.

He had become Buddha, the enlightened one, and he now felt that he had positive knowledge of the answer. On the basis of the conclusions reached during this day of thought, Gotama Buddha developed a system of explanation which was destined to capture the religious imagination of Asia's millions.

With their gift for poetic imagery, the later followers of Buddha tell the following story of how he came to preach his gospel. Mara, death, saw that Buddha had learned the secret of existence and was therefore in a position to threaten his hold over the world. To combat this threat to his power, Mara sent his three daughters, Desire, Discontent and Lust, to steal the eternal knowledge from Buddha. But these temptations were of little consequence since Buddha had already risen above the distinctions of love and hate. Buddha now knew what the illusions of this world were, and the usual instruments of Mara were too coarse for such a well-armed adversary. There was one temptation, however, that might turn the trick. If Mara could convince Buddha that the knowledge he possessed was too exalted for the masses of people and too deep for normal comprehension, Buddha would not give up his life to preaching the good news. He would simply enter Nirvana at once and the secret would die with him. The followers of Buddha never tire of singing the praises of the man who was capable of putting this temptation behind him. Such was the final defeat of Mara. "Like as when some cruel chieftain slain, the hateful band is all dispersed and scattered, so the host of Mara, disconcerted, fled away. The mind of Buddha now reposed peaceful and quiet." Armed with a mind at peace he set out to find the five disciples who had deserted him.

Buddha found his disciples at Benares and immediately set to work to explain his saving discovery. The so-called Sermon at Benares, which was preached to the five ascetics, states the basic elements of the new doctrine. In it is found the enumeration of the Four Noble Truths and the Eightfold Path.

Top left, Ganesha, the elephant-headed son of
Siva. He is a popular god of prosperity, good
luck and wisdom among the Hindu Sivites.
(*Courtesy Bush Collection of Religion and Culture.*)

Top right, A small stone relief of Surya, the
Hindu Sun God. Here he is pictured in his
chariot with his driver Aruna, two attendants and
seven horses. (*Museum of Ethnography, Berlin.*)

Right, Brahma is on his wild goose holding the
four Vedas and a rose wreath. *Vishnu* is pictured
with his attributes: lotus, conch, discus and mace.
Siva is shown as an ascetic. (*After von Glase-
napp.*)

The procession of Nagas (naked ascetics) was held in connection with an annual fair and religious festival at Allahabad. The Nagas are regarded as especially holy and are worshiped by the people. (*Courtesy Bush Collection of Religion and Culture.*)

This woman is gathering sacred soil over which the ascetics have walked. (*Courtesy Bush Collection of Religion and Culture.*)

This is a Sadu lying on a bed of spikes and holding a rosary in his hand. All pictures taken at Allahabad in 1918. (*Courtesy Bush Collection of Religion and Culture.*)

THE NEW DOCTRINE

As would be expected, Buddha begins with an analysis of suffering. The Four Noble Truths are: the universal nature of suffering; the original or universal cause of suffering; the assurance that this cause can be removed; and finally, the means by which it is removed. The fact that suffering is universal and that all men participate in it should be a self-evident truth. "Birth is suffering; Decay is suffering; Death is suffering; Sorrow, Lamentation, Pain, Grief, and Despair are suffering; not to get what one desires is suffering." By these words Buddha seeks to show that no mortal can possibly live without some experience of suffering.

All suffering springs from one source. Man errs when he searches for a source of each of his sufferings; by so doing he only sinks farther into despair and travels farther from the truth. The Second Noble Truth is recognized when one sees that "it is craving which gives rise to fresh rebirth, and, bound up with pleasure and lust, now here, now there, finds ever fresh delight. There is a sensual craving, the craving for eternal existence, and the craving for temporal happiness." Thus Buddha reduces the source of human misery to desire, which is not unlike the source propounded by the writers of the Upanishads. Men suffer because they desire well-being, they thirst after pleasure, and most particularly, they desire eternal life. To be free from these desires is to attain perfect freedom; indeed, it is to be totally unconditioned by the world of men and things.

Once this source of human misery is discovered, the question arises about the possibility of eliminating it. The Third Noble Truth is the simple fact that there is a way of getting rid of the craving which fills the world with suffering. Buddha not only states the fact, he goes on to assure his followers that he has found the way. Salvation can be achieved by any who are willing to follow the Eightfold Path. This Path is the middle ground between indulgence in sensual pleasure and self-mortification. Both of these extremes are to be avoided. "A life given to pleasures, devoted to pleasures and lusts; this is degrading, sensual, vulgar, ignoble and profitless. And a life given to mortifications; this is painful, ignoble, and profitless." The road to true enlightenment and final Nirvana lies between and is characterized by the following virtues:

1. Right Understanding
2. Right Mindedness
3. Right Speech
4. Right Action
5. Right Living
6. Right Effort
7. Right Endeavor
8. Right Concentration

"This, O Monks, is that middle path, avoiding these two extremes, discovered by the Tathagata—that path which opens the eyes, and bestows understanding, which leads to peace of mind, to the higher wisdom, to full enlightenment, to Nirvana!" [3]

As soon as this new method of salvation was announced, Buddha attracted a large number of disciples. At first the majority were from his own class and principally from among those who had already become ascetics. From its inception Buddhism was without caste differentiations, a way of life for all men in all conditions. As the number of disciples increased, missionaries were sent to all parts of the land to preach the good news. The order grew rapidly, drawing its converts from the Jains, Brahmans and independent seekers. Its growth was not only in numbers but also in power and wealth. After

[3] Buddhist Suttas, trans. by T. W. Rhys Davids, in *The Sacred Books of the East*, Vol. XI, p. 147. (London, Oxford Press, 1881.)

forty years of preaching, Gotama the Buddha gave up his body and attained Parinirvana,[4] leaving to the world a religious order which now claims more adherents than any other.

Like many of the other philosophies and religions of the time, Buddhism declared that man was required to find his own salvation without the aid of gods. The Vedic gods were without power; in fact they were subject to the same cycle of birth and rebirth that haunted men. The older Vedic practices of sacrifice and worship were fruitless since the ultimate ground of the universe could not be conceived of as a personal god. In effect, primitive Buddhism was as atheistic, in a Western sense, as Jainism, and certainly much more so than the religion of the Upanishads. The evil from which man desired salvation was the physical world itself. Man yearned to be free of all fetters, to be unconditioned by time and circumstance, and to attain release from an existence burdened by the sins of the past. In this, Buddhism was much the same as the other heretical movements of the time. Heretical, that is, from the viewpoint of the Brahmans, for the Brahmans still held to the authority and revelation of the Vedas.

The idea of a universal natural law was developed in the Upanishads but did not become a part of popular belief until the time of Buddha. Buddha considered belief in the existence of natural law a prime requisite for understanding the universe. Like all other beings, man is subject to regularity, and there is just as much natural regularity in the moral life as there is in the physical universe. Here there is no room for an interfering supernatural. The laws of nature are the laws of life, and he who knows them is enlightened. By placing the idea of natural law on the level of popular belief, Buddha effectively released morality from the domain of supernatural religion and its practicing priests. At the same time he raised

---

[4] Parinirvana is possible only after death, while Nirvana is possible and can be enjoyed during life.

the conception of human nature and restored to it some of the dignity it had lost through the preaching of the Brahmans and the ascetics. In this Buddha was well within the tradition established by the writers of the Upanishads.

THE SOUL

MANY commentators have emphasized the close connection between the thought and spirit of Buddha and that of the Upanishads. This is probably valid with the exception of one great doctrine which is essential to Buddhism but contrary to the previous Indian tradition. All previous systems had assumed the existence of a soul or ego in man. Both the Upanishads and the Jain Sûtras had been emphatic in their declaration that the true soul of man is ultimately unconditioned by the material or mental changes of the world. The man another person knows is a union of the soul with material elements. He is, indeed, a synthesis or organization. The argument for believing in a soul which counted most heavily with Buddha's predecessors is a potent one: there has to be in the individual something permanent and unchanging, something which represents the pure essence of humanness. This is the "real" individual. Those aspects that are temporal, changing and conditioned by life seem to lack permanence; therefore there has to be a static, unchangeable center—the soul.

It was at this point, over the contention that there is anything called a soul or ego in man, that Buddha differed most radically from the earlier and contemporary systems of religious philosophy. He looked at the world and found that it revealed perpetual change. Man only deludes himself when he sees it otherwise.

"This soul of mine can be perceived, it has experienced the result of good and evil actions committed here and there: now this soul of mine is permanent, lasting, eternal, has the inherent quality of never changing, and will continue for ever and ever!"

This, brethren, is called the walking in delusion, the jungle of delusion, the wilderness of delusion, the puppet show of delusion, the writhing of delusion, the fetter of delusion.[5]

Our consciousness tells us only that our sensations, our emotions, and our ideas are moving, never stationary. We see things always in terms of process and never as static, finally fixed entities. On what basis, then, do we postulate the fixed eternal soul which never becomes but always is? Such a postulation is only a "doctrine of fools." The body can never be separated from its functions and capacities. The object we call an "individual" is a combination of five different factors (Skandhas): physical mass, perception, sensation, consciousness and predispositions; and all five of these are released at death, leaving nothing of what was once the "individual." The following dialogue between Milinda, a king, and Nāgasena, a Buddhist teacher, illustrates the type of argument employed in this connection:

The king said, "How is your reverence known? What is your name?"

Nāgasena replied, "I am called Nāgasena by my parents, the priests, and others. But Nāgasena is not a separate entity."

To this the king objected, very much as a modern Christian might, that in that case there could be no virtue, nor vice; no reward, nor retribution (in other words, no "sanction"). He then mentioned one after another all the parts of the body, and mind, and the *Skandhas* just described, and asked of each whether it was Nāgasena. All these questions were answered in the negative. "Then," said the king, "I do not see Nāgasena. Nāgasena is a sound without meaning. You have spoken an untruth. There is no Nāgasena."

The mendicant asked, "Did your majesty come here on foot, or in a chariot?"

[5] Buddhist Suttas, *op. cit.,* p. 299.

"In a chariot," was the answer.

"What is a chariot?" asked Nāgasena. "Is the ornamental cover the chariot? Are the wheels, the spokes of the wheels, or the reins, the chariot? Are all these parts together (in a heap) the chariot? If you leave these out, does there remain anything which is the chariot?"

To all this the king said, "No."

"Then I see no chariot, it is only a sound, a name. In saying that you came in a chariot you have uttered an untruth. I appeal to the nobles, and ask them if it be proper that the great king of all Jambudwīpa should utter an untruth?"

Rather neat, doubtless, and not undeserved. But the king is not convinced. "No untruth have I uttered, venerable monk. The cover, wheels, seat, and other parts all united or combined (chariot-wise) form the chariot. They are the usual signs by which that, which is called a chariot, is known."

"And just so," said Nāgasena, "in the case of man"; and he quoted the words of the Teacher, where he had said, "As the various parts of a chariot form, when united, the chariot, so the five Skandhas, when united in one body, form a being, a living existence." [6]

However the argument strikes, it is certainly true that Buddhism feels that any statements regarding the permanent nature of the soul go far beyond the facts of experience. To speak of inscrutable mysteries, and then to base systems of salvation upon them, is not a mere theoretical error, according to the Buddhist, but a positive set-back to the religious life. Man must first have right knowledge, he insists, and this does not include fanciful notions about a soul he cannot experience. True understanding of man is possible only when the metaphysical basis for the soul is discarded and an empirical basis is substituted.

[6] T. W. Rhys Davids, *Buddhism*. Society for Promoting Christian Knowledge, London, 1917, pp. 96-97. By permission.

Since Buddha denies the existence of an eternal soul, he has difficulty in establishing a belief in Karma and rebirth. However difficult it might be, the doctrine has been consistently maintained throughout the history of Buddhism. Indeed, it forms one of the keystones for the entire Buddhist structure.

PROCESS AND DETERMINISM

GOTAMA postulated the existence of reincarnation, but not the transmigration of souls. The life which comes after death is in reality a totally new life; no single phase of the new existent can be considered part of the past. However, the life which passes is the cause of the new life. One life runs its course and dies, but the very fact that it has achieved a discernible result is sufficient to give birth to a new life. The new life (angel, man or animal) is produced according to the law of Karma, which simply means that it is produced out of the Karma of the old and as a result of the "thirst" or the "cleavage" to which the previous life was bound. The law of Karma is thus responsible for the constant round of birth and rebirth, the existence any single individual now has being the result of the past. This doctrine expresses for the Buddhist the close interconnection between all life histories, and it asserts the moral cause of suffering and apparent tragedy in the world. No individual begins at birth; he has actually been "in the making" for ages. And no individual ends until all Karma is destroyed.

It is apparent that this conception of Karma is closely related to the idea that the total world is in process, always becoming and never arriving. Any individual man is simply a "link in a long chain of cause and effect where no link is independent of the rest." The dynamic of the process is the "thirst" or the grasping after the fulfillment of desires in this life. The source or ground of this "thirst" is ignorance. Once man learns the truth and no longer desires the illusions of existence, the fatal cause-and-effect series is broken. It is by this knowledge and the consequent right living that Karma is dried up and man is able to enter Nirvana. At death such a person attains perfect Nirvana, or Parinirvana. After this there is no rebirth, and final deliverance from bondage is secured.

On the face of it, this appears to be a deterministic system; the present life is determined by the Karma of the past. If this is so, is not the present action determined by the present self, which is loaded with Karma? But then there would be little sense in asking man to follow a different path or initiate a new course of action. Buddha offers a solution to this problem. According to the law of Karma there is a flow out of the past into the present. Although the past is directly connected with the present, there can be no assumption of a mechanical causality. What a man will be is determined by his present choices. He is thus presented with the possibility of salvation. He can act as the cause of his own future, and in so doing, the "opportunity is afforded for the entire extinction of misery."

It is obvious that Buddha did not confront the problem of freedom and determinism on a philosophic level. Indeed, he expressly rejects the problem as being speculative and ultimately incapable of rational solution. He was much more interested in asserting the continuity of all things and the necessity for man to work out his own salvation. Buddha eschews metaphysics in favor of ethics. Karma expresses the orderliness of man's moral estate and the necessity for spiritual growth. Any attempt to translate this essentially moral principle into metaphysical categories is to make it meaningless.

NIRVANA

THE problem of Nirvana is much the same. Buddha spent little time trying to describe Nirvana and no time at all trying to describe its exact dimensions or its position in space. To do so would be to engage in metaphysical speculation. He simply asserts that once the great truths of existence are recognized, the mind is released and all distinctions vanish. "The mind released is like the extinction of a flame." And the word Nirvana is often translated as "blowing out." This Nirvana of Buddhism is in no way to be confused with the ultimate release of the Ātman in either the Upanishads or the theories of Mahavira. Nor, on the other hand, does it mean the complete annihilation of the individual. Rather, it is the "blowing out" or extinction of the "thirsting" of mind and heart which would otherwise cause a new rebirth. Here again is an essentially moral rather than a metaphysical idea. Nirvana becomes for the Buddhist a state of "perfect peace, goodness and wisdom."

The person who has attained Nirvana (the Arahant) is still encumbered by a body which is the result of his former errors. As time passes, this body withers away and the Arahant ceases to be alive or to be in existence in any way whatever. Here is the final and complete extinction called Parinirvana.

Those who have applied themselves studiously with a firm mind and free from desire to the commandments of Gotama, have obtained the highest gain, having merged into immortality, and enjoying happiness after getting it for nothing.

The old [Karma] is destroyed, the new [Karma] has not arisen, those whose minds are disgusted with a future existence, the wise who have destroyed their seeds (of existence, and) whose desires do not increase, go out like this lamp.[7]

ORGANIZATIONAL DEVELOPMENT

THE ordinary life of man is far too complicated and full of distractions to permit a person to follow the pathway of

[7] Ratanasutta, 7, 14. In *The Sacred Books of the East*, Vol. X, pp. 38, 39. (London, Oxford Press, 1880.)

Buddha to salvation. The life of a father or businessman, for example, could not admit of such a rigorous spiritual regime; so Buddha requested all those who were really serious to forsake their families, social and business ties, and enter his Rule as monks. Monasteries were opened and a definite set of proscriptive rules promulgated to aid the monks in their quest. The most important of the monastic rules were summed up in ten commandments: (1) Refrain from killing; (2) Refrain from stealing; (3) Refrain from unchastity; (4) Refrain from lying; (5) Refrain from intoxicants; (6) Refrain from solid food after midday; (7) Refrain from dancing, music and the theater; (8) Refrain from using flowers, perfumes and salves; (9) Refrain from using high broad couches; and (10) Refrain from accepting gold and silver.

To this decalogue was added a large number of lesser rules which eventually came to control the monk's every movement. No monk was allowed to work, or to wear hair on his head or face. All monks were required to dress alike in three simple garments with no ornamentation. The only survival of more ancient religious practice was the maintenance of two appointed days each month for fasting. It was on these days that the monks tested their consciences and determined according to detailed questions the purity of their minds and hearts.

For those who could not give up the responsibilities of daily life to enter the Rule as monks, lay organizations were established. They were in many ways similar to the lay orders found among the Jains. Laymen, just as monks, could come from any caste, but they differed from monks in so far as they could not attain Nirvana, their discipleship to Buddha being necessarily limited since they were unable to devote their full time to the religious life. They could look forward, however, to a more favorable reincarnation. Then it would be possible for them to lead the life of a monk and ultimately achieve the status of an Arahat. Here and now they were required to live up to the first five commandments of the decalogue and to perform other rigorously defined duties, including the support of the monasteries.

Reluctantly Buddha consented to allow an order of nuns to develop. Early Buddhist texts contain passages which depict women stirring desire in men and leading them to a false way of life away from the path of high moral renunciation. However this might be, Buddha finally admitted that women as well as men could gain salvation. With this admission, he was forced to establish a sisterhood. It was always to be dependent upon the brotherhood of monks, however, and it was compelled to operate under rigid regulations.

Buddhism and Jainism represent the great heresies which arose out of the ferment and unrest of the Upanishadic period. Both follow in the general tradition of Indian thought with the great exception that they deny the existence of savior gods. Although both religions speak of beings who inhabit the wondrous worlds outside the earth, in no way are these beings considered an aid to man in his quest for salvation; both heresies place this responsibility directly upon the shoulders of man himself. But it must be remembered that Buddhism and Jainism were at first relatively small sects. The great mass of Indians still worshiped their highly personalized deities, and even many of the laymen who served in the Jain and Buddhist cults continued the liturgical practices of their fathers. The inherited religions were affected and changed by these heresies but they were never supplanted, because the metaphysical abstractions and the ascetic practices of the Buddhist and Jain sects were far too difficult and much too arid for the majority of Indians. It was not until much later that Buddhism developed into a universal religion. And when it did its character was greatly changed.

6

THEISTIC HINDUISM

AFTER the heresies, the older Vedic religion and culture underwent profound changes, but these changes
were unconscious and required no violent revolution
in thought and practice. The new beliefs invoked by the Upanishads and the heresies were accommodated to Indian life in a
slow evolutionary process. Out of it we find two of the lesser
deities of the old Vedic religion, Vishnu and Siva, rising to
prominence and displacing the ancient Indra and his equals.
Just when they began their rise is lost in history, but it is
known that these two deities have held the central places in
Indian religion from a century before Christ to the present.

In general they symbolize two aspects of the Indian character. Siva is a dark god, the personification of the wild savage
life of the mountain tribes. He dances or sits in deep thought
high in the icy stillness of the mountains. He represents a kind
of ascetic irritability which expresses itself in irrational destruction and bloody battle. It is often said that Siva is the
expansion and development of the Vedic god Rudra. Worship
directed toward him was necessarily bloody, sacrificial and
orgiastic. Like human beings of this temperament, Siva could
be a powerful friend or a terrible enemy.

Vishnu, on the other hand, has a mild and merciful character. He performs his feats and wins his friends by love, and
it is love and mercy toward all that his will respects and
teaches. His followers worship him by faith and devotion to

that ideal, dealing with other human beings in charity and mercy. The earlier character of Vishnu as the sun-god of the Rig-Veda is maintained by his later worshipers. He is warmth, a source of strength and a dispeller of gloom. In the Bhagavad-Gitā he (or Krishna, one of his many incarnations) is worshiped as the supreme monotheistic deity who rules over paradise and saves man from the despair and tragedy of existence. His saving power is manifest in love, a sharp contrast to the coldly capricious wrath of Siva.

THE BHAGAVAD-GITĀ

THE Bhagavad-Gitā is the New Testament of the Vishnuite religion. The god of the Gitā is Krishna, an incarnation of Vishnu, who teaches men a method of salvation that is universal in scope, yet simple and direct in manifestation. In poetic fashion the Bhagavad-Gitā summarizes the basic lessons of philosophy, ethics and religion. It was produced in an age when the Brahmans, since they exacted large gifts for sacrifice, dealt only with the rich, and when the sects and heresies called for a renunciation of the world which was possible for only a few. To the great mass of people the Gitā preaches a simple doctrine of bhakti, the love and devotion of man for god.

The poem takes the form of a conversation between Krishna, the god-man, and Arjuna, one of the heroes of an earlier epic, which is supposed to take place before a great battle between the two branches of the royal family. The Mahābhārata, the epic which tells of the battle, is probably based on an actual incident of Indian history in the tenth century B.C. By the time the Gitā is written, the story of the fight has become a national folk-tale. As with most folk-tales, a germinal historical event here becomes a mighty earth-shaking turn of history. The Mahābhārata is an attempt to synthesize the many stories into one great epic that could be handed down in concrete form from generation to generation. It thus becomes the crystallization of the Indian heroic tradition.

Before the battle Arjuna is faced with the possibility of killing many of his own relatives, and is torn between his duty as a soldier and his feeling that such killing would be wrong and ultimately unjustifiable. In replying to Arjuna's questions, Krishna develops a complete view of life and the nature of human destiny. It is thus against the dramatic background of a bloody family fight that the Gitā preaches its mystical doctrine of salvation.

The history of the Gitā's deity, Krishna, is lost in the unrecorded development of Indian religion. It is supposed, however, that he was probably the deified head of a local tribe. How he attained the honor he holds in the Bhagavad-Gitā of being regarded as the incarnation of Vishnu is also shrouded in mystery. Where he appears in the Mahābhārata, he is spoken of in purely human terms as a great and powerful chieftain.

However this may be, Vishnu is the ultimate deity of whom Krishna is only an incarnation. The Gitā conceives of Vishnu as the all-pervading first principle of the universe. "There is nothing else that is outside of Me; on Me this All is strung like beads of pearls on a string. . . . Also the seed of all beings, that I am. There is no being, moving or motionless, that is without Me." Such statements seem to indicate a close connection between the theism of the Gitā and the Brahman of the Upanishads. In many places the concept of Vishnu as a kind of pantheistic deity is strong and overt, yet the burden of the poem indicates the belief that Vishnu is a separate deity who creates, sustains and "makes the wheels of the universe go around." He is at the same time in all natural processes and all human beings and above them. As the transcendent god he is the object of all knowledge and the creator of all things. As the immanent god he is the "soul of all" and the reality of all things. The Gitā is never consistent in its emphasis upon either of these aspects: at one point Vishnu is "both immortality and death, both existence and non-existence . . . the beginning and the middle and the end of being"; while in another place Vishnu says, "I am the strength of the strong, free from lust and passion; I am desire in all being but not such desire as is opposed to righteousness."

There is no question that the worshipers of Vishnu are monotheistic. The evidence points in this direction rather than towards pantheism. Nevertheless it would be false to assume that either the author of the Gitā or the Vishnuites in general were clear about their conception of god. Vishnu is shrouded in mystery and can never be caught within the bounds of conceptual knowledge. No matter what is said, the words are always inadequate. This very inadequacy of words tends to produce confusion and contradiction when the god is an object of speech or writing. Vishnu is known in some of his aspects: he is revealed to man through sacred knowledge, through spiritual exercise, through observation and introspection, through love and devotion; but his totality always remains hidden.

Not the multitudes of gods, nor the great sages know my source; for I am in every way the origin of the gods and great sages. Of [all] mortals, he who knows me to be unborn, without beginning, the great lord of the world, being free from delusion, is released from all sins.[1]

One of the more remarkable ways in which Vishnu reveals himself is by incarnation as an avatār. The concept of Krishna symbolizes one of the many times Vishnu condescended to

[1] Bhagavad-Gitā, Chapter X. In *The Sacred Books of the East*, Vol. VIII, p. 86. (London, Oxford Press, 1880.)

become man so that the human race could be set upon the right road to salvation.

Even though I am unborn and inexhaustible in [my] essence, even though I am lord of all beings, still I take up the control of my own nature, and am born by means of my delusive power. Whensoever, O descendant of Bharata! piety and religion languishes, and impiety is in the ascendant, I create myself. I am born age after age, for the protection of the good, for the destruction of evil-doers, and the establishment of piety.[2]

It is thus for the benefit of mankind that Vishnu, choosing this manner of expressing his infinite and unbounded love for the children of his hand, takes on human form and walks the earth. But even one who knows Krishna or one of the other avatārs cannot be said to know Vishnu in his entirety. The great Vishnu cannot be known "with the eye or mind" of man.

VISHNU AND SALVATION

THERE is only one way that man can attain complete knowledge of Vishnu. If Vishnu so desires, he may, by a supreme act of grace, reveal himself completely in a mystical vision. There are only a few who can claim to have been so elected; for the mass of his followers, the other avenues of partial knowledge must suffice. The Gitā reports that Arjuna, who experienced Vishnu through his meeting with Krishna, was the first of all mankind to receive this gift, but that it was through no merit of his own. The reasons for choosing Arjuna are, of course, lost in the mysterious councils of the supreme god.

O Arjuna! being pleased [with you], I have by my own mystic power shown you this supreme form, full of glory, universal, infinite, primeval, and which has not been seen before by any one

[2] *Ibid.*, pp. 58-59.

else but you, O you hero among the Kauravas! I cannot be seen in this form by any one but you, [even] by [the help of] the study of the Vedas, or of sacrifices, nor by gifts, nor by actions, nor by fierce penances. Be not alarmed, be not perplexed, at seeing this form of mine, fearful like this. Free from fear and with delighted heart, see now again that same form of mine.[3]

All Arjuna can say about the experience is that it is "made up of all marvels."

The Gitā is catholic in its concept of salvation. Man can be saved by knowledge, as the Upanishads taught, or by a renunciation of the world. The hard path of the ascetic can lead him to a peace which transcends the tragedy and despair of this life. Likewise, perfect knowledge can release man from the inevitable round of birth and rebirth. The source of rebirth and evil is here, once again, desire. And desire can be overcome by both knowledge and asceticism.

However, the most effective and the easiest path to salvation is found in bhakti—the love of god. This is the method most strongly recommended by the Gitā. If the believer fills himself with love and respect and devotion to Vishnu, he will be made secure in perfect faith and thus saved. The individual must give himself up completely, abandoning his own petty desires and ambitions for a perfect trust in one supreme being. The chief end of man is to devote himself unceasingly and untiringly to the love of God. In so doing salvation will be his.

Those who being constantly devoted, and possessed of the highest faith, worship me with a mind fixed on me, are deemed by me to be the most devoted. But those, who, restraining the [whole] group of the senses, and with a mind at all times equable, meditate on the indescribable, indestructible, unperceived [principle] which is all-pervading, unthinkable, indifferent, immovable, and constant, they, intent on the good of all beings, neces-

[3] *Ibid.*, p. 98.

sarily attain to me. For those whose minds are attached to the unperceived, the trouble is much greater. Because the unperceived goal is obtained by embodied [beings] with difficulty. As to those, however, O son of Pritha! who, dedicating all their actions to me, and [holding] me as their highest [goal], worship me, meditating on me with a devotion towards none besides me, and whose minds are fixed on me, I, without delay, come forward as their deliverer from the ocean of this world of death. Place your mind on me only; fix your understanding on me. In me you will dwell hereafter, [there is] no doubt.[4]

WORSHIP AND MORALS

IN SO FAR as Vishnu is concerned, there is no one way of worship. There are some few sections of the poem in which the more highly ritualistic practices of the popular religion are condemned, but in the main, Vishnu's attitude is tolerant. He is, after all, so high and so universal that the worship of any deity or the practice of any kind of devotion is really worship of Vishnu. Approval is therefore given to any form of sincere religious worship. Even though the worshiper is mistaken about the nature of the object he is worshiping, the object of all true devotion is always Vishnu, so it is easy to see why the worship of Vishnu varies from temple to temple and according to the part of the country. Vishnuism thus becomes a syncretistic religion which encompasses virtually any kind of religious expression. The only real condemnation is saved for those who "say that the world is untrue, without any basis, without God, not produced in orderly sequence, in short, governed by chance." But although each religion contributes something, Vishnu can always recommend the highest and the best. The highest worship is found in the idea of bhakti as expounded in the Gitā.

[4] *Ibid.*, pp. 99-100.

Although moral ideas are relatively unemphasized in the Gitā, the moral life of the Vishnuite has an important religious function. To be immoral, that is, to place the desires of this world above the love of god, is fatal to ultimate salvation. This kind of worldly life does nothing but add Karma to the soul and cause the rebirths to continue. The closest thing to an ethical principle of a positive nature is found in these words: "For beholding the same Lord [universal soul] residing in all beings, a man does not injure himself [his own self in others] by himself; so he goes to the final goal." This would appear to be an early Indian example of the Golden Rule doctrine found in Western religion: "Do unto others as you would have them do unto you."

Aside from this positive principle, Vishnuite morality makes the standard provisions that love and charity be practiced and duties fulfilled. The caste system is accepted as one of the methods for defining duty, and the religion tends to solidify the caste lines and make them more absolute. We find here, then, a much greater concern with devotion to god than with social change or popular ethics.

VISHNU'S FOLLOWERS

THE religion of Vishnu is a synthesis of three separate strands of Indian religious thought. Vishnu is first of all a Vedic deity who belongs to the hieratic ritualistic religion of the early Aryans. As such he maintains a direct continuity between the past and the present. Moreover, he is a localized hero-god of the people. Some commentators have said that this is essentially a Dravidic characteristic, because those who were on the Indian peninsula when the Aryans came apparently had local hero-deities to an extent never achieved by the Aryans. Added to these two is the fact that much of the Upanishadic monistic philosophy is found in the Gitā. The philosophic absolute of the Upanishads becomes the god of the Gītā. Although it is true that Vishnu never takes on the complete pantheism of the Upanishads, he does become Absolute Being, that which is behind all things. As we have seen, this mixture is never a perfect blend. Inconsistencies of one kind or another appear continuously and are not resolved. Here we see a popular attempt to quiet the religious ferment created by heresy and speculation. The Vishnuite religion is not so much a reform movement as an effort to create a synthetic religion which will express the complex religious consciousness of the Indian, and in so doing, it tries to take the best from philosophy, tradition and popular mythology. In many ways it further represents the seemingly innate urge of the Indian to find the unity which lies hidden behind the diversity of the world. In Vishnu it is found to be love, charity and devotion.

As time went on, the Vishnuite religion split into sects according to different emphases. In one group there was controversy as to whether or not Buddha had been an incarnation of Vishnu. Others split off on philosophic grounds. Still other groups formed because of varying interpretations regarding the place of women and the possible existence of a female counterpart to Vishnu. One northern group, formed in the thirteenth century, preached that Vishnu's consort, Lakshmi, is also infinite and uncreated and can be the object of worship. The southern school did not deny Lakshmi's existence but maintained that she was a created being and could not be the object of saving worship.

The most serious conflict arose between the northern and southern schools over the doctrine of grace. The northern group felt that Vishnu required a certain degree of cooperation from man. They developed the famous "monkey doctrine" in which they compared man to a baby monkey and Vishnu to the mother monkey. When danger threatens, the baby monkey holds on to the back of the mother monkey while she runs for safety. This, according to the northern school, is the way man is saved by Vishnu. Vishnu cannot do it alone; man must cooperate at least to the extent of "holding on." The southern school countered with the "cat doctrine." Man is like a baby kitten. When danger threatens, the mother cat picks the kitten up by the skin of its neck and runs for safety. The kitten has nothing to do with its salvation; the mother cat does it all. Out of this conflict grew many further ones, until India now contains uncounted numbers of Vishnu-ite sects. Each differs from the other in some small particular, yet all go back to the Bhagavad-Gītā for inspiration and light.

SIVA AND HIS CONSORT

THE other great branch of popular Hinduism worships not Vishnu but Siva, who has evolved from the early Vedic god, Rudra. It must be remembered that in the Vedas, Rudra is the personification of the more terrifying aspects of nature. Siva worship has none of the incarnations found in Vishnuite religion, but there are other gods who are often identified with him. Although he never loses his character as a dread deity, he does acquire a number of benevolent qualities and is both the originator of life and its ultimate destroyer.

Sivaism never produced a document such as the Bhagavad-Gītā. Although there are many references to Siva in the Mahābhārata and in various other parts of the epic literature, a systematic presentation of the god's position is never given in any one place. For the most part, the worshipers of Siva adopted the theistic form of an Indian philosophic system known as Sankhya-Yoga. This system is clearly pluralistic, dividing the universe into three parts: the soul, matter and god. Each of these parts is distinct from the others and each is eternal. Matter, or prakriti, is the chaotic blind mass upon which the divine creative energy works. The soul of man is married to prakriti and is consequently separated from god. Because of this separation man is subject to error, death and rebirth. Matter anchors man's essence to this world, and neither true happiness nor true knowledge is possible under such conditions. Man is often likened to an animal that is chained to the world. The chain which binds him is matter, and the function of the religious life and practice is to break the chain and allow the soul to ascend to Siva. Siva is pure spirit uncorrupted by taint of matter. When he manifests himself within the world he does so "not of matter, but of force."

Siva, like Vishnu, is thought of as the absolute uncaused cause of all things and of all motion. He is omnipotent, but out of his infinite wisdom he grants to man a degree of freedom. For most Siva worshipers, therefore, there is something man can do by way of gaining salvation. This concept is not a universal one. The Pacupatas, a sect of Sivaism, maintains a strong belief in predestination and the absoluteness of Siva's grace. Man can do nothing of himself; he must always consider his actions, deeds and adventures to be a determined part of Siva's divine grace. The members of the Saivadarsana, another great sect, leave the responsibility for salvation entirely in man's hands.

The female deity is much more important in Sivaism than in any of the other religions of India. Each of the gods has a consort who embodies the female principle, but Siva's goddess has an important metaphysical and religious function which goes beyond that of any of the others. This female deity is known by a number of different names. In the Mahābhārata she is often called Umā, which means mother. In other places she is called Devi, the goddess; Sati, the faithful wife; Gauri, the lustrous one; Kali, the black one; Parvati, the child of the mountains; Karala, the horrible; and Bdrairavi, the terrible. As indicated by her names, she has an ambivalent character. Sometimes she is represented as being kindly, warm and faithful, while at other times she is wild and sensuously awe-inspiring.

WORSHIP IN SIVAISM

MUCH of the worship of Siva and his consort is in celebration of the reproductive powers of nature. In some sects the sex act is used as a form of worship, and the bull, which unites savage force, rage and generative power, is the sacred symbol of the religion. To this day the sacred bull of Siva is allowed to wander the streets and highways of India unmolested. The consort of Siva is often thought of as the universal womb in which the world was formed after union with Siva. The final union of a man and woman symbolizes in religious worship the beginning of the world and celebrates the creative power of nature. When sexual intercourse is carried on under these religious auspices, the man identifies himself with Siva and the woman identifies herself with the goddess.

In addition to this sexual emphasis, Siva worshipers sometimes engage in complicated rites which ultimately lead to the sacrifice of a human being. Usually these sacrifices are offered to the goddess under her name of Durga or Kali. The sects which engage in both of these practices are generally secret mystery-cults. Final union with the divine can only be achieved within a circle of true believers, so to practice the necessary acts where nonbelievers might see them is to commit sacrilege against Siva.

This does not mean that the public worship of Siva lacks emphasis upon the reproductive powers of nature. The symbol of male creativity, linga, and that of the female sex organ, yoni, are a part of the equipment of every Siva temple. Often these symbols are worn around the necks of believers, and due homage is paid them as representations of the divine.

The outstanding characteristic of Siva worship is provided by the dual nature of the god. The worship is at once a celebration of creativity and destruction. It is both wild and tender and uses male and female symbols indiscriminately. Salvation is attained by equally contradictory practices. Sometimes the votary is required to cover himself with ashes (occasionally human, but more often the ashes of animals), while at other times he worships in laughter and dancing. Always the worship is a reflection of the way in which the god himself acts. He is both ascetic and sensuous, powerful and weak. True salvation comes to the believer by identifying himself with the god or goddess and thus obtaining final release from matter. In death his soul is forever freed and finds its eternal home with Siva.

As would be expected, Sivaism is insistent upon the idea of bhakti or faith. In earlier times it was of little importance, but as the religion has grown, faith has gradually become the most popular method of attaining blissful union with Siva. With the emphasis upon bhakti the more sensuous and bizarre elements have receded into the background. However, it is impossible to give a single characterization since Sivaism is split into a large number of sects with multifarious emphases.

POPULAR THEISM

ALTHOUGH the older Vedic polytheism generally shunned the use of temples and idols, theistic Hinduism abounds in them. In both the Vishnu and Siva religions, worship occurs in a definite place and usually under the auspices of a priestly group. Many of the idols represent lesser gods or godlike manifestations of the supreme god. To Western eyes they appear grotesque and repulsive. Often the idols are part animal and part human or have a multiplication of heads and arms. The wise god Ganeśa, for example, represents the art of writing and clear thought. This god has the figure of a man with the trunk of an elephant. Idols representing knowledge are given a third eye in the middle of their foreheads. The Indian represents the supernatural in extremely unnatural forms.

In describing Hindu theism it would appear that the sectarian lines were clearly drawn and consciously held, but this is not the actual case. The majority of Indians may class themselves in one general group, but they do not have the Western attitude of exclusiveness. Even if one god is raised to the highest level, the other gods are not denied existence. The Indian pantheon is large and the range of acceptable gods wide. Often the worshiper of Vishnu will observe the holy days and some of the sacred practices of a Siva sect. This is not to say that there have been no bitter and unresolved sectarian wars; rather, it points to the syncretistic aspect of the Indian religious consciousness. A very real element in this consciousness is mysticism, and the mystic knows no ultimate and final contradictions. In almost every home can be found shrines and idols of different and, in a theological or philosophical sense, contradictory faiths. But for the majority of the people these ideological differences are relatively unimportant. The great thing is to be saved from despair and from bondage to this world of flux and change. Such salvation can be achieved in a number of ways, no single theology or practice being able to claim it as its exclusive and private possession. To do so would deny the basic Hindu characteristic of searching for a unity above and beyond all things.

In view of this emphasis upon unity and its consequent philosophic expression, it is not surprising that the guru, or teacher, holds the place of honor among men. His is the great task of bringing enlightenment and establishing peace of mind. Unlike the priest, he does not bargain with the gods. Rather he shows the student the true nature of evil, man, the world and the gods. Salvation may come by bhakti, but even then it is not only the emotional love of god, but also the intellectual. Bhakti often becomes reverent and pious knowledge which consists more in understanding mystery than in knowing the will of god. The will of god which manifests itself in ethical commands and moral prescriptions is secondary to the secret knowledge of the nature of all things. It is not a question of knowing in order to act, and then acting in order to be saved. In Hinduism knowing and salvation are often one and the same thing.

In late centuries India has been the object of many foreign invasions. Early in the fourteenth century the Mohammedans gained a strong foothold in the west central portion of India. Christian missionaries from England, Germany, France and the United States have been going into India in ever-increasing numbers since the early nineteenth century. Traces of Persian influence can be found, and not a little Tibetan and Chinese teaching sifted down into the peninsula. With all these varying pressures, Hindu worship and thinking have undergone considerable change and modification. The foreign influences have been responsible for a large number of reforming sects. The Sikhs, for example, attempted to combine some of the major elements of Hinduism with the strict monotheism of Islam. A strong Christian influence can be seen in the religious community which goes under the name of Brāhma Samaj. This "Brahman society" attempts to correlate the Gospels of the New Testament with the idealistic philosophy of the Vedānta. In so doing it has developed a worship not unlike that of Western Protestantism, and the group has also developed a system of social ethics much akin to Christianity.

The existence of these groups further indicates the syncretistic tendency in Hinduism. During the nineteenth century, however, the strong movement in India toward self-determination expressed itself in religious terms. In one sense the Indian Nationalistic movement, as led by Tilak and Gandhi, is a protest against the so-called materialistic and selfish culture of the West. Often this aspect of Western civilization has been identified with Christianity.

In the modern day there have been constant attempts to revive and glorify the religion of India and to associate the political movement toward independence with this glorification. Bal Tilak, who died in 1920, was a fiery revolutionary. His bombing raids and organized destruction of the English garrisons were often conducted in the name of Siva or Siva's consort even though he was a well-known scholar of the Bhagavad-Gitā. The soldiers who gave their lives in the fight for independence were promised eternal blessedness and final salvation. The cause of nationalism was the cause of Siva and his lesser gods. It is interesting to compare this rationale with the entirely opposite one used by Gandhi. Gandhi was more in the tradition of the Vishnuites. His method emphasized the power of love, "nonviolent resistance" and moral supremacy. It is not by destruction but by the power which comes through the love of god that India will be freed from foreign domination. Gandhi, like Tilak, identified the cause of national salvation with personal salvation. Both represent modern examples of theistic Hinduism.

SECTION SUMMARY

THIS entire discussion of Indian religion is a summary. It has of course been impossible to discuss or even point to all the varied beliefs and practices which go to make up the religion of such a mass of people. A final history or treatment of Indian religion can never be written. The records are too scanty and the difference between the written word and the actual belief too great. At best we can only get a glimpse of the way in which the spirit of the Indian has reached out for explanation and order.

The religions of India, like all religions, serve to give life and action a meaning which transcends the particularity of existence. The Indian systems have seen fit to fuse the speculations of the mind with the yearnings of the heart, so Indian religion and philosophy are inextricably mixed. Both enterprises have the same end, the attainment of peace for the human soul. The Indian spirit is alien to departmentalization. The quest is one, just as the answer is one.

The religious expressions we have studied seem obsessed with the notion that there is something eternal and unchanging behind the temporal and changing. Although man may reach the limits of his logic, there is always some method by which he can reach the light that dispels all gloom and all doubt. Hindu religions cry out their affirmation of the fact of salvation.

The ultimate salvation may be achieved through sacrifices, as in the Vedas; or through philosophic contemplation, as in the Upanishads; or through sacred rites and formulae administered by the priests, as in the Brāhmanas; or through bhakti, as in the Bhagavad-Gitā and the later theism. Whether it is by works, knowledge or devotion, the end is always the same— man can be saved and despair need not be his destiny. Within the varied traditions of India, the Indian finds his spiritual meaning and his escape from the confusion and transcience of this world.

III

THE EXPANSION OF BUDDHISM

III

7

THE LATE INDIAN DEVELOPMENT

AFTER the death of Gotama the Buddha (circa 500 B.C.), the order he established continued in a fairly unified form. In its early stages it was quite small in relation to the size of the Hindu sects and could not be considered a very important power. It was spreading throughout India very slowly, giving no indication of the triumphs to come. For the most part, it was confined to the northeastern section and appears to have exerted little influence elsewhere.

While the teachings of Gotama were gaining adherents, India was invaded by Alexander of Macedon. Alexander's armies had come overland, conquering all countries between Greece and the Indian Ocean. In 327 B.C. his forces reached Kabul and announcement was made that he was to be the ruler of the Punjab. Since most of the Punjab princes failed to acknowledge the conquest, Alexander was forced to go farther to the city of Taxiles, the capital of the province known as Taxila. It was here that he realized that the country he had invaded could never be conquered in the ordinary fashion. It was disorganized to the point of chaos, its area was so extensive that effective occupation was out of the question, and the terrain held too many hiding-places for attacking bands.

After leaving a skeleton force to symbolize his conquest, Alexander turned back to Babylon. The garrisons which he left in India were in no wise capable of maintaining themselves under attack. One of Alexander's Indian officers turned against the remaining Greeks and finally cleared them out of the Punjab. In doing so he established himself as king of Magadha. He reigned for twenty-four years and consolidated considerable power in his own family. The lesser princes and chiefs of this northern area paid homage to Sandro Cottus, as Greek history calls him, and allowed him to found the great Mauryan dynasty.

However great Sandro Cottus (he is sometimes known as Chandra Gupta) was, his grandson Asoka was greater. In 272 B.C. Asoka came to the throne of the Mauryan dynasty and extended its control over a large part of southern India. When in 263 B.C. Asoka became a Buddhist, he caused that religion to gain in influence and power. In a sense Buddhism became the state religion, endowed with civil authority. Its major battle with Brahmanism was easily won. The idea of a middle ground between sensualism and asceticism appealed to the Indian mind, so that many of the popular Hindu sects absorbed Buddha and made him one of their chief gods. Preaching the simple doctrine of Gotama, missionaries moved out beyond the borders of India proper into Siam, Burma and Ceylon. In his late years Asoka himself became a Buddhist monk, and his sons were Gotama's most ardent missionaries.

Obviously the skeleton of primitive Buddhism offered ample room for elaboration. Gotama had taught an uncomplicated doctrine—a "way" of life without metaphysical explanations. His interest had been solely in salvation, of which he had found the secret in the human soul. There was no worship, no explanation of the origin of the world, no explanation of why men are on earth, and no assurances regarding the friendliness of the cosmos. With regard to these questions Gotama had been silent. Indeed, he had preached an agnosticism which pointed to the ultimate futility of all metaphysical speculations. Man had no need of the supernatural; all he required was sufficient self-knowledge to attain final annihilation.

It would be quite incorrect to assume that the ordinary lay Buddhist followed the simple path of Gotama. There was a sizable accretion from the common beliefs of Hinduism to Buddhist thought and practice, leaving the popular cult liberally endowed with deities, miracles and cosmic explanations. This caused confusion and dissension among the monks, so that the principal problems of Buddhism were now doctrinal rather than disciplinary. In the latter years of Asoka's reign he required that the teachings of Gotama be codified and that this code be henceforth known as the true teaching. The canon thus established by Asoka was written in the Pali language and is known as the Tripitaka, or the three baskets. It is divided as follows:

1. *Vinaya Pitaka*—Discipline basket—deals with the monastic life. It includes the rules and regulations governing entrance and conduct.

2. *Sutta Pitaka*—Sermon basket—is the true teaching of Gotama. Taken primarily from the early records of Gotama's own ministry.

3. *Abhidhamma Pitaka*—Exposition basket—contains the various expansions and explanations of the Buddha's teaching.

The Tripitaka is only a part of the large Buddhist literature of the time. There was much other material, largely theological and poetic, which could not be included in the canon but which held a high place on the fringes of sanctity.

Although Asoka officially designated the Buddhist canon, the general movement continued to grow farther and farther away from the founder's teaching. Each new convert required some kind of explanation and some theological framework for justifying the basic ethical teachings. The monks and students continued to find new meanings and new interpretations of life in the words of the master. More important, the devotion and veneration paid Gotama slowly turned to worship. He became a kind of god, and the shrines which were originally built to house a statue of the Buddha for purposes of veneration became real temples of worship.

Coincident with this development was the revival of Brahmanism. The ancient authority of the Vedas was reasserted, and Buddhism was forced to come to grips with problems its master had not answered. The battle between Brahmanic religion, the rising Hindu theisms and Buddhism was engaged at the level of thought as well as practice. The decline of primitive Buddhist agnosticism can be traced in part to the revival of the more indigenous theistic faiths of the Indian. By 125 A.D. there had developed a definite schism between the more eclectic north and the advocates of traditional teaching in the south. The schism was inevitable from the day Asoka was converted. Gotama's simple formula was not designed for a mass movement. It left unanswered too many fundamental questions, and it did not meet the need of a people for an object of worship.

The schism between north and south resulted in two different types of Buddhism. The northern branch, which is known as *Mahayana*, expanded the original doctrine to include a great deal of the popular magic and superstition of the local Hindu sects. The southern school, called *Hinayana*, eschewed additions and claimed to represent the older, more monastic teaching of the founder. Mahayana is often translated as the "Greater Vehicle" or "High Path," while Hinayana means "Low Path" or "Lesser Vehicle." Although these two schools have continued to exist side by side, sometimes in the same monastery, the Mahayana branch produced the great missionary movement which went out to evangelize Asia.

MAHAYANA AND HINAYANA BUDDHISM

PRIMITIVE Buddhism, like the other salvation religions of India, was strictly individualistic. Gotama placed primary emphasis upon the importance of each person's working out his own salvation, and since this was essentially a matter of ridding the empirical soul of Karma, there was nothing anyone else could do. The goal of the Buddhist believer was to become an Arhat, then a saint, and finally to enter Nirvana. If, on his way to becoming an Arhat, he chose to preach and tell others of the Four Jewels and the Eightfold Path, he could do so; but this was neither mandatory nor would it save the hearers, for after seeing the light it would still be up to them to work out their own salvation.

Mahayana offers man a chance to become a Bodhisattva. A Bodhisattva is one who takes the hurt and misery of the human race to his heart and conscience, and consequently works for the final salvation of all beings. In effect, the Mahayana school offers everyone a chance to become a savior of mankind—not a saint, but a kind of Buddha. Involved in this is a new code of ethics, a belief in the existence of supernatural beings, and a new doctrine of salvation.

First of all, the Mahayanists believe that Gotama was not the first of the Buddhas. Whenever true religion has gone into decline and men have lost their way, new Buddhas have arisen to reestablish proper order. Behind the physical world and all temporal events stands the *Dharmakaya*, which is true existence conceived as being totally indestructible, the permanent which lies behind the flux of material existence. There is no way of describing the Dharmakaya as a person or a being. Rather, it is the eternal ground upon which all beings rest. The Mahayana conception of Dharmakaya is much the same as the Upanishad conception of Brahman. When Dharmakaya assumes bodily form and enters history as a Buddha, it is known as *Nivmānakāya*. Gotama was such an incarnation, and the Buddhist believes that the next one will go under the name of Maitreya. Thus the Buddhas are simply manifestations of the highest rather than being absolute in themselves. The third aspect of Mahayana theology is *Sambhogakāya*. Sambhogakāya is the power by which the Buddha is capable of imparting saving knowledge to the community of believers. It is the spirit or power of salvation.

These three metaphysical principles are aspects of *Bodhi*, meaning enlightenment or knowledge of the kind which made Gotama a Buddha. It is from this word that the Bodhisattvas take their name. These are earthly beings, filled with Bodhi, who love their fellow men so completely that they refuse to achieve for themselves the ultimate salvation, electing out of their compassion for mankind to stand midway between Nirvana—which is the state of utter blessedness, but from which no help can be given—and earthly existence. From this vantage point they can guide, protect and aid the suffering souls of men on their long march to glory.

The Bodhisattvas are substitutes for the multitude of deities in popular religion. Since all men are striving to become Buddhas, there must be many who have stopped at that midway stage before entrance into Nirvana. Consequently, man must have a host of cosmic friends who watch over him and guard him. As would be expected, many of the gods of the Hindu pantheon become Bodhisattvas and many local heroes are deified and worshiped after this fashion, thus fulfilling, in Mahayana Buddhism, the need of popular religion for an object of worship.

With the development of the idea of Bodhisattva, the ethical content of Buddhism changed. In Hinayana and primitive Buddhism the achievement of Arhat was the highest goal of man. This produced an intensely individualistic and essentially

disinterested monk. Social ethics, in so far as they were operative at all, were of a negative character. There was no idea of
cooperation or "I am my brother's keeper," for every man was
concerned to save himself and only himself. When the ideal
shifts from an Arhat to a Bodhisattva, there occurs a remarkable change in social attitude. The Bodhisattva, far from being
uninterested in the welfare of others, is intimately involved
with all mankind. Whereas Hinayana emphasizes its lack of
social idealism, Mahayana preaches the necessity for unselfish
assistance to all men. The Bodhisattvas who, but for their compassionate love for all men, could escape the endless round of
death and rebirth, represent the ultimate dedication to this
great goal.

Such a radical change of concept caused the Eightfold Path
to be further elaborated and, in a sense, socialized. One of the
new vows called for a resolution never to enter salvation until
the whole world be redeemed and purified. The true believer
must give up all traces of egoistic struggle and devote himself
to the saving of mankind. With this the asceticism of earlier
Buddhism is relaxed, and the married Buddhist who partici-
pates in the affairs of the world has as much chance to meet
the conditions for salvation as the monk in the monastery. The
good becomes the practice of love and comradeship with one's
fellow beings. Nor is there here any distinction of caste or
race. All men can become Bodhisattvas by practicing the art
of love and turning evil to good.

While the monistic philosophy, religious polytheism and
ethical idealism of Mahayana continued to spread, the rather
arid asceticism of Hinayana caused the southern school to be
much less popular. Although Hinayana allows the worship of
the Buddha, there is no place in its thought for a god. The
philosophy of the group has always remained apart from its
actual religious practices, creating a tension between these two
aspects of the tradition which has never eased. The heart of

the believer cries out for an object of worship, but his doctrine maintains that there can be no such object. The ethics of the Hinayana sect drives the individual away from the joys and delights of this world into the cold asceticism which leads to annihilation. Although Hinayana is probably truer to the original teaching of Gotama, it lacks the warmth and idealism of Mahayana, so it is little wonder that Mahayana caught the imagination of people to an extent never achieved by Hinayana.

THE DECLINE OF INDIAN BUDDHISM

As MAHAYANA Buddhism spread, it increasingly absorbed local Indian religious and magical practices. In about the seventh century A.D. the worship of Siva and his consort produced a body of literature which went under the name of *Tantras*. Much of the Tantras is devoted to the worship of Sakti, Siva's consort, and to magical means for gaining salvation. Often sexual intercourse is a form of worship, and such things as drunkenness are prescribed for their saving power. In addition to physical inducements of the ecstatic state there are also a number of formulae that carry magical power.

Tantrism and Mahayana were intermingled with many of the older Dravidic practices. As time went on, the Buddhist element became practically indistinguishable from the beliefs and practices of Sivaism and Tantrism, its older aspects of stern asceticism disappearing in the welter of popular sensual belief. As a result it lost its individuality and became easy prey for the more rigid religion of the Brahmans.

In addition to the loss of its essential characteristics, Buddhism also suffered vigorous persecution by the states. India was subject to invasions from the East, and with each invasion the first object of attack was always a religious stronghold. Sind, for example, one of the greatest Buddhist headquarters, was invaded by the Arabs in 711 A.D. Moreover, the local princes were often enrolled in the ranks of Brahmanic orthodoxy and as a result fought anyone who denied the authority of the Vedas. Although the Brahmans tried to stamp out all heresy, the Buddhists were especially hurt, because even though the newly rising Hindu faiths offered just as much as Buddhism, they were, in a sense at least, embedded in the Vedic past. Thus Buddhism was forced out of the land of its birth by a complex of political and religious factors, not the least of which was the loss of its positive and definable character.

8

PRE-BUDDHIST CHINA

AS EARLY as the time of Asoka, in the third century B.C., missionaries were being sent from Buddhist India to other parts of Asia. Actually we know very little of their enterprise and next to nothing of their real influence. According to tradition Buddhism, in its Mahayana form, entered China at the request of the Emperor Ming in the year 61 A.D. We are told that Ming had a dream of a large golden figure hovering over the emperor's palace. At first he was frightened and called for one of his wise men to interpret and explain the symbol. The wise man, Fu-yih, assured the king that the gigantic figure was a reflection of the great Buddha who was known to the Indians. As a result, Ming is said to have ordered some of his men to India with instructions to gather information about the new god. After some six years the men returned with sacred writings, relics and two Buddhist monks. This is the traditional beginning for Buddhism's conquest of northern Asia.

However accurate the story, it is generally conceded that Buddhism moved from India into China sometime during the first century after Christ. It was the Buddhism of the period when Mahayana was most flourishing and distinctive, before it had begun to take on the characteristics of popular Hinduism or fallen under the sway of Tantrism. It must be remembered, however, that both Mahayana and Hinayana went to China, existing there for many years side by side and with varying degrees of influence. Chinese Buddhism nevertheless derived most of its character from Mahayana, the rigid asceticism of Hinayana being relegated to a secondary position.

The China into which Buddhism was transplanted was an old and established culture. Although it is impossible to assign completely accurate dates to the various Chinese dynasties, it is known that the Emperor Huang was reigning as early as 2704 B.C. If this date is accepted, we are given some idea of the tremendous tradition that was already ancient by the first century of our era. As would be expected, there was a well-established religious and moral system in operation. This system presented a challenge to Indian Buddhism which made necessary certain fundamental changes. The fusion and conflict between Indian Buddhism and the traditions of the Chinese produced a religion of a new and essentially different character.

Prior to the advent of Buddhism it is impossible to describe Chinese religion apart from the general stream of Chinese culture, for the conception of religion as a separate and distinct part of life had not yet come into existence. What records we have of the beliefs and worship of the early periods are all found in philosophical, political and moral treatises. In no case do we find philosophy or speculation placed opposite religion or religious beliefs. The religion, if the term can properly be applied, was a fusion of all these interests into a general view of the world. Consequently, religious conceptions permeate the whole of the ancient culture, all aspects of life being found to possess religious meaning or implications.

NATURE WORSHIP

THE basic attitudes of Chinese religion are derived from nature worship and beliefs regarding the continued existence of the dead. From the earliest times, according to the records, these two aspects formed the basis for a systematic set of beliefs. No single individual can be designated as the founder of the religion, and no specific date can be set for its origin. By the time the Chinese had ceased their nomadic wanderings and established a more settled life, the religious and cultural foundation for their later development was well secured.

In the early period, worship was directed toward many of the same objects of nature that were deified in the Rig-Veda. There were gods of the sky, the wind, the rain, the mountains and forests. Much attention was paid to the crops in the field and to the gods who could produce good harvests. In general, all aspects of physical nature were endowed with souls or spirits.

In one of the oldest of the ancient Chinese books, the universe is conceived of as consisting of two souls and their manifestations. Yin, one of the souls, is found in coldness, death, darkness and the earth. Yang, the other soul, is represented by warmth, life, creativity and the bright heavens above. These two souls or principles animate all of nature and everything that can be said to exist. Most objects are a combination of the two. Thus the entire world, including man, is construed as a mixture of good and evil, light and dark, and the various other opposites.

In this conception man is not thought of as being essentially distinct or different from the other aspects of nature. He is as much a part of nature as a tree or rock or a star in the heavens. He is a transient mixture of Yin and Yang which upon death will be dissolved, the Yang going back to heaven and the Yin returning to the earth. The evil side of man is sometimes called Kwei and the good side, Shen. In many cases these two names are used to refer to the good gods (Shen) and the evil gods or devils (Kwei). All the world teems with Shen and Kwei. They move the stars in their courses, they cause the good to suffer. At night the Kwei perpetrate their greatest works of evil, while by day the dangers are kept in check by the benevolent Shen. The demons Kwei cause pain at childbirth, whereas the gods Shen are responsible for the joy when a perfect child is born. In short, the personification of the two principles, Yin and Yang, furnished the ancient Chinese with an explanation of good and evil, joy and suffering. In addition, it provided many gods for many special purposes and for many special needs.

ANCESTOR WORSHIP

IN SOME mysterious fashion the soul of man is thought to continue in existence after death. Since all members of the human race have both Shen and Kwei, all are, in a sense, gods. Considered in this light, the concept means further that gods can either reside in human bodies or have had bodies at one time. And here is found the basis of ancestor worship. The dead still form a vital part of the family unit. They are, indeed, in an extremely enviable position, for not only do they see and understand all that is happening, but they also take part in the various activities of the living. If they are properly cared for by those still alive, they can be counted on for protection and help in the affairs of life. Because in this way man occupies a place among the gods, each family owes it to its members to see that the ancestors are properly venerated. Ancestor worship formed the basic private religious exercise of the culture, whereas nature worship was usually public and often the exclusive prerogative of the governing group.

Since there was a rather heavy traffic between heaven and earth, it was not unnatural for the Chinese to feel that men were divine even while alive. Because of this identification of men with gods, the great and virtuous heroes of the living were often accorded religious attention, their rank being designated, in general, by virtue of their wisdom and knowledge.

The most usual living object of worship was the emperor, and to him all manner of sacrifice and deference was paid. As we shall see, the sage or philosopher, who usually held the place of highest dignity in the community, also often came within this category. Although the instances of living objects of worship were many, by far the vast majority were elevated to this position after death.

Ancestor worship performed a very important function in the life of the Chinese. Through it was maintained a sense of continuity from past to present to future. To be constantly surrounded by the spirits of the departed meant to be ever aware of the past. The rules formulated by parents and their forefathers were remembered, and respected and adhered to as necessary duties. The moral life of the living was thus always bound to the thought and practice of the past, the present being considered more or less as a temporary interlude in the ongoing process of nature and time. In these circumstances the Chinese could never feel alone in an alien world, as many of the Indians did. Rather, they felt themselves to be intimately related to the entire universe in all of its parts. Questions of procedure were answered in terms of tradition, and questions of ethical conduct were answered by recourse to the record of the past. Such a conception elicited tremendous veneration for historical tradition and standardized modes of conduct. Violent revolutions and the introduction of new institutions were not consistent with the Chinese world-view. The sage, with his knowledge of sacred history and established magical formulae, here becomes the most valued of all men.

These beliefs found much of their expression in highly ritualized practices of worship. Not only were the actual creeds handed down from generation to generation, but the ritualistic aspects of the religion were also crystallized. A given rite had to be performed exactly as in the past; no slight variation from its established pattern could be countenanced. With such a conception of worship it is easy to see how piety became formalized into an elaborate structure. Family prayers were often hours long and full of intricate and difficult physical movements. Nature worship, the state religion, became a formalized public ceremony celebrated by the mandarins for the benefit of the populace. This emphasis upon stylized worship was a further indication of the Chinese conception of an orderly nature. There was a suitable way for doing everything. There was a way imbued with Yin, which was evil, and a way filled with Yang, which was right and good. All actions had moral importance, and all aspects of nature, family, state and ceremonies were permeated with moral responsibility. For the ancient Chinese there was no escape from Yin and Yang.

CONFUCIUS

IN 551 B.C. the third great historic dynasty of China was drawing to a close. The social conditions of the period were anything but calm, and a repressive feudal system had been established. In this year Confucius, for whom the orthodox religion of China is named, was born in the small state of Lu. Much of the ancient tradition had fallen into the dim recesses of men's minds. The state was no longer as vitally interested in the people as it had presumably once been, and it was now being used as a powerful instrument of coercion by the feudal barons. Wealth was piling up in the hands of the overlords, while the poor continued to work out the meager existence possible in China's rocky soil. The age into which Confucius was born was politically decadent and morally bankrupt.

Confucius was neither the founder of a new religion nor a reformer of the old. As he saw it, his function was to resurrect and publicize the ancient tradition, making men realize that the old days, the days when they knew their ancestors and worshiped the spirits of the departed, were really the happy days. It was to the pattern of ancient life that Confucius called his hearers.

Although he added next to nothing to the religious thought and spirit, Confucius did edit and systematize certain of the Chinese classical writings, thus providing an authoritative foundation for much of the later tradition. The books he was responsible for, a set of nine, serve as the basic writings for Confucianism. They were certainly not written by the man born in 551, but they were compiled by him and his school. By the time of the Han Dynasty (206 B.C.–221 A.D.) these texts were accepted as the final orthodox teaching.

Confucius was primarily a moral rather than a metaphysical teacher. In this he was well within the tradition of the earlier Chinese. He emphasized over and over again the necessity for recognizing the existence of a universal order of all things (*Tao*), of which man's moral life is as much a part as the changing seasons or the rising sun. "The Moral Law takes its rise in the relation between man and woman; but in its utmost reaches it reigns supreme over heaven and earth." This quotation from the Confucianist Scriptures indicates the transcendent nature of the universal moral law. All nature, so the Sage observed, operates on a legal basis. There is no chance or accident; there are only regularly recurring events. To see in nature no cause-and-effect relationship is to be blind to the obvious. Nature is not confusion: it is balanced design. If man follows the order of which he is a part, he will escape confusion and chaos, since the universe is one system and not many. His moral life can be separated from the requirements of law with no more success than his physical existence can. Salvation, then, will come to man through the achievement of absolute conformity to natural moral law.

After stating the existence of an ethical law it became necessary for Confucius to discuss it in practical, workable, everyday terms. Here again he goes back into the early tradition.

The first and greatest moral commandment is filial piety. Look to the teaching of ancestors, obey fathers and mothers, pay due respect to cousins, uncles, sisters and brothers, and consider the emperor the great earthly father of all. If man begins in this wise he will ultimately achieve the goal of Confucianist religion—the good life. In more concrete terms, salvation comes through the good works and personal efforts of its seeker.

Confucius, like Gotama, was not a philosopher who loved to speculate on the mysteries of existence. His concern was for this world and man's place in it. When he speaks of god, he uses a moral frame of reference with few metaphysical connotations. Actually avoiding the use of the term god, he more often refers to heaven. "Heaven produced the virtue that is in me." The Tao, or ultimate order of things, is felt to be impersonal, in no way giving salvation by grace. "He who offends against Heaven has none to whom he can pray."

Confucius never tired of emphasizing the basic goodness of man and the so-called "doctrine of reciprocity." All men, he said, are created with a moral reason that should make it possible for them to follow the eternal Tao. If they stray from the straight path of order, they are doing so against the better natures with which they are endowed. Often parents and teachers are responsible for moral deviations because they fail in giving proper instruction. Every child should be taught at the earliest possible age that "what you do not want done to yourself, do not do to others." This is the practical rule by which all mankind should live. Filial piety is the worshipful acceptance of family obligations, but the "doctrine of reciprocity" is the rule for all social intercourse. The practice of these two commandments is both possible and mandatory. Through them man realizes that ultimate goodness which has been latent within him since birth.

When Confucianism became the state religion of China it

was expanded to reintroduce the neglected elements of deities and public prayer. In a religious sense the original Confucianism contained nothing of importance beyond its system of ethics. In the state religion, however, the emperor became the object of worship and sacrifice. He mediated between the people and Tao and made himself responsible for the religious welfare of all his subjects. The state thus became a religious community with the administrative officers as priests and teachers. While on the popular level there were nature deities and ancestral spirits who received a portion of the worship, none of these gods could be considered absolute, for that attribute was the exclusive possession of the universal impersonal Tao. Nevertheless, the deities could aid man in his attempt to conform to the moral law and could grant the emperor the supreme virtue that was necessary for his divinity. Some five centuries after his death, Confucius was raised to the level of a deity, and in that status was second only to the supreme Tao.

LAO-TSE AND THE TAO

ALTHOUGH Confucius used the idea of Tao in a very practical fashion, further possibilities for the concept did not escape the speculative philosophers. One of Confucius's elder contemporaries, Lao-tse, used it as the basis for the development of a mystical cult known as *Taoism*. The sacred book of Taoism, the Tao-Te-King, deals with metaphysical problems not unlike those found in the Upanishads. In the latter section of the King the problems of ethics and politics are defined and given rather obscure solutions.

Lao-tse was impressed by the way in which nature operated. He wished to penetrate its changing appearances to find the one eternal and immutable principle. What lies behind heaven and earth and the glittering stars, behind the existence of transient man? These are questions which have troubled speculative minds the world over, and China was no exception. Like the philosophers of India, Lao-tse found that the ultimate reality behind all things temporal was an inexpressible absolute. In the opening of the Tao-Te-King these words appear:

The Tao that can be expressed is not the eternal Tao;
The name that can be defined is not the unchanging name.
Non-existence is called the antecedent of heaven and earth;
Existence is the mother of all things.
From eternal non-existence, therefore, we serenely observe the
    mysterious beginning of the universe;
From eternal existence we clearly see the apparent distinctions.
These two are the same in source and become different when
    manifested.
This sameness is called profundity. Infinite profundity is the gate
    whence comes the beginning of all parts of the universe.[1]

However unknowable this final reality, its manifestations are everywhere evident in the world of sense. Tao is the power of nature and is in all things. When the eagle soars to the heavens, that is Tao; when the crops produce in good season, that is Tao; and when the spirit of man triumphs over tragedy, that too is Tao. The whole universe bears witness to the one great absolute that is in, above, behind, and below all things.

CHAOTIC MYSTICISM

THIS type of philosophy leads to a mystical kind of religion. The salvation of man is found in his final achievement of Tao —his absorption into the reality behind all realities. The goal can best be seen in the words of the Tao-Te-King:

Attain to the goal of absolute vacuity;
Keep to the state of perfect peace.

[1] *The Bible of the World*, Taoist Scriptures, Vol. I (New York: Viking Press, 1939), p. 471.

All things come into existence,
And thence we see them return.
Look at the things that have been flourishing;
Each goes back to its origin.
Going back to the origin is called peace;
It means reversion to destiny.
Reversion to destiny is called eternity.
He who knows eternity is called enlightened.
He who does not know eternity is running blindly into miseries.
Knowing eternity he is all-embracing.
Being all-embracing he can attain magnanimity.
Being magnanimous he can attain omnipresence.
Being omnipresent he can attain supremacy.
Being supreme he can attain Tao.
He who attains Tao is everlasting.
Though his body may decay he never perishes.[2]

Such a mystical doctrine of salvation produces an ascetic ethical structure and a fundamental emphasis upon individual, as opposed to social, redemption. The Taoist sees little need for trying to reshape the world when such an enterprise can only lead to frustration and failure. The best course is inaction. And this is true not only in matters of social practice but also with regard to learning and the accumulation of knowledge.

He who pursues learning will increase every day;
He who pursues Tao will decrease every day.
He will decrease and continue to decrease,
Till he comes at non-action;
By non-action everything can be done.[3]

The practical ethics of Confucius and his insistence upon correctness of worship have no place in such a system as this.

[2] *Ibid.,* XVI, p. 477.
[3] *Ibid.,* XLVIII, pp. 490-491.

Lao-tse was appealing primarily to mystics and those who wished to leave the life of the villages for quiet contemplation in the mountains. Although Taoism carried on a part of the Chinese tradition, it was the part most unimportant to the masses. There were no gods who could be worshiped, no ethical norms which could be counted on for guidance through the complexities of daily life, and no dynamic which would produce a missionary enterprise. Had it not been for the introduction of popular magical and superstitious elements, Taoism would probably have remained a small ascetic sect.

The tendency in China at the time of the introduction of Buddhism was for all the various beliefs which found themselves unassimilated by state Confucianism to congregate around Taoism. The high mystical attainment preached by Lao-tse and his philosophic followers made little impression on the minds of the people. They tended to convert the doctrine of Tao into a proof for the immortality of the soul, thus reasserting the divinity and supernatural power of man. In some worship practices Tao was thought to exist primarily in the intoxicating juices of plants, and a magical potion was developed to guarantee eternal life and bliss. At one stage Lao-tse himself became a deity, and he reigns today as a chief god of popular Taoism. Besides multiplying its gods (mostly local heroes and natural forces), the popular religion developed strict and complicated rituals. The result was an elaborate organizational structure built around Taoist priests and holy men.

Most of the degeneration of Taoism took place at the time its rival, Buddhism, was gaining ground in China. The state religion considered them both heretical and even went so far as to initiate consistent programs of persecution against their centers of worship and learning. Being lumped together in persecution created something of a bond, and the two sects borrowed freely from each other. For example, the Taoists borrowed from the Buddhists their form of organization, their use of idols and a great deal of their worship service. The Buddhists in turn found it possible to assimilate many of the Taoist gods and beliefs. Buddhism could absorb a great deal without losing its intrinsic character, for it was at this time firmly established in its mother country. Taoism, on the other hand, had become so chaotic and had departed so far from any standard of orthodoxy that its absorption of Buddhism was disastrous to its individuality.

9

CHINESE BUDDHISM

BUDDHISM was able to expand in China because it offered more than either Taoism or the state religion. Confucianism, it is to be remembered, was virtually nothing more than a patriotic gesture. The people performed no rites and did not really participate in the religious worship; the government officials did it all for them. Since the state religion was so aloof and Taoism so cluttered with magical practices and chaotic superstitions, the people turned quite naturally to the moral idealism and the warm, friendly polytheism of Mahayana. The brand of Buddhism imported from India was lush with imagery, bright colors, robed priests and impressive temples. All these external factors contributed to the ultimate triumph of Buddhism in China.

Moreover, Buddhism propounded a theory of life after death. The Chinese already believed in immortality to a certain degree, but the connection between a person's continuing existence after death with his moral life on this earth appealed to their sense of justice. Ultimate salvation was dependent upon the way a person lived. It was not a question of virtue for virtue's sake, but virtue for the sake of eternal blessedness.

THE WHEEL OF LIFE

CHINESE Buddhism interpreted the cycle of birth and death in terms of "Lun-Luei," the wheel of life. At the highest point of the wheel the gods exist in an almost perfect heaven. With them in this near-perfection are the good men, those who have lived up to their duties and obligations and followed the Eight-fold Path. The perfection is not absolute, however, since final Nirvana can only be attained in the step beyond, pure Bud-dhahood. The system thus provides for a number of "heavens" in which the Bodhisattvas (in Chinese, Putisato or Pusa) live and work toward the final redemption of mankind. Their achievement of one or the other of them is dependent upon the degree of virtue they reached in this life. The gods still go through the cycle of rebirth, but always on a higher and higher level, everything being dependent upon the deeds of the previous life. It was not merely an affair of this world, but a drama which went on long after death. In Chinese this con-cept of cosmic reward and punishment is called Yin-Kuo, the law of retributive justice.

Obviously, man can move down the wheel as well as up. He can just as easily (or maybe more easily) become a demon as a god. The demons are half good and half evil, and they are in continuous warfare with the ultimate goodness of the Buddha. They dwell beneath the cold ground and in the dark waters, in a hell of horrible suffering and cruelty. They are not happy, and at times they cry out because of their sur-roundings and their internal conflicts, and are heard by those dwelling on earth.

Just as there is a hierarchy of heavens, so also of hells. There are eighteen, over each of which rules a stern master who, with inflexible justice, exacts payment for past sins. It is interesting to note that both heaven and hell contain administrative offi-cers who are charged with keeping a record of man's activi-ties. No deed is committed without the knowledge of both supernatural spheres. By means of an accurate accounting and a rigorous legal system, each man receives in this or some fu-ture life his due return in punishment or reward. In order that the records may be kept straight, the mythology has the earth divided into sections and each section into districts. There is an overlord per section who does the recording from the material brought in by the various district superintendents. Because of the complexities of urban life, cities of any size often had their own special superintendents. The countryside, with its simpler existence, could assign one superintendent to a much wider area.

This development of local deities was not introduced by Buddhism but is rather what the conquering Buddhists made of the local hero-deities of the ancient indigenous religion. Temples which had been built to the local deities became Buddhist temples, each usually containing two groups of gods: those representing the hells and those representing the heavens. And in the religion itself the total process of retribution and after-life was reinterpreted in Buddhist terms.

MASSES FOR THE DEAD

HOWEVER rigorous the Chinese might be in their notions of justice, they found it impossible to witness the eternal torment of their sinful ancestors. It was natural enough, therefore, that some means should be developed whereby souls could be aided in their slow ascent from hell to heaven. One of the basic tenets of the Chinese Buddhist system came into existence to meet this need. The basis for the development of masses for the dead was found in a legendary tale told of Gotama and one of his followers, Ananda, who saw all the writhing and thirsty souls being tortured in hell. Out of compassion for them he asked Gotama if there were not some way in which he could help to redeem these lost ones. After due consideration Gotama told Ananda that the living could offer special prayers in front of the statue of Buddha and thereby aid the sinful departed. According to the legend, monks were required to offer the prayers in the presence of the "assembled congregation." Although the story is obviously apocryphal, it enabled the Chinese Buddhists to build an elaborate ritual which made them feel that they were participating in the ultimate salvation of the ancestors they venerated.

One of the most famous of the masses is known as "The Feast for the Wandering Souls." It is begun after the death of a man who is thought to have been a sinner in the eyes of Buddhist law. It can be held in a monastery, a temple, or, if the situation permits, in the courtyard of a relative. After much preparation, such as the construction of symbolic paper houses, horsemen and statues, the mass begins, usually at sunset. There are long readings from the Buddhist Scriptures and the sacred music is played. Offerings of food and drink are placed on the altar and many of the paper symbols are burned. Before things actually get under way, for example, the paper horseman is burned to indicate a messenger leaving the world of the living to inform those in hell that their mass is beginning. The ceremony moves through its various stages, all carefully worked out in terms of ritualistic motions and words, until at midnight it finally ends. Each act symbolizes the progress of the souls as they are guided over the "sea of pain." At midnight the new day is begun with the souls safely across the bridge and now traveling the road to light.

There are many types of masses for use in various situations. The very wealthy can afford to pay for numerous monks and fine offerings while the poor must be content with a simpler ceremony. But whether elaborate or simple, the periods in which the feasts occur are religious holidays, some of which take on a most spectacular appearance. For example, masses for the souls of those who have been taken by drowning are often conducted on summer evenings on boats that are lit by thousands of candles, making a beautiful picture as they float gently down the river. The size and elaborateness of the mass is not always determined, however, by the wealth of the living relatives. In some cases the monasteries themselves, out of their own funds, conduct gigantic masses for those killed in battle. During both World Wars and immediately following, masses of this kind were said for all those killed on the battlefields of Europe.

The formalization of the masses does not prevent their being more or less elaborate, but it does insist that they go through the various stages which symbolize the entrance of Yin-Yang-Ssu into hell and his leading the souls over the "sea of pain" into the light of redemption. Yin-Yang-Ssu is the most famous and most widely used of the guides since he is considered to have access to heaven, to hell, and to the land of the living.

THE PURE LAND SECT

As ONE might expect, many sects with varying emphases have developed within Chinese Buddhism. They are not mutually exclusive, however, and should perhaps more properly be called different strains of theological thought. Virtually all temples utilize monks of different persuasions, and it is often impossible to make important distinctions.

The most famous of the Buddhist schools is known by the name "Pure Land." It is also probably the oldest, and an accurate dating of its famous scripture, "The Awakening of Faith," is impossible. Its founders are supposed to have been Nagarjuna and Asvaghosha, who were instrumental in the split between Mahayana and Hinayana. In its original form the Pure Land group was probably a part of the reform movement that attempted to break away from the formalism represented by the ascetic traditionalists. "The Awakening of Faith," therefore, is filled with philosophical criticism of asceticism and rigid formal structure. In their place the School preaches the importance of a sincere heart and a strong faith.

Much of the Pure Land doctrine is taken directly from the Taoist Scriptures, and its mysticism is almost indistinguishable from that of Taoism.

The School emphasizes the necessity of faith in Amitabha, the person designated by Gotama to save the world from its miserable existence. According to Pure Land Scripture, there has been a line of eighty-one Buddhas. During the time of the last one, Gotama, a monk called Dhamakara went to him and asked how he too could become an eternal Buddha. Then he inquired as to how a perfect Buddha country should order its affairs. After being given the desired information regarding both Buddhist countries and the requirements for becoming a Buddha, Dhamakara (later to be known as Amitabha) made the following vow:

"When I become Buddha, let all living beings of the ten regions of the universe maintain a confident and joyful faith in me; let them concentrate their longings on a rebirth in my Paradise; and let them call upon my name, though it be only ten times or less; then, provided only that they have not been guilty of the five heinous sins, and have not slandered or vilified the true religion, the desire of such beings to be born into my Paradise will surely be fulfilled. If this be not so, may I never receive the perfect enlightenment of Buddhahood." [1]

This emphasis upon the primacy of faith held great appeal as a pragmatic arrangement for a large number of Chinese. Salvation could be attained by praying such prayers as, "I turn to Amitabha, in reverence and trust," without the costly and sometimes arid works prescribed by the more ascetic Buddhists. Moreover, in such a doctrine distinctions regarding earthly possessions and estate had little meaning. Even learning and knowledge of ancient lore were unimportant. Faith could

[1] Quoted in Karl Ludvig Reichelt, *Truth and Tradition in Chinese Buddhism* (Shanghai: The Commercial Press, Ltd., 1927), p. 142.

be achieved by men of all stations and of all degrees of intellect. In many ways the Pure Land emphasis had the same kind of leveling influence that the idea of bhakti brought to Hinduism. To worship in faith requires no aid from either ecclesiastical or state organization.

THE VINAYA SCHOOL

THIS exaggerated emphasis upon faith led to a general discounting of the moral pathways. But since the single individual could not be counted upon for orthodox behavior if he threw out the Middle Way and Eightfold Path concepts, the final achievement of salvation had still, in some sense, to be dependent upon the quality of action. This reaction to the individualism of the Pure Land School came from Vinaya, an opposing school, which stressed the necessity of works. The Vinaya School, established by Tao Hsüan around 625 A.D., reintroduced what were essentially Hinayana conceptions of ascetic discipline. Ethical actions were not the only question: the scriptures also were subjected to intense study. The Vinaya School accepted faith but thought it could be efficacious only after a period of profound ascetic study and meditation. For this legalistic School, Amitabha was relegated to a relatively unimportant position; ultimate bliss was achieved by man through the original Buddha and his teachings.

T'IEN T'AI PHILOSOPHY

CHINESE Buddhism absorbed both of these general strands of thought and practice without allowing either to dominate completely. The faith of Mahayana and the works of Hinayana both find a place in the philosophico-religious thought of the Buddhist. The most important single school of philosophy, T'ien T'ai, accords importance to all forms of religious expression and exclusiveness to none. Within this rambling and often contradictory philosophic structure can be found Pure Land faith, Vinaya legalism, Taoist absolutism, and the filial piety of the Confucianist. The eclectic and composite nature of this system gives ample proof of the all-inclusive character of Chinese religion. The strict sectarianism that often bedevils Western thought is not to be found within Chinese Buddhism.

Although the T'ien-T'ai School has a loose philosophic structure, it rises out of a basis which distinguishes it from all other Chinese systems. Chi-K'ai, the founder, placed his major stress upon an epistemology designed to ensure perfect intelligence. He had been a monk of the Ch'an-men sect which emphasized the value of contemplation, consequently recommending the abolition of the study of the sacred scriptures and, in fact, of all intellectual discipline. The Ch'an-men sect had gone so far in this direction that it even discarded the words of the original Buddha. Nirvana was to be achieved solely by introspective contemplation. As a reaction to such doctrine, which seemed to be excessive, if not heretical, Chi-K'ai went back to the original Sutras and developed a system which he considered to be the embodiment of Gotama's teaching.

The basis of salvation, said Chi-K'ai, is to be found in universal reason. All men, indeed all living things, are possessed of a degree of rationality which is a gift from the Buddha. Any perfection of human nature lies in the development of these rational capacities through instruction in the sacred scriptures and through the correct observation of human action. These two processes alone can save man from the illusion and error which clutter the phenomenal world.

The entire structure is thus built upon a theory of education. As the instruction begins, the votary is known as a disciple; after leaving the stage of discipleship he becomes wise, then perfectly intelligent, then a Bodhisattva, and finally the Buddha. The purpose of the course of study is not to produce a keener awareness of social obligations and moral distinctions; rather it is designed so to increase man's knowledge of the temporal world that he is sure everything is flux and illusion. Through education, then, the votary comes to realize that his material desires are vain and that physical existence is simply an unfortunate result of ignorance. The T'ien-T'ai system of the books is atheistic. It lacks the sensuous Western paradise of the Pure Land sects, and its religious life is directed toward the expulsion of evil by getting rid of error.

Although the book philosophy explains the popular gods as illusions due to ignorance, the T'ien-T'ai School permits the mass of people to worship and venerate idols and Buddha representations. The reason for this is found in the T'ien-T'ais' conviction that true knowledge is possible only for the few highly intelligent monks who devote themselves entirely to becoming utterly vacant. The majority of people are on a level of knowledge where gods have reality, and they must therefore worship them. This conception of an intellectual elite allows the entire pantheon of popular Buddhism to be incorporated into the worship of the T'ien-T'ai School. Further, it sets the monk on a pedestal from which he can look with ill-concealed contempt upon the poor souls who still require gods and thus continue to live in ignorance.

The T'ien-T'ai School, which becomes the Tendai sect in Japan, was undoubtedly influenced by the teachings of Indian Brahmanism. Its philosophy, if theistic at all, is certainly pantheistic, and its social theory is both aristocratic and exclusive. Moreover, there are obvious borrowings of its scriptures from Hindu theism. Hindu mythology, too, is used more extensively by the T'ien-T'ai group than by any other sect in China. The popular worship exercises call upon Brahma, Vishnu and Siva as well as many of the lesser Hindu deities. All these various influences and borrowings combine to form one system which, with a number of distinctly Chinese additions, is presented as the true legacy of Gotama.

POPULAR BUDDHISM

ALTHOUGH Buddhism has made a rather phenomenal conquest of China, it has never become the official religion. Confucianism still offers it the most direct competition. However, the character of Buddhism has been so changed by its invasion of China as to be now more Chinese than Indian. For example, the basic Chinese tendency toward a profound appreciation of nature and its essential continuity has not been altered. But the Buddhists did offer new ways of expressing the old faith and the old beliefs, and in so doing greatly increased the richness and variety of Chinese religion. The moral structure of the nation has remained unchanged with the possible exception of the introduction of the Buddhist conception of compassionate faith. Certainly the Buddhist influence has tended to intensify those elements of mysticism that were already present in Taoism. In many instances Buddhism has given this mysticism an ethical twist not to be found in primitive Taoism. But for the Chinese the world is still good, and man remains an essentially good creature.

Buddhism contributed a great deal to the popular Chinese custom of "making gods," for within its structure room can be found, on the level of either Buddha or Bodhisattva, for an infinite variety of worship objects. Even human beings, especially heroes, can easily attain the status of divinity since Buddhism, like Taoism, encourages such elevation. Nor need the gods be considered only in connection with heaven. Their earthly representations in the temples and shrines offer unlimited opportunity for variations in color, craftsmanship and other forms of that artistic expression which is so well developed in the Chinese. Their sense of drama is more than satisfied by the stirring stories of many heavens, hells, and wandering spirits without home or rest. In Buddhism the Chinese have been able to write their national romance and satisfy their yearnings for immortal blessedness. But they have not neglected to combine with these their traditional concepts of morality and retributive justice.

10

BUDDHISM IN TIBET

IF THE type of Buddhism that was introduced into China can be called high, the type that went to Tibet was low. China received its original Buddhist missionaries from the golden age of expanding Mahayana. Although there was a certain degree of superstitious belief in magical incantations and mysterious controls, the main burden of the Chinese importation was more distinctly religious and ethical. Tibet, on the other hand, drew its Buddhism from the period of the Tantras, consequently acquiring a large body of Indian magical practices.

THE INDIGENOUS PÖN

ALTHOUGH we have few accurate sources of information regarding it, the indigenous religion of Tibet prior to Buddhism was called Pön, which was a form of nature worship. The priests, who exercised tremendous power in the society, were more nearly witch-doctors and magicians than teachers of religious doctrine. In so far as we have evidence, the philosophic content of this native religion was slight, but the number of its specific gods and rites was extremely large. Devils, some of whom demanded the burning of scarce foods in time of famine, roamed the land, and there were rites for their exorcism. There were good gods also, many of whom nevertheless demanded the sacrifice of human beings and animals.

The Tibetan Wheel of Life. In the center are the three basic sins: lust (dove), igno-
rançe (pig), and anger (snake). The first circle shows mental development; the second
is Karma with the six realms of life; and the third circle indicates causal law. (*Courtesy Bush Collection of Religion and Culture.*)

A thirteenth-century painting on silk of the Japanese Buddha (Sakyamune). He is understood to be preaching Mahayana doctrine. (*Boston Museum of Fine Arts.*)

There appears to have been no sacred scripture within which the pantheon was elaborated, but there is evidence of a developed oral tradition.

As in most nomadic groups, the religious exercises centered around the tales of national heroes and their exploits. The most famous Tibetan epic concerns King Ke-Sar and his prowess in hunting and war. The action in the story is violent and has a large amount of supernatural coloration. Ke-Sar was supposed to have been the son of the king of the gods. Upon petition by the people the king of the gods sent his son, who was forced to prove himself by remarkable exploits, to lead a war-like people in conquest. The story of Ke-Sar is still looked upon as the basic Tibetan national hero epic.

The names of such heroes as Ke-Sar were called upon for all kinds of favors. Some of the so-called priests of the "Black Pön" could place a curse or hex upon a whole village by the proper use of a hero's name in a magical formula. Evil spirits could be exorcised from one individual and introduced into another, or eliminated entirely from any given region. The people of Tibet considered the works of the magician of indispensable value in coping with the problems of existence. They are to be distinguished from other primitive practitioners of magic, however, in that they usually associated the power of the practice with the name of an ancient and honorable hero. In this association is found an identification of magic and religious worship. The line between the natural and the supernatural is so blurred that it becomes almost impossible to ascribe one form of magic to the mundane and another form to the divine. For the Tibetan, spirits and gods were as real as men, and much more powerful.

TANTRIC BUDDHISM

INTO this land of demons and spirits the Tantric type of Mahayana was introduced. Both because of the nature of Tibetan religion and for political reasons, most of the Buddhism which was imported came from Bihar and Nepal rather than China. The spirit of the Tibetan was much more warlike than that of the Chinese and his powers of reflection much less developed. Certainly the middle-ground ethical position was foreign to everything in him. The mythology and demonology that had developed in the Indian Tantras made this particular form of Buddhism seem to be a codification and extension of much that was indigenous to Tibet.

The sexual emphasis of Tantric mysticism found immediate acceptance in Tibet, where the folklore is filled with references both to the necessity for reproduction and to the religious significance of fertility. Indeed, the uniting of the male and female deities is one of the oldest and most widespread conceptions of how creation began and is sustained. The wild and reckless abandon which comes with certain types of sexual expression was closely akin to the character of the Tibetan peoples, containing as it does symbolization of both creativity and destruction, passion and peace.

It was not until nearly a hundred years after the introduction of Buddhism into Tibet that it became an important religion. There were many obstacles in its way. First, the sacred texts had to be translated. Then, the Pön priests fought the establishment of an ecclesiastical organization. And finally, many of the emperors considered it a threat to their power. Tibet was at that time the major military power of Asia, and the quietistic doctrines of Gotama were hardly in keeping with the royal family's desire for greater conquests. Nevertheless, it was a Tibetan king who was responsible for bringing Padma Sambhova, a Tantric Mahayana monk, into the country. By 749 A.D. he had established the first great center of Buddhist learning in a monastery built near Lhasa. From that time forward Buddhism spread throughout the land and was finally able to assimilate most of the important Pönist doctrine. Padma Sambhova, the "Lotus Born," became the great teacher, and to this day his images are worshiped.

In many respects he was a peculiar monk. His face is usually represented with an angry twist to the mouth, and he has more the appearance of a warrior than of a calm saint. He had two wives and never felt it necessary to follow the more orthodox pattern of celibacy. As he went preaching from place to place, he emphasized always the superior nature of the gods and spirits of his own religion. Often he proved his contention by engaging Pön priests in contests. According to tradition, his supernatural powers invariably triumphed, forcing the Pönist to retire in defeat. His miracles included such things as making crops grow in barren soil, healing lame or diseased animals, and bringing water to places where no stream or well existed. By these methods the great leader and his disciples proved the superiority of Buddhism over all other religions.

THE LIVING BUDDHAS

The local hero and nature deities were quickly absorbed into the Buddhist pantheon. Most of the important teachers (such as Atisa, Marpa and Milaraspa) were known as Bodhisattvas, and their wives were considered to be manifestations of various goddesses. Tibetan Buddhism, however, has a distinctive concept of the Buddha. As in other places, there are many Buddhas who reside in Nirvana. But there are also the "living Buddhas." These are figures who have left their heavenly paradise and descended to earth to aid men and guide them to the final fulfillment. This conception of an incarnate Buddha forms the basis for a monastic theocracy which rules both the religious and the secular life of the nation. The incarnations themselves are recognized by their performances of various supernatural acts. Often the Grand Lama, or head, of a monastery is considered to be the incarnation of that particular monastery's founder. In such cases the founder may or may not be ranked as a Buddha; he may be only a Bodhisattva. In any event, the problem of deciding precisely which one a given Lama incarnates must be faced in each individual instance. No general principle seems applicable to all.

In the fourteenth century the position of the incarnate Buddhas was consolidated by a reformer named Tsong-Ka-Pa. Tsong-Ka-Pa was both zealous and fierce in the fight he waged against the extravagances of Tantrism. He was in stern opposition to the marriage of monks and the use of alcoholic beverages as an inducement to religious experience. His emphasis was upon strict conformity to the rules of monkish discipline, and in general he tried to raise the priesthood to a more spiritual and less material level. Under his direction, mass prayer festivals were organized and the scriptural writings were canonized and stripped of many of their early Tantric passages. His followers were called Ge-luk-pa, those of the virtuous way, and they started to wear yellow hats as a mark of distinction. The older sects used the red hat.

When Tsong-Ka-Pa died in 1419, he left a large, well-established monastery known as Gan-den which became the center for the more ascetic monks and spread its influence out into Tibet and Mongolia. The strong leadership of Tsong-Ka-Pa was continued by his successor, Gedün Truppa, who founded another monastery, called Drepung, which was to become the center of the theocratic state of Tibet. After a time the abbots of Drepung sent missionaries to Mongolia and successfully converted a number of the most important chieftains. As Drepung grew in importance, the head abbot assumed the name

of Dalai Lama and became the head of both state and church.
The first Dalai Lama was so named by a Mongolian chief out
of gratitude for his conversion.

The incarnation of the Buddha, supernatural perception,
and the highest spiritual authority were all combined in the
person of the Dalai Lama. Under him the priesthood exercised
the most extreme powers of life and death over all the inhabitants of Tibet. The Yellow Hat group did not have to depend
solely upon the force of their doctrine or the spiritual authority of their leaders for growth, for in back of their words and
deeds stood the might of the Mongolian army. With this joining of religious authority and military power, the supremacy
of the Dalai Lama could hardly be resisted. During the period
of the fifth Dalai Lama (died in 1680), the concept of a living
Buddha reigning over both church and state was well established and impossible to break. It was at this point that the
triumph of Buddhism over the religion of Pön was complete.

POPULAR TIBETAN BUDDHISM

THE Buddhism of Tibet, like that of China, became an expression of the national temperament and consciousness. Therefore the essential quality of the early Pönism was not lost; it
was merely put into Buddhist forms. The people themselves
still believed in the magical and supernatural powers of their
priests and in the efficacy of certain words and bodily movements. Buddhism offered Tibet an organizational structure
that was long lacking in the indigenous religion. Moreover, it
was a structure that was able to unify this portion of Central
Asia into one nation under one ruler. Now the various tribes
and local chieftains are bound to the central authority in Lhasa
by bonds which their people recognize as essentially religious.
Tibetan Buddhism thus offers a striking example of the way
in which religion can be used to centralize government and

exert wide and tyrannical control over a large population.

The peaceful and nonviolent doctrines of Buddhism have left their mark on the once warlike tribes of Central Asia. With the consolidation of both secular and religious power in the hands of the monks, the Tibetan and Mongolian peoples have lost much of their aggressiveness and have been generally content to eschew foreign conquest. In spite of the gulf between Tibetan Buddhism and the ideas of Gotama, there is still an essentially quietistic attitude toward life expressed by the monks. Buddhist influences have pronounced against the training and maintenance of armed services and have specifically described the evil of war and violent conflict. The Dalai Lama and his regents have not always been able to live up to the Buddhist ideal, but the tendency is certainly in a more peaceful direction.

One of the most distinctive contributions of Buddhism to Tibet is found in the arts. Huge temples of stone and wood construction have been built all over the country. Inside these buildings, craftsmen have fashioned multicolored images to represent various heavenly figures and their efforts to aid man in his search for Nirvana. In addition to these plastic art forms, the Buddhist mythology has offered innumerable opportunities for dramatic expression. The Lamas are thought to be the suppressors of the devils in hell, and in this role they protect the world of men from attack. The mystery plays, which are given at regular intervals throughout the year, enact scenes of writhing devils who are cunningly trying to gain control of the world. As the plays progress, the Lamas are shown to be more cunning than the ambitious devils and, moreover, in possession of a magical formula that finally thwarts them. Though built around a serious theme, these plays offer ample opportunity for comic relief and artistic expression.

At various times since the introduction of Buddhism into

Tibet, the Lamaistic form has seeped through its borders into other parts of Asia. China has received more than any other country, and much of the purer Mahayana of the Chinese has been infused with Tantric influence by way of Tibetan missionaries. If a religious or political leader of Tibet is exiled, it is usually to China, and with him goes his religion and often a missionary zeal. This is quite natural, for any group of people so strongly imbued with a belief in the reality of spirits and magical exorcism is bound to have a missionary attitude which makes its impression wherever it goes. Thus, much of the religious practice of the Chinese must be viewed with a knowledge of Tibetan changes in the original Mahayana.

The influence has not been entirely one way, however. Chinese missionaries have at one time or another penetrated the mountain fastnesses of the Lamas and brought with them their morality and their belief in ancestor worship. These Chinese ideas have reinforced an emphasis upon the importance of death rites and the necessity for making proper provision for the protection of departed souls. In the popular religion of Tibet this protection is, of course, against the demons who inhabit the spirit world. The Chinese concepts of retributive justice and moral responsibility have done much to tame the Tibetan and Mongolian savagery.

In late years Lamaistic Buddhism has maintained its tight grip on the peoples of Central Asia by a pronounced doctrine of isolation. Commerce between Tibet and the other parts of Asia has been heavily taxed and consistently discouraged. Foreign influences have been rigorously rejected in favor of local institutions and beliefs. As a result of this enforced isolation, the eight million people of Tibet and Mongolia have concentrated upon their own salvation, evolving a state and a religion peculiar to their area and their tastes. Gotama's brand of Buddhism was probably more conquered than conquering in Central Asia.

11

SHINTO AND BUDDHISM

BOTH China and Tibet obtained their Buddhism directly from the source in India and assimilated it into their own cultural traditions. Buddhism, again of the Mahayana type, came to Japan out of the southwestern corner of the Korean peninsula during the sixth century A.D. Legend has it that the chief of a small Korean state sent a statue of the Buddha along with other presents to the emperor of Japan as part of a gesture to gain Japanese support against some nearby enemies. Such is the probably apocryphal story of the beginning of Japanese Buddhism.

It is known, however, that Buddhism got its start in Japan under the aegis of a royal family that was on the throne at the beginning of the seventh century of our era. The Empress Suiko Tenno, who reigned between 593 and 628 A.D., took the imported Chinese Buddhism for the religion of her court and quickly converted most of the aristocracy. Actually it was not only Buddhism that was imported from China. Virtually all the exportable aspects of the older Chinese civilization—its law, political philosophy, classical literature and religion—became a part of Japanese culture during this period.

NATURE WORSHIP

BUT in order to make such importations popular, it was first necessary that a very ancient religion of the Japanese islands be supplanted by the new structure or incorporated into it. The primitive indigenous religion of Japan was much like that of China. The worship of nature deities and the vague veneration of ancestors was fused into a religion called *Shinto*, "the way of the gods." The name Shinto was not applied to it until, in the sixth or seventh century, it became necessary to distinguish it from Butsudo, "the way of the Buddha." Japanese tradition before the sixth century A.D. was not codified and is therefore not anywhere near as trustworthy as that of China. Indeed, it is doubtful whether the Japanese were even measuring time or recording their historical experiences prior to the introduction of Chinese civilization. Nevertheless, we do know that the islands of Japan were inhabited long before the beginning of any written records, and throughout its history there developed a popular religion with its own peculiar emphasis and mythology. The oldest literature, which was compiled in the eighth century A.D. from the oral tradition, contains the basic mythology of Shinto. The Kojiki is the ancient history book, while the Nihongi consists of descriptions of worship practices and much of the local mythology.

For the most part the gods of Shinto were derived from various forces and objects in nature. There were deities of storm, rain, mountains, fire, and other aspects of the phenomenal world. In return for the worship of their believers, these deities were expected to furnish proper protection and provide coveted rewards. The character of the early Shinto gods and ritual indicates very clearly the Japanese feeling of dependence upon the forces of nature. The good life was conceived in terms of physical well-being, and this well-being could best be obtained by propitiating the proper powers of the world above. The nature deities are personal, and they have a very direct relationship to the affairs of men on earth.

THEORIES OF CREATION

WITHIN Shinto mythology there are a number of different stories regarding the origin of man and of the earth. One of the most popular is told in the Kojiki and repeated in the Nihongi. Out of an original chaos, the heavier part settled and became the earth while the lighter portion rose and became heaven. From this separation appeared a reed-sprout which became a Kami, or god. According to some mythology this god, Ama-no-Minaka-Nushi-no-Kami, is considered the source for all the other gods. At any rate, new gods were created with the normal sex differentiations. Two of them, Izanagi (Most Inviting Male) and Izanami (Most Inviting Female), came together at the command of the original Kami and gave birth to the Islands of Japan. At this time Izanami and Izanagi were standing on a bridge between heaven and earth. After thrusting a jeweled spear into the waters below, the divine pair descended to the island of Ono Koro-juina which was formed by the drops which fell from the end of the spear. Other sacred beings were created, and after the birth of the fire god, Izanami died and went to Hades.

The loss of Izanami caused Izanagi to follow her to Hades in an effort to take her back to their idyllic island. However, by the time he got to her she was so thoroughly corrupted by the demons of the foul nether region that he could not get her away. When at last Izanagi returned, he was forced to take an extended bath to purify himself. As the water from the bath fell to the ground each drop became a Kami, and in this way a large portion of the Shinto pantheon came into existence. As he was bathing his left eye a drop fell and became Amaterasu, the Sun Goddess. (Amaterasu is the central deity of the later pantheon, and one of her attributes is absolute cleanliness.) As he washed his right eye, the wild storm god Susa-no-wo was created, only to be ultimately banished for having insulted the Sun Goddess.

All through this rather ornate mythology gods were created out of water and nothingness. Each special act of the primitive Japanese had a Kami in charge who required some kind of propitiation. For the most part these early gods were jealous and certainly as quarrelsome as their human counterparts. They ate and drank large quantities of the best food and wine, and they engaged in wild dances and expressed themselves with reckless abandon in sensuous orgies. From the few data now extant it is almost impossible to construct a meaningful theology. There seems to have been no consistency about the ethical demands of these gods: in fact we are distinctly conscious of a lack of any supernaturally sanctioned moral code. The only duties of the primitive Japanese appear to have been obedience to the emperor, who was a divine descendant of Amaterasu, and worshipful fear of the gods. The one moral commandment seems to have been physical cleanliness, and this in the strict sense of constant bathing.

OFFICIAL SHINTO

MUCH of the early religion centered around human sacrifice. Many of the gods demanded that living human beings be killed in special ways to insure their good graces. The gods of the sea, in particular, required that men be drowned to make the fishing boats safe. When large buildings were to be constructed, men were buried alive in the foundations to assure a permanent and long-standing structure. Many of the generalized worship rites included the cutting or burning of beautiful young girls for the glory of the various gods.

Order was brought to this wild vitalism of the primitive religion by the conquering Yamato tribe. As the Yamato, or Mikado, family extended its political control, the Shinto religion was transformed into state worship. The Mikado claimed to be the direct descendant of the highest deity. He had been sent, so the tradition relates, as the controller and organizer of the divinely created islanders. According to Shinto chronology, Jummu Tenno, Japan's first Mikado, was enthroned in 660 B.C.

Under the leadership of successive Mikados Japan became a partially integrated nation. Various officials of the government became the leaders of the worship held in shrines throughout the land. From the time of Jummu Tenno until the close of World War II, the government of Japan has been a theocracy in which politics and piety were inextricably mingled. Governmental actions as well as worship practices carried an air of sanctity and absoluteness. Since the Yamato clan was largely engaged in agriculture, rituals and prayers for good crops, protection of the harvest, and sufficient sun and rain assumed greatest prominence. Through everything, however, ran constant references to the good health and long reign of the Mikado.

Ancestor worship, as opposed to veneration, was probably borrowed from the Chinese. Prior to the introduction of Chinese culture in the sixth century A.D. there is no reference to the worship of either ancestors or the dead emperors. With the coming of Chinese Buddhism the emperor's spirit assumed an important position in the pantheon, but still, with one or two exceptions, it failed to achieve a rank equal to that of the established nature deities. Even Buddhist influence could not counteract what seems to have been a marked tendency to forget the emperor once he had left this mortal life. With the revival of Shinto in 1868, the government made a definite attempt to establish imperial ancestor worship as a more prominent part of the cult, but despite this added impetus, only four annual rites for deceased emperors found their way into the Shinto calendar.

The ordinary worshiper in Shinto was obligated to a tremendous number of gods. The various prayer services became long and involved, and sometimes as much as an hour would be consumed simply with an enumeration of names. Besides the emperor and natural deities, the ancestors of the family required attention. The sun was worshiped both morning and night, while the various local deities who graced the Karnidana, or god-shelf, of each home demanded almost constant worship. This confusion of deities was an additional factor in making the introduction of Buddhism comparatively easy.

THE COMING OF BUDDHISM

THE brand of Buddhism which entered Japan was equipped with remarkable powers of assimilation. It had a pantheon of Buddhas and Bodhisattvas that could easily be reinterpreted to include the complicated mass of native Japanese gods. Further, it had a theology which considered life after death, salvation, moral excellence—all problems which had been almost totally neglected in the sacred traditions of the Kojiki and Nihongi. These theological and mythological elements found immediate acceptance with large numbers of Japanese. But they were not the only basis for assimilation. Japan's pre-Buddhistic Shinto had been practically devoid of artistic expression. The temples were low rude huts with little or no ornamentation, and the statues of the gods were plain and uncolored. Up to this time the only art known to the Japanese was highly abstract monochrome paintings imported from the Chinese mainland. With the coming of Buddhist priests the whole character of esthetic expression changed. Buddhism was nurtured in southern Asia where color and delicate craftsmanship had long been an expanding tradition. The Buddhist priests were clothed in bright gold, black, and red robes, the altars to the various avatars were carved in exquisitely fine lines, and the idols were a blaze of color. The richness and luster of gold was indispensable to the Buddhist temple: golden threads were mixed with the cloth and used as wall hangings, gold leaf covered the statues of the gods, gold plating appeared on the pillars of the shrines and temples, and the worshipers were often required to wear gold rings and offer food in gold cups. Such a use of precious metal, far as it was from the simple alms basket of Gotama, fired the imagination of a people completely unused to such drama in their religious worship with a vision of the golden future offered by Buddhism.

KŌBŌ'S SYNTHESIS

THE great task of synthesizing primitive Shinto and Chinese Buddhism was left to Kōbō Daishi, a remarkable teacher of the ninth century A.D. Kōbō was well schooled in Chinese lore and Buddhist theology, but he was equally well versed in the ways of the national gods of Japan. After studying the Chen Yen doctrine in China, he returned to Japan to announce that all the deities of Shinto were either incarnations of the Buddha or, at the very least, avatars. The Chen Yen school, which was strongly influenced by the Indian Tantras, maintained that all the nature deities, as well as those of the spirit, should be considered valid manifestations of the One Highest Buddha. Kōbō added to this doctrine the fact that the Shinto gods were being worshiped by the Japanese even before Gotama had received enlightenment in faraway India. Then he went even further and declared that the supreme Buddha could make himself known as a god (Kami), or as a teacher (Confucian sage) or as a Buddha (Hotoké). In short, Kōbō really attempted a synthesis of Shinto, Confucianism and Buddhism.

In addition to the identification of the Kami with avatars and Buddhas, various national sages and heroes of Japan were raised to the rank of deities. Every day in the month and certain special holy days were assigned a Basatu (the Japanese for Bodhisattva), who watched over and protected the twenty-four hour period. Statesmen, priests, literary men and warriors were given places in the pantheon and worshiped for their special powers and talents. They, as well as the forces of nature, became known to the Japanese as Dai Miō Jin, Great Enlightened Spirit. It is probable that this custom came in with Kōbō, and it has lasted down to the present time.

The work of Kōbō was so successful that the Mikado joined in the movement toward synthesis by announcing the new "twofold divine doctrine" as the official religion of Japan. Under the Shingon sect, as Kōbō's followers were called, it was possible for the emperor to maintain his theocratic control while at the same time publicly declaring his Buddhist faith. Such a system kept Buddhism from becoming a threat to the royal family. In return, governmental sanction facilitated the spread of Buddhism throughout the islands and the ultimate establishment of a rich and powerful church.

It is difficult to say whether Shinto was overcome by Buddhism, or Buddhism by Shinto. Certainly the amalgamation of the two traditions produced both a new Shinto and a new Buddhism. Indian Tantric magic and superstition met, as it entered Japan, equally strong local traditions. Formulae for controlling nature and the gods were little changed since they were capable of manifold interpretations. The basic concepts of Shinto mythology were put into Buddhist molds, even though many contradictions remained. In this early period the life of the ordinary Japanese seems to have been enriched by a new art and new gods, but the fundamental characteristics of his worship remained much the same.

Ancient Shinto, at least from the rise of Mikadoism, demanded unswerving loyalty and obedience to the divine emperor. This nationalistic duty took precedence over all other obligations to family, friends or even the memory of ancestors.

The earthly descendant of Amaterasu was the final and complete authority for all things, both temporal and spiritual. One would expect that at this point the Chinese idea of filial piety and family loyalty would run completely counter to the traditional Japanese conception. But here again Shinto solved the problem with mutual satisfaction. The emperor was still the divine monarch, and loyalty to him took the place of loyalty to the more intimate family. In Japan this feeling came naturally, for the feudal nature of the economy and political organization substituted loyalty to the feudal lord for loyalty to father or mother. By this process the whole of the nation was conceived of as a huge family with a set hierarchy of duties, rights and responsibilities. Particularization of duty into the simple filial piety of the Chinese variety never gained headway. The compromise at this juncture shows more Shinto than Buddhist influence.

12

JAPANESE SECTARIANISM

AS THE mixture of Shinto and Buddhism spread, monasteries were opened and thousands of Japanese became Buddhist monks. The political supremacy of the monks was unquestioned, and much of their tremendous numerical growth can be attributed to the general privilege and economic advantage they enjoyed. Political activities, however, were only a part of the function of the developing priesthood. Scholars were designated to explore the possibilities of the Mahayana Sūtras and the various imported Tantric Mantras and Mudrās. From these and the original Shinto documents elaborate rituals and theological structures were developed. But although the monasteries became the centers of learning and culture, they also gave impetus to the inevitable rise of sectarianism.

THE ZEN SECT

ONE of the more important sects was established in the latter part of the twelfth century by a monk named Eisai. According to tradition Eisai went to China in 1168 and studied a special form of Buddhism which had arisen in the early part of the eighth century. When Eisai returned to Japan in 1187 he built a Zen shrine and started preaching his "reformed" Buddhism. After a number of setbacks, such as the destruction of Kyoto by an earthquake which was attributed to the existence there of a Zen shrine, Eisai established the seat of Zen Buddhism in Kam-a-Kura. From this center the sect expanded until it became one of the most powerful and influential groups in Japanese Buddhism.

The Zen sect claimed to be in the direct tradition of the great Gotama. The various accretions of both a doctrinal and a ritualistic nature which, through the centuries, had come to be considered a part of Asiatic Buddhism were denounced by the founders of Zen as being heretical and alien to the Pranjna, or transcendental wisdom, of the original. Zen proposed to penetrate the outward forms and recapture the spirit of Buddha.

Once again is asserted the early Buddhist idea that the meaning of life is to be found by going behind the world of sense experience and entering the timeless, limitless, undifferentiated Nirvana. This is the transcendental wisdom of the Buddha. Coupled with this is the doctrine of *Karuna*. Karuna, which means love or compassion, is free to operate only when man has ceased worrying about his empirical existence and has prepared himself spiritually for fulfillment in Buddhahood. Knowledge and intellectual activity only cloud the true meaning of Buddha's discovery. According to Zen, man has become interested in the outward signs, the ritual, the mythology, and the work of his mind and hand, with the result that he has lost his true orientation and bound himself more completely to Karma.

Obviously Zen found it difficult to propagate such a doctrine. The very necessity of coherent language had to be denied, since its use would be an admission of defeat. In order to achieve acceptance of its reform doctrine, Zen had to develop some other method. A story told by Goso Hōyen, a twelfth-century Zen monk, illustrates the nonverbal method of Zen instruction:

If people ask me what Zen is like, I will say that it is like learning the art of burglary. The son of a burglar saw his father growing older and thought, "If he is unable to carry out his profession, who will be the bread-winner of this family, except myself? I must learn the trade." He intimated the idea to his father, who approved of it. One night the father took the son to a big house, broke through the fence, entered the house, and, opening one of the large chests, told the son to go in and pick out the clothing. As soon as he got into it, the lid was dropped and the lock securely applied. The father now came out to the court-yard, and loudly knocking at the door woke up the whole family, whereas he himself quietly slipped away through a hole in the fence. The residents got excited and lighted candles, but found that the burglar had already gone. The son who remained all the time in the chest securely confined thought of his cruel father. He was greatly mortified, when a fine idea flashed upon him. He made a noise which sounded like the gnawing of a rat. The family told the maid to take a candle and examine the chest. When the lid was unlocked, out came the prisoner, who blew out the light, pushed away the maid, and fled. The people ran after him. Noticing a well by the road, he picked up a large stone and threw it into the water. The pursuers all gathered around the well trying to find the burglar drowning himself in the dark hole. In the meantime he was safely back in his father's house. He blamed his father very much for his narrow escape. Said the father, "Be not offended, my son. Just tell me how you got off." When the son told him all about his adventures, the father remarked, "There you are, you have learned the art." [1]

The whole area of human discourse is negated by the Zen Buddhist. Neither logic nor language and its structure can furnish truth in matters of religion. Language is built upon the necessity for making distinctions, and true religion deals only with the utterly indistinguishable. When words, no mat-

[1] Daisetz Teitaro Suzuki, *Zen Buddhism and Its Influence on Japanese Culture*, The Ataka Buddhist Library IX (Kyoto: The Eastern Buddhist Society, 1938), pp. 5-6.

ter how poetic, are applied to the final judgments of faith, the results can only be false. If a Zen monk were to ask his teacher a question such as: "What is the most miraculous event in the world?" the teacher would respond with a meaningless statement of this kind: "I sit here all by myself." For no intellectual interpretation can or should be given to the origin of the world, the nature of death, or the requirements of man. The Zen method is one of personal, unmediated experience of truth in which the use of symbolization is idolatry.

As would be expected, Zen is in opposition to all forms of science or philosophy. Anything which smacks of abstractness or even representation must be discarded in favor of the reality it conceals. The Zen believer, abandoning the complex art of the Chinese, produces artistic creations with simple, narrow lines, vast spaces, and a minimum of ornamentation. Zen art, like Zen doctrine, looks for the unity of experience in the all-pervasive oneness of life.

From its very inception Zen Buddhism has been identified with the controlling military group in Japan. Although Zen does not preach war, neither does it teach peace. Salvation is achieved by discovering the Buddha within, not through the development of a specific kind of society or the promulgation of a particular ethical system. The life of a warrior is simple and direct with little time wasted upon philosophical investigations into the cause and nature of things. This rather necessary military trait finds strong support in Zen. The Samurai is free to go about its bloody business with no fear of religious sanction or supernatural retribution.

Zen requires that life and death be regarded with equal indifference. True achievement is measured by introspective self-realization and not by objective historical acts. The believing spirit is supposed to rise above life and death, and to view all reality from a vantage point which makes such distinctions meaningless. Much of the instruction given the Samurai, or warrior group, is a constant emphasis upon the necessity for mastering any fear of death by finding meaning and strength in the eternal Buddha who is neither alive nor dead. In the *Hagakure*, a Zen document for the Samurai, the following appears:

Bushido means the determined will to die. When you are at the parting of the ways, do not hesitate to choose the way to death. No special reason for this except that your mind is thus made up and ready to see to the business. Some may say that if you die without attaining the object, it is a useless death, dying like a dog. But when you are at the parting of the ways, you need not plan for attaining the object. We all prefer life to death and our planning and reasoning will be naturally for life. If then you miss the object and are alive, you are really a coward. This is an important consideration. In case you die without achieving the object, it may be a dog-death—the deed of madness, but there is no reflection here on your honour. In Bushido honour comes first. Therefore, every morning and every evening, have the idea of death vividly impressed in your mind. When your determination to die at any moment is thoroughly established, you attain to perfect mastery of Bushido, your life will be faultless, and your duties are fully discharged.

Zen teaching is not so much a denial of life as an indifference to it. As such, it makes excellent instruction for the military. Although Zen is supposed to be without ritual and dogma, a great symbolism has developed around the sword. "The sword," so an old Japanese saying goes, "is the soul of the Samurai." It represents the spirit of both self-discipline and patriotic militarism. On the one hand it is used to defend and conquer, which is the business of the Samurai. But it also carries a religious meaning. The sword is supposed to be used to slay the passions of greed, anger and capricious action. For example, the individual who carries the sword or places it in a prominent shrine within his home is continually reminded of the necessity for unswerving loyalty to his chosen profession. In Shinto the sword is supposed to be vested with supernatural power for wreaking destruction on the enemies of the state. In Zen it is a constant reminder that personal desire is nothing, and that duty is everything.

The self-discipline and intuitive epistemology of Zen Buddhism have made it possible for a variety of moral systems to be taught in its monasteries. At no time should any ethical pronouncement be considered absolute or endowed with supernatural sanctions. The ethics of this group is more a matter of expedient absorption than adherence to strict principle. In this respect the followers of Zen are much like the adherents of earlier Shinto. The insight they possess is capable of meeting the demands of any type of political system or any type of moral structure. Political decisions are made by the emperor and, if they involve fighting, implemented by the Samurai. The question of their validity never arises; the Zen Buddhist's sole duty is to carry them out. The same holds true of the moral code: the one in current use is the one to be followed, and this without questioning or doubting. Such attitudes are conservative in the extreme but they solve problems which haunt the lives of other men.

One of the fundamental characteristics of the Japanese cultural consciousness is its almost fanatical love of nature. In cherry blossoms, the view of Mt. Fuji, or the sunset, the Japanese finds glory and wondrous beauty. Zen Buddhism capitalizes on this trait and asserts that there is no essential distinction between man and nature. Nature must be respected as it is found; any violation is considered evil. For this reason, asceticism of the self-mortification variety is never permissible. Except for that inordinate drive which causes man to exploit the physical universe for his own selfish pleasure, natural desires and wants are to be fulfilled rather than denied. All of nature, whether animate or inanimate, is ultimately destined for Buddhahood. Through this doctrine Zen promotes what it calls a "friendly cooperation" among the various aspects of nature. True asceticism, it believes, is living in accord with the totality of nature.

Closely akin to this kind of asceticism is the esthetic side of Zen's teaching. The subject-object relationship upon which science and language are founded is denied by Zen. Man and nature are one. The tree and the rock are "continuous" rather than distinct. As one Western writer has put it, the world, conceived thus, is a vast "undifferentiated esthetic continuum." This sense of continuity is, of course, beyond all speech and, except in rare instances, beyond pictorial representation. The beauty of a painting or a flower is not to be judged by its form, but by its ability to capture the onlooker and absorb him into itself. For the Zen this is the religious quality of beauty. Through its agency man can lose his self-consciousness and be at one with the undifferentiated absolute. The Zen poet Kanzan attempts to express the spirit of this concept in the following words:

> My mind is like the autumnal moon;
> And how clear and transparent the deep pool!
> No comparison, however, in any form is possible;
> It is altogether beyond description.

The primary aim of Zen is to rid man of his sense of discontinuity and restore him to his original state of purity.

It is interesting to note that Zen achieved its greatest popularity only within the warrior class. Its lack of colorful ritual together with its emphasis upon periods of quiet contemplation put it outside the interest of the mass of Japanese. Moreover, few of the uneducated could appreciate its philosophical positivism, which allowed no discussion of the life after death or the origin of the world. Since most of the Japanese were farmers and hunters who had to support a rather burdensome warrior and aristocratic class, it would have been difficult to convince them that they did not stand in constant opposition to a nature which was only waiting for the slightest relaxation on their part to crush them completely; for those on the lower economic levels of this society were required to wrest what they could from an unyielding nature or be thrown into prison to starve.

THE JODO SECT

The Jodo sect, which developed in the twelfth and thirteenth centuries, filled the needs of the less-favored political and economic groups. Jodo was founded by a monk, Genku, who patterned it after the Chinese sect of the Pure Land. He was convinced that the people had fallen so low that there was little possibility of their being able to follow the Noble Eightfold Path to salvation. In an age of health the Noble Path could be used for guidance, but the Japanese people were far from spiritual health. Genku and his followers reached the conclusion that man in this state could not be saved by his own works but would have to be dependent upon some kind of supernatural aid. Thus, as in China, Nirvana was to be achieved by faith rather than works, and Amida (Amitabha) was established as the great saving power.

At its inception Jodo was a reaction against the moral laxity and corruption of the monasteries and court. Both groups had begun to feel that they were beyond good and evil, and many of their practices outraged the general populace. Large groups of Japanese paid the necessary lip service to their superiors but fell away from whatever spiritual guidance they might offer. Jodo Buddhism filled the gap by preaching the simple doctrine of faith. The authority for the sect was derived from one of the early Sūtras which was supposed to be in the words of Buddha. In this Sūtra Buddha is speaking to the wife of an Indian king and closes his sermon with these words: "Let not one's voice cease, but ten times complete the thought, and repeat the formula of the adoration of Amida." The formula, "Namu Amida Butsu"—Glory to the Eternal Buddha—can be heard to this day in the Jodo temples.

Whereas the Zen Buddhists eschewed ornamentation and metaphysics, the Jodo sect abounded in artistic creations and dramatic stories of life before and after death. The traditional Japanese deities were employed to work miracles and lead men to the Pure Land, the home of Amida. Both magical formulae and ritualistic acts were incorporated into the faith. Indeed, there was very little in the popular superstitions that did not find a place of some kind within the expansive folds of Jodo, which nevertheless must be considered a purer form of Buddhism than the Shingon started by Kōbō.

Zen Buddhism insists upon the ultimate unity of all nature, while the Jodo sect sees this world as a road of thorns, a progression of birth, disease, old age, death. A follower of Jodo must completely reject the phenomenal world and eradicate all desire for attachment to it. He who clings to material objects, or even views life as joyous and good, is incapable of keeping his eyes fastened upon the holy Amida. All of man's attention must be directed toward absolute faith and trust in the saving power of Amida. For only Amida can save from the eternal round of birth and death; only Amida can lead to the paradise of Pure Land in the western sky. A great deal of the power of Jodo lies in the fact that it recaptured a portion of the original Buddhist pessimism and coupled it with a stirring description of life beyond tragedy.

THE SHIN SECT

WITHIN the Jodo school different cults and sects grew and flourished. They all held to the importance of faith, in varying degrees. Some felt that a combination of faith and works would give the greatest assurance of Nirvana. Others of the Amidaists thought that constant reiteration of the worship formula was sufficient. Then there were those who permitted prayers and requests to be directed to Buddhas other than Amida. Among these sects there was also a strong controversy regarding the nature of prayer. Some authorities granted the validity of prayers for material benefits, while others maintained that true religion should be completely unconcerned with temporal existence.

Out of this medley of belief a monk by the name of Shinran organized what he called the "True Pure Land Sect." It is often referred to as Reformed Buddhism, and Shinran has sometimes been called the Luther of Japan. The Shin sect believed with other Pure Land groups that faith was necessary for salvation, but Shinran went far beyond Genku and his Chinese counterpart, Horen. According to the Shin sect, man is utterly incapable of initiating any good action; in his heart he is "black, foul, and false." Because of this diseased condition he is unable to follow a path of virtue and obviously cannot aid in his own entrance into the Pure Land. It is only out of the infinite compassion and mercy of Amida that anyone at all can be saved from the eternal effects of Karma.

For all practical purposes the Shin sect is monotheistic. Amida is the only means of grace; therefore the only avenue of salvation is through faith in Amida. No knowledge is necessary, but neither will a simple repetition of the Amida formula suffice. Shinran asks for a reorientation of the heart of man. By faith he means a complete spiritual trust in the overwhelming goodness of Amida. Metaphysical systems are considered important but without efficacy for salvation. According to the Shin sect, man can be saved in spite of his doctrine but never because of it. The weakest sinner may attain salvation, while the champion of law and order may be condemned to the cycle of birth and rebirth.

The original historic Buddha of ancient India is virtually forgotten in both the Jodo and Shin sects. Since Amida was the creation of a much later theological development, many Buddhists, in Japan and elsewhere, consider the Pure Land sects to be both heretical and without adequate historical foundation. Although their conception of salvation is the purely Buddhistic idea that man is to be saved from the wheel of rebirth and sanctified into Buddhahood, the means for attaining this salvation is totally foreign to the original tradition. In effect both Jodo and Shin depend upon the merit of another, Amida, rather than upon the semi-ascetic rigor of the Eightfold Pathway. This development in Buddhism closely parallels the similar growth of the Bhakti sects that we found in India.

As one might expect, the Pure Land doctrine of salvation by faith was either enthusiastically accepted or vigorously attacked by the people. Many saw in it an easy method for achieving the same end indicated by the more difficult Eightfold Pathway. Further, the idea that all men were so internally corrupt as to require the grace of Amida tended to minimize the difference between monk and layman. Since everyone had an equal chance, the honor which was traditionally accorded the Buddhist monk tended to vanish. In this life, according to Jodo and Shin, there can be no differentiation between the good person and the evil person: all are equally corrupt. Such doctrine could not long be tolerated either by the monks or by those interested in the moral welfare of the people. A reaction in favor of salvation by works was almost inevitable.

THE NICHIRENITES

THE reaction came in the person of Kominato, later to be known as Nichiren, a priest of the Shin sect. The Nichiren sect, which he founded in 1282, made a direct attempt to win the acceptance and favor of the masses. Its first attack was against the exclusive power of Amida and the emphasis upon the efficacy of faith. Japan, preached Nichiren, is a holy land created much as the early Shinto myths proclaimed. Although the Japanese have many Buddhas to guide them in their search for final release from the fetters of existence, salvation itself is still up to each individual: man will enter Nirvana by his own efforts or not at all. Honor the gods, honor those who have achieved Buddhahood, but work out your own salvation.

The pantheon of the Nichiren sect began to fill up with ancient heroes and nature deities. The historic Buddha stood at the apex and guided the lesser Buddhas, Bodhisattvas, and gods in their appointed chores. He had revealed once and for all, especially in the Saddharma Pundarika Sūtra, how man was to travel from the temporal to the eternal. And this method depended upon the moral energies of man.

The Nichirenites developed a lush mythology replete with miraculous happenings. For example, Nichiren himself, considered to be the product of a virgin birth, was supposedly endowed with all knowledge of the great Buddha through supernatural agency. His personal history is filled with tales of bloody battles, romantic adventures, and constant communications with supernatural beings. Animals, humans, rocks, trees—all are felt to have supernatural importance and are consequently placed in the Nichiren temples alongside the idols of Buddha. Surrounding each of these objects of worship is a body of magical practices and superstitions.

One of the outstanding characteristics of Nichirenite worship is its use of bells and loud gongs. Moreover, a pungent incense is burned and colorful dramatic presentations are common. There is little formalism and a great deal of spontaneous emotionalism. Whereas the other sects have more rigid codes of propriety in reverence and praise, the Nichirenites allow themselves complete freedom of expression. The noise and color of their services is not unlike the more primitive vitality of the earlier Shinto worship.

Most of the other sects are at least semi-tolerant of their Buddhist brethren of different persuasion, but the Nichirenites heap verbal and physical abuse upon all those who disagree with their doctrines. In general the sect is violent, intolerant and exceptionally nationalistic. The monks, who are perhaps the most reactionary, have led bloody battles against other sectarians, especially the Pure Land groups. In their laymen's handbook, warning is issued against intermarriage and even day-to-day social contact with other Buddhists. This exclusiveness of the sect has been strengthened rather than minimized with the passage of time. The good works insisted upon by their Buddhist scriptures are ignored where people of a different conviction are involved. "A thousand years in the lowest of the hells is the atonement prescribed by the Nichirenites for the priests of all other sects" was written by a Nichirenite in describing his faith.

LATE JAPANESE BUDDHISM

IN JAPANESE Buddhism there is discernible a constant dispute involving pantheism, polytheism and monotheism. Each sect tends to emphasize one of these "theisms," and there is no clear authority to which appeal could be made in an effort to settle disputes. The early mixed Buddhism and the late Nichiren sect espouse a definite polytheism and an inconsistent blend of Shinto, magic and Buddhism. Zen and certain doctrinal groups within Nichiren seem to border on, if not embrace, a pantheism in which temporal distinctions vanish in a haze of comprehensive unity. Jodo and Shin both lean toward, but never quite achieve, a monotheism not unlike that of various forms of Protestant Christianity. Japanese Buddhism is nothing if not chaotic in its theological orientation.

Its sects have maintained a consistent separation. Many are identified, sociologically if not theologically, with specific feudal classes. There is a unity among them, however, in their extreme nationalism and veneration of the emperor. Although some sects, particularly Zen, have a theoretical universalism, they all practice national exclusiveness. There seems to be little in Japanese Buddhism, at least on the practical level, that would engender international good will or trust. Part of this is perhaps due to the amazing amount of Shinto that has been pressed into Buddhist molds and preserved by Buddhist reinterpretation.

Since the nineteenth century Buddhism has been disestablished as a government-financed enterprise. With the restoration of the imperial throne in 1868, Shinto was designated as the official state religion and Buddhist idols were removed from the Shinto shrines. But this has by no means caused a collapse of Buddhist influence in Japan. Buddhism still holds the central position while Shinto has become a channel for patriotic expression. In the constitutions of 1889 and 1946, there is official recognition of freedom of religion, and all people are supposedly guaranteed complete religious liberty. Japanese Buddhism is today fighting for its life against a revival of "Pure" Shinto and an aggressive Christian missionary movement.

One of the striking aspects of Japanese Buddhism is its lack of a rationalized ethical structure. The traditional sects maintain the double standards for monks and laymen. But any further development in terms of modern applications or deeper penetrations into its meaning and significance has been negligible if not nonexistent. The real roots of Japanese morality are found in an imported version of Confucianism and in the duty concepts born of the feudal system. Popular morality is based more on customary modes of procedure than on principles derived from supernatural revelation. Japanese Buddhism has been far more concerned with salvation from despair and material want than with the proximate problems of religious ethics.

SECTION SUMMARY

THE origin and growth of Buddhism is a long story of protest against formalism and the establishment of formal structures. The Hinduism out of which Buddhism grew had succeeded in destroying most of the original vitality which characterized the early Vedas. As Buddhism spread throughout Asia, it in turn lost much of the dynamic power and enthusiasm which had once led large numbers to forsake their homes and follow Gotama, the enlightened one. Buddhism was never able to rise very far above the prevailing ethos of whatever country it happened to be in. In India it lost its character completely and was simply absorbed into the current theistic cults and Tantric magic; in Tibet, Buddhism took over most of the ancient Pön and became largely a magical system; in China Buddhism borrowed much of its content from Confucianism and Taoism; and in Japan, Chinese Buddhism was mixed with the ancient Shinto.

To be sure, some of the principles of Gotama's teaching survived in the varieties of later Buddhism. The Eightfold Path and the Four Noble Truths have been venerated consistently, even though interpretations without number have been given them. To a greater or lesser extent Gotama has remained an important figure. In Mahayana his influence is less, for innumerable Bodhisattvas are more regularly and piously worshiped than he is. In Hinayana the worship of Gotama the Buddha has finally been permitted, but his teaching and the self-reliant seeking of Nirvana are of primary concern.

Within very general limits it is possible to formulate a description of the Christian world-view. Such a statement, however, is impossible for Buddhism. Dating from a time shortly after Gotama's death, the number of metaphysical teachings which have called themselves Buddhist has been too great for recording. Each branch has produced literally thousands of theologies. In Buddhist countries there has never been that drive toward a scientific doctrine and a generally accepted dogma which characterizes Western thought. As a consequence, Buddhist theology abounds in contradictory statements and assertions for which no evidence is offered and no authorities cited. Although such confusion makes general statements regarding Buddhism next to impossible, it has been one of Buddhism's major strengths in conquering Asia. The Buddhist missionary has never had great difficulty in establishing rapport with those he wished to convert.

One of the most pervasive characteristics of Buddhism is its attitude toward the phenomenal world. Practically all branches hold to the idea that the totality of phenomena is part of an originless causal series. Life, down to its most minute detail, is caught within a structure of necessity from which there is but one escape. The Buddhist theory of salvation, however variously it is elaborated in the different traditions, concerns itself with this means of escape from necessity. In normal phenomenal existence there is little but misery and frustration. These are the results of basic causes, most especially desire, thirst and ignorance. To be saved is to leave the causal sequence, escape from the necessity of being born again, and enter into that state which is neither Being nor non-Being —Nirvana.

Although many branches of Buddhism, such as the Pure Land Sect, have a sensuous heaven in which glory is depicted in extremely human terms, the idea of a distinctionless Nirvana is never completely absent. Consequently, the various forms of the religion emphasize the unimportance of this world with

Scenes from a Chinese funeral, Peiping, 1936. The first picture shows the head of the procession with one of the pair of demonic guardians. The second is a paper house representing the abode of the dead in another world. The house will be burned in the court of the temple. The third picture is of the catafalque, fully decorated and awaiting the remains of the dead. It is covered with a scarlet and yellow cloth and many gilded ornaments. (*Courtesy Bush Collection of Religion and Culture.*)

Lao-tse riding the water buffalo which was supposed to have come to carry him away from earthly life. (*Art Museum, Worcester, Mass.*)

The shrine of Confucius is to be found in various places in China. The one which is shown here is that in Chinchow. This shrine is said to have been built about 800 years ago, and has undergone repairs several times since then.

In China, Confucius has been venerated as the god of learning, and the existence of the shrine has much encouraged the local people to study. As a matter of fact, Chinchow has produced many celebrated scholars in the past.

all its subject-object distinctions, and affirm the primary importance of that which is beyond all states of being. The pilgrimage of Buddhism travels a road of mystic contemplation through the different levels of earths and heavens until desire, thirst and being are as nothing. This mystical road may never be accurately described since all words presuppose distinctions among beings. Language and scientific knowledge are both dependent upon the conditioned existence which man now possesses; when the unconditioned is achieved, such tools of discourse and earthly learning must be abandoned.

In most of its phases, Buddhism is other-worldly and transtemporal. The gods, whatever they might be called, are not the ultimates of the universe. Rather, they are stages along the way. Sometimes they are helpful to man in his quest for Nirvana; other times man recognizes that "he is his own helper; there is no one else to help." The true ultimate in the universe is the "spiritual continuum" toward which man strives, but from which he receives no aid or guidance. No logic is applicable to a discussion of it, and no soul may enter it and return to tell of its wonders. The positive reality can only be described *via negative*.

Since such a conception of ultimate reality is bound to lead to an emphasis upon detachment from the world, Buddhism becomes the great religion of monks who spend their lives trying to negate self and achieve the timeless Nirvana. Metaphysical beliefs are subordinated to monastic discipline, and the practice of mystical contemplation is raised to the highest level of sanctity. Buddhism in its most distinguished aspects is therefore not a popular religion of the masses, but a way of liberation for those who have the time and spiritual courage to renounce the ordinary existence of man for the life of a monastery.

Popular Buddhism remains to this day a fantastic welter of uncodified belief in magic, superstition, theology and customary moral practices. Almost any kind of belief is tolerated on the popular level since true salvation is usually restricted to those who inhabit the monasteries. The spread between the monk and the layman is probably wider in Buddhism than in any of the other great traditions of the world.

The romance of Buddhism is the story of much of Asia. Within its history can be found a feeling of contempt for the world expressed by its low estimate of science and government, and that exaltation of mystic reverie which is so characteristic of Eastern art. Buddhism remains the most inclusive and structureless religion that has ever captured the imagination of millions of human beings. To the Western mind it will always be an enigma, known in part, but never thoroughly understood.

IV

THE HEBREW TRADITION

13

HEBREW ORIGINS

JUDAISM, Christianity and Islam, three of the great religious traditions, had their beginnings in a small but important section of the world known as the Middle East. The peoples from whom these traditions received their first impetus occupied the Arabian peninsula, Mesopotamia and much of the fertile land on the slopes of the Mediterranean. In general they formed the groups known to history as the Aramaeans, Assyrians, Babylonians, Phoenicians, Arabians and Hebrews.

When the Israelites (or Hebrews) came into being as a distinctive group, they did so in an area that was already well advanced in civilization. The earliest of our records indicate that Babylon was founded by Sargon sometime between 2650 and 2000 B.C. and that the Babylonian civilization was the center of a highly developed Western Asiatic culture. However, the records show that even before this date Egypt had a long-established tradition. Indeed, most investigators have concluded that Egypt and Babylonia are among the oldest centers of civilization on the globe. The Egyptian calendar is supposed to have begun in 4241 B.C. Whether or not these dates are accurate, the Middle East was nevertheless well on its civilized way by the time Moses entered the scene of history.[1]

[1] The historical problems concerning the tribes and peoples of the Middle East are so vast and complex that no accurate statements can be made in

The group later to become known as the Hebrews was originally a part of the Semitic tribes which wandered from Mesopotamia into the land of Canaan (roughly, what was later known as Palestine) sometime during the fifteenth century B.C. The Canaanites were a tough and sturdy people and easily repulsed the earliest of the Hebrew invasions. Since the Hebrews were unable to gain control of these fertile valleys and plains, they were forced to move up into the mountains. In the small settlements possible in the hills, the Hebrews were under constant attack from the better-established Canaanites. Undoubtedly many of the Hebrews were taken as slaves and became a part of the Canaanite population.

THE EARLY CANAANITES

THE PEOPLE of Canaan appear to have had a rather highly developed civilization built around commerce and craftsmanship in metals.[2] In addition to these urban pursuits, agriculture was well advanced. At this stage there appear to have been an ample water supply and a fecund earth. The arts of weaving and cloth dyeing were also well developed.

Much of the commerce between Babylonia and Egypt was required to pass through Canaan. Since these two great powers to the north and south controlled large armies, the rulers of Palestine were forced to guarantee the safe conduct of both commercial and military caravans. To aid them in the discharge of this duty, large fortifications and military bases were established. Such contacts with the two major seats of Middle Eastern culture were bound to leave their mark on

summary fashion. Middle Eastern scholarship has recently made momentous discoveries, but the evidence is yet to be sifted and assessed. Until such material is available we must be content with cautious and tentative generalizations.

[2] A great deal of the data regarding the Palestinian civilization is gained from archeological excavations and the lists made by Egyptian armies.

the total Canaanite civilization. In fact, Canaan at the time of the Israelite invasions was to such an extent a composite of Egyptian, Assyrian, Hittite and Babylonian influences that it is now impossible to reconstruct the "pure" Canaanite culture.

The city-states of Canaan were controlled by kings or a board of "elders" who were absolute despots. They were responsible for wars, religious exercises and the general economic production. For the most part the total country was without organization, each ruler making individual treaties with Egypt and Babylon. As one might expect, intercity wars were usual occurrences, and the forces of the two great powers were often used as allies. The only ruler common to all the Canaanites lived either in Egypt or Babylon, but it was Egypt which maintained the most constant supremacy. Thus from the beginning Palestine was, in a political sense, a center of strife and conflict.

The religion of the Canaanites was concerned with special divine places and objects of nature. As elsewhere, mountains, stones, trees and fire held central places in the nature worship. As might be expected, these desert, and at times nomadic, peoples raised water, and the springs from which it came, to a place of the highest importance. The most famous temple in the land was situated on the shores of the divine lake Aphaca. The Phoenicians, a group within the Canaanite complex, were the ones to lay the greatest stress upon water. It is interesting to note in this respect that most of the temples were placed either on high mountains or by a spring or lake.

The temples of the Canaanites were filled with carved statues supposed to represent the various deities. Many of these deities have been identified as members of the Egyptian and Babylonian pantheons. Osiris, Ptah, Nephrit and Thoth along with the goddess Astarte all find their home in Canaan. Among these idols of human figures, archeologists have uncovered representations of animals which were obviously used in worship. Serpents and in some cases dragons were apparently believed to be possessed of supernatural powers which could be used to aid man in his efforts. Often the goddess was represented by the serpent symbol, and in this guise pictured as a healer and a destroyer of disease.

Each village seems to have had a local deity who presided over the destinies of his people. In each case, however, he not only had this general function but was also responsible for certain specific events. Baal Zebub, for example, was the god of Eknon, but he also controlled the activities of flies and insects. In this instance insects were associated with disease, and thus Baal Zebub had the further function of building and maintaining health. Others of the local deities protected the food supply, saw to the necessary rain, guarded against invasion and guaranteed the fertility of man and nature. In the fertility aspects of Canaanite religion the representation was usually in the form of a cow (for the goddess) and a bull (for the god). In areas where fish were sacred the goddess was often represented with the head and bust of a woman and the tail of a fish. There were so many local and special deities that a complete catalogue would be cumbersome and serve no real purpose.

The close association of the divine with animals is often looked upon as a survival of primitive totemism. It is undoubtedly true that the Canaanites of this period considered certain animals to be endowed with supernatural potency. Whether it was assumed that these animals were originally ancestors, or whether they were thought to have a power in excess of the human, can only be a matter of conjecture. Some scholars have pointed to the identity of name between some of the tribes and certain animals. This has supplied evidence for the first alternative. Others have pointed to evidence which concludes that animals became divine because man longed for the power he thought they possessed. In any event, there seems to have been a kind of totemic atmosphere in the early Palestinian religion.

The area of the sacred also included the sun, moon and rain. These aspects of nature appeared against a cosmic backdrop and were either the result of the deities' action or were themselves gods. In the Babylonian pantheon Sin, the moon-god, was worshiped as the "Father of the Gods" and the character of life. Sin stood in the exalted position of being the creator and sustainer of life while the sun was looked upon as the destroyer. In the presence of the sun all stars disappeared and the green of the fields withered and died. The Babylonian astronomer also knew that the sun caused the moon to be reduced to a pale sliver each month. The Babylonian myth speaks as follows regarding the monthly "disappearance" of the moon:

His light was darkened, he [the moon] sat not upon his throne.
The evil gods, messengers of their king Anu, bringing to pass that
    evil enters into the head [of man] makes them tremble. . . .
They seek after evil,
They break forth from the heavens like wind over the land.
From heaven Bel saw the darkening of the hero Sin.[3]

Interestingly, the moon-god and sun-god relationship was reversed in Egypt. Here the moon-god was lord of the underworld and in charge of the evil spirits that prey upon man. The sun-god, on the other hand, was in charge of all things good and was recognized as the great helper of man. Both of these influences had a part in the pre-Israelite religion of Canaan, but the major borrowing was from the Babylonian conception. The Canaanite gods, Ba'al and Moloch, cor-

[3] Translated by Alfred Jeremias in *The Old Testament in the Light of the Ancient East* (New York: G. P. Putnam's Sons, 1911), Vol. I, p. 112. By permission.

respond most completely to astral gods of the Babylonians.

The religion of the settled Canaanites was polytheistic, but there appears to have been a strong tendency toward unity, or at least unification. The title Ba'al came to be applied to many local deities whose characteristics were fused into a "Lord of the heavens," or one supreme Ba'al, known as Ba'al Shamen. This development has led some commentators to suggest that monotheistic worship was a part of the Canaanite religion long before the Israelites achieved their famous escape from Egypt. However this might be, it is not as yet a settled question. It is most probable that the Canaanite pantheon, filled with local gods and goddesses, remained as polytheistic as those of Babylonia and Egypt. For it was from these two great powers that the pre-Israelite Palestinians received their inspiration and most of their religious teaching.

Although some of the Semitic tribes which moved from Mesopotamia to Canaan in the fifteenth century B.C. probably stayed within the nation, others continued their nomadic wanderings in the deserts of the South, not far from the border of Egypt. According to Israelite tradition some of the tribes, especially the clan under Jacob, went into Egypt in search of food. The Pharaoh, Rameses II (1301-1235 B.C.), later forced the descendants of this group into slave labor camps, and it was from this captivity that Moses is supposed to have delivered the Israelites.

MOSES AND THE ORIGIN OF A NATION

THE oppression of the Israelites afforded Moses his opportunity. The diverse tribes which settled in Egypt were in need of some strong leader who could bring together the exploited tribesmen and throw off the Egyptian yoke. According to tradition, as recorded in the Book of Exodus, Pharaoh commanded that every male child be destroyed at birth. Moses

escaped death by a ruse of his mother and was subsequently
adopted by the Pharaoh's daughter. After he grew to man-
hood he went back to his Israelite brethren and "looked on
their burdens." On one of his visits he saw an Egyptian overlord flogging a Hebrew and was prompted to kill the guard.
After a time his deed became known, and Moses was forced
to flee Egypt for a mountainous region called the "land of
Midian."

The Midianites were a relatively peaceful pastoral people
and offered sanctuary to Moses. Jethro, one of the Midianite
priests, took Moses into his family and allowed a marriage
with one of his seven daughters. In this fashion Moses became
a keeper of Jethro's flocks. But more importantly, he was
thrown into close contact with the Midianite religion and thus
came to know the god Yahweh who lived on the summit of
Mount Sinai or, as it is sometimes called, Mount Horeb.

Although it is common for scholars to assume that Moses
came to know Yahweh through Jethro, the Jewish scripture
speaks of a different introduction. One day, so the tradition
runs, Moses was out feeding his flocks near Mount Sinai.
While in the desert he noticed that a bush was burning but
that it was not being consumed. As he watched, a voice came
from the bush saying, "Moses, Moses, draw not nigh hither:
put off thy shoes from off thy feet, for the place whereon thou
standest is holy ground. . . . I am the God of thy fathers,
the God of Abraham, the God of Isaac, the God of Jacob."
Although Moses was awestruck, God went on to tell him that
He, Yahweh, had noticed the plight of the Hebrews in Egypt
and that it was his purpose to free them and give into their
possession a promised land "flowing with milk and honey."
It was, according to Yahweh, Moses' duty to return and lead
the Israelites out of Egypt. Although Moses was impressed by
Yahweh and his orders, he was unimpressed with his own abilities. But Yahweh answered these fears by promising to be

with the Israelites at all times. Moses was thereupon directed to go to Egypt and announce that "Yahweh, the God of your fathers, hath sent me."

Although the tradition is undoubtedly a romantic story, it is nevertheless with Moses that the Israelite nation and religion are born. Yahweh chose the Israelites, and the enslaved tribes in Egypt eventually, under the leadership of Moses, chose Yahweh. The job which Moses was called to do was predominantly a practical one. He had to create a nation around the center of a new national religion. According to Biblical tradition, Moses was greatly aided in his task by a series of miracles made possible by Yahweh's power. Whether or not this was actually the case, Moses succeeded in unifying the Israelites on the strength of their conviction that their God had great power and that he would save them from bondage. This overawing sense of Yahweh's power tended to distinguish the national God of the Israelites from other national gods of the time. There was certainly no monotheism in the belief: at most it was simply a belief in Yahweh as being more powerful than the other national gods.

As the Israelite tribes collected themselves for their flight from Egypt, Yahweh was constantly with them, giving advice and directing the preparations. It was thus unnecessary for Moses or his lieutenants to develop a code of ethics or a body of theology: Yahweh was always present to be consulted. The only thing required was the covenant between the people and Yahweh. In return for Yahweh's services the Israelites pledged themselves to him and agreed to make him the center of their national religion. This did not mean, however, that lesser deities could not be worshiped in the home.

If we accept the written record, Yahweh fulfilled his part of the bargain. After the Israelites left Egypt, Pharaoh sent troops with instructions to bring them back. When the two groups met at the Red Sea [4] the Israelites were sure they were lost and would be returned to bondage, but Yahwen commanded the waters to recede and allowed his people to escape by means of a dry path through the sea. As the Egyptian forces tried to follow, Yahweh released the waters and the Egyptians were drowned.

> Sing ye to Jehovah,[5] for he hath triumphed gloriously;
> The horse and his rider hath he thrown into the sea.
>
> (Exodus 15:21)

Though one might question its historicity, this is the great act of deliverance to which all subsequent Jewish religion pays homage. The original faith in Yahweh, preached by Moses, was vindicated and the Israelites were henceforth under strong obligation to the God who chose to save them.

After their rescue from the Egyptians, the tribes are supposed to have gone on to Mount Sinai where Yahweh renews his covenant and makes a further promise.

> Ye have seen what I did unto the Egyptians, and how I bare you on eagles' wings, and brought you unto myself. Now therefore, if ye will obey my voice indeed, and keep my covenant, then ye shall be mine own possession from among all peoples: for all the earth is mine: and ye shall be unto me a kingdom of priests, and a holy nation.
>
> (Exodus 19:4-6)

After this Yahweh issues the following commandments which bind the Israelites to specific rules and regulations:

---

[4] This is the translation from the Greek Septuagint. The Hebrew *Yam Sûph* is usually translated "Sea of Reeds." In any event the name does not refer to what we now call the Red Sea. It was probably the upper part of the Gulf of Suez.

[5] *Jehovah* and *Yahweh* are two different spellings and pronunciations of the same Hebrew name for the God of Israel. *Yahweh* is closer to the original pronunciation, but since the fourteenth century A.D. most Biblical translations have used *Jehovah*.

And God spake all these words, saying,

I am Jehovah thy God, who brought thee out of the land of Egypt, out of the house of bondage.

Thou shalt have no other gods before me.

Thou shalt not make unto thee a graven image, nor any likeness of any thing that is in heaven above, or that is in the earth beneath, or that is in the water under the earth: thou shalt not bow down thyself unto them, nor serve them; for I Jehovah thy God am a jealous God, visiting the iniquity of the fathers upon the children, upon the third and upon the fourth generation of them that hate me, and showing lovingkindness unto thousands of them that love me and keep my commandments.

Thou shalt not take the name of Jehovah thy God in vain; for Jehovah will not hold him guiltless that taketh his name in vain.

Remember the sabbath day, to keep it holy. Six days shalt thou labor, and do all thy work; but the seventh day is a sabbath unto Jehovah thy God: in it thou shalt not do any work, thou, nor thy son, nor thy daughter, thy man-servant, nor thy maid-servant, nor thy cattle, nor thy stranger that is within thy gates: for in six days Jehovah made heaven and earth, the sea, and all that in them is, and rested the seventh day: wherefore Jehovah blessed the sabbath day, and hallowed it.

Honor thy father and thy mother, that thy days may be long in the land which Jehovah thy God giveth thee.

Thou shalt not kill.

Thou shalt not commit adultery.

Thou shalt not steal.

Thou shalt not bear false witness against thy neighbor.

Thou shalt not covet thy neighbor's house, thou shalt not covet thy neighbor's wife, nor his man-servant, nor his maid-servant, nor his ox, nor his ass, nor anything that is thy neighbor's.

(Exodus 20: 1-17)

Thus under Moses was the nomadic band welded into a nation, which was essentially a religious community, with a definite code of ethics.

MOSAIC RELIGION

Iт is undoubtedly true that Yahweh was seen by the Israelites in the volcanic action of Mount Sinai. He was a God of wrath, and his noise could be heard for miles. When he manifested himself the earth would shake, fire would spout to the sky, and black smoke would cover the sun. The people were in constant fear of Yahweh's tremendous power. Indeed, this thunderous power was the prime characteristic of Mosaic religion. Further, Yahweh was not some far-off deity with abstract qualities, but rather a violent, jealous deity of volcanic proportions who had a definite place of residence on Mount Sinai.

Yahweh was not only a god of power: he also demanded ethical action and religious duties. In the Ten Commandments, eight of the propositions deal with ethics, while only two are devoted to the Israelites' ritualistic obligations. The religion which developed during these stormy nomadic days was primarily practical. What should be the course of action? Thou shalt not steal, commit adultery, or bear false witness. Here are found rules for social action, the very rules that are necessary for a society on even the most primitive level. Yahweh, as interpreted by Moses, appears to have wanted above all else a unified nation. Coupled with these proscriptions against human conflict, Yahweh makes it clear that he is to be worshiped as a mighty power, superior even to representation in images. There were to be no pictures or statues, but instead symbols, such as the ark and the metal serpent. Yahweh could dwell *within* the ark, and certainly the ancient Israelites believed that he did, but the *ark* was not *Yahweh*.

Although the Mosaic religion did little to define with any clarity the nature of Yahweh and his relations to other gods and to men, it pointed the direction in which later Hebrew

[2 2 1]

religion would go. The primary factor of Mosaic religion was its emphasis upon history. There was no heavenly salvation promised; rather, the saving work of Yahweh was to be wrought within the limits of historical time. These chosen people were to be watched over and guided by a god who was concerned with their day-to-day actions and their historical destinies. History has a purpose—Yahweh's purpose—and it moves according to Yahweh's plan. Yahweh's interest was not, at this stage, to keep the stars in their courses, or explain the origins of nature, or even to rule over a paradise achieved by death. On the contrary, he was a social god committed to building "a kingdom of priests, a holy nation." Yahweh was thus a god of historic action, not of metaphysical abstraction.

THE SETTLEMENT OF CANAAN

ACCORDING to Biblical tradition, Moses died before the Israelites invaded Canaan. Into the place of leadership came Joshua, one of the most trusted of Moses' lieutenants. It was his duty to lead the small nation of some 1200 to 1500 men with their women and children in an invasion of the established and fertile land of Canaan. The Canaanites were well armed, and their civilization, in both material production and the arts, was incomparably superior to that of the ragged, semi-nomadic Israelites.

The walled city of Jericho stood directly in the path of the invasion and offered the first real challenge to Joshua and his fighters. The later Hebrew historians who wrote of this situation remained true to the Mosaic pattern. Yahweh caused the walls to crumble and the city was taken. As was customary with jealous national deities, Yahweh required the death of all living persons within the city (Rahab was saved because she aided Joshua's spies) and the destruction of all of Jericho's valuable property. This destruction was considered to be

Yahweh's due for his goodness and a commemoration of his military help. It was further an expression of his utter disregard for the Canaanites and their gods. To his people the fall of Jericho was but another instance of Yahweh's might and favor.

After this initial success the Israelites moved forward and invaded other towns. Bethel and Ai were taken by military force, but again with the help of Yahweh as chief strategist. Fortunately for the Israelites, Canaan was not one cohesive nation under a single king and with a single military establishment. Had it been, none of the Israelites' conquests could have been made, and it is almost certain that they would have been pushed back over the desert borders. Instead, the various city-states of Canaan were in a constant state of war among themselves, and their mutual distrust enabled a comparatively small but well-organized group to overpower them in successive stages.

However, the march was neither continuous nor consistently successful. The Israelites moved slowly and often made treaties in preference to fighting. Extermination such as that practiced at Jericho was discontinued in their desire to establish peace and settle the land. As rapidly as this new policy could be put into effect, the Israelites adopted the agricultural and industrial methods of the Canaanites. With each generation intermarriage became more and more common until the two populations were completely fused with regard not only to blood but also to culture.

As was customary, the god of the conquering people became the god of the merged group. However, those of specific Canaanite heritage were as attached to their gods as the Israelites were to Yahweh. In addition to this, Yahweh was essentially a thundering war-god bound to the task of conquest and to the destiny of a given people. The Canaanite gods, on the other hand, were designed to deal with the problems of an agricultural community. They protected the crops, guaranteed abundant harvests and supplied the proper ratio of sun and rain. Yahweh had no experience with crops, and was consequently in danger of being superseded by the Canaanite baals.

In all probability the worship of the baals and Yahweh was carried on side by side without too much conflict. The Yahweh of Sinai could not be forgotten since he was the national deity who released the Israelites from captivity and made possible the conquest. It was perfectly possible for Yahweh to remain supreme in his area while the various local baals were accorded the worship necessary for prosperous agriculture. Since he claimed no competence in that area, Yahweh could hardly object. To meet the demands of their new mode of existence, the Israelites for the first time added the worship of a goddess, Astarte, to their religious expression. Here was a development which cut directly athwart the ancient patriarchal conceptions of the Mosaic period. Under the aegis of Moses it would hardly have occurred to the Israelites that a god could be female, but in an agricultural setting nothing seemed more natural than to symbolize fertility and regeneration by the female figure.

Although the common man of Palestine tended toward syncretism in his religion, the officials of the state and Yahweh's priests waged an unceasing battle for the exclusiveness of the Mosaic God. Over and over again they warned of the misfortune and disaster to befall were the covenant broken. The Israelites were still in conflict, especially with the Philistines, and the good grace of Yahweh was essential to their triumph. His wrath could mean nothing but national destruction. The Philistines, who had entered Canaan about the same time as the Israelites, presented a constant threat. Their military power was well known and properly feared. After Saul became the first king of Israel, the conflict between the two began in earnest and continued all during his reign. The very survival of the Israelites depended upon their unity and military prowess, and in these areas Yahweh was undoubtedly supreme.

This conflict with the Philistines together with the amazing personality of David, Saul's successor, produced a unified nation under Yahweh. David succeeded in establishing a real governmental organization and a centralized capital with an official court. The political aspirations of the people, all their hopes and dreams, were embodied in the capital at Jerusalem. It was the dwelling place of Yahweh and the primary center of his worship. David had the ark, supposed to be Yahweh's abode, moved to Jerusalem, and he also made plans for a sumptuous temple which, when actually built by his successor, Solomon, was of such magnificence that it outshone all other places of worship in the country. By these various processes David was able to establish his kingdom upon the ancient foundations laid by Moses. He felt he was completing the task begun by Yahweh's famous feat of rescue.

While Saul, David and Solomon were building the Hebrew Kingdom, Yahweh was appropriating to himself the attributes and functions of the Canaanite baals. He first took over their places of worship, then their titles, and finally their agricultural and pastoral functions. His priests made no move towards establishing an orthodoxy that would exclude him from any of these. David apparently introduced into the Hebrew worship music and psalms which made it possible for Yahweh worship to include virtually any kind of religious expression. The one absolute requirement was that Yahweh be recognized as the *only* god of Israel and the *only* power beyond man's own efforts. Any subsidiary functions or attributes desired for him by the people could be absorbed with ease.

14

THE PROPHETS

PRIOR to the middle of the eighth century B.C., the religious development of Israel is to be seen in the fragmentary remains of political and social history. The teachings of Moses formed the basis upon which Israel was to build, and the land of conquest, Canaan, set the conditions. The worship of Yahweh and the fate of Israel became inseparable. In the middle of the eighth century, however, there developed a new and very different phase in which the religious progress of Israel could be seen through the lives and teachings of a small number of great men. Such men as Amos, Hosea, Isaiah and Micah gave to Israelite religion the ethical character which has lasted to this day in both Judaism and Christianity.

The prophets were well within the Mosaic tradition. They should not be thought of as creating some new form of religion, for they all looked back to the great days of Yahweh's leadership and simply wished for a wholehearted return to former glories on the part of the Chosen People. These prophets were not tied to the temple or to the lesser places of worship; their only support came from the authority of their pronouncement that they came as Yahweh's messengers to warn against evil and provide for its correction. As they wandered from place to place, they found sympathetic audiences among the poor who were subject to exploitation and oppression by the rich. For this reason the major content of their message, always in the name of Yahweh, was directed against social evils.

In most of the other religious traditions of the world, major advances in both thought and practice come from within the priesthood. Hinduism, Buddhism and the non-Jewish religions of the Middle East all have this priestly influence. Israel, however, in its emphasis upon prophecy, represents a unique contribution to the world of religion. Although much of that prophecy has been lost or was never written down, some has been preserved and is to be found in both the Jewish and Christian Scriptures.

AMOS

THE Israel into which Amos came (c. 760 B.C.) was both wealthy and corrupt. The Northern Kingdom was the center of a thriving merchant trade, and the king's armies were more than successful in their raids against Syria. All this afforded opportunity for the development of a fairly large luxury class which could spend its time and money on fabulous houses and nonproductive, yet expensive, comfort. If we can trust the record left by Amos, the courts were rigged for the benefit of the rich while the taxes were paid and the work done by the poor. The old feeling of community solidarity was disappearing in an emergent class society in which the poor were becoming poorer and the rich richer.

In general, the religious life of the times was strong on sacrifice, and the various holy places were crowded with communicants. Feast days were set aside and observed both publicly and privately. Worship services became more elaborate by their use of music and solemn parades. Yet little of this increased religiosity was translated into ethical action. According to the conception then popular, it was possible to treat men like cattle while at the same time worshiping Yahweh as the one supreme God. Much of the earlier Israelite emphasis upon conduct and social justice had been lost, and the wealthy rulers of society forbade the new preachers to recall it.

Amos, a herdsman out of the hills of Tekoa, enters this scene with a warning that Yahweh's judgment on his people will be fearful and terrible if conditions are not ameliorated.

Hear this word, ye kine of Bashan, that are in the mountain of Samaria, that oppress the poor, that crush the needy, that say unto their lords, Bring, and let us drink. The Lord Jehovah hath sworn by his holiness, that, lo, the days shall come upon you, that they shall take you away with hooks, and your residue with fish-hooks. And ye shall go out at the breaches, every one straight before her; and ye shall cast yourselves into Harmon, saith Jehovah.

(Amos 4:1-3)

Judgment is seen in Assyria's might which would come as an instrument of Yahweh. It is obvious from the way Amos talks that he, at least, feels that Yahweh is the only God and that as such he will use the nations to suit his purposes. The whole of mankind is here considered to be under one great monotheistic deity who moves not only history but the natural process. Although a similar concept can be found in the earlier Elijah, Amos expands it into the first clear statement of Jewish monotheism. The other gods are relegated to the position of idols which blur the vision of the one true and all-powerful God.

You only have I known of all the families of the earth: therefore I will visit upon you all your iniquities.

(Amos 3:2)

Amos further attacks the pretentiousness of Israel's priests in claiming that Yahweh is interested only in those he brought out of Egypt. All peoples have been saved by the one God: the "Philistines from Caphtor and the Syrians from Kir." Whether Amos really meant all that these words imply is a disputed point. Nevertheless, they hold a unique position in Old Testament literature as the first real glimmerings of faith in a universal savior God.

Amos is not solely concerned, however, in proclaiming military catastrophe at the hands of the Assyrians. He wants to see the poor raised and the rich cut down, for to worship God and deal in corruption and fraud is to him the worst of all religious crimes. Such worship is false and a "stench in the nostrils of Yahweh." God requires justice rather than sacrifice, kindness rather than parades, righteousness rather than feasts. From Amos come some of the most stirring lines ever written in this tradition: "Away from me with the uproar of your hymns, and the music of your lyres let me not hear. But let justice flow like water, and righteousness as a mighty stream." God is to be seen, understood and approached through right-eousness and truth rather than through prayers and sacrifices.

Although Amos offers Israel a chance to redeem herself, he knows that she will not take it. He sees no hope for the future. Rich and poor alike are to be swept under by the Assyrian invaders, for the Jews gave up their chance for life when they decided to be their own saviors. The doom of Israel is irrevocable:

The Virgin of Israel is fallen; she shall never rise again; she lies prostrate upon her land, there is none to raise her up.

(Amos 5:2)

HOSEA

By the time of Hosea (c. 745 B.C.), the condition of Israel had not changed, except perhaps for the worse. The strong central government had collapsed after Jeroboam II closed his reign in 743 B.C. In quick succession a number of kings held the throne, many of whom were murdered or fled, and the condition has often been described as close to anarchy.

The religious message which Hosea brought was similar to that of Amos, but if anything, more dramatic. Yahweh required Hosea to marry a prostitute and have children by her. "Go [says Yahweh], take thee a wife who is a prostitute and have children by a prostitute; for an utter prostitute is the land, departing from Yahweh."

Hosea was pointing to the fact that Israel and Yahweh were partners in a marriage relationship. Each had freely selected the other, and now Israel was playing the harlot by following other gods and her own selfish desires. Yahweh was not being truly loved; he was asked to be content with sacrifices and burnt offerings. Against his express commandments, idols were being made and worshiped, adultery had become common, fraud was practiced in high places, and stealing was an ordinary and accepted practice. All such evils Hosea conceived to be the fruits of ignorance of Yahweh. Earthly fame, kingly fortune and social status were worshiped to the exclusion of the great Yahweh, who had saved his people from bondage and given them the wealth and glory of Canaan. For such disloyalty Israel could expect nothing but destruction.

Whereas Amos could see *only* destruction, Hosea saw an ultimate reconciliation between Yahweh and Israel. Yahweh would be just and punish the infidelity of his chosen wife, but after the punishment a "remnant" would be saved and the Jews would finally be restored to their high and holy place.

And Jehovah said unto me, Go again, love a woman beloved of her friend, and an adulteress, even as Jehovah loveth the children of Israel, though they turn unto other gods, and love cakes of raisins. So I bought her to me for fifteen pieces of silver, and a homer of barley, and a half-homer of barley; and I said unto her, Thou shalt abide for me many days; thou shalt not play the harlot, and thou shalt not be any man's wife: so will I also be toward thee. For the children of Israel shall abide many days without king, and without prince, and without sacrifice, and without pillar, and without ephod or teraphim . . .

(Hosea 3:1-4)

The restoration of Israel to Yahweh gives Hosea a chance to speak of the power of God's love—a power which transcends the righteous indignation of a husband for a harlot bride. Beyond all the mistakes and blunders of Israel stands the infinite capacity of divine love. Yahweh is not simply engaged in a contract; the relationship is that of a love-union. In such a case rigorous righteousness is tempered by compassionate mercy. Here Hosea has gone far beyond the justifiable doom predicted by Amos. In fact, he attributes to Yahweh a characteristic he has never lost—forgiving love.

ISAIAH

AMOS and Hosea prophesied in the Northern Kingdom of Israel, while Isaiah (c. 740-700 B.C.) was giving the same message with variations to the Southern Kingdom of Judah. Both the earlier prophets were concerned with the welfare of society and the implementation of Yahweh's righteous will in international, national and personal affairs. Isaiah was interested in righteousness and love, but went further to point out the essential holiness of Yahweh. The true worship of Yahweh demands absolute trust and obedience, it demands love and righteousness; but it also prescribes a recognition of Yahweh's complete transcendence and his nonworldly moral purity. Man must never confuse himself with God, for all his puny strivings and little efforts are "as nothing in God's eyes."

Such ideas give Isaiah a basis for attacking all foreign alliances and the prevalent faith in the ability of an army to save those whom Yahweh had chosen. The conception of a "remnant," which is dimly seen in Hosea, becomes a specific doctrine in Isaiah's thought. Foreign nations, especially Assyria, are destined to overrun both Israel and Judah, and the "daughter of Zion . . . [will be] as a besieged city." Yet a few will return to build on the ruins and give honor and service to Yahweh. From this group the holy city of the future will be peopled, and through it Yahweh will be truly known.

This redeemed and purified remnant will have an ideal king, usually translated as the Messiah, upon whose shoulders will rest the government and upon whose wisdom will depend the glorious future.

> For unto us a child is born, unto us a son is given; and the government shall be upon his shoulder: and his name shall be called Wonderful, Counsellor, Mighty God, Everlasting Father, Prince of Peace. Of the increase of his government and of peace there shall be no end, upon the throne of David, and upon his kingdom, to establish it, and to uphold it with justice and with righteousness from henceforth even forever. The zeal of Jehovah of hosts will perform this.
>
> (Isaiah 9:6-7)

This concept of a golden age to be ushered in by the Messiah forms the cornerstone of much of the later prophecy. In each age the various prophets who speak in Messianic terms picture the Messiah and his kingdom according to their own training and social backgrounds, but the hope that Yahweh will send a "redeemer" or "an anointed Lord" never leaves the Hebrew consciousness. Although it is certainly true that Isaiah did not originate Messianism, he gave it its most brilliant early expression.

THE FALL OF PALESTINE

DURING this period of prophecy, both the past and the future were idealized. The period of Moses was looked back upon as perfection in religion and as somehow free of the vexing problems the Hebrews now faced. The future was idealized in the Messianic conceptions. This left the contemporary world of the prophets as a valley of shadow and death between the two golden ages. However, the present was transient. History was moving in an inexorable fashion toward final and complete fulfillment. No matter how terrible the injustices, the fraud, the deception and the slavery, the eternal pattern of the holy, righteous and loving Yahweh was ultimately to be completed. History was the theater within which Yahweh was acting out his portentous drama, and in the events of history could be seen the signs of the future, both for good and ill.

The dire predictions regarding Israel's fall were justified shortly after the death of Jeroboam II. In 738 B.C. the reigning king of Northern Israel, Menahem, sought to bolster his tottering regime by ceasing any resistance to Assyrian pressure. Four years later Tiglath-Pileser, the Assyrian king, led his armies in a final conquest of Galilee and Gilead and made these areas a part of the new provincial government he had established in Damascus. During Tiglath-Pileser's lifetime the whole of Palestine fell under Assyrian control and quickly became a troublesome but relatively unimportant province of the great Empire. A rebellion in 724 B.C. brought the Assyrian armies into Palestine again with the result that Sargon, who had succeeded to the throne, captured Samaria, capital of Israel, and forced the country into complete submission. For a while at least, the Jews lived in relative peace under their ruler, Hezekiah.

Although the Assyrian Empire was backed by a trained and experienced army, its unity depended largely upon the personality of the king. Sargon was strong, and while he lived the Empire was without peer. At his death in 705, however, the various subject provinces started to revolt. Sennacherib, his successor, was forced to battle for each one. Although he was at least partially successful, the period represents the first real crack in Assyrian hegemony in the Middle East. As a part of this general upheaval, Hezekiah began an intensive religious reform. His major task seems to have been to drive out the foreign cults and reassert the exclusive worship of Yahweh. In retaliation, and for reasons connected with Sennacherib's operations against the Egyptians, the whole of Judah, in southern Palestine, was laid waste and Hezekiah was subjected to terrific penalties.

After Hezekiah's death, Manasseh, his successor, attempted a reconciliation with the Assyrians. Manasseh reintroduced foreign rites, and in general appears to have tolerated the growth of cults dedicated to the gods of the Phoenicians and Assyrians. It is usually considered that Manasseh initiated the practice of sacrificing the firstborn of every family. Although he clothed the ritual in the language of the earlier prophets, the ideological basis for such sacrifice certainly came from outside. The religious situation became more and more chaotic and the older worship, advocated by the prophets, descended to a relatively unimportant position.

During the reign of Josiah, who followed Amon, the son of Manasseh, the final destruction of the Assyrian Empire was begun by the Scythians, who came out of the north on wild attacks and ravaged the fertile crescent. How much damage they did to Josiah's kingdom is unknown, but certainly their disorganized marauding invasions contributed to the collapse of Assyrian power.

THE DEUTERONOMIC CODE

DURING the decline of Assyria, Josiah set to work in an effort to reorganize Jewish religion and politics. The Temple at Jerusalem had fallen into disuse, and the number of foreign gods and strange cults had increased. According to Biblical tradition the reforms of Josiah were guided by the Book of Deuteronomy, which was supposed to have been discovered by a priest, Hilkiah, as he was making repairs in the Temple. This new law book was considered to be an ancient revelation from Yahweh which had been forgotten, or perhaps never completely known.

With the Deuteronomic code as his guide, Josiah demanded that all foreign gods and alien ornamentation be stripped from the Temple. There was to be no more human sacrifice, and certainly no toleration of other deities. Yahweh was reaffirmed as the only God, all others being snares and delusions. Yahweh was strong. Yahweh was a savior. Moreover, he was so holy as to transcend physical shape, thus precluding the use of any idols or representative statuary in the place of worship. Indeed, Yahweh was so great and so complete a unity that there could be but one place of worship, and that the appointed temple at Jerusalem. The sacrifices and the feast days could be efficacious only if they were properly performed in Jerusalem, the city of Yahweh. This new exclusiveness resulted in the smaller shrines and altars about the countryside being torn down and their priests taken to Jerusalem. Now, for the first time in Hebrew history, Jerusalem became the spiritual as well as the political capital of Yahweh's people. By centralizing political and religious functions in the capital city, Josiah helped to root out some of the last vestiges of the earlier Canaanite worship while at the same time dramatizing the essential unity of the Hebrew people. One God, one nation, one altar; and within this unity there was strength to meet attacks from the outside world.

The ethical aspects of Deuteronomy were further designed to give social health and internal strength to this unity. Righteousness, devotion, social justice and charitable dealings were required of all men. Yahweh's laws even went so far as to prescribe the cancellation of all debts every seven years. Indeed, much of the book is given over to a detailed treatment of all manner of laws that would direct the total society into paths of benevolence and compassionate generosity.

As might be expected, the reforms of Josiah incorporated little of the universalism seen in the earlier prophecies of Amos, Hosea and Isaiah. Yahweh was now interested only in the resurrection of those he had chosen so many years ago. The benevolence, justice and humility urged upon the Jews were not required of others. As in his earliest days, Yahweh was in conflict with all who would not call upon his name or worship him exclusively. He was still jealous of his people—so jealous that the Deuteronomic writers pay special attention to prohibitions against mixed marriages and other forms of foreign alliance. Whatever else this reform movement was, it was nationalistic and devoted almost entirely to building a strong and pure state that could resist both military and religious attack.

THE BABYLONIAN EXILE

THE period of reform, however, was brief. Babylonia was rising to take the place of Assyria, and she had already begun her assault by making a fortunate alliance with the Scythians and the Medes. As usual, Palestine found itself caught between two aggressive powers: Babylonia out for the Assyrian possessions, and Egypt fearful of her position if Babylonia were able to take the whole of the North. Necho, the Egyptian king, decided that Judah was hostile, and he defeated and killed Josiah at the battle of Megiddo. With this event Judah was thrown into a panic, and finally Jerusalem was sacked and the whole movement toward religious and political centralization ended for the time being. Again the followers of Yahweh brought in foreign deities and established the outrageous idolatries that Josiah had abolished. Necho was defeated by the Babylonian Nebuchadnezzar at the famous battle of Carchemish in 605 and all the Middle East fell under his sway. This was the last Egyptian bid for world power.

In 597 Nebuchadnezzar first conquered Jerusalem and took into captivity the major portion of the upper ruling classes. Later, after an attempted revolt, he returned to Jerusalem, burned the city, razed the Temple and destroyed the fortifications. This time he deported the skilled workmen and left only the peasants to work the land. The Promised Land was now in ruins, and those who were not forced into slavery fled to Egypt or other places of refuge. Under Gedaliah an attempt was made to revive the Hebrew state, but it proved futile and the last vestiges of independence were destroyed.

With their country gone and their Temple in ruins, the people of Yahweh were confronted with a fateful challenge. If the customary procedure were followed, the conquerors would impose their gods upon the conquered, and by slow assimilation Yahweh would die as a functioning God. He was, after all, a national God; he began his career with the Hebrews when they were first organized into a nation by his prophet Moses. Now these same people were dispersed throughout the vast Babylonian Empire. They had no nation, and certainly no national dignity. Even their numbers were not large. How were they to maintain their distinctive religious culture while they lived as slaves of a seemingly permanent conqueror?

The challenge was met by a great number of Jews by simply giving in to the situation and becoming Babylonians, religiously as well as politically. This was probably the easiest form of reconciliation. On the other hand, there was a large group who reconciled themselves by recalling the faith and predictions of the prophets. This exile was punishment inflicted by Yahweh because of the apostasy of his people. His prophets had issued their warnings, and the actuality could hardly be more difficult than Amos or Isaiah had promised. In this fashion the captive Jews looked upon the whole series of events leading to their exile as acts of *their* God and not as a victory for some foreign deity. The nations had been moved: Assyria had been raised and crushed, Egypt had been defeated, and Babylonia had been given victory, all because of the infidelity of Yahweh's Chosen People.

The duty of the exiled Jew was clear and obvious. He should maintain his religion in its purest possible state. Intercourse with his captors should be superficial, and he should never allow himself to fall into their ways or their beliefs. Thus at least a portion of the dispersed Jews formed themselves into separate communities. Here they worshiped with devotion and prayed for the day when the Messiah would arrive to usher in the Golden Age of Yahweh. Their sins had caused the Temple at Jerusalem to be destroyed, but they had an abiding faith that it would some day be rebuilt with an even deeper meaning. The record of the past was studied, and the pious found within it conclusive proof that Yahweh was still the one God and that he was peculiarly interested in the Hebrews. Out of these communities of dispersed but loyal Jews came the institution of the synagogue which at a later time became so central to Hebrew religion.

JEREMIAH

Even during the exile the Hebrews were not without the aid of prophecy. Just prior to Nebuchadnezzar's conquest, Jeremiah (c. 626-585 B.C.) began his forecasting of doom and destruction. He lived long enough not only to see his prophecies fulfilled but also to preach courage and perseverance to his exiled countrymen. Jeremiah wrote that it was possible for the followers of Yahweh to be just as loyal in Babylonia as in Jerusalem. He castigated those priests who had been left behind because they denounced the exiles as being out of favor with Yahweh. For Jeremiah religion was spiritual, not national; and there was thus little necessity for temples and organized priesthoods with special privileges and functions. True religion could be practiced by any man who worshiped with devotion and scored his ethical life against rigid divine standards. Here was an individualism quite unlike the previous tradition. Now man was responsible, in an individual sense, to his God. This responsibility could not be discharged by being a member of a specific nation or by worshiping with a temple cult. It could only find fulfillment in the inward change of heart brought about by right relations with Yahweh. All else was not only incidental but, more often than not, positively harmful to the religious life. Jeremiah must indeed have been a comfort to those faithful Jews who, having lost their Temple, searched for a religious meaning beyond time and place.

> Behold, the days come, saith Jehovah, that I will make a new covenant with the house of Israel, and with the house of Judah: not according to the covenant that I made with their fathers in the day that I took them by the hand to bring them out of the land of Egypt; which my covenant they brake, although I was a husband unto them, saith Jehovah.
>
> (Jeremiah 31:31-32)

EZEKIEL

WHILE Jeremiah was writing such sentiments to the exiles, Ezekiel was actually in Babylonia combating the common conviction that a God who allowed his people to be destroyed thereby proved his impotence. Like Jeremiah, Ezekiel preached individualism and roundly condemned those who believed that Yahweh's purposes had been thwarted simply because the outward forms of the Jewish nation had been destroyed. Yahweh knew what he was doing, Ezekiel maintained. The fault lay with the Chosen People because they had denied Yahweh's holiness. They had thought that their national unit was more important than Yahweh's holy name, and finally, they had allowed their worship to become corrupted beyond recognition.

Above all, Ezekiel taught the close connection between purity of heart and ritualistic observance. He was not concerned with the anti-institutional arguments of Jeremiah. According to Ezekiel, God makes his will known in laws and gives equal weight to ritual and ethics. Man cannot depend simply upon a pure heart without recognizing that this very purity is further dependent upon the purity of his worship practices. But this ritualistic emphasis was not nationalistic; rather, it stands at the point of transition between the Hebrew state and the Jewish church. Here Ezekiel appears to be discarding the more ancient theocratic conception of a unity of religion and politics. When the two are separate, true religion with all its ritual and institutional structure can operate under any conqueror and in any geographic area. Yahweh is thus absolved from the necessity of preserving a nation as a physical unit. For these reasons Ezekiel is often referred to as the father of Judaism.

15

POST-EXILIC TIMES

WHILE the religion of the Jews was being spiritualized and legalized by the Exilic writers, the political complexion of the Middle East was undergoing a further change. The new Empire of Babylon was overcome by the gigantic Persian military power under the direction of Cyrus. Cyrus followed a rather unusual policy with conquered peoples. Whereas Nebuchadnezzar and his successors had pursued a course of deportation and enslavement, Cyrus respected national differences, especially in the area of religion. Early in Cyrus's reign the Jews were permitted to return to Palestine, and a small group under the leadership of Sheshbazzar left Babylonia in 538 B.C. The prophets of Yahweh had foretold such a day, and Cyrus was therefore looked upon by the Jews as fulfilling a divinely appointed mission.

Although the captives probably looked to Palestine as a panacea, actual conditions there were quite difficult. The land they had left some sixty years before was now inhabited by other tribes who had migrated from both East and West. The only remaining areas feasible for the Jews to inhabit were the ruins of Jerusalem and a small section around the city. The farm lands that were not held by the other groups had gone to weeds and the houses were quite dilapidated. Thus the once luxurious and proud nation of Judah, in addition to being ruled by a Persian puppet, was to suffer dire economic poverty, having nothing but the crumbs left by others.

Uppermost in the minds of those who returned to Palestine was the rebuilding of the Temple. All during the Exile the emphasis had been shifting from sacrificial performances at the Temple to the reading and veneration of Yahweh's law, yet this love of Torah and its consequent non-Temple worship had always been considered a substitute. The Jews felt that in his own good time Yahweh would restore the worship to its rightful center in the Jerusalem Temple. Soon after they arrived, the work of rebuilding was begun, but life was so hard that first attention had to be given to the dwellings and the fields. Consequently, for fifteen years little progress was made. Added to the problems of physical reconstruction was a severe depression, caused by a number of droughts and crop disasters. It appeared that both men and nature were conspiring to keep the Jews from economic and religious security.

The records indicate little with regard to their progress during the next two centuries. There was, however, a continuation of the religious movement begun in Exile. It was all too obvious both during and after the Exile that the Jewish religion was to become more churchly and less national; the ecclesiastical institutions had to be rebuilt out of past history and shown to be independent of the vague fortunes of the nation. The writings which embody the fruits of this movement are commonly called Priestly and are to be found in the early books of the Jewish Scriptures.

THE PRIESTLY WRITERS

THE Priestly writers took what sources they had in both oral and written tradition and composed stories about the beginnings of man, rituals and the law. Although they were primarily concerned with the origin of sacred institutions, they wove this study into the general history of the Jewish people. Such a combination of sacred and profane history resulted in the books of the Pentateuch,[1] whose authors, it must be remembered, were not trying to establish something new, but rather were showing that the tradition was of such a nature as to indicate the God-given character of the ritual they hoped to promote.

In terms of later developments, the stories of creation told in the first chapters of Genesis are perhaps the most important parts of these writings. They indicate a strict monotheism, with Yahweh as the creator and sovereign of nature and all mankind.[2] The Priestly influence can be seen in the emphasis upon the holiness of the Sabbath day, even to the extent of having God use it as a day of rest. From the oral mythology then current throughout the Middle East, these writers took the nostalgic account of a lost paradise, the reasons for woman's suffering in childbirth and man's work in gaining the fruits of the earth, and the story of the flood. The tale of God's saving Noah allowed the Priestly writers to establish the Jewish custom of eating bloodless (Kosher) meats, since it tells how Yahweh permitted Noah and his family to eat animals only after their blood had been drained. The ritualistic practice of circumcision was given foundation by the story of Abraham's covenant with God. All of Abraham's descendants, who were to be the residents of the Promised Land, Canaan, had to be circumcised as a symbol of their relationship to Abraham and their fidelity to his covenant.

[1] Genesis, Exodus, Leviticus, Deuteronomy, and Numbers in the Jewish-Christian Scriptures.

[2] During the whole of pre-Mosaic history, according to the Priestly writers, the one great God was known as "Elohim" and "El Shaddai" rather than as Yahweh. After the escape from Egypt, which established the various feasts of unleavened bread and the Passover, God was revealed to his Chosen People as Yahweh. During this period he made his covenant with Moses and required the use of the Ark and the construction of a tabernacle.

It is obvious from what we know of the actual history of the Jews and their religion that most of these stories and statements of origin are without foundation in fact. The Priestly writers were seeking support for the existing sacred institutions rather than engaging in historical research. Many of the stories, particularly those regarding the flood, were taken over from Babylonian mythology with the changes necessary to make them fit the pattern of Israel's thought. In the main these writings can be considered as a level of interpretation woven around a core of legend remembered in the folklore of the Hebrews. The interpreters were concerned to place the events of history within a total cosmic process initiated and guided by the one true God. By so doing they were able to establish the sacramental importance of thousands of rules regarding disease, eating, childbirth, public sacrifice, death, and so on *ad infinitum.*

The vast body of law codified by these writers dealt principally with the problem of purification. Physical purity was as important as the more spiritual kind recommended by the prophets. Indeed, there was no clear distinction made between the two. All impurities were rooted ultimately in "sin," which was largely a ritualistic term. To violate ceremonial prohibitions was considered just as much a sin as to violate a moral commandment. A great deal of the moral fervor of the prophets who spoke of the spiritual concerns of Yahweh and his consequent disregard for outward form was lost to the Priestly writers. For them Yahweh was much more interested in the affairs of the church than in those of the heart.

As one would expect, the office and person of the priest attained an extraordinarily high degree of importance. As the chief representative of God it was his duty to act as intermediary and see to it that the proper ritual was conducted. On one of the great annual purification festivals, the Day of Atonement, the High Priest was first required to purify himself by "sin offerings" and then to place the sins of the community on the back of a goat. The goat was sent from the city carrying all the sins and was finally pushed over a cliff to ensure its not returning. Throughout this elaborate ceremony the priest was entirely responsible, the people being merely passive recipients of his ministrations. In addition to officiating at sacrifices, he became the chief expositor of the law and the chief judge of what was and what was not a sin. By one means and another, principally through the assumption of such tremendous powers, the priestly caste came to be the dominant and controlling group in Jewish society.

In spite of the legalistic and priestly emphasis of this period, the conception of a moral God with a loving nature did not die. The Priestly writers were, in a sense, building upon the firm foundation of prophecy laid in pre-Exilic days. The following centuries produced such writings as Psalms, Proverbs, Job, Ecclesiastes and the Wisdom of Solomon. In all these the inscrutable majesty, the holiness and the moral purpose of God are constantly affirmed. But there is a new spirit. The spontaneity of the earlier prophets gives way to tender piety and open skepticism. Their fire and passion is replaced in these subsequent religious utterances by a kindly and often friendly tolerance. The Book of Proverbs is an excellent example of this later ethical writing.

THE BOOK OF JOB

THE Book of Job is a classic treatment of the problem of evil from a nonprophetic point of view. The author of this book examines the question of why men suffer and considers at least five answers: first, and least important, Satan has goaded God into testing Job to see whether or not he is really as good as God thinks he is; second, suffering is punishment for evil; third, God is by his very nature unjust; fourth, evil is a device for training and educating man; and finally, Yahweh uses apparently unearned suffering to show man his own ignorance. All these are discussed and analyzed by the author, and he arrives at the conclusion that man is incapable of learning the inscrutable ways of God. Instead of following the prophets' procedure of making an absolute declaration of God's justice, Job is forced to rest in blind faith. The older belief that God deals with men according to their actions, that the pious are rewarded and the evil punished, is questioned by this book in a way quite foreign to the earlier tradition.

PROVERBS

HOWEVER, the writer's criticism did not change the prevailing conception with regard to the idea of retribution. That is, it assumed that evil is punished and good rewarded. The Book of Proverbs, written by men of the orthodox tradition, was much more widely influential, and in general represents a more accurate picture of the thought of this period.

In Proverbs the wise man is idealized. And to be wise is to be happy, contented, reasonably prosperous, and enlightened in self-interest. The contrast between the counsel of the wise and that of the passionate prophet is illustrated by such words as these:

> Rejoice not when thine enemy falleth,
> And let not thy heart be glad when he is overthrown;
> Lest Jehovah see it, and it displease him,
> And he turn away his wrath from him.
>
> (Proverbs 24:17-18)

> If thine enemy be hungry, give him bread to eat;
> And if he be thirsty, give him water to drink:
> For thou wilt heap coals of fire upon his head,
> And Jehovah will reward thee.
>
> (Proverbs 25:21-22)

ECCLESIASTES

WHEREAS Job finds no rationale for evil and suffering and the wisdom writers find a doctrine of retribution as an explanation for evil, Koheleth, the writer of Ecclesiastes, sees the world of experience as "Vanity of vanities, all is vanity." Here there is no room for the blind faith finally arrived at by Job. Happiness, pain, misery and joy are all ultimately meaningless and give no indication of the character of God. Morality is not to be considered part of the motive power of the universe. Just a look at the simple facts of existence gives ample proof that righteousness does not ensure happiness, nor each action a suitable reward or punishment.

The wise man's eyes are in his head, and the fool walketh in darkness: and yet I perceived that one event happeneth to them all.
Then said I in my heart, As it happeneth to the fool, so will it happen even to me; and why was I then more wise: Then said I in my heart, that this also is vanity.

(Ecclesiastes 2:14-15)

I returned, and saw under the sun, that the race is not to the swift, nor the battle to the strong, neither yet bread to the wise, nor yet riches to men of understanding, nor yet favor to men of skill; but time and chance happeneth to them all.

(Ecclesiastes 9:11)

HELLENISM

WHILE these changes were evolving in the religious thought and practice of the Jews, great events were taking place in the Middle Eastern political arena. Out of the small and comparatively rude country of Macedonia, a father and son made conquest of the entire world as it was then known. Philip, father of Alexander the Great, conquered Greece in 338 B.C.

and started a series of events more momentous for the ancient world, and in many respects for the modern world, than any which had occurred in the history of man. Alexander, who came to the throne after the murder of his father, was trained in Athens, the seat of Hellenic learning, by Aristotle, one of the world's greatest philosophic minds. With a conviction that Hellenism was the most desirable way of life, Alexander set out to convert the world, albeit more by the sword than by persuasion.

The Hellenic culture to which Alexander was dedicated based its faith in man and his rational powers rather than in the revelation of a supernatural deity. It is usually held that scientific thought began in the Mediterranean world with Thales of Miletus, who flourished around 600 B.C. Whether we wish to establish this particular date or not, Thales nevertheless posed the question which occupied the thoughts of early Greek philosophers: "What is the origin of the things of the universe?" This same question had been asked by the Hebrews, and, as we have seen, was given a mythological answer by the Priestly writers. The Greeks, however, were searching for an answer that would validate itself to their senses and to their reasons. In other words, Thales asked the question in such a way as to elicit a scientific rather than a religious answer.

Thales was quickly followed by other thinkers, notably the Pythagoreans and Eleatics, who further developed conceptions of nature and offered different solutions. Underlying all of their speculation was a rational and in some ways a scientific search for the secret of physical existence. Plato and Aristotle, the two great founders of Western philosophy, tackled the problems and produced the first real systematic philosophizing.

With poetry and philosophy, Hellenism developed a man-centered skepticism regarding traditional religion and its gods.

Euripides and the Sophists not only subjected theological conceptions to critical analysis, but they went further and discussed conventional morality. In the hands of the Sophists the established bases of morality were turned into matters for argument rather than propositions of conviction. The Sophists, some poets and the physical philosophers joined in emphasizing the primary role of human reason and the necessity for a man-centered rather than a god-centered universe. Protagoras, one of the most famous Sophists, is credited with a succinct expression of the essence of the Hellenistic spirit: "Man, the measure of all things."

CONFLICT WITH HELLENISM

Such intense appreciation of man's capacities together with the inevitable recognition of the intrinsic value of each individual was a direct threat to the life of Hebrew religion and its distinctive culture. Cultivated Jews felt an almost immediate pull toward the expansive self-confidence of the Hellenizers. The upper reaches of Hebrew society were rich; they had personal power and certainly a developing sense of their own importance. What surprise, then, that the older Mosaic ideas of human sinfulness and unimportance in the sight of Yahweh should seem both unnecessary and repulsive? Life could be richer and more enjoyable, they thought, if the strict legal prescriptions of the established religion were modified or even discarded. Included in the Hellenistic view of life was not only freedom, but also an awareness of the possible esthetic dimensions of human existence. While the Hebrews had been shying away from artistic expression, the Greeks had raised it to the highest possible level. And now beauty, goodness and truth were more appealing to these Hebrews than sin, humility and faith.

However, not all Jews viewed Hellenism with a clear eye

of approval. To the freedom and so-called democracy of the Greek humanist, there was a large admixture of human slavery and—at least so it seemed to the Jew—moral corruption. No matter how enlightened the human mind, it was still possible for injustice to be condoned and human pride to ride rough-shod over the rights of a communal society. For many Jews the very fact of self-confidence and the consequent lack of humility indicated the ultimate falsity of the Greek spirit. Add to this religious distrust the intense desire of the Jews for cultural independence, and it is not difficult to understand their violent opposition. It should be emphasized, however, that there were two distinct groups: one embracing Hellenism and the other fighting it, both with equal zeal.

The conflict between these two views of life was carried into the priesthood and ultimately led to the civil wars known as the Maccabaean Revolts. In 175 B.C. Antiochus IV, Epiphanes, an ardent Hellenizer, became king of Syria, which controlled Palestine, and appointed another Hellenizer, Jason, as High Priest. Immediately the two set about trying to establish Greek customs and even Greek religious notions. A Greek gymnasium was built in Jerusalem and a youth-training program was begun. Instruction in the Laws of Yahweh was suspended by many priests in favor of a physical education patterned after the great games of Greece. Jason, who had attained position by bribing Antiochus, pushed his Hellenization scheme so fast that he was ultimately forced out when Melenaus, another but perhaps more moderate Hellenizer, offered a larger bribe. This appointment was a supreme affront to the traditional Jews. Not only did Melenaus buy the office, but he was not even a member of the priestly families.

As the revolts flared up against Melenaus, Antiochus, who was then engaged in a war with Egypt, decided to visit Jerusalem and put an end to this Jewish flouting of royal authority. Much blood was spilled and many of the Jewish temples and holy places were razed. Celebration of the Sabbath was forbidden, sacred books were burned, circumcision was outlawed, and an altar of Zeus was placed upon the sacred altar of burnt-offering in the Temple. Such indignities were not confined to Jerusalem. Throughout the country altars were raised to Greek gods, pigs were offered up in sacrifice, pork became required food. And all these new rules and prohibitions were rigorously enforced by Syrian troops.

This sort of treatment resulted in increased unrest among the persecuted Jews and inspired in them a violent hatred. Throughout their long history the Jews had never been faced with such an alternative: either to give up their religion or to suffer physical torture, possibly death. For those already Hellenized the problem was not grave, but for the more traditional it was a case of either fleeing the land or organizing an armed revolt. The immediate cause of the series of revolts came when one of the Syrian king's agents was killed in the small country town of Modin. An elder of the community, Mattathias, took his five sons and some of the other loyalists to the hills and there organized a revolutionary army under the leadership of Judas Maccabaeus, one of the sons.

For some time the small band waged guerrilla warfare against the Syrian troops which were sent against them. The Maccabees, as the guerrillas were called, gathered larger and larger numbers to their arms and finally, in 165 B.C., they were able to capture that portion of the Holy City which held the Temple. The Temple was purified, the Zeus altar removed, and the traditional worship of Yahweh once more established. Syria was in so many difficulties that she could not remove the revolutionaries. Normal worship was carried on in the Temple until its final destruction in 70 A.D.

APOCALYPTIC WRITINGS

THE Book of Daniel was written in the midst of this crisis caused by the Maccabees. It was written to encourage the revolutionaries and at the same time to reassert the ancient faith of Israel against the foreign influence of Hellenism. The promise of salvation, of a glorious future in which Yahweh would rule his children in peace and righteousness, was added to an exaggerated account of the ways in which Hebrew believers of the past had successfully overcome the tempting and corrupting powers of the world. One of the most typical is the story of Shadrach, Meshach and Abednego. When these three had refused to worship the golden idol set up by Nebuchadnezzar, they were thrown into a fiery furnace. They did not perish because Yahweh had guarded them with one of his angels. Story after story of this kind was told to describe Yahweh's mighty deeds in protecting those who worshiped and served his holy name. In each instance earthly kings were thwarted by the superior power of the Jewish God.

The literature of the two-hundred-year period prior to the Christian schism concerned itself with the reconciliation of worldly distress with the power and justice claimed for Yahweh. All through Jewish history the promise of a Golden Age was held out to true believers, yet many centuries had already passed with nothing but increased misery and disappointment. The great centers of power had shifted, but the Hebrews were always caught and subjugated. The Apocalyptic writings, which the Book of Daniel inaugurates and which characterize the literature of the intertestamental period, attempt to deal with this problem by recalling the glories of the past and prophesying the speedy coming of the Kingdom of God. The divine providence of Yahweh is traced through history, with

the fury of the current struggle indicating the final battle before victory. These writings do not offer a long-range hope,
but rather a salvation to come just after the next, and possibly
worst, clash.

For the most part the Apocalytic writings do not add anything new to the general prophetic tradition. They are primarily a rewriting and a reinterpretation, applied especially
to ancient prophecy which appeared to be wrong in the light
of later facts. The author of Daniel reinterprets Jeremiah's
prophecy that the Kingdom of God would arrive seventy
years after the Exile to mean that it would arrive in seventy
weeks of years, or four hundred and ninety normal years.
According to this chronology, only half a week or three and
one-half years remained before complete salvation. In other
Apocalyptic books the seventy years is interpreted in various
ways, but the theme is always the same: the prophets of old
were right; the Golden Age is almost here.

Much of the change that was taking place in religious
thought is obscured by the extensive use of imagery and imaginative symbolism in the Apocalyptic writings. The earlier
writings of the Jewish tradition are amazingly straightforward
and direct when compared with the early records found in
Buddhism and Indian religion. The Apocalyptic writers, however, symbolize their concepts in much the same way as
Eastern religious thinkers. In doing so they offer a surprising contrast to the earlier Jewish tradition. There are many
reasons given for this increased use of symbolism. Some have
thought that it represents an attempt on the part of the writers
to obscure their meanings so that they might escape persecution. Other commentators have urged that it indicates the
authors' desire to lend their work an air of antiquity, designed
to give authenticity to their assumed use of an ancient hero's
name. For whatever reason the new method was used, it did

succeed in creating an atmosphere replete with supernatural coloring and miraculously wonderful happenings.

For these writers, probably laymen who represented a cross section of current belief and practice, Yahweh was the One God. He ruled his world from a heavenly Paradise far off in the sky, and surrounding him were hosts of angels, archangels and a remarkable number of servants and messengers. Heaven was conceived to be the most ideal of all places, where every comfort and every magnificent creation gladdened the lives of the purified and redeemed. Yahweh was supreme, and by his side were his ministers and those to whom he delegated various responsibilities.

SADDUCEES AND PHARISEES

OUT of the deep roots of conflict between the Hellenized and the orthodox came not only the Apocalyptic literature but also the most important religious division among the Jews: the difference between Sadducees and Pharisees. The Sadducees were mostly upper-class people of wealth and culture who had by this time become fairly well Hellenized. By this very process they had developed the importance of a Jewish *state* as distinguished from a Jewish *nation*. To the Sadducees, as to the Greeks and Romans, a state meant a political unit within a specific geographic area. This was considered to be the essential organizing principle, while the particular religion of the people within that state was looked upon as a civic duty and an important expression of patriotism. Thus the Sadducees were primarily interested in maintaining the status of the Jewish state, and they placed less emphasis upon the purity of the Hebrew religion wherever it might be found.

The Pharisees, on the other hand, were more representative of the lower and middle classes and less under the influence of Greek ideals and concepts. For them, the Sadducees were denying one of the great achievements of the earlier Jewish tradition. From the time of the first great Exile the nation, for the pious Jews, was quite different from the state. There needed to be no central state for Yahweh's people to be a unity. No matter where the Jews might find themselves, however the forces of history might move them and their places of residence change, the ethnic unity of Israel would remain. The Pharisees hoped to maintain this distinction between nation and state so that never again would religious integrity be dependent upon the fortunes of war and political structures. True Judaism, they maintained, was far greater than the geography-bound state.

As would be expected, the Sadducees were the most violent protectors and defenders of Israel against all foreign invasions, while the Pharisees were more passive except when the forceful introduction of an alien religion was part of the conqueror's plan. Indeed, there were some among the Pharisees who urged the complete annihilation of the Jewish state and welcomed the invading forces. These Pharisees, like many of the prophets before them, considered the state to be an instrument of evil since it tended to turn the devotion of the people from the proper worship of Yahweh to patriotic love of the political unit.

In our modern sense of the word, both groups were nationalists. The essential difference lay in the aspects of the problem which seemed important and in their methods for dealing with them. In working out these methods each group developed individual emphases. The Sadducees expressed their nationalism in a love of the state and consequently of the written law. They maintained that the law, as it was written, was the basic authority, and that as such it demanded the rigid adherence of the people. The Pharisees, on the other hand, insisted that the true authority was to be found in the oral tradition, a living and ever-changing growth of customs and beliefs. To the Pharisees the Jewish ethnic group was a dynamic whole which continually adjusted itself to new conditions. In his active relations with men, Yahweh was best seen and understood in terms of historic existence. The Sadducees, on the other hand, sought a permanent and unchanging written revelation. Yahweh had revealed himself once, they felt; therefore religious life could not be thought of in terms of progressive revelation.

Because of the Sadducees' strict and literal acceptance of the Torah (the Law of Moses), accretions from other religions which had become a part of the general Jewish religious community became more obvious. Ideas of personal immortality, held by both Persians and Greeks, came to be accepted by the Pharisees. Nowhere in the earlier law could such conceptions be found. The closest it could come was a belief in the eternal existence of the Jewish people, but this was hardly adequate in an era of rising individualism. The Maccabaean wars resulted in a heightened tendency to believe in reward for those who died in the cause of true religion. Thus the oral tradition came to be filled with doctrines of immortality and the resurrection of the righteous.

In a sense, these concepts answered the doubts raised by the discrepancy between the promises of Yahweh and the facts of history. The proclamations of the prophets regarding the Golden Age could be readily transferred to an essentially other-worldly setting. The Messiah would eventually come, and when he did the dead would be resurrected to live in eternal peace and blessedness. The destiny of the individual was thus inextricably linked with the ultimate destiny of the nation.

And many of them that sleep in the dust of the earth shall awake, some to everlasting life, and some to shame and everlasting contempt.

(Daniel 12:2)

Within the structure of this resurrection theology, it is also possible to see the ideas of retribution changing. Previously Yahweh saw to it that man received his just reward or punishment while he was still alive. Now the stretch of history was extended beyond the sequences of natural time. The end of history would not only see the redemption of those who were then living, but the righteous Israelites of the past would also regain life and attain peace under the absolute reign of Yahweh. Those who had revolted against Yahweh and his word when they were alive would either remain dead, and therefore annihilated, or be consigned to Sheol, or Hell.

In addition to conceptions of immortality and resurrection, the Pharisee theologians developed an angelology, again much to the displeasure of the Sadducees. This doctrine of possible mediators between God and man resulted from their constant need to unite a perfect God with an imperfect world. In the first books of the Jewish tradition angels were thought of simply as heavenly messengers, but now the popular religion was developing a conception which endowed them with lives and wills of their own. The saints, heroes and martyrs of earlier days were looked upon as spiritual entities who could intercede with Yahweh and gain favors for the people. Altogether, the universe of the average Jew of the second and first centuries B.C. was as filled with angels and demons as his ancestors' had been with manifold gods. The angels, however, were not gods; rather, they stood between God and man as beings of superhuman, but not ultimate, power. Satan, who had previously been an instrument of Yahweh's power, now became the supreme embodiment of evil. And his demons and God's angels were in constant conflict.

Such dualistic conceptions found their roots in Hellenistic mystery cults and the Zoroastrian theology of the Persians. As the cultural influences of this Middle Eastern area played gradually over the population of Palestine, foreign ideas were probably accepted without thought of their origin. The Pharisees, who best represented the thinking of the common man, were not speculative theologians who looked for logical contradictions in their systems. Their primary concern was with the popular power of the religion and, consequently, with its more practical aspects. The wonderful and fantastic stories of the Apocalyptic writers caught the imaginations and stirred the religious consciousness of the people. Therefore, whether or not they were orthodox in the way in which the Torah was orthodox for the Sadducees was of little consequence.

The very fact that the Pharisees denied the crucial importance of the political state led them to be concerned with the religious practices and beliefs of those of Jewish origin who were spread throughout the Hellenistic world. Since it would have been impossible to make the Temple at Jerusalem the center of all Jewish worship, the Pharisees encouraged the establishment of synagogue congregations. It will be remembered that this congregational movement had begun during the Exile and had continued to grow throughout the various dispersions. These non-Palestinian congregations were naturally more interested in the aspects of Jewish heritage upon which geography had no influence. Thus the proper observance of the Sabbath was accorded great importance, and education in the Torah and the oral tradition was firmly established as a further function of the congregation.

DIASPORA MISSIONS

THE Jews scattered in exile through the Old World are known as the Jews of the Diaspora, or dispersion. As they became accustomed to their new life, their occupations gradually changed from agriculture to trade and commerce. In terms of their religious theory they were not supposed to have any relations with the pagans outside of business. Nevertheless, a large majority of the non-Palestinian Jews took over many of the practices of the Greek world. They used the Greek language for their Bible and even in religious services; many took Greek names; and practically all developed pagan friendships. This assimilation did not necessarily mean a loss of distinctively Jewish religiosity. On the contrary, many set out with intense missionary zeal to evangelize the pagans. They were motivated, at least in part, by the ancient prophetic notion that the one true God had put them on earth to lead all nations and all peoples to his everlasting throne.

Such missionary activity was not new to the Greek world. Many of the Greek mystery cults, the various Egyptian religions, and even the sects of Persia had a sense of divine commission in establishing the exclusive power of their god. In a way, the least interesting of all these religions to the pagan was Judaism, and more especially so when its lack of images and its emphasis on a high ethical idealism became apparent. In spite of these disadvantages, however, the Jewish propaganda made progress. The pagan world at that time was in a state of moral and religious confusion, and the rather simple, straightforward affirmations of traditional Judaism were at least definite and unambiguous. If we are to follow such ancient writers as Josephus, Seneca and Philo, the number of Judaized Greeks was staggering. The Roman authors, Horace, Persius and Juvenal, write of a similar conversion record.

The question of admitting ethnically non-Jews to the religious community raised many difficult problems. The Jewish religion had always maintained a high degree of particularity, especially in the idea of a "Chosen People." Many of the Jews of the Diaspora, however, had sloughed off much that was peculiar to Judaism, and they now adhered simply to a monotheistic faith which was ethically centered. Even the question of circumcision had become subject to debate, with some missionaries demanding it and others denying its importance. The problem raised by the "Chosen People" argument was met by reinterpreting it to mean that Israel was chosen as the priestly nation which was to serve all peoples. Such universalist and liberal doctrine gained headway among the Jews of the Diaspora, but those remaining in Palestine usually looked upon talk of this kind with horror, or at least with suspicion. For the Christian missionaries to come, however, this movement was a boon and has always been considered one of the major factors contributing to the success of Christianity.

THE SHIFT TO ROME

WHILE Hellenistic culture was conquering the Mediterranean world, the center of political power was shifting from the Greek islands to Rome. Between 500 and 300 B.C. Rome extended her control throughout the Italian peninsula. In this process of expansion she unified a large number of people in a fashion never achieved by any of the Greek states. As time went on, Rome was able to extend her military and political control until she became one of the greatest empires the world has ever known.

In the early periods of the Roman Empire the conception of local self-government was highly developed. Wherever the Romans found a well-developed city organization they delegated the power of government and the right to collect taxes. Although the nature and extent of local autonomy varied from place to place, the general tendency was toward controlled decentralization. Above the city-states the Empire was divided into provinces. Ruling each province was a governor who represented the central government in Rome and acted as a supervising agent. This rather loose organization proved a benefit to those within the conquered countries while at the same time contributing money and power to Rome with the least possible effort.

As the Empire grew stronger and, particularly under Augustus, more highly organized, the position of the Jews became increasingly difficult. Throughout their long history they had maintained their ethnic and religious identity despite all conquerors. Now that the Roman Empire was becoming more and more homogeneous, the Jews stood out as radically different from the other peoples. Moreover, there was question as to the correct legal status of the Diaspora Jews with their quasi-religious and quasi-political allegiance to the government in Palestine. For example, throughout the entire Empire Jews alone were not forced to comply with one of the most important civic obligations. Whereas all others were required to participate in the worship of the *genius* of the Emperor, the Jews, for whom this would have been outrageous blasphemy, were exempt. Yet many of those affected lived and had lived for centuries outside the political borders of Palestine. Such special treatment, when coupled with the extreme sense of loyalty and community which the Jews felt, made their assimilation into the Greco-Roman population impossible.

16

THE FRUIT OF HELLENISM

THE Jews in the first century of our era were not organized into a homogeneous religious or political unit. The Jewish communities spread throughout the Empire were broken up into sects and were increasingly taking on the color of Hellenism. The Pharisees, who had formerly been the great advocates of a freer interpretation of the tradition, became more and more formal in their emphasis. They, as well as the Sadducees, allowed the spirit of the Prophetic tradition to wane, substituting for it a kind of self-righteous piety toward the law. Although Pharisees and Sadducees still differed in doctrine, their attitudes were now identical. The learned Scribes and leaders of the two great divisions looked down upon the Am ha-Arez, or country people, as ignorant and incapable of practicing the highly disciplined and legalized worship of the city dweller.

Since the educated considered themselves a group apart, it was natural that the gap between the official religion and the practices and beliefs of the masses increased. Magical practices borrowed from the Chaldean and Babylonian astrologers became popular. Various foreign demonologies and angelologies slowly usurped the place of the more austere legalistic ethics propounded in the schools and synagogues. The Yahweh of the Pharisees and Sadducees had become so unattainable that the common people had little other choice. Along with this increased popularity of spirits and magic there was a parallel growth of asceticism. The Essenes cried out against the evils of urban life and advocated the establishment of monasteries where men could devote their lives to religious worship and be freed of the distractions of this world. This wing of the Pharisaic movement tried to purify Jewish religion by taking literally some of the utterances of the desert prophets of an earlier age.

MESSIANISM

ONE of the beliefs most common in the Palestinian community concerned the coming of the Golden Age. God had promised it, and as the political, economic and religious situations worsened, the great expectation seemed nearer and nearer at hand. Events were moving so rapidly that the signs all seemed to point to a speedy coming of the Messiah and the end of misery. Prophets of one kind and another walked the land announcing it, and bands of people following them gathered in desert spots to await his arrival. The spirit of the time as one of immediate hope was building to a climax. For some in the Palestinian community that climax was reached in the person of Jesus of Nazareth, for them the Messiah.

One of the itinerant preachers who roamed the hills of Palestine was John the Baptist. His message concerned the popular belief that the end of the world was at hand and that God was about to pronounce judgment on the sinners, who would perish, and on the righteous, who would live in eternal blessedness. He exhorted his hearers to repent, confess their sins and receive absolution by immersion in the waters of the Jordan. Although John was only a prophet announcing the coming of the Messiah, the suspicions of Herod Antipas were aroused. In view of the multitudes who listened and were baptized, it looked to the authorities as if a revolution were brewing. In order to forestall any such political unrest, Herod Antipas had John arrested and put to death. The loss of their leader, however, did not destroy the feeling of the people that his predictions were trustworthy—that the Golden Age would soon appear, ushered in by the coming of the Messiah.

JESUS OF NAZARETH

AMONG the vast number who received baptism from John was Jesus, the son of a carpenter from Nazareth. Although the sources regarding the life of Jesus are obscured by the writings of his followers, it is probable that he was carrying on the trade of his father and perhaps caring for his brothers and sisters. In any event it is at this point that the oldest of the Gospel records, the Book of Mark, begins the story of Jesus and his earthly career. Immediately upon baptism, according to Mark, Jesus became aware of his divine consecration and thus embarked upon his ministry. It was, however, a ministry much like that of John, conducted within the framework of the Jewish apocalypticism so popular in Palestine.

Whatever education he received was from the hands of the Pharisees and in terms of their interpretation of the Law and the Prophets. Like any other young man of his time, his beliefs were formed by the school, the synagogue and the traveling preachers. The Messianic hope was strong everywhere, and the sense that the world was waiting on the edge of great events filled most religious minds.

After his baptism Jesus went into the desert where, the tradition relates, he was tempted by the Devil to give up his great mission. Having rejected the temptations, he then returned to Galilee to begin his public ministry. There he attracted a number of disciples who together constituted a preaching company. As the little group traveled about the country, the words of Jesus were heard in the market places, around the desert

[264]

wells and in the synagogues. In addition to gaining a reputation as a teller of great truths he was also known as one who could perform miracles, cure illness and exorcise evil spirits. As his travels broadened and his fame spread, crowds came to hear his words and see his miraculous deeds.

As the popularity of Jesus grew among the people, his position in religious and political official circles became difficult. In preaching the happy news of the imminent Golden Age, he tended to slight, and on occasion directly challenge, some of the most rigidly held Pharisaical practices. He considered the keeping of fast days to be a sign of somber mourning completely out of place in the joyous days of redemption. The rigid observance of the Sabbath, which for the Pharisees was an essential requirement of religion, was rejected by Jesus with the statement that man is more important than ritual. When such offenses as this were added to the fact that Jesus was taking upon himself the authority to forgive sins, which had always been the prerogative of God alone, the gap between Jesus and the official religious leaders widened.

Throughout, however, Jesus had never once proclaimed himself to be the Messiah. He was not preaching himself, but he was preaching a doctrine which could have serious repercussions. In his discussions of the "Kingdom of God" he emphasized that it was based on peace among men. To the Zealots, who formed a kind of subversive party of resistance, this meant disapproval of any fight against the Roman yoke. Indeed, Jesus's famous phrase, "Give unto Caesar the things that are Caesar's . . . ," was interpreted to mean paying taxes and pledging political loyalty to Caesar. Moreover, he advocated the supremacy of "spirit" over law, a position which denied, or seemed to deny, the concepts of both state and nation. Both Jews and Romans immediately became suspicious since Roman imperialism was built upon a sanctification of the state, and Judaism, in its major forms, seems to have been a synthesis of nationalism and statism.

For these various political and religious reasons resentment against Jesus increased, but he continued to preach his message without qualification. If anything, his zeal increased and his actions became more overt. At one juncture he drove the money-changers, who had a monopoly in selling objects of sacrifice, out of the Temple. He criticized more and more strongly the Pharisaical lawyers because, he insisted, they were killing the spirit of religion by their strict demands for literal observance of the Law. Consequently, two days before the Feast of the Passover the chief religious authorities decided that the time had come for the removal of Jesus. Added to concern for their own positions was a fear that the movement would culminate in an uprising against the government, especially since word had reached them that Jesus had decided to declare himself as the Messiah at the Passover. Such a declaration by a popular figure would inevitably lead to a disruption of the *status quo* and to serious Roman reprisals.

While the chief priests and Scribes were debating the method of disposing of Jesus, they were visited by Judas, one of his disciples. Whatever Judas's motives might have been, he agreed to lead the priests to Jesus. After Jesus's arrest at Gethsemane he was taken to the high priest, who then turned him over to Pilate. The charge against him was that he had posed as the King of the Jews. As such he was pronounced an agitator. Pilate knew full well that there was more to the charge than rebellion and sent the prisoner to Herod, who ruled the province of Galilee. Herod sent him back and finally Pilate was forced to pass judgment. He gave the people an alternative: he would release either Jesus Barabbas, a popular anti-Roman hero, or the man alleged to be Jesus the Messiah. By this time the crowd had been won over by its leader, and

Barabbas was released while Jesus of Nazareth went to the cross.

JEWISH CHRISTIANITY

By all normal standards, especially when viewed in the light of previous occurrences of this kind, the movement generated by Jesus should have died with him. How could mere men possibly kill the Messiah if he were the true Messiah? And at first his death did seem to negate the promise held out by his work and preaching. According to Christian tradition, however, Jesus did not remain dead. On the Sunday following the crucifixion he arose from his tomb and appeared to his disciples and later to all the apostles. After his first appearance in Galilee, he and his disciples went to Jerusalem, where he appeared to some five hundred other people. It was here, according to the Whitsuntide story, that the first church was organized and its leaders confirmed in their offices by the Risen Lord. Thus the resurrection of the man killed by his ecclesiastical and political enemies gave the cult of Jesus fresh impetus.

The members of this first church were Jews who had no thought of starting a new religion. They were still interested in living up to the Torah, they still worshiped at the Temple, and they still accepted the general Pharisaical interpretation of the sacred Jewish writings. The only major difference between them and their brethren lay in their conviction that the Messiah had arrived and that he would soon return to bring God's kingdom to earth. His miraculous resurrection placed the seal of divine authority upon his teaching. It was the duty of those bound together in the Messiah's church by their experience of the Risen Lord to convince other Jews of this, the most momentous historic fact since creation. In spreading the faith, baptism, fasting and other rites borrowed from contemporary Judaism were used as symbols of repentance, for only those who repented of their sins and acknowledged Jesus as the Messiah could hope to participate in the bliss of the Golden Age.

PHILO OF ALEXANDRIA

WHILE Jesus and his followers were developing and preaching the eschatological faith of Palestine, various Jewish philosophers of the Diaspora were attempting a synthesis of Hellenism and Judaism. The only writer in the field whose works have been preserved in anything but fragmentary form is Philo of Alexandria (c. 20 B.C.–50 A.D.). Philo was a man well instructed in Greek culture; but he was also a Jew with national and religious convictions. The Mosaic Law and the tradition of prophecy were his bases for ultimate truth. With them he attempted to combine the metaphysical and ethical insights which he found in the writings of Plato, the Pythagoreans and the Stoics. Because of the radical difference between philosophical and religious thought, his system was never complete or structurally unified. Nevertheless he formulated some of the fundamental problems and concepts which were used later by both Jewish and Christian theologians.

Philo was convinced that the Mosaic Law and the Greek philosophers (especially Plato) were discussing essentially the same thing. The Law had been revealed to man by God in the form of concrete precepts and symbolic object-lessons. The philosophers, on the other hand, were searching out truth with reason and consequently spoke in abstract terms. Although there is no fundamental conflict between the two methods, says Philo, it is obvious that the truth of God is more complete when grasped by the intellect than when revealed by the Bible. Once man has progressed to the use of his intellect he can no longer be content with an easy acceptance of revelation. Indeed, the business of the philosopher is to penetrate beneath the historical outer garment of revelation to the abstract and eternal truths of God beneath.

The basis of the Philonic system is found in Plato's radical separation of essence and matter. Philo makes God into absolute essence, or pure spirituality, and matter into the object upon which God works. God is the metaphysical absolute and is beyond description. The specific definitions used to differentiate among the objects of sense perception cannot be applied. Indeed, the ancient answer given to Moses when he asked Yahweh who he was is all that can ever be said:

> And Moses said unto God, Behold, when I come unto the children of Israel, and shall say unto them, The God of your fathers hath sent me unto you; and they shall say to me, What is his name? what shall I say unto them?
>
> And God said unto Moses, I AM THAT I AM: and he said, Thus shalt thou say unto the children of Israel, I AM hath sent me unto you.
>
> (Exodus 3:13-14)

All that can ever be affirmed about God is that he exists.

Philo's conception of deity raised a problem concerning the nature of the relationship between passive matter and God. Since God is nameless and without definable attributes, it would be impossible to assign to him actions which entailed his mingling with the inert matter of the world. To do so would be to state an attribute. In order to escape this difficulty Philo is forced to postulate *Logoi Spermatikoi* (seminal principles) which exist between God and matter. These *Logoi*, which correspond to the Ideas in Platonic philosophy and to the angels in the Scripture, are spiritual beings who carry out the will of God. They are immanent within all matter and give to the various facets of creation form and vitality.

THE "LOGOS" DOCTRINE

THESE operative *Logoi* are the active causes of all order and animation within the world, yet they are also unified into one *Logos* which has its existence outside the phenomenal world but its work within it. This would seem to mean that the *Logos* is at once in God, and at the same time immanent in the material universe. In such a position *Logos*, which is probably most accurately translated as Reason, is both the representative of God and a priest for man. As God's agent it stands as the force which created the world, and as priest it is capable of mediating God's will to man. Consistent with this position Philo introduces a kind of salvation by philosophy. Through philosophic contemplation upon the eternal *Logos*, the soul of man is able to rise above and beyond the trammels of physical existence to the true bliss of the divine. The most complete, or at least the highest, form of worship consists in a state of rapture during which the soul of man is infused with divine radiation.

Philo also uses his conception of *Logos* to solve the problem of creation. Through the mediation of the *Logos*, formless and chaotic matter was created into the world of objects and things. Again on the basis of Plato and the Jewish tradition (Genesis 1:2), Philo asserts that the world was not created from nothing, but that the chaos which was already existent was *formed* into a meaningful unity. Only certain aspects of the world, then, can be considered "good"; others would naturally possess a greater degree of chaos. The closer the connection with earth or matter, the more removed from God and consequently the less pure. By this reasoning the spirit of man is immortal and good because "it was breathed into clay by God," whereas man's body is evil and the source of all his pain and distress. The evil of life is therefore not

These two pictures first appeared in the Nuremberg Chronicle, a history of the world published in 1493. They show how Yahweh fashioned Adam on the sixth day of Creation, and how Eve was literally created out of Adam's rib. (*Courtesy of Harvard College Library.*)

These two scenes picture two Jewish festivals. The synagogue ceremony is Rosh Hashanah, the beginning of the New Year when a ram's horn is blown. The other picture is of the Seder feast, an ancient ceremonial meal around the paschal lamb. Those sitting around the table are dressed to symbolize the flight from Egypt.

attributable to God, but to the "waste, void, darkness and water" from which God fashioned the world of the senses.

As would be expected, Philo's ethical teaching is directed toward freeing the soul from involvement in the world of sense experience. Alone and unaided, man is unable to put aside his earthly desires and sensuous cravings for material satisfaction. It is only by the "grace of God" as mediated through the *Logos* that man is given the strength to overcome ignorance with wisdom, lasciviousness with self-control, cowardice with courage and injustice with justice. All true ethics are therefore ultimately based in "piety and holiness . . . which we cannot obtain without the worship of God." Since both piety and holiness are the fruits of divine illumination, all good action is dependent upon man's relationship to God. For Philo, the Stoic sense of self-reliance was destined to end in moral disaster. The final point of ethical achievement is found only when the soul is freed of its worldly attachments and is at one with the will of God.

The actual content of Philo's ethical teaching is taken from the Law of Moses, and its essentially Jewish character is seen in his constant references to the relations obtaining among men. The extreme individualism of certain Hellenistic ethical schemes was always rejected by Philo. In spite of his philosophic abstractions he never tires of calling God "the Father of all" and human beings "his sons." And because all are sons of God the Father, "assuredly there is in the soul of every man, however undistinguished he may be, a detestation of evil," which binds one to another in love and justice.

The synthesis which Philo attempted was in reality a compromise between Hellenism and Judaism. It tended to obliterate the absolute lines of difference between the two traditions and offer the basis for a common recognition of truth in both. Although Philo accepted the Jews as a "Chosen People," he did so in a religious rather than a national sense. The age-old claim of the Jews that their Torah was something unique and unparalleled and that their ethical monotheism was without counterpart in other human societies was nullified by the implications of Philo's philosophy. The deeply rooted conviction that there *should* be opposition between Judaism and Hellenism tended to negate Philo's influence among the Palestinian and Babylonian Jews. The Diaspora Jews who had drunk freely of the Hellenistic way of life found his marriage of philosophy and religion much more compatible. It was finally left to Christianity, especially as expressed by Paul and John, to utilize the tools of compromise which the main body of Judaism rejected.

PAUL OF TARSUS

In the years immediately following the death of Jesus a large number of Hellenistic and a smaller number of Palestinian Jews were converted to the new sect. For the most part they were opposed by all of the Sadducees and the more rigid of the Pharisees. The basis for conflict lay in the belief of the converts that the Messiah had arrived and that the "new age" had been ushered in with his coming. In terms of a prevalent interpretation, this meant that the old legal code, which gave minute prescriptions for ceremonial observances, was no longer applicable. This break with tradition was much easier for the Hellenistic Jews since, to an extent at least, they were denationalized and therefore removed from the more rigid provisions of the Law.

Saul, a Cilician Pharisee, was one of the most zealous of the persecutors sent against the Christian sect. It is probable that he had something to do with the stoning of Stephen, and in his own words he did much to uproot the blasphemous sect of Hellenistic Nazarenes. When some of the disciples fled the persecutions in Jerusalem and started preaching in Damascus,

Saul obtained permission to pursue them with an eye to their arrest and forcible return to Jerusalem. According to the Gospel records, it was on this trip to Damascus that Saul had a vision of Jesus as the Risen Lord.

And as he journeyed, it came to pass that he drew nigh unto Damascus: and suddenly there shone round about him a light out of heaven: and he fell upon the earth, and heard a voice saying unto him, Saul, Saul, why persecutest thou me? And he said, Who art thou, Lord? And he said, I am Jesus whom thou persecutest: but rise, and enter into the city, and it shall be told thee what thou must do. And the men that journeyed with him stood speechless, hearing the voice, but beholding no man. And Saul arose from the earth; and when his eyes were opened, he saw nothing; and they led him by the hand, and brought him into Damascus. And he was three days without sight, and did neither eat nor drink.

(Acts 9:3-9)

From this moment on Saul becomes Paul, the first Christian theologian and popular unifier of Judaism and Hellenism.

Paul had studied under Gamaliel, one of the greatest Pharisaical teachers, and had lived a good portion of his life in Tarsus, where the winds of Hellenistic doctrine blew with increasing strength. For him Christianity was the fruition of the long history of struggle and expansion which characterized Judaism. Like Philo, Paul always remained essentially a Jew whose thinking was colored and infused with rabbinic learning. Again like Philo, Paul thought that many of the ancient laws concerning diet, the Sabbath and even circumcision were now outmoded as rules of practice. Justification before the throne of Yahweh, the one true God, could not be achieved by living up to the Law of Moses, but rather by faith in Jesus as the Christ. The national body of Israel, organized as it was around the Law, was to give way to the Universal Israel of the spirit.

[273]

When the uniqueness of Judaism as a chosen nation of God should be destroyed, the preaching of Jesus as the Christ could be directed toward Gentiles as well as Jews. Although Paul consistently preached first to the Jews, his universalist and de-nationalized doctrine eradicated the historic barriers between the Jews and the rest of mankind. The demand for a "new life in the spirit" placed faith in Jesus as the Christ above and beyond all ceremonial law. Whether Paul meant to or not, it was he who laid the groundwork for the ultimate separation of Christianity from Judaism.

17

ORTHODOX JUDAISM

DURING the course of the long Roman rule, the Jews in Palestine had engineered a number of revolts. Internal dissension resulting from the conflicting religious and political ideas of the first century A.D. increased the unrest and further stimulated the uprisings against Rome. From the death of Herod in 4 B.C. to the beginning of the fatal war in 66 A.D. the Roman conquerors and their governors had known no peace with the Jews. The end of the revolts came in 70 A.D. when Titus sent his armies into Jerusalem and destroyed the Temple for the last time. From this time on the Jews of the Diaspora could no longer look to Jerusalem as a political and religious center. The priests of the Temple were dispersed throughout Palestine, Babylonia and the rest of the Roman world. Nearly one million Jews were killed and untold thousands were taken captive and sold into slavery. With the Temple gone and the people scattered it looked as if the long history of the Jews had finally come to an end.

THE TALMUD

HOWEVER, Judaism was much too deeply rooted in the minds and souls of Abraham's descendants to be crushed by either Rome or Christianity. Within its oral and written traditions was the foundation for an extensive system of religious practice and education. No matter where the Jews might be there could always be a synagogue, that very useful institution developed through necessity during the first Exile and perfected by the Diaspora; and the Law could always be read. The Pharisaical tradition had long since made it possible for the Chosen People of Yahweh to maintain their national existence independent of any political state. In a sense, then, the Jews were already prepared for the new dispersion. The school and the synagogue became the true core of their life. And these institutions could be organized under any government and in any climate.

Together with the political state went the destruction of the Sanhedrin, which had been the chief administrative council, and also the influence of the priestly aristocracy and their major supporters, the Sadducees. This left the field of instruction in the hands of the Pharisees, who had always maintained that Israel had been given two authoritative revelations at Sinai: the written and the oral traditions. It was now possible for them to establish the necessity for some formulation of the oral tradition that could be easily read and taught. The result of this systematic codification was the Talmud. At the same time (second century A.D.) the canon of the Jewish Scriptures was fixed and closed. The days of prophecy, so the rabbis said, were over.

The canon of Jewish scriptures was divided into three general groups:

1. The Law (*Torah* or *Pentateuch*)—Genesis, Exodus, Leviticus, Numbers and Deuteronomy.

2. The Prophets (*Nebiim*)—Joshua, Judges, I and II Samuel, I and II Kings, Isaiah, Jeremiah, Ezekiel and others.

3. The Writings (*Kethubhim*)—Psalms, Proverbs, Job, Song of Songs, Ruth, Lamentations, Ecclesiastes, Esther, Daniel, Ezra, Nehemiah and I and II Chronicles.

As we have seen, the writing of these books extended over a period of time beginning with the earliest days of Judaism and ending with Ezra in the second century before Christ. There were many books, such as the Wisdom of Solomon and the books of the Maccabees, that were judged unworthy of the canon.

Down through the ages of Hebrew history the rabbis (teachers) had been making repeated studies and interpretations of the written Torah which were handed down from one generation to the next in the form of the oral tradition or, as some called it, the oral law. The rabbis had long insisted that the two were inseparable, since the oral law was necessary if the written law were to be made applicable to the daily lives of the Jews. As long as Palestine remained the center of Jewish learning, there was never any real need for codifying the oral tradition. However, when the armies of Titus destroyed the Temple and the schools which surrounded it, the leaders of Judaism, fearing that the oral tradition would be lost, began the tremendous job of collecting the interpretive teaching which had formed the basis for lectures and discussions during the previous centuries.

Actual preparation for putting the Talmud into final form was originated by the Scribes, or Sophirim, who began their intensive work some time during the Babylonian exile. It is to them that both Judaism and Christianity owe the preservation of the writings which form the Old Testament. In addition to this work, which was ultimately canonized, they committed to memory, and in some cases to notes, the oral tradition of exposition and interpretation. After the destruction of the Temple in 70 A.D., their work was carried on by a school of rabbis who were known as the Tannaim. It was this school that was primarily responsible for the form in which the Talmud was finally written. After the Tannaim, who flourished from 70 to 200 A.D., the codification was carried on by the Amoraim, until in the sixth century the Saboraim gave the Talmud its final editing and closed the book. Since that time there have been no additions or deletions in this amazing collection of sayings.

Of the two centers of Jewish learning, Palestine and Babylonia, by far the more erudite was Babylonia. Both centers produced a Talmud, but the technical and intellectual superiority of the Babylonian Jews is easily seen in their collection. The Palestinians seemed to be much more interested in face-value interpretations than in the dialectical profundity which characterized the work of the rabbis of Babylonia. Although the Palestinian collection was earlier, the obvious superiority of the Babylonian Talmud made it the authoritative version for all succeeding generations of Jews. Moreover, it is complete, whereas the Palestinian version contains only a part of the Mishnah and none of the Gemora, the two great divisions of the Talmud.

The word *Mishnah* literally means repetition or reproduction. It has special reference to the period when the laws and interpretations of the tradition were memorized and handed down orally from generation to generation. A list of its contents [1] will give some idea of how extensive a structure this was:

I. Laws concerning Seeds and Fruits.

1. Benedictions or Prayers; liturgical rules.
2. Treats of the corners and gleanings of the fields, the olives and grapes to be left to the poor.
3. Buying from people who may not have paid the tithes.
4. Prohibited mixtures.
5. The Sabbatical year.
6. Heave offerings.
7. Tithes given to the Levites.
8. Second tithes.
9. Dough, or priest's cake.

[1] From Dudley Wright, *The Talmud* (London: Williams and Norgate, 1932), pp. 32-34. By permission.

10. The Uncircumsized, fruits of tree during first four years after planting.
11. The first fruits.

II. Laws concerning Seasons and Festivals.
 1. Sabbath.
 2. Combinations, extensions of Sabbath boundary.
 3. Passover.
 4. The yearly half-shekel.
 5. The Day of Atonement.
 6. The Feast of Tabernacles.
 7. Days of Holy Convocation.
 8. The New Year.
 9. Fasts.
 10. Purim.
 11. Minor Festivals.
 12. Feast and private offerings.

III. Laws relating to Women.
 1. Levirate and forbidden marriages.
 2. Deeds and settlements.
 3. Vows and their annulment.
 4. Laws concerning the Nazarite.
 5. Adultery.
 6. Divorces.
 7. Betrothals.

IV. Injuries, Punishments, and Reparations.
 1. Damages and injuries and their remedies.
 2. Buying, selling, lending, hiring, and renting.
 3. Real estate and commerce, hereditary succession.
 4. Courts and their proceedings, capital crimes.
 5. Stripes, false witness, cities of refuge.
 6. Oaths.
 7. Traditional laws and Rabbinical decisions.
 8. Idolatry.
 9. Fathers and ethical maxims.
 10. Decisions, true and false.

V. Sacred Things.
   1. Sacrifices and how to be offered.
   2. Meat and drink offerings.
   3. Profane things, slaughtering of animals, dietary laws.
   4. Laws of the first-born of men and animals.
   5. Valuation of devoted things.
   6. Exchange of sanctified things.
   7. Excisions and expiation by sacrifices.
   8. Sacrilege and profanation of sacred things.
   9. Daily sacrifice.
   10. Measurements of the Temple.
   11. Offerings of the poor.

VI. Pollutions and Purifications.
   1. Pollution of vessels and garments.
   2. Tents and dead bodies.
   3. Leprosy and its cleansing.
   4. The red heifer, water of separation.
   5. Sundry pollutions and purifications.
   6. Wells and reservoirs for ritual purifications.
   7. Pollutions and purifications of women.
   8. Preparations, pollutions, and purifications of seeds.
   9. Running issues.
   10. Pollutions not removed till sunset.
   11. Washing of hands.
   12. Stalks and shells of fruits.

The *Gemora*, which means complement, is the commentary on the Mishnah. Thus the Mishnah is the commentary on the Torah and the Gemora is the commentary on the commentary. As such it is a mine of information and interpretation regarding the trials and suffering endured by the Jews.

The orthodox Jews of later centuries looked upon both the canonized Scripture and the Talmud as being the self-revelation of God. Since only through knowledge of the Law could God's will be known, and only by the existence of such Law could God's peculiar love of the Jews be recognized, it was felt that there could be no higher calling than that which sent a man to study the divine Law and its equally sanctified interpretation. Study and scholarship were therefore accorded the highest possible place in the community. In the synagogues and schools throughout the world, public instruction in the Law took the place of the worship which had centered in the Temple at Jerusalem, with its physical altar and material sacrifices. An inward reverence and the study of Yahweh's will became the principal matters of religious concern. Thus were all exigencies met. Political overlords could burn their buildings and institute all manner of persecution, but the essentials of worship would remain. The Jews, both as individuals and as a nation, had finally succeeded in "building a fence" around their faith.

THE JEWS AND THE WORLD OUTSIDE

Since Yahweh's will often ran counter to Roman and Persian law, however, it was impossible for his people to be assimilated into the general population of the cities in which they dwelt. An example of a clash between Roman law and Jewish law is seen in their respective attitudes toward marriage. In the Old Testament and in traditional Jewish practice a man was permitted any number of wives he felt he could afford. The Romans, on the other hand, prescribed strict monogamy for all those who held the rights of Roman citizenship. When in 212 A.D. the law of Caracalla made all Jews citizens, they became subject to Roman law and were therefore required to be monogamous. Their own tradition, however, still permitted polygamy. The result of this conflict was severe persecution for many Jews, especially after the official religion of Rome became Christianity.

In Persia and Egypt the problem of marriage within a family arose. In both these countries the marriage of brothers and sisters and even of parents with their children was not only practiced but actually recommended as a means of maintaining the purity of the family strain. On this subject the Jews had definite Biblical commandments which forbade incestuous relations of all kinds, so that the orthodox among them simply refused to comply with the prevailing custom. Once again they were looked upon by their non-Jewish neighbors as persons set apart.

The gap between the Jews and the other peoples of the Mediterranean culture was further widened by their peculiar economic ideas. The Talmudic Law constantly stressed the collective responsibility imposed upon each Jew by virtue of his membership in the ethnic group. No child of Yahweh's could be permitted to live in poverty while his brethren enjoyed the fruits of wealth. As a result of this social obligation the various synagogues became centers of charitable activity, and philanthropy was preached as a sacred duty. The Talmudic Law went even further and designated certain occupations as being suitable for Jews to enter and others as not suitable. All in all, the economic and social laws were sufficiently varied and stringent to provide the rabbi with tremendous control over those who formed his congregation.

Although the Jews had bulwarked themselves for continued existence without a political state, they never lost the hope that some day the promised Golden Age would be ushered in. For some the hope had a purely political cast, while for others it took on spiritual meaning. Those who thought in political terms dreamed of the day when the house of Israel would be freed of foreign domination and they could return to the Promised Land to live under the wise rule and blessing of God. For the others the Golden Age would have arrived when all mankind knelt at the throne of the one true God, Yahweh. This would be complete consummation, the realization of the goal toward which all history had been moving.

This concept of universal salvation was, of course, in terms of Judaism. Those Jews who had been selected by God as his holy priests and ambassadors would still hold their high positions. Jerusalem, in that Golden Age, would be the center of worship to which the other nations of the world would pay homage. The prayers of the dispossessed Jews were for the speedy coming of the Kingdom and the establishment of final peace. On this day of gladness all the righteous, especially those buried in Palestine, would be resurrected to take their places beside those who were fortunate enough to be alive. In some cases the Mishnah included Gentiles among the company to be resurrected, but most often the favored group was confined to Jews of right belief and right practice according to the dictates of the Torah. However, any attempt to state positively and systematically the attitude of orthodox Judaism toward either resurrection or the Messiah always ends in frustration. The Talmud offers ample evidence for a number of interpretations.

ORTHODOX WORSHIP

In the order of prayer which was standardized during this period of developing orthodoxy, the general character of Jewish piety becomes evident. Throughout each prayer there is constant emphasis upon the almighty majesty of God and the sinful ignorance and immaturity of man. In most of the standard prayers recorded in the authoritative Daily Prayer Book and in the Talmud, requests are made for a clean heart, for knowledge, for forgiveness of sins, for love of the Law and for the speedy coming of the Messiah. Some excerpted examples of orthodox prayers follow:

O our Father, the merciful Father who showest mercy, have mercy upon us, and put it in our hearts to discern and to understand, to hear, to learn, to teach, to keep, to do, to fulfil, all that is learned by the study of the Law, in love.

.   .   .   .

Magnified and hallowed be his great name in the world which he created according to his will; and may he make his kingship sovereign in your lifetime and in your days.

.   .   .   .

May salvation from heaven, with grace, lovingkindness, mercy, long life, ample sustenance, heavenly aid, health of body, a higher enlightenment, and a living and abiding offspring that will not break with, nor neglect, any of the words of the Law, be vouchsafed unto the teachers and rabbins of the holy community, who are in the land of Israel, and in the land of Babylon, and in all the lands of our dispersion; unto the heads of the academies, the chiefs of the captivity, the heads of the colleges, and the judges in the gates; unto all their disciples, unto all the disciples of their disciples, and unto all who occupy themselves with the study of the Law. May the King of the Universe bless them, prolong their lives, increase their days, and add to their years, and may they be saved and delivered from every trouble and mishap. May the Lord of heaven be their help at all times and seasons; and let us say, Amen.

.   .   .   .

What are we? What is our life? What is our worship? What is our righteousness? What help is there in us? What strength? What courage? What can we say before thee, O Lord, our God and our fathers' God?

The core of orthodox Jewish piety is always the sense of complete and utter dependence. The things of this world are good only when they are given by God. Nor does anything that man can do or make have any meaning in the sight of God's tremendous power and glorious majesty. It is interesting to note the emphasis upon thankfulness for learning and requests for continued enlightenment in the Law. These, and requests for a pure heart, are the most usual subjects of the formal daily prayers prescribed for the orthodox of Judaism.

Faith in the promises of God, dependence upon God's providence and obedience to the Torah all point to the basic orthodox conception of sin. To sin is to refuse to recognize that God is God and that man is at best only a creature of his hand. To deny God his sovereignty, to be "proud of heart," or to raise oneself to a level of independent importance is to drive the "presence of God from the face of the land." There must be no pride in piety, learning or earthly treasures; there must be no praise of man and no honor except to the "poor in spirit." In the Talmud, Rabbi Phineas ben Jair describes the following stages in the progress of Jewish piety:

Heedfulness leads to cleanness; cleanness to purity; purity to holiness; holiness to humility; humility to fear of sin; the fear of sin to saintliness; saintliness to the [possession of the] holy spirit; the holy spirit to the restoration of the dead; the restoration to life brings him to Elijah [the herald of the Golden Age] of sacred memory.

The opposites of all these qualities, especially humility, are considered to be sin. The whole of Israel's history, from Adam on down, offers ample proof of God's hatred of pride and love of the lowly.

In order to increase piety and at the same time preserve continuity with the ancient past, orthodox Judaism after the final exile maintained many of the festivals and holy days which had been developed during the national life in Palestine. Most of these festivals had had agricultural significance when they were first instituted, but after the dispersion they took on more general moral and religious meanings. Some of the important ones can be described as follows:

Passover, *Pesach*, was originally of pastoral origin but came to be the celebration of the successful exodus from Egypt. It is a time for reflection upon the way in which the Providence of God operates in history and also upon the nature of Israel's covenant with God. It is a feast of joy and an expression of hope. The Passover occurs in Nisan (April) from the fifteenth to the twenty-second day.

Day of Atonement, *Yom Kippur*, is the holiest of all Jewish religious days. While the Temple stood this was a day of continuous sacrifice and confession carried on by the High Priest. After 70 A.D. a liturgy of confession, reconciliation and repentance became standard in the synagogues. On this day God's forgiveness is sought and promises of steadfast holiness are made. The Day of Atonement is the tenth day of the New Year, which begins in September.

Feast of Tabernacles, *Sukkot*, which occurs in October, is the regular harvest-time festival of thanksgiving. Also originally an agricultural festival, it became a time for giving thanks for God's goodness and care. Instead of making sacrifices, as had been customary at the Temple, charitable gifts for the poor were prescribed. The last day of this seven-day feast is given over to *Simhat Torah*, Rejoicing in the Law. At this time the yearly cycle of Torah reading is finished and the new reading is begun.

There are numerous other feasts, fasts and festivals which celebrate political and historical events. The fast of *Tiskha 'B'abh* mourns the destruction of the Temple; the *Hanukkah*, the Feast of Lights, is in remembrance and commemoration of the cleansing of the Temple which occurred with the Maccabean victory; and *Purim*, the Feast of Lots, is a patriotic celebration of ultimate deliverance. Through them all runs the combination of history, personal piety and love of the Law.

The weekly observance of the Sabbath, the seventh day in the week, was continued in orthodox Judaism both as a day of rest and as a day commemorating God's creative activities. It was also linked with the idea of deliverance from Egypt. The synagogues of the Diaspora held their major services on this day, and the congregations assembled to hear the Law read. Talmudic Judaism relaxed some of the more rigid Pharisaical proscriptions against Sabbath activity by pronouncing that "the Sabbath was made for man and not man for the Sabbath." In spite of this teaching, some rabbis who were particularly interested in having Sabbath observance represent the solidarity of the dispersed Jews often made outlandish ritualistic requirements for Sabbath observance. These, however, were the exception rather than the rule. In general, the day was given over to worship and the study of the Law, and orthodox Judaism came to look upon the Sabbath much as orthodox Christians look upon Sunday.

18

JUDAISM IN THE MIDDLE AGES

THE formulation of Jewish orthodoxy was completed in the twilight days of the Roman and Persian Empires. The center of intellectual and religious Judaism had shifted from Rome-dominated Palestine to Babylonia, which was under the rule of a more tolerant Persian government. But even here the zealots of Zoroastrianism succeeded in persecuting the Jews and their religious offspring, the Christians. With the conversion of Constantine to Christianity, the basis was laid for a new civilization in the West; and with the rise of Mohammedanism, a new culture was forming in the East. Nevertheless, the existence of a Jewish orthodoxy made it possible for the children of Yahweh to maintain their essential individuality despite pressures from all sides.

ISLAM AND JUDAISM

IN MANY ways the Jews and the Christians were the parents of the new religion which began with the prophet Mohammed. All through the northern Arabian kingdoms of Palmyra and Hira, Christian immigrants had been carrying on a missionary enterprise for at least four centuries. In the south, especially in Yemen, a strong Jewish population had made their homes. And throughout all Arabia both Jewish and Christian slaves were numerous, and sometimes very prosperous. The monotheism of these settlers was in striking contrast to the primitive polytheism of the pre-Islamic Arabians. The Arabs had developed little in the way of mythology; their priests were magicians rather than the officers of a hierarchy; and the most specific religious expression was to be found in the fear of some totem. There was little danger that the relatively sophisticated Jews or Christians would take over pre-Islamic Arabian belief, but there was a good chance that the ethical monotheism developed in Palestine might influence the Arabs.

Although the early life of Mohammed is clouded by the legends and stories created by his followers, it is known that he was born about 570 A.D. and that much of the first part of his life was spent traveling about the Middle East. When he was approximately forty years of age he used to spend considerable time fasting and, if the tradition is correct, studying writings of Jewish and Christian origin. In any event, after one of his periods of seclusion on a mountain near Mecca, he felt a call to become a prophet of God. The Koran (the scriptures of the Mohammedans) records that the angel Gabriel appeared to Mohammed in a dream and said to him:

> Recite! in the name of thy Lord,
> Who created man of a clot of blood.
> Recite! thy Lord is most gracious,
> Who taught by means of the pen,
> Taught man what he knew not.
>
> (Koran, Sura 96, 1-5)

The basic religious concepts preached by Mohammed came from the Jews and Christians. He denounced the polytheism of his countrymen in the name of the one true God. Further, the God he called upon had all the attributes of forgiveness, mercy and law-giving possessed by Yahweh. There could be no images made of him, and, as in popular Judaism and Christianity, he was to be pictured as seated upon a throne in a far-off heaven surrounded by angels and messengers. Like the

God of the Old Testament, Mohammed's God was all-wise, all-seeing and directly interested in the affairs of this world. With his absolute power and sovereignty, subject to limitation by neither man nor nature, he predestined some to salvation and others to damnation. "God leads astray whomsoever he wills, and guides aright whom he wills."

Mohammed believed that the religion he preached was the same as that revealed by God to the long line of prophets from Moses to Jesus. He used the Torah and the Christian Gospel as his basic scriptures and fundamental guides to God's will. Therefore, when his own countrymen rejected him and asked for miracles and "signs" to prove the validity of his doctrine, he naturally turned to the Jewish and Christian populations for support. It is probable that a number of converts were made from these groups, but the majority saw little room for another prophet. Those Christians who knew the fundamentals of their faith were sure that the Messiah had already arrived; there was no need for further revelation. Orthodox Judaism spurned this Arabian prophet who had neither Jewish blood in his veins nor any substantial learning in the Scriptures.

Although this initial rejection did not change Mohammed's basic ideas regarding God and the imminence of judgment, it completely altered the direction of his religious movement. Mohammed's avowed purpose had always been to unite Arabia and establish political control. When he had thought it could be done on the basis of Judaism, he had declared Jerusalem to be the Holy City and had ordered the observance of the Day of Atonement. After being rejected, however, he declared that it had been further revealed to him that Mecca (the Arabian city of his birth) was holy and that both Judaism and Christianity were perversions of the true religion which had actually been given, in its pure form, by Abraham himself to the Arabs many centuries earlier. As a result of this switch, Islam (the Mohammedan religion) was completely severed from Judaism and began its own career as the latest great religion of the world. From this point on, Mohammedanism played a double role: not only was it the Arabian national religion, but it also laid claim to being the most complete and final revelation for all mankind.

As the religion of Islam continued to develop as a national expression, the armies of Mohammed became increasingly successful. By the time of his death in 632 A.D., the groundwork had been laid for a unified Arabia. After several internecine struggles for control, the Arabian religio-political community was organized into an empire by a series of aggressive campaigns against Persia and Rome. Within twelve years after Mohammed's death the Caliphate [1] of Omar had an empire which extended from India to Cyrene.

Within this vast and necessarily loose empire, religious sectarianism spread. It would be as impossible to describe a single unified religious system as being followed by all who were under the political rule of the Caliphate as it woud be to say that all Jews believed the same things. The Middle East was filled with a variety of religious systems, some with a Messianic hope, others based upon Chaldaic magic and astrology, and still others founded upon mysticism and Persian Zoroastrianism. All these left their mark on Judaism as well as on Islam. Most of this sectarianism was definitely linked with political ambitions and strong nationalist feelings. Religion and politics have never been more inextricably linked.

LEARNING AND THE KARAITES

IN THE eighth century a conflict which started over the problem of succession to the Exilarchate (the Exilarch was the head of the Jews in Babylonia) developed into a schism which

[1] Caliph means "Vicar of the Apostle of God" and was the title assumed by the head of the Arabian State.

began the medieval emphasis of Judaism upon philosophic learning. Tradition has it that Anan was in line for succession but that certain of the elders had reason to be suspicious of his orthodoxy. As a consequence they elected his brother Hananiah to the post. Anan went to the Caliph and protested the election. At the same time he made it plain that his followers not only recognized Mohammed as a prophet but that they also denied that the Talmud was the only authoritative basis for interpreting the scriptures. With the help he received from the Caliph, Anan was able to establish himself as the representative of a separate body of Jews.

Anan and his followers, who were called *Karaites*, went beyond their denial of the authority of the Talmud; they maintained that each man should read the Law and interpret it for himself. Among their number was a strong group of nationalists who refused to admit any of the universalist implications of the Messianic idea and agitated for the re-establishment of Palestine as the Holy Seat of Zion. For them all other facets of the Jewish faith were subordinated to their zeal for political independence. The Pharisaical doctrines which had become a part of the Talmud were rejected in favor of the long-buried ideas of the Sadducees. The Written Law was re-established as the primary authority, while the Oral Law, with all of its implications, was discarded. The Karaites (meaning readers) prayed for the rebuilding of the Temple and the abandonment of the synagogues, which they considered to be symbols of a defeated Israel.

The tendency of all branches of the Karaite movement was toward asceticism and rigid legal observances. They went back to the Deuteronomic code and reinstituted dietary, marriage and health laws which had long since ceased to be binding. Feast and fast days were multiplied in number and the regulations governing Sabbath work and activity were strictly enforced. The use of alcoholic beverages, condemned by Mohammed, was prohibited by the Karaites until Palestine should be freed from foreign domination and the Temple rebuilt. The Karaite schism had such a profound effect upon Judaism that until this day orthodox Jewish Law prohibits marriage with a Karaite.

Most of the rabbis teaching in the Babylonian schools until the time of the Karaites, not being particularly interested in an intellectual defense of the Jewish faith, were content to make legal deductions from the Oral and Written Law. The short spell of metaphysical speculation characterized by such men as Philo found little place in these schools. However, the challenge presented by the Karaite doctrine of individual exegesis of the scripture was taken up by the rabbis, who made a concerted effort to prove the heretics wrong by means of rationalistic apologetics. Utilizing the tools of analysis which Mohammedan theologians had borrowed from the Greeks, they attempted to show that the revealed truth of the Torah and the Talmud was not inconsistent with truth arrived at by human reason.

The introduction of philosophical theology into the tradition set the pattern for the development of Judaism through the Middle Ages and into modern times. Questions which had never before been of serious concern pushed themselves into the consciousness of the Jews. How is God omnipotent? If he is omnipotent why didn't he prevent Adam and Eve from eating the apple? How could Satan be evil if God created all things good? If God is omniscient why did he allow Job to suffer when he already knew the outcome? In addition to such theological questions as these, the Jewish philosophers began to wonder why their people were always under the heel of a conqueror while nations not possessing the Law lived in prosperity and health. The problems of history, morals and metaphysics were demanding some rational explanation and justification beyond the simple statement that God's will is inscrutable.

A mixture of Arabian Aristotelianism and neo-Platonism gave Jewish theologians their answers. The existence of God was not questioned, but the ability of man to see and understand his attributes was. God became less personal and more of a philosophic absolute. He was the source and ground of all being; his divine will (identical with Philo's *Logos*) created the world of sense experience and physical life. The Bible came to be looked upon as a book which presents the great philosophic truths in common symbolic language, without, however, contradicting in any way propositions which validate themselves to man's rational faculties. This concept obviously necessitated an allegorical interpretation of many of the Biblical passages and in some cases a complete retranslation. Thus were many of the traditional tenets of Judaism virtually explained away. Reason, rather than revelation, had now become the highest court of appeal.

MAIMONIDES

ALTHOUGH the movement toward rationalistic theology started in the Babylonian schools, the center of intellectual and religious Jewry soon shifted from East to West. The greatest of the Jewish philosophers, Moses ben Maimon, known as Maimonides (1135-1204), was born in Spain and spent most of his life in Egypt. He was a thoroughgoing Aristotelian, maintaining that a religious faith which was not rationally grounded was worthless. In his *Mishneh Torah* he rationalized the principal teachings of the Talmud, while his *Guide to the Perplexed* furnished an Aristotelian basis for Jewish faith.

Following Aristotle, Maimonides proves the existence of God by causal analysis. All things are a mixture of actuality and potentiality. An acorn is actually an acorn, but it is also potentially an oak tree. If all things can be explained this way, then it must also be true that before all potentiality there is some actuality. Before the oak there is an actual acorn, and before the acorn there is an actual seed. There must, then, be an actuality which is both eternal and prior to all things. This is Aristotle's prime mover or first cause, the fundamental principle of the whole world. It is complete within itself, potentially nothing, utterly simple, incorporeal and absolute. It is the final and supreme substance, or God. On this basis the existence of God is proved from the nature of the phenomenal world, and no revelation is required.

But how was this philosophic abstraction to be identified with the Old Testament picture of God as a gigantic personal being: the God who walked in the cool of the evening with Adam and Eve—who expressed fear when he found that all the peoples of the earth spoke the same tongue—and who took an active partisan stand in the affairs of history? Such a God could hardly be confused with the austere pure actuality of Aristotelian logic. Maimonides solved the problem by using the same device Philo had. In such parts the Bible was allegorical, its true meaning being concealed beneath the concrete imagery of folklore. For Maimonides the only thing that could be said of God is that he is perfect and totally unlike anything in phenomenal experience. Any attempted description of God's positive attributes results merely in a man-made image of man. Such a subjective anthropomorphic concept of God must never be taken as a literal representation of the divine. The closest man's finite language can come to a true description is the simple statement that God, in his unity and perfection, exists. This does not mean that concrete verbal images cannot be used in worship and prayer, but it does mean that their fictional character must be recognized lest they become idols of man's own creation.

In all Maimonides's work the influences of Talmudic Judaism, Arabian science and Aristotelian philosophy can be discerned. After proving the existence of God he went on to describe the nature of medicine, mathematics and astronomy. The world of sense experience as revealed by science and philosophy gave further confirmation to Maimonides's faith in the ultimate goodness of God's creation. The evil which obviously exists cannot be blamed on God; rather, it is the result of the defective matter with which he must work. This is not a permanent state, however, for God has implanted in man the power to overcome evil with rationality and moral goodness. The peak of "active intelligence" was reached in the prophets and it is for each man to follow in their steps, in loving devotion to the Torah. Maimonides's synthesis, which was aimed at raising Judaism to the highest philosophic level, has remained to this day the backbone of rationalistic Jewish philosophy.

THE KABBALA

In both Eastern and Western religious traditions rationalism has always existed side by side with nonrational mysticism. In Judaism such mystical expression is found in the Kabbala movement, which began in the early years of the Christian era. The increasing importance of this movement was coincident with the spread of the teachings of Maimonides and their acceptance by the orthodox. The medieval founder of the Kabbala was Isaac the Blind, who flourished about the end of the twelfth century and the beginning of the thirteenth. The most famous publication of the group was a book by Moses de Leon entitled *Zohar*, which was an esoteric and mystical commentary on the Pentateuch.

The Kabbala doctrine, given impetus by Isaac the Blind and ultimately adopted and accorded a certain degree of authority by Nahmonides (1195-1270), one of the greatest of the medieval Talmudists, was based in neo-Platonism. It started from the assumption that God was above and beyond all things, even beyond existence and thought. Therefore, it maintained, it cannot even be said of God that he exists, and certainly it cannot be said that he thinks, wills or acts. All such categories are human and imply restriction or limitation upon his unthinkable absoluteness. The only title the Kabbalist could give God was *En-Sof*, which in Hebrew means eternal. Then the question arose, if the En-Sof is so transcendent and inconceivable, how can he have relations with the world of men and history? Indeed, how can this obviously imperfect and finite world have been created at all by the infinite and perfect En-Sof?

To furnish acceptable answers to such problems as these, the Kabbalists constructed an entirely different theory of creation. God must not be looked upon, they felt, as the immediate cause of the world. (At this point Maimonides was considered to be in error.) The perfect and complete En-Sof is not active; he does, however, radiate, or emanate, a spiritual substance which is not himself, but which in some ways partakes of his infinity. This substance, which is called *Sefira*, then radiates a second, which in turn produces a third and so on until the number of ten is reached. These the Kabbala calls the Ten Sefiroth. It is then supposed that by means of these forces or Sefiroth the phenomenal world comes into existence. The world of man's experience is the last of a series of worlds which the Sefiroth have created; all things of sense experience are simply copies of the original forms which exist in the higher worlds. Thus everything in this lowest of worlds has meaning and purpose only when related to the higher world.

Man himself is the epitome of all the various worlds. His soul is divided into animal (the lowest state), moral (the intermediary), and finally pure spiritual intelligence. Because of the privilege he enjoys of occupying a position both above the world and of the world, he is in immediate contact with all of the Sefiroth. His duty is to overcome the fear which characterizes this world, rise to the next, which is conditioned love, and finally to achieve oneness with God in pure and perfect love. On the side of knowledge, he is to proceed from reflection to intuition and finally to pure and perfect contemplation. Through both of these processes, which are actually two sides of one ascent, man leaves the world behind and returns to the undifferentiated absolute source of all being.

This general structure has been utilized by mystics of all religious traditions, but the Kabbalists added certain factors which made it peculiarly Jewish. They reinterpreted the Bible, saying that whenever it was recorded that God spoke, it really meant that the Sefiroth was in physical form, walking and talking with men. Further, they contended that Israel had been chosen by the Sefiroth to be the vehicle of revelation to all men; consequently it was to them, and only them, that the true Law and ceremony had been given. Moreover, the deep spiritual significance of this ceremonial Law could be caught only by the pure intelligence of pious men. The Temple, with its ritual and sacrifice, was in reality a copy of the heavenly Temple; each event in its long career, even its destruction, had an abiding spiritual meaning which gave insight into the nature of the worlds above. All prayers and worship forms, even to the raising of ten fingers in the priestly blessing, were signs of the hidden secrets entrusted to Judaism. Thus, while the philosophical theologians were busily explaining away many of the ancient practices and beliefs of Judaism, the Kabbalists were giving them increased importance through mystical interpretation.

Much popular folklore and superstition was included in the Kabbalistic system. The rather limited doctrine of immortality which Maimonides's Aristotelianism allowed had more appeal for the philosopher than for the ordinary member of the synagogue congregation. Kabbalist teaching included the idea that all souls had been created at the beginning of this world and that they were destined to spend a certain amount of time in physical form before being freed for entrance into the spiritual world of the Sefiroth. Some men, however, allowed their thoughts and actions to be bound to this earth. They were doomed to rebirth and could never attain that unity with God which was possible for the righteous. This idea is reminiscent of the ancient Jewish doctrine of retribution. It also satisfactorily explained to orthodox Jews why some men who were both rich and corrupt seemed to escape just punishment. Secret symbols and even amulets came into use in an effort to ward off evil, achieve purity, and thus be saved from transmigration. Such beliefs and practices resulted in an intermingling of magic and religious faith.

Closely connected with the idea of transmigration is the Kabbalist attitude toward the Messiah. In the articles of faith derived from the Talmud by Maimonides and his fellow philosophers, emphasis was always placed upon the eventual coming of the Messiah and the consequent resurrection of the Jewish people. It was difficult to explain, however, why the Messiah had not yet arrived, and equally difficult to prophesy the time when he could be expected. The Kabbalists contended that the soul of the Messiah had been created at the beginning of the world, but that he could not enter the sphere of men until every created soul had dwelt in a human body for its appointed length of time. This condition seemed to postpone his coming indefinitely because of the innumerable sinners doomed to repeated incarnations, and most Kabbalists were incapable of leaving the future so open. On the basis of some calculations found in the *Zohar* they predicted that the end of the current age and the beginning of the Golden Age would occur in either 1648 or 1666. Indeed, the later followers of Kabbala considered Isaac the Blind to be the Ephramite

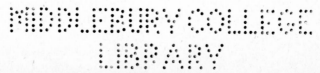

Messiah who, according to prophecy, was the herald of the approaching Davidic Messiah.

CONFUSION AND PERSECUTION

BY THE end of the Middle Ages the people of Israel had spread throughout the continent of Europe, establishing their synagogues and holding orthodox services wherever ten believers could meet. The same intellectual influences which swept through the Christian academies became a part of their religious culture. Arabian science and Aristotle were introduced to the Christians by way of Jewish scholars and rabbis. But like the Christians, neither they nor their congregations could agree on doctrinal and philosophic issues. Fifty years after the death of Maimonides there were three separate factions within Judaism: the philosophic rationalists, who followed the course established by Philo and Maimonides; the Kabbalists, who had absorbed popular superstition and neo-Platonism; and finally the rigid Talmudists, who cared for neither philosophy nor mysticism but contented themselves with literal deductions from the Talmud. The passage of time only seemed to solidify the opposition of these groups toward each other, the result being a very poor intellectual climate indeed for original research and creative thought.

These internal dissensions were intensified by consistent persecution from the dominant Christian church. Official papal commands such as that issued in 1415 by Benedict prohibited the Jews from the study of the Talmud and from any direct intercourse with Christians. In many places they were denied their civil rights in the courts and were barred from holding public office. Certain trades were closed to them by law, and many a Christian ruler forced the Jews in his realm to attend at least three Christian services each year. To escape

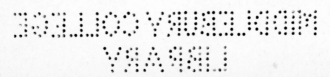

such treatment the Jews became wanderers over the face of Europe, entirely stripped of political power, subject to economic discrimination, and suffering from internal insecurities caused by the conflicting interpretations of their heritage in the Torah.

19

AFTER THE GHETTO

HAVING been pushed both physically and spiritually into isolated ghettos by the triumphant Christians of the Middle Ages, the Jews of Europe entered the modern era almost completely demoralized. The greatest number of their rabbis had given up even the most elementary Talmudic learning for a belief in sorcery and the power of amulets. Science, art, the impressive philosophic tradition begun by Maimonides, all languished. In many cases even the Law was given only lip service, with the actions of the people becoming consequently less and less controlled. From time to time, there were reports of various Messiahs who were followed by large groups of Jews, but even these movements had little religious vitality.

MOSES MENDELSSOHN

THE renaissance of Judaism started in Italy, Holland and Germany at about the same time that Humanism and the Reformation broke the unity of medieval Catholicism. But it was not until the days of Moses Mendelssohn (1728-1786), a learned German Jew, that traditional Judaism took on new garb for its modern career. Mendelssohn had sound training in both Maimonides and the Talmud. He was a philosophic writer of equal stature with his close friend, Gotthold Lessing, yet he was a "Jew of Judaism" from the depths of his being.

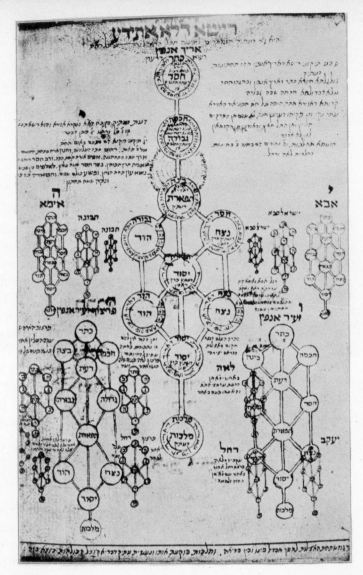

A page of Kabbalistic diagrams with the "sacred tree" of the Sephiroth. Reading from top to bottom, the ten spheres are Crown of mercy, Severity, Beauty, Glory-victory, Foundation, Glory-victory, Foundation, Kingdom. The central pattern is repeated with variations along the sides.

After the Exposition of the Law, the scroll is held aloft face up so that all may see it. The worshipers sing a benediction. (*Courtesy Bush Collection of Religion and Culture.*)

This picture of the Torah scroll shows the mantle, silver bells, pointers and the parchment scroll of the Pentateuch in Hebrew. This is an eighteenth-century scroll made in Smyrna.

Throughout his active life he was not only venerated by the Jewish community but respected by Christian philosophers as well. In many ways Mendelssohn has become in Jewish history the symbol of the emancipation from the ghetto. More importantly, however, he formulated some of the basic concepts of contemporary Judaism.

According to Mendelssohn, Judaism is not a system of revealed articles of faith. Whatever external truths it possesses are the eternal truths of all human religion. Judaism cannot claim sole possession of specific dogmas which must be accepted as final. Reason, an instrument common to all men, is to be the basis for the understanding and formulation of belief, an area in which revelation is unacceptable since God reveals himself in "nature and events, but never in words or written characters." Nevertheless, according to Mendelssohn, the Law is a revelation of what men should do though not what they should believe. It was revealed to a priestly nation (Israel), which then was morally bound to propagate throughout the world the way of life it taught. To philosophy and reason was left the task of establishing sound belief.

Interpreted in this way Judaism was not so much a religion, considered in the traditional sense, as it was a structure of "revealed legislation." The Jews, now dispersed through the Western world, were thus relieved of all their old purely national commandments which had depended for their existence upon the operations of a Jewish state. Such laws, said Mendelssohn, had been obsolete since the destruction of the Temple. Because following God's moral commandments was an entirely individual matter, the Jews need never again base their religious integrity in political unity. Thus emancipated, they could and should become good Frenchmen, good Germans, good Russians, and good Italians without compromising their essential loyalty to Judaism; for to be constant in the spiritual heritage of Israel did not imply inconstancy with regard to civic duties and obligations imposed by a foreign power. Indeed, Jews were no longer to consider themselves as foreigners resident in an alien land; rather, they were to be as much a part of the nation as any other person or group. But they should always remember that the "personal commandments, duties which were imposed on a son of Israel, without any consideration of the Temple service or landed property in Palestine, must be observed until it shall please the Most High to make our conscience easy by loudly and openly proclaiming their abrogation."

LIBERTY AND REFORM

THROUGHOUT Europe and the expanding new nation in America, the Jews emerged from the ghettos and took their places with the general population. The religious wars touched off by the Reformation culminated in the wide acceptance of a principle of religious liberty. State governments came to recognize the necessity for permitting Catholics, Protestants and Jews the free exercise of their respective consciences. Jews and the various Christian sects alike were accorded full legal rights and the benefits of complete national citizenship.

However, to achieve their assimilation into modern culture, many changes had to be made in the ancient tradition of Judaism. One of the primary cementing forces which had held the Jewish community together all through the years of wandering and persecution was their faith in the eventual coming of the Messiah and the re-establishment of the holy state in Palestine. Under the Reform Movement, which was begun in the early part of the nineteenth century by Israel Jacobson (1768-1828), such beliefs had to be reinterpreted or discarded, for to maintain them not only would be unpatriotic, but also would ultimately lead to the exclusiveness which had characterized the ghetto. The Reform leaders consequently taught that be-

lief in a personal Messiah was no longer valid: the belief in the
Messiah really meant a hope that soon or late all of mankind
would accept ethical monotheism as their saving faith. When
this should happen an age of peace and justice—the true Messianic age—would be ushered in. Toward this end the Jews of
the world should bend their efforts.

By such a process of reinterpretation and discard, Reform
Judaism, like many Protestant sects, became a creed rather
than a structure of law. Indeed, many emancipated Jews assumed that there was no essential difference between Judaism
and Christianity except the belief in the Messiahship of Jesus.
The Talmud and the Torah began to lose their significance,
and many of the formerly obligatory ceremonial laws fell
into disuse. Rabbi Holdheim, a radical reformer in Germany,
held that marriage between Jews and persons of other persuasions was not only permissible, but advisable. The ancient
Jewish laws of marriage, divorce, circumcision, diet and even
in some cases the Sabbath, were abandoned in favor of a
wholehearted acceptance of the mores of modern society. The
foundation of the most radical reformers is seen in the plat-
form of the Frankfort Society issued in 1843:

> We recognize the possibility of unlimited development in the
> Mosaic religion. The collection of controversies and prescriptions
> commonly designated by the name Talmud possess for us no au-
> thority from either the doctrinal or the practical standpoint. A
> Messiah who is to lead back the Israelites to the land of Palestine
> is neither expected nor desired by us; we know no fatherland but
> that to which we belong by birth or citizenship.

The popularity of Reform Judaism was by no means general throughout Europe and America. To a large group of
Jews the loss of national consciousness, of Talmudic authority, and of the Messianic hope seemed the end of true Judaism
and a complete capitulation to secularism and Christianity.

Many among them, such as Rabbi Geiger, wished to avail themselves of modern scholarship and the benefits accruing to those who lived within the framework of modern culture, without giving up the traditional faith. From this group came a more modified but nevertheless Reform type of Judaism. On the other hand, there developed a "conservative" Judaism which attempted to retain the validity of the Torah and the Talmud, at the same time allowing for freedom of individual interpretation. For them the new age in which Judaism was to establish itself presented a challenge, a test of vitality and strength. The attitude of all but the most radical assimilationists and reformers is cogently expressed by S. R. Hirsch:

> I bless emancipation if Israel does not regard it as the goal of its task, but only as a new condition of its mission, and as a new trial, much severer than the trial of oppression; but I should grieve if Israel understood itself so little, and had so little comprehension of its own spirit that it would welcome emancipation as the end of the Galut and the highest goal of its historic mission.[1]

SECTION SUMMARY

IT is a long way from Judaism's beginnings in primitive polytheism and nature worship to its present-day philosophical and religious sophistication. As a people the Jews have gone through the most harrowing persecutions imaginable, and yet, in large part, they have stood by the distinctive beliefs separating them from the other groups which have come to comprise Western civilization. Within Jewish history can be found the extremes of magical practice, ethical idealism and philosophic monotheism, but with all its divergencies and historical ac-

[1] Quoted from *The Nineteen Letters of Ben Uziel* in S. W. Baron, *A Social and Religious History of the Jews* (New York: Columbia University Press, 1937), Vol. II, p. 258.

cidents, the fundamental structure of Judaism has remained unchanged since the time of the return from Babylon.

Judaism has been and continues to remain a religion of history. Yahweh has always had a direct regard for men's actions and for the events which move nations and establish kings. From the earliest days of Moses, the Jews have derived from a supernatural source the rules governing their everyday lives. Moreover, they have been taught to interpret the march of history as a determined course which will result in the fulfillment of God's promises and the establishment of peace and justice on earth. Consequently the Jews have never been able to conceive of historic progress or retrogression as meaningless meanderings of meaningless men. From the Law and the Prophets to the rabbis and the mystics, life is freighted with cosmic significance and moves toward a cosmic goal. The goal has been seen in different terms in different stages of development, and with clear or clouded vision; but the religious Jew has never lost sight of the fact that a goal exists. Judaism has ever been unwilling to be absorbed by other religions, and for the most part it has never been completely able to accept non-Semitic converts as true fellow-religionists. The meaning of Jewish religion is found in the history of the Jewish people.

As the mother of Christianity and Mohammedanism, Judaism has contributed both its scripture and its sense of historic destiny. In both cases the daughter religions still feed upon the religious vitality and moral insight of those ancient men who declared God to be one and without equal. The two offspring are today quite different from the parent, but through them the numerically insignificant Jews have exercised the most pervasive force in Western civilization. Their fellow creators of the West, the Greeks, have lived only in spirit, whereas the Hebrews have lived in fact as well.

The internal controversy between those who saw in Judaism a universal religion and those who saw a narrow, particular religion has never been decided. It was during the Hellenistic period that universalism had its greatest chance for success, but the creation of a defensive orthodoxy killed the vision. Christianity became the universal religion of the West, and the Jews of Judaism retired from the evangelistic battle. As we have seen, however, this retirement did not lead to death, although it did often result in rather sterile and arid legal deductions. Judaism's consciousness of historic mission kept it alive through the excesses of rationalism, mysticism and legalism. At times it has led to arrogance and a smug sense of superiority, but such movements have always been counterbalanced by the deep-seated sense of humility which has remained an important part of Jewish faith and practice.

From Old Testament times to the present, the main tradition of Judaism has emphasized an essentially this-worldly conception of salvation. To be saved is the fruit of faithfully keeping the laws of God which were established in the original covenant and handed down by written and spoken word. God has given man freedom to choose; to make the right choice is to be saved. Although God is merciful and generous in his forgiveness, he nevertheless demands rigorous observance of the Law. Such achievement is possible within this life, and so is salvation. Maimonides gives classic expression to this concept of earthly salvation in the following words: [2]

Not immortality, but the power to win eternal life through the knowledge and the love of God is implanted in the human soul. If it has the ability to free itself from the bondage of the senses and by means of the knowledge of God to lift itself to the highest morality and the purest thinking, then it has attained divine bliss, true immortality, and it enters the realm of the eternal Spirit together with the angels. If it sinks into the sensuousness of earthly existence, then it is cut off from eternal life; it suffers annihila-

[2] Quoted by K. Kohler, *Jewish Theology* (New York: Macmillan, 1928), pp. 284-85.

tion like the beast. In reality this life eternal is not the future, but is already potentially present and invariably at hand in the spirit of man himself, with its constant striving toward the highest. When the rabbis speak of paradise and hell, describing vividly the delights of the one and the torments of the other, these are only metaphors for the agony of sin and the happiness of virtue. True piety serves God neither from fear of punishment nor from desire for reward, as servants obey their master, but from pure love of God and truth. Thus the saying of Ben Azai is verified, "The reward of a good deed is the good deed itself." Only children need bribes and threats to be trained to morality. Thus religion trains mankind. The people who cannot penetrate into the kernel need the shell, the external means of threats and promises.

In keeping with this feeling for "eternal life in the present," Judaism has always emphasized the fact that God's purposes are realized through and within history. The very minute detail of the six hundred and thirteen laws in the Pentateuch indicates the cosmic importance of each act in man's life; for to be moral, to follow the law, is to aid in the fulfillment of historical destiny. However, Judaism does not conceive this to be a simple individual decision. Rather, it is related to the status of the entire nation. Each Jew is in a very real way responsible for the actions of all Jews, since the aims and goals of the whole transcend the desires of the individual. Moreover, the eternal life of the nation far outweighs the importance of individual immortality or resurrection. For this reason Judaism emphasizes the idea of "a chosen pepole" rather than the idea of "a chosen person."

Having lost their homeland through the peculiar vicissitudes of history, the Jews have become a nation without a state. Consequently they have had to divorce their religious institutions from the territory in which they grew and from the form of government which grew with them. Thus the Jewish faith has been spiritualized and intellectualized to a much

[309]

greater extent than other religions which have lived solely in their own homelands. Rather than resulting in a loss of national character, this spiritualization has extended the nationalism of Judaism beyond the bounds of territorial states. Throughout his wanderings, the pious Jew has remained a citizen of two nations: the nation of his birth and the nation of his spiritual heritage. The recent re-establishment of the Jewish state in Palestine by the United Nations cannot radically affect this result of such a long development. Judaism is significantly outstanding among the world's religions because it has been able to combine particularity with universalism in a meaningful pattern of devotion and action.

V

CHRISTIANITY

20

THE CHRISTIAN GOSPEL

THE cultural heritage of Jesus of Nazareth was much broader than Judaism. The world in which he lived was extremely cosmopolitan, containing amazing crosscurrents of thought and belief. Thus the Christian faith, with all its institutional and theological variations, was born out of not only Jewish religious consciousness but also Greek mystery religions, speculative philosophy and Roman conceptions of law and organization. The New Testament, which contains the basic documents of the new faith, was composed over a period of at least one hundred and fifty years. It embodies such a variety of religious notions that later ages have found within its pages support for innumerable sects and doctrines. All those, however, which could justifiably call themselves Christian have maintained one common principle: God entered history in the person of Jesus, in whose life and teaching man has been given the perfect revelation. On the meaning and interpretation of this tenet there has never yet been agreement within the Christian community.

THE RESURRECTION FAITH

ALTHOUGH in his preaching Jesus was probably conscious of a divine mission it is highly doubtful that he shared the conviction of his followers regarding his messiahship. Moreover, it is probable that faith in Jesus as the Christ (the Messiah) did not spring up until after the crucifixion. Whether the disciples stayed in Jerusalem or returned to their former occupations in Palestine is not known, but shortly after the crucifixion there spread among them the belief that Jesus was not dead. For many this meant a complete revision of their idea of messiahship. The traditional interpretation of the Messiah as a political leader who would eject all conquering tyrants and establish a prosperous and free Jewish theocracy was changed to a conception of a transcendental Messiah residing in heaven. The apocalyptic imagery which had become so important to the Jews since the time of Daniel was immediately taken over as suitable to the Messianic Jesus. So adorned, Jesus' message concerning the speedy coming of the Kingdom gained much wider popular support.

The antinationalistic emphasis of the resurrection believers was quite foreign to the main body of Judaism. Jesus had paid no real attention to the problem of organization, and his activities were never directed toward the development of a group which would wield powerful influence over the affairs of state. This very lack gave further support to the belief that the end of historical time was at hand; to have built an organization in such circumstances would have denied faith in the coming of the Great Day. Although Jesus, like the prophets before him, preached love, righteousness and justice, he made no direct attack upon war, slavery or the maldistribution of wealth. Such unconcern for the political, organizational and economic welfare of the people aroused protest from the traditional Jews, but it also served as confirmation of the apocalyptic faith.

Throughout the major portions of the New Testament there is little criticism of Rome. Indeed, Paul is credited with describing Rome as being "ordained of God," and in the Gospels and Acts there is an open attempt to exonerate the Romans from any complicity in the crucifixion of Jesus. However one might explain these facts, it is nevertheless true that they tended to create additional friction with the orthodox Jews, for to side with Rome, the conqueror, meant acceding to and abetting the extermination of a kind of Judaism which had a large number of zealous followers. On the other hand, such a treatment of Rome resulted in a softening of attitude toward Rome on the part of those who could see nothing but annihilation in resistance to the conqueror. For this group the resurrection faith, with its acceptance of the political status quo and its claim of being the fulfillment of the long history of the Jews, seemed to be the answer to both temporal and transcendent problems. It is easy to see why the sect prospered, and just as easy to see why it was so cordially hated.

CONFLICT WITH STOICISM AND THE GREEK MYSTERIES

THE new faith in Christ Jesus was forced to combat not only Judaism but also the philosophic and religious societies generated by the thinkers and pietists of Greece. Stoicism, a self-confessed materialist philosophy founded by Zeno about 308 B.C., was the outgrowth of Greek science and the product of the general deterioration of Greco-Roman culture. For the Stoic the universe is a finite sphere existing in infinite space. This totality (or cosmos) is living and possessed of intelligence, and it is to these characteristics that man refers when he speaks of God. God is that form of matter (fire) which is diffused throughout all things; it gives all things their special attributes, and it also moves them and holds them together. In short, God is not a transcendent being existing in some fashion outside the created world; rather, it is immanent, it is responsible for all existence.

Although the Stoics were interested in propagating their materialistic metaphysics, they were principally moral teachers. They carried a mental picture of an ideal wise man—not unlike a composite of Socrates and Antisthenes—who was free of all emotional involvement in the affairs of this world. To be virtuous or wise (the terms are synonymous in Stoicism) is to be entirely independent and detached from all concern for wealth, health or pleasure; the conditions of earthly existence are matters of complete indifference. The only thing that really counts is obedience or disobedience to world law, and world law is expressed in human nature by reason. To be happy is to be virtuous; to be virtuous is to be rational.

This ethical teaching was incorporated into the Stoic metaphysic by identifying the rational spirit with the unifying cosmic matter, God or Fire. The resulting world appears to be one vast closed system with each part tending toward its own particular perfection. All evil exists for the sake of good, and man's true freedom is found in his choice of reasonableness over passionate unreason. "Man must live his life in accordance with nature," by which is meant in accordance with his rational soul, the highest expression of his humanness.

The religious significance of Stoicism is found in its elevation of duty to the level of divine obligation. To live "according to nature" is to live according to God. To sin is to deny reason and the duties which moral reason imposes upon the individual. In the performance of duty there is no matter of degree: there is only good or bad, wise or unwise. All virtuous actions are of the same degree, and none takes primacy over another. The same is true of evil actions. God, who exists in all men, is constantly pressing for justice and benevolence. The good man gives to each of his brothers his due while at the same time offering unbounded good will and sympathetic understanding to all. Moral reason demands that everyone be treated with forgiving respect, with gentleness and liberal charity, and with courage and honor. The noble man, the wise man, the good man is in, yet not of, the world. His duties are rigorous, his thought is pious, and his good will is boundless.

Although Stoicism was admittedly a religious philosophy, its pantheistic piety was hardly material for popular consumption. The Stoic preacher with his poor clothing and his doctrine of the self-sufficiency of virtue had a difficult time with those who were wedded to the worship of particular deities. The vast majority of the Greek people looked for help and salvation from some force outside themselves rather than from within. In the popular mind at least, man could not lift himself by his own bootstraps, and "worship in the mind" was poor substitution for the rites and services directed toward specific and powerful deities. The Hellenistic mystery religions of Attis, Isis, Mithras and Osiris were far more attractive than the intellectualizations of Stoicism.

These mystery religions, which began as primitive nature rites, had become spiritualized by the time Christianity arose. They were largely built around a secret body of esoteric revelation and rites of purification. The elaborate initiation required of the novice introduced truth, usually in the form of an incarnate god, and promised both deliverance from the despair of this world and the achievement of blissful immortality. Like Stoicism, the mysteries were essentially individualistic. But this individualism was an individualism of the cult in the sense that the esoteric knowledge was shared by only a few and could not be the common property of all who would read. Further, the cultus practiced certain sacramental rites which tended to bind the worshipers together in a secret communion from which the uninitiated were excluded.

Aside from its sacred doctrine and its promise of immortality, the mysteries were filled with mystical experiences which brought about a regeneration of the individual. The sacraments were most often interpreted as the eating of the deity and the consequent deification of the worshiper. The holy substance was constantly becoming incarnate in the things of this world for the benefit of man. The magical practices resulting from such a conception permeated the mysteries and encouraged their borrowing from Babylonian astrology and Egyptian folklore. For the most part the mysteries expressed the desire for holiness and salvation from guilt rather than the search after righteousness. The gods of the cults were subject to magical manipulation; they bore little resemblance to the stern and other-worldly Yahweh. Whereas mystical absorption into the divine was the rare occurrence in Judaism, it became standard practice in the Greek mysteries. Nevertheless, the eschatology of Judaism and the eschatology of the mysteries drank from the same oriental source, so it is not surprising that there were elements common to both.

Although the Christian sect was officially opposed to both the Greek mysteries and Stoicism, it borrowed a great deal from them. Much of the sacerdotal practice of the early Church could hardly be distinguished from the type of worship found in the mysteries. And from Stoicism, Christians gained a Greek vocabulary for their ethical concerns as well as reinforcement for their traditional Jewish emphasis upon discipline of the will and the search for righteousness. The average pagan of these early centuries could find included in Christianity most of the elements which appealed to him in both Stoicism and the mysteries.

PAUL

HAD it not been for Paul, the Christian sect would probably have developed into a half-Jewish, half-Greek mystery religion. Paul was born a Jew and studied under the most rigid rabbinical influences, yet he was also a citizen of Hellenistic Tarsus with its crosscurrents of religious and philosophic speculation. As we have seen, Paul's pre-Christian career found him a zealous defender of traditional Judaism against all seeming deviations. In spite of his Greek environment Paul was utterly convinced of the divine character of the revelation given to the Hebrews, and from this conviction no amount of glamour or drama inherent in the Greek mysteries could sway him. To this strong Jewish background, however, he added a certain mysticism and an understanding of the person of Jesus that was at least partially Greek.

The earliest followers of Jesus had generally maintained that he became the Messiah, or *Christos*, the Greek equivalent, at the time of his resurrection. Although Paul considered the resurrection an important proof of the messiahship, he placed his major faith in an experiential meeting with Jesus as a risen heavenly figure. Jesus was not a mere man who had been sent of God; rather, he was a heavenly figure who had come to earth, lived among men, and had then been resurrected to sit again with God. The career of the carpenter of Nazareth did not begin with his birth, it began with God at the origin of all things. In Paul's own words Jesus was "the first-born of all creation" who gave up his heavenly riches and "on your account became poor," poor in that he "emptied himself . . . and was found in fashion as a man." In one place Paul even refers to Jesus as having once "existed in the form of God." Thus does Jesus as the Christ become Jesus Christ, and often Paul calls him simply Christ.

In maintaining this doctrine of the "pre-existent Christ" Paul leaves his Jewish tradition for a conception essentially Greek. The universe was not created by God, but rather God created Christ, and Christ then became responsible for all else.

. . . for in him were all things created, in the heavens and upon the earth, things visible and things invisible, whether thrones or dominions or principalities or powers; all things have been created through him, and unto him.

(Colossians 1:16)

[319]

Clearly, Paul gave the historic figure Jesus much less emphasis than the heavenly first-born Christ. Whether or not he actually deified Jesus and thereby broke with the strict monotheism of the Hebrew tradition cannot be settled on the basis of the extant evidence. Apparently he himself could not make up his mind on this point.

The death of Jesus was interpreted by Paul in the typical sacrificial terms of Judaism. In some places the death of Jesus is considered to have vicarious efficacy: "Our Lord Jesus Christ gave himself for our sins that he might deliver us from this present evil age" (Galatians 1:3-4). This idea of vicarious atonement receives little by way of further explanation. Somehow, Paul thought, the destruction of the earthly Christ took away the sins of the world and made possible the advent of a new age. On the other hand, the death of Jesus is often referred to as the sacrifice which God was willing to make in order to shock his people into a recognition of his love, mercy and righteousness. The magnitude of the sacrifice was to bring all men to their knees in repentance for their sins. "Ye do not belong to yourselves, for ye were bought with a price" (I Corinthians 6:19).

Whatever interpretation Paul places on the death of Jesus, he is convinced that the cross is no substitute for the sinner's own conversion of heart. In order to be redeemed, man must have faith, he says—faith in Christ and him crucified. This is the new way of salvation, the way which is to take precedence over adherence to the old Mosaic Law. The death of Jesus ushers in the new age of justification by faith rather than works. The love of God, the forgiveness of God, the power and majesty of God are all to be seen in his sacrificial act. To take advantage of this new approach to the Throne of Grace, faith in Jesus Christ as Lord and Redeemer is mandatory. By such faith man is freed from his bondage to sin and is no longer under the wrath and condemnation of God. A new relationship exists between God and man: in Christ, God and his creatures are reconciled.

Justification, however, is not the same as salvation. Faith in "Jesus Christ as Lord and Master" automatically reconciles the sinner with God, but the final attainment of salvation will come only with the second appearance of Christ on earth. Like the other early Christians, Paul believes the Golden Age to be close at hand, but man, he says, has no way of knowing the exact time. In the meantime, each justified person is to engage himself in a moral struggle on the side of righteousness. Pauline theology thus tries to blend that joyous personal experience of the divine with which the Greek mysteries are primarily concerned with the rigorous ethical demands of his own prophetic inheritance.

Once man finds himself wholly committed to Christ Jesus, he recognizes a new power in his soul. He is from this time on capable of performing good actions; and further, he is much more likely to win at least partial success over his tendency to sin. Paul, like other Jews, was bound to a doctrine of original sin. This is the same sin which caused the expulsion of Adam from the Garden of Eden, and it has been transmitted from man to man in the form of a "depraved" nature. The "old Adam" is in all men, and the "natural man" (i.e., man without Christ) is doomed to live in moral blindness and spiritual weakness. For Paul there is a kind of mystical identity of Adam with all mankind. It is the function of the "new Adam," or Jesus Christ, to break this identity and allow the spirit of man to rise to the heights of godliness. Thus Paul speaks of men being "in Christ," or of the justified as being "not in the flesh but in the Spirit," or that "it is no longer I that live, but Christ who lives within me." After justification there is a mystical identity with Christ rather than with Adam. But the identification is only partial: man is still subject to the sin which dwells within him. Nevertheless, the chances of ultimate victory in the moral struggle are now weighted most heavily on the side of God.

It is readily seen that Paul drew the major portion of his theology from his own personal experience. As a strict Pharisaical Jew he had tried with all the desperation of a fanatic to live up to the Oral and Written Law. But the more he tried, the more impossible such a life seemed to be. With his conversion to Christ, he surrendered his life and placed the burden of justification upon God. This surrender meant for him giving up willfulness—the same kind which had caused the fall of the original Adam—and thereby becoming a child of God living in conformity with his will, an admitted creature of his hand. "Wretched man that I am! Who shall deliver me from this body of death? I thank God that I am finding deliverance through Jesus Christ our Lord."

The radical individualism implicit in Paul's experience and theology gave rise to a highly spiritualized conception of the church. He, like the other early Christians, believed that Jesus Christ would very shortly return to earth. This belief, when coupled with his spiritual individualism, tended to make ecclesiastical organization insignificant. To be sure, he felt that there should be churches (i.e., assemblies) where groups of Christians could meet for instruction and a public profession of their faith in the Lord. But as far as we can tell from the record, the organization was to be not only simple but, in the general scale of values, relatively unimportant. The universal community of saints, spiritually conceived, took precedence over any mere social gathering of Christians. This spiritual body of saints, with Christ as its head, was to receive the mysterious knowledge of God's plan for the world which it was duty-bound to proclaim to all men.

Now I rejoice in my sufferings for your sake, and fill up on my part that which is lacking of the afflictions of Christ in my flesh

for his body's sake, which is the church; whereof I was made a
minister, according to the dispensation of God which was given
me to you-ward, to fulfil the word of God, even the mystery
which hath been hid for ages and generations: but now hath it
been manifested to his saints, to whom God was pleased to make
known what is the riches of the glory of this mystery among the
Gentiles, which is Christ in you, the hope of glory: whom we
proclaim, admonishing every man and teaching every man in all
wisdom, that we may present every man perfect in Christ; where-
unto I labor also, striving according to his working, which work-
eth in me mightily.

(Colossians 1:24-29)

Paul's dedication to the "body of Christ" took him on long
missionary trips through Asia Minor, Greece and Macedonia.
At first he was sent on these journeys by the church at Antioch, but as time went on he became more and more an independent evangelist, moving from city to city and supporting
himself by whatever means possible. In each place he would
go first to the synagogue and there describe his personal experience and interpret its meaning for Jews. His message took
the following pattern. The Messiah who was prophesied in the
Scriptures has arrived. He has been killed, it is true, but he is
very soon to return, ushering in the Golden Age. The old Law
has been superseded by faith in Christ. Although Paul was
probably given a hearing in most of the Diaspora synagogues,
his doctrine was rejected by the major portion of his hearers.
Nevertheless, out of many of the congregations small groups
formed which called themselves followers of Jesus. These
constituted the churches to which Paul wrote his famous letters outlining his conceptions and encouraging the converts
in their new faith. Since he believed these churches to be
directly guided by the Spirit of Christ, Paul could see little
need for the establishment of a set organizational structure.
As Paul and the other missionaries spread Christianity

throughout the Mediterranean basin, many questions of procedure developed. The most important concerned the relation of the Gentile Christians to Mosaic Law. Some of those within the Christian community felt that anyone who professed their faith and received baptism could be considered a member of the church. Others, who thought of Christianity as an extension of Judaism, demanded that all Gentile converts submit to circumcision and declare their allegiance to the Torah. In this controversy Paul stood directly opposed to the Judaizers, affirming his belief in Christ not only as a substitute for the Mosaic code, but more than that, as its fulfillment. The question was officially settled at the Jerusalem Assembly in 50 A.D. when James, the brother of Jesus, and Peter, one of his chief disciples, declared that ritual Law was not binding upon the Gentiles. This was the first step in the relatively short process of making Christianity a Gentile religion.

It is to be remembered that Diaspora Judaism of the first century was marked by a strong missionary zeal. Before Jesus went to the cross, the religious hunger of the Greco-Roman world had been satisfied by Stoicism, the mysteries and Judaism. Gentile converts to Judaism were an easy target for the Christian missionaries—much easier than the traditional Jew. Although Paul and his fellow travelers hoped for the ultimate conversion of the "Chosen People," their final aim was more universal. As time went on, Jewish Christianity became less and less important, and the Gentile groups gradually took over major control. To be sure, some Jews saw within the Christian faith a chance to obliterate the barriers between Jew and Gentile, but by far the greater number felt that they would lose more than they would gain in the transaction.

THE SYNOPTIC TRADITION

THE small churches established by Paul and others were largely disowned by the orthodox Jews and looked upon with disinterested contempt by the pagans. In order to keep alive the vision of Jesus Christ and offer the necessary facts regarding his life, there developed a biographical literature which covered the areas neglected in Paul's letters. The three earliest of these biographies are called in the New Testament Matthew, Mark and Luke. In all probability Mark was written first, somewhere around 70 A.D.; Matthew second, about 80 A.D.; and finally Luke, some ten years later. These Gospels were supplemented by the Gospel of John which was probably written between 95 and 100 A.D. All four purported to tell the story of the life of Jesus in such a way as to clarify his mission and his historical character, and it was upon these records that the early church was forced to depend. Paul had been less concerned with the historical Jesus than with a theological interpretation of the meaning of Christ. Such a concern was important for both missionaries and members of the various congregations, but the core of the new faith was still felt to be the supreme revelation received through an historical person. Without the Gospels, Christianity could easily have been absorbed into the unhistorical mysticism of the competing mystery religions.

All the Gospel records are written in the conviction that Jesus is the Son of God, that he is now raised from the dead, and that he will soon come again "on a cloud of glory to judge the quick and the dead." It is therefore impossible to look upon these records as being dispassionate objective biography. The followers of Jesus, like the followers of Gotama Buddha, elaborated upon the life of their master, meanwhile coloring the facts with specific interpretations to suit their purposes.

This is a very normal, natural situation. The real surprise would come if anyone had actually bothered to record a simple chronology of events. The life of the early Christian communities was too fraught with a sense of impending glory to permit much worry about historical accuracy. The Kingdom of God was at hand, history was rushing toward a speedy conclusion, and the Golden Age was to be experienced within this very lifetime.

Matthew, Mark and Luke, which form the Synoptic tradition, are the only important records of the life of Jesus. In these Gospels Jesus is represented as having been from the very beginning conscious of his Messianic mission. Although Mark starts his story from the beginning of Jesus' ministry, Matthew and Luke maintain that certain people were aware of the advent of the Messiah even before his birth. In Matthew, Joseph is told the good news during a dream; in Luke, the angel Gabriel announces the coming. Those people destined to be close to Jesus were not the only ones to know; the demons and evil spirits of popular belief were also aware that the arrival of the Messiah meant that their days were numbered.

Although the Christian communities were still predominantly Jewish, the Synoptic Gospels show considerable evidence that they were written for persons of Hellenistic learning and background. Mark, who was probably writing for what was almost entirely a Gentile church, constantly leaves out material that would be of interest only to the Jews. Moreover, he uses such phrases as "Son of God" which obviously had greater significance for the Greek than did the Hebrew term, "Messiah." Matthew, on the other hand, was writing for the Jews and therefore places the whole story of Jesus in terms of Old Testament prophecy. Jesus came, says Matthew many times, in order "that the scripture might be fulfilled." As might be expected, Matthew is never quite consistent on the question of who will enter the Kingdom: sometimes it is only the Jews, at other times only the Gentiles. No other Gospel shows quite so clearly the ambivalent nature of Christianity in its early years.

Luke, who was writing after Christianity had become a much larger movement, is frankly out to convince the Gentiles. Matthew's concern for Jewish prophecy is here dropped in Luke's effort to establish the universal validity of Christianity for all men regardless of their origins. Jesus is not simply a descendant of the line of David, but more importantly his ancestry is traced back to the first man of all men, Adam. In a sense Luke infers, if he does not say directly, that it was pure accident for Jesus to have been born a Jew rather than a Greek or even a Roman. Indeed, the whole story of the crucifixion is written in such a way as to relieve Pilate and the Roman courts of complicity and to place the blame squarely upon a perverted Jewish leadership. Whereas the earlier Gospels show a marked Pauline influence, Luke is content to tell the story of Jesus in terms of the emotional imagery that appealed to the Greeks and without any theological interpretation. Paul, and to a lesser degree Mark and Matthew, seek to prove the Christian claim by scripture and theology; Luke presents the biography of Jesus as the only important fact.

The rapidly growing Christian communities were dependent upon the Synoptics, the Pauline letters and other writings, such as I Clement and "The Shepherd of Hermes," which were not accepted when the New Testament was finally assembled. The emphasis of Paul and others upon mystical salvation and the transcendental nature of Christ was bound to appeal to the mystery cultists of the Hellenistic world. As the devotees of the mysteries entered the Christian communities, heresies of one kind and another developed; specifically, there was an attempt to turn Christianity into a speculative system. By the end of the first century the Gentiles far outnumbered the Jews in the movement, and they brought with them their own categories of thought and their own special religious interest. This general syncretistic tendency served to introduce into Christianity a body of variegated beliefs which usually goes under the name of *Gnosticism*.

THE FOURTH GOSPEL

THE Fourth Gospel, which tradition assigns to John, was written at this time. Much of it is an attempt to meet the challenge of Gnosticism while at the same time preserving the mystical character of the early tradition. In John's hands Christianity becomes firmly anchored in the historicity of Jesus, yet his interpretation of Jesus successfully meets the religious needs of his Hellenistic brethren. To accomplish this end John had to reject the Jewish apocalyptic ideas of his predecessors and turn to the philosophic categories developed by Philo and popularized by the Stoics.

In general, Greek secular thought had raised reason (*Logos*) to be the ultimate principle of the universe. Being a monotheistic Jew, Philo had refused to equate reason with God, but he had established reason as the effective cause of all things temporal. The *Logos* was subordinate to God who, in Philo's thought, was completely unknowable; yet it was responsible for creation and divine action in history. John, taking his cue from this conception of *Logos* (which is also translated as Word), interprets Christ as the divine *Logos* who has been in existence from all eternity. The Jesus who came to earth, who worked at carpentering in Nazareth, who preached and healed during his short ministry, was actually the incarnation of the *Logos*, a physical embodiment who came to earth that men might have eternal life. The Christ of John's Gospel was never really burdened with the cares of the world or the temptations of the flesh. "In the beginning was the Word [*Logos*], and the Word was with God, and the Word was God. The same was in the beginning with God. All things were made through him; and without him was not anything made that hath been made. . . . And the Word [*Logos*] became flesh, and dwelt among us (and we beheld his glory, glory as of the only begotten from the Father), full of grace and truth" (John 1:1-3, 14).

Whereas both the Synoptic Gospels and, so far as we can tell, Jesus, placed their emphasis upon the speedy coming of the Kingdom of God, John bases the Christian teaching on "eternal life." Mere men, creatures of the flesh, cannot hope to live a divine life unaided and in their natural state. Christ came "that they might have life, and have it more abundantly." This new life of which John speaks is attained by a mystical oneness with Christ, the eternal *Logos*. Salvation as conceived by the Jewish apocalyptic writers and the early Christians was usually thought of as the promise of the future. With John it is the present state of any person who finds union with Christ. Like the Greek mystery writers, the author of this Gospel considers man's natural life to be death; endless, true life is the possession of the redeemed. John has Jesus say, "He who hears my Word, and believes him who sent me, has endless life and does not come into judgment, but has passed from death to life" (John 5:24). Christ's work on earth, then, is to give the gift of life to all men. With it, the bonds which bind man to his animal, sightless existence are broken and the spirit is released to its higher destiny.

This Gospel is dated some seventy years after the death of Jesus when some of his followers were beginning to wonder just when the Messiah would come on his cloud of glory to usher in the New Age. John writes not only to the Greeks but also to this group. Christ has already returned, he says, but in a different fashion from that looked for. Just as no one really expected the Messiah to come in the guise of a humble carpenter of Nazareth, so people have not been able to recognize the form of the second advent. John is sure, however, that Christ is now on earth—on earth in the hearts of true believers. At his death on the cross, Christ unburdened himself of the limitations imposed by space and time; by so doing, he became free to dwell in the inward parts of men and thus to be both closer to his people and more effective in his work. The cross is actually a symbol of victory, a beginning of the living presence of Christ in history.

The extreme individualism of John's mystical religion produced a conception of the church more akin to the Greek mysteries than to the Jewish synagogue. The writers of the Synoptic Gospels were too much concerned with the imminence of the Kingdom of God to worry much about organizational matters, and Paul, at least in his early days, shared the Synoptic view. John, however, saw the church as a spiritual fellowship within which Christ lives and works. This fellowship required little or no organization, but it did presuppose meetings at which additional revelation was received from the presence of the *Logos*. By John's time the small Christian communities were subject to ridicule by the Romans and persecution by the Jews. Such general condemnation by the "sinful world" was bound to draw the believers closer and closer together in a life of sacred fellowship. It was therefore natural for John to look at the Christian communities as being composed of people "chosen out of the world" who, having had their sins washed away, were now standing in union with Christ. The Gospel of John must have contained remarkable solace for the persecuted and despised "spiritual Israel."

In spite of the variety of their interpretations, all the Gospels agree that God entered history in the person of Jesus. Each writer's understanding was different, and he probably directed his remarks to believers of different backgrounds. Certainly Mark and John spoke from obviously diverse perspectives, yet both were convinced that the entrance of Jesus into history was the fact of primary importance. Much of this diversity of interpretation can be explained by the existence of Judaism in an alien Greco-Roman culture. The whole of the Greek tradition, with its advanced science and philosophy and its polytheistic religions, was foreign to the metaphysical monotheism and prophetic temper of the Hebrews. The variety inherent in the Gospels is indicative of the cosmopolitanism of Mediterranean culture.

21

EXPANSION AND HERESY

AS THE Christian movement spread throughout the Mediterranean basin, the original church at Jerusalem gradually decreased in importance. Jewish law and the customary Jewish modes of thought gave way to Hellenism. The Gospels, the writings of Paul, and the other literature which forms the New Testament corpus give only the vaguest hint of the radical transformation which was well under way by the beginning of the second century. The center of Judaism was already shifting to Babylonia when, in 70 A.D., the Temple at Jerusalem was finally destroyed by Rome. As Judaism moved East, Christianity went West. Although Christianity never lost its essentially Jewish foundation, it developed in altogether different channels.

THE CHRISTIANS AND ROME

AMONG the phenomena of Hellenistic-Roman religion, the expression most offensive to the Christians was the worship of the Emperor. The religious veneration of the chief of state had its basis in the ancient Greek notion that in every human being there dwells a *daimon*. In great men this *daimon* is particularly powerful and indicates their exalted position as favorites of the gods. After the time of Alexander the Great, who was considered by both Egyptians and Greeks to be the son of Amnon Zeus, many of the Hellenistic kings and Roman

[332]

officials were revered as manifestations of deity. By the beginning of the second century this worship was made mandatory for all living within the borders of the Empire. For the early Christians, however, it seemed to entail a denial of their Lord and an affirmation of the ultimate divinity of the Roman Empire. They faced a choice—a choice between Caesar and Christ. The two could never be reconciled in the minds of these men, for they could see no salvation other than the personal kind offered by the Gospels in the name of Jesus.

This problem did not seem to bother the adherents of the various other religions of the time. Their roots were not so deeply embedded in exclusive monotheisms of the Hebrew type. Rather, they were indebted primarily to oriental influences and could much more easily absorb a number of different religious expressions. Their own particular deities received private worship while the Emperor filled the need for public worship. For the most part, devotees of the non-Semitic religions could satisfy themselves, in a way impossible to Jews and Christians, that the peace and prosperity offered by Rome was divine and ultimately good. The Jews were imbued with a political concept which made Rome a conqueror rather than a savior; the Christians felt themselves to be "chosen out of the world" in a highly select group which was concerned with matters of the spirit rather than material or cultural welfare. There could be no divided loyalty, no private worship distinguished from public worship. The Christian Gospel demanded absolute commitment to "Jesus Christ as Lord and Master."

With the Christians following this course at a time of serious internal difficulties, those responsible for the Empire had no choice but to institute a program of persecution. By 180 A.D. the church was fairly well organized, and it had members in all the Roman provinces. The threat of Empire-wide organization at first produced sporadic condemnation by local governors and then developed into full-scale persecutions of an intensity rarely felt by any religious group. In a letter written by Pliny the Younger to the Emperor Trajan (98-117), the general procedure is outlined. At first, Pliny says, he would ask a person if he were a Christian. If he said yes, he would then be asked to renounce his faith. If the renunciation was not forthcoming, Pliny would subject the offender to some kind of physical torture. Trajan's reply approves this method, but maintains that Pliny need not bestir himself to seek out Christians. They should only be dealt with when brought to his attention from some outside source.

The earliest reign of terror came with Marcus Aurelius (161-180), who was a famed Stoic philosopher and man of general good will. However, his pet abomination was enthusiasm, especially of the religious variety; moreover, he considered the idea of immortality to be an affront to intelligence. Since the Christians were both enthusiastic and believers in immortality, he not only permitted, but even fostered, the persecutions. During his reign a number of high-ranking churchmen, especially Justin Martyr, Polycarp and Pothinus, were put to death. However, it was not until the time of Emperor Decius (249-251) that the persecutions became universal. The Empire was at the point of disintegrating, and Decius concluded that Christianity was one of the most important factors contributing to its decline. In his edict of 250 the Christians were offered the alternatives of either renouncing their faith or having their goods confiscated and facing possible torture and death. The climax was reached some years later when Diocletian (284-305) burned the church buildings of the Christians and offered them only one alternative: apostasy or death.

MOTIVES FOR CONVERSION

DURING this long period of persecution the Christian churches grew both in number and influence. The pattern of conversion was much the same as in the expansion of Buddhism. At first a few strongly committed individuals renounced their conventional associations with various social institutions. Following their lead, whole families and then the larger units of society declared their faith. One of the most outstanding mass conversions was initiated by Gregory Thaumaturgos, a person of high aristocratic position who used his political and social power to swing a whole populace and have Christianity declared a matter of state policy.

It was not without mixed motives that one became a Christian in those early days. Some adhered to the new faith because they felt that its record of miraculous power proved ultimate authenticity. There were certainly others who were impressed by the argument that Christ was the fulfillment of Old Testament prophecy and were thereby given an important sense of kinship with the historic past that was lacking in the competing philosophic and mystery faiths. Salvation from the despair of a meaningless future was given to some by the Christian doctrine of the Second Coming of Christ. One of the primary motives seems to have centered in the ethical vitality and absoluteness of the new faith. Heavenly rewards were promised to the morally upright, and disastrous punishments were to be meted out to those who persisted on a path of evil. The early Christians were fortunate in having the long Hebrew tradition upon which to build and from which they could draw their code of morality.

Economic and political factors also played an important role in conversion. Early Christianity had an extensive system of charity which gave generous aid to the materially unfortunate.

The poor always knew that they would be taken care of in times of distress, especially if they were members of the church. From all we can gather from extant records, large numbers of the early converts came from the less fortunate economic groups; they found within the church not only a spiritual home together with badly needed respect and friendship, but also food, clothing and sometimes even housing. The church considered military service to be unchristian, and no true member of the faith was allowed to join the army or engage in war. Such stipulations were bound to draw into the congregations a number of pacifists along with those who resented the inconvenience and social loss involved in army training. Others, those simply opposed to the Roman government, found refuge and likemindedness within the Christian fellowship.

THE APOLOGISTS

IN ADDITION to emotional, political and economic motivations for conversion, there were those who found within Christianity the answer to their most perplexing intellectual problems. This group of literate searchers after truth was addressed by the *Apologists*, usually converted philosophers who made their living by teaching and lecturing. For them the Christian faith offered not only what they considered to be true philosophy, but also the final answer to such perennial human problems as the nature of God, revelation, immortality, ethical demands and the nature of man himself. Indeed, the documents of this new faith seemed to give satisfactory answers to such eternal human questions as, Where does man come from? Why is he here? and Where is he going?—origin, purpose and destiny.

Whereas the writings which now compose the Christian Scripture had simply *proclaimed* the truth of the Gospel, the Apologists now *argued* it. In rejecting the method of proclamation, they took over the logical methods of philosophic debate, attempting to show the *unreasonableness* of polytheism and the mythology of pagan thought and the inherent *reasonableness* of Christianity. In so doing, they used the categories of thought and the essential concepts of Greek philosophy. The movement toward the Hellenization of Christianity which was begun so early in the first century was finally completed by the Apologists in the second.

JUSTIN MARTYR

By far the most important of the early Apologists was Justin Martyr, a Greek philosopher who taught in Rome during the first half of the second century. Justin had a Greek intellectual's love of philosophy and maintained that it is "a knowledge of that which is and an understanding of the truth; and happiness is the reward of this knowledge and wisdom." His personal experience with the various philosophic systems of the time (he had been an adherent of Stoicism, Pythagoreanism and finally Platonism) left him with a feeling of incompleteness and doubt. He was a practical man in search of a firm basis for moral decisions as well as a philosopher in search of a consistent speculative structure. For Justin, life was one indivisible whole in which happiness and wisdom were inextricably bound. This union of the moral and the speculative, the practical and the theoretical, is seen in his own account of his principal interests even before he became a Christian. The essence of philosophy, and thus of life, is to be found in the knowledge of God. This knowledge of God is not to be interpreted as being some secret insight into the "mysteries of divine Being" as the mystery cults had supposed; rather, it is the knowledge that God is the moral governor of the universe and that his very character bespeaks of justice, love, mercy and righteousness. The greatest intellectual sin, according to Justin Martyr, is to conceive of God as being impartial about good and evil. From this standpoint much of the popular religion of the day stood condemned.

In Christianity Justin felt that he had found a unification which asserted the primacy of moral demands. The ethical monotheism of the Jewish tradition made it plain that the ultimate reality of the world was God, a God who would reward virtue and punish evil. The beginning of the Christian life was repentance, and this act was always rewarded by the forgiveness of past sins and the entrance of the believer upon a new life of virtue. The new life did not mean, as it did with the Jews, a rigorous observance of the ancient Mosaic Law. The new life entailed a new law which came into the world with Christ, and which, though in essence the same as the old, relieves man of its spelled-out particulars. Christ's law is simple: love God, love your fellow man. The Jewish Law had had the single purpose of constantly reminding the Jews of God's existence and their obligation to worship him. The social duties it prescribed were not performed out of love of man, but simply because God commanded them. With Christ the motivation changed; loving service was placed on the same level as worship. God has always really required this combination, says Justin, but until Jesus walked the earth the Jewish revelation was incomplete, or at best, misunderstood.

The superior morality of Christianity is directly related to the fact that Christ came from God. First, the Old Testament gives ample evidence that such a person as Jesus was promised and expected over a period of many years. It would be wholly unreasonable, Justin argues, to suppose that such a long tradition was erroneous, especially when the person of Jesus apparently fulfilled all the essentially spiritual conditions. This argument from history need not stand alone. It is strongly supported by philosophic considerations. Justin takes over the general *Logos* doctrine common to the author of the Gospel of John and other religious philosophers. He, too, considers the *Logos* to be divine reason, created before the beginning of the world, and through which the world itself came into being. The God that created the *Logos* is above and beyond all human knowledge and is certainly not identifiable with the deity of the Old Testament. Nevertheless, Old Testament writers and prophets were spoken to by the *Logos*, as are men of reason in all countries and under all conditions. Indeed, the presence of the *Logos* in various forms accounts for all the truth that men have ever known. The greatness of Christianity is that "the whole *Logos* . . . became Christ, body and mind and soul." On such a basis Justin is able to maintain that "whatever things have been rightly said by anyone belong to us Christians." Socrates, Heraclitus and all "who have lived rationally are Christians even if thought to be atheists"; but those who live in Christ Jesus live in the fullness of truth.

It is readily seen that Justin was concerned to show the tolerant breadth of the Christian faith. As a Hellenistic philosopher, he was bound to make the universality of truth his major touchstone, and by identifying it with Christ he established the final authority of Christianity. In this scheme Christ became the savior and fulfillment of all men who were searching for truth. The *Logos* became incarnate because man had been incapable of correctly understanding God's revelation in morals and metaphysics. The presence of the historic Jesus confirmed man's deepest insight while at the same time making possible the complete banishment of ignorance. For Justin, redemption was not a change of heart or a new will, as it was for Paul; it was a change in religious ideas.

In essentials, Justin and the other Apologists were in agreement. They all argued that the world must be conceived as a creation of the *Logos* for the sake of man; that God, although abstract and metaphysical, is the moral ruler of all; that human reason reveals truth which finds its completion in the incarnate

Lord; and that good is rewarded while evil is punished. In all the writings man's freedom is affirmed and his responsibility as a creature of God directly emphasized. Christianity is not an esoteric cult among other cults, but the final system of thought and practice, open to all men of right mind and right action. The Apologists completely separated Christianity and national Judaism; and thus the new religion became intellectually armed for its conquest of the West.

THE HERESIES

THE rapid expansion of the Christian movement and the consequent elaboration of its theological structure was bound to produce a variety of doctrines, each claiming to be the true statement of faith. The piety of the common man within the Christian communion was replete with demons, angels, magical practices and an extraordinary quantity of superstition. The Greco-Roman world was being invaded by Eastern mysticism, Babylonian astrology, and the gods of many traditions. In the resulting syncretism it was almost impossible to keep a single religious movement "pure" in the sense of adhering to the fundamentals of its founder and his immediate followers. Christianity was certainly no exception. Its battles with the Gnostics and Montanists finally produced a fairly unified dogma, but the battles were not easily won.

THE GNOSTICS

THE tendency of the primitive tradition, represented in Paul and John, was toward a mystical religion in which salvation was dependent upon union between man and Christ. The Gnostics, who had drunk deeply of oriental mysticism, felt that this emphasis was directly in accord with their own conception of the duality of the world. For them there were two worlds, one represented by the material phenomena of bodies and sense perception, the other a world of spirit. The world of matter was evil, and as long as man was tied to it his soul could never find rest in union with God. Man's great problem in life was his need to escape the influence of matter. According to the Gnostic, God had nothing whatever to do with matter; in fact, matter was so irremediably evil that it constituted the principle diametrically opposed to the principle of God. Since it defied improvement, all man could do was to try to free himself of it. Paul's dualism of flesh and spirit was ethically, if not cosmologically, as radical as that of the Gnostics. Although John had written his Gospel in defense of the historicity of Jesus, his emphasis upon divine union and knowledge gave considerable impetus to Christian Gnosticism.

The Gnostics, with their conception of the absoluteness of the supreme being and the complete separation of infinite spirit and the material world, naturally could see little sense in the idea of incarnation. Long before the time of Christ, Gnostics had conceived of a divine savior coming to earth to liberate the spirits of men. But this savior only *appeared* to assume human form; he certainly could not be born of woman, nor could he suffer and die. If these characteristics could be eliminated from the conception of Christ in Christian theology, they could call themselves Christians. As Gnostics became more numerous within Christian circles, they taught that the earthly body of Christ was an illusion and that his entire career was appearance rather than reality. The true Christ could never be nailed to a cross, could never hunger and thirst; indeed, he could never be so closely bound to matter as to have a body at all. As Gnosticism spread, there was a general weakening of both the ethical and the historical roots of Christianity. Most especially, Gnosticism cut itself off from any connection with Judaism.

The struggle with the Gnostics came to a head about the

middle of the second century when Marcion, a wealthy shipper, attempted to reorganize Christian theology. Marcion was probably ignorant of the elaborate mythology of Gnosticism, but he was certainly under the influence of various types of oriental mysticism. He maintained that the church had wandered far afield from Paul's original formulation and was now dangerously close to being apostate. Paul and the Gnostics agreed not only regarding dualism, but also in their ideas of limited salvation. The Gnostics held to a belief that only certain human beings were capable of rising to a purely spiritual level. The great majority of mankind would always be tied to its animal existence and would be annihilated at death, just as animals are. But there were others (in Paul, those who were predestined to salvation) who were elected to salvation because they possessed within themselves a spark of the divine. The universalist tendencies of the Apologists and others ran counter, Marcion thought, to this express teaching.

But Marcion's most important criticism concerns the Christian use of the Old Testament. The God of the Old Testament creates the world and has a specific interest in all that goes on within it. The writings are filled with laws and rules for the conduct of everyday life, even down to the mention of such disgusting functions as procreation and eating. The spiritual Christ of the New Testament is bound to suffer degradation by association with the Jewish God. The Redeemer-God who manifested himself in Christ has always been, both before and after his appearance, the direct antithesis of this worthless, evil, material existence. The whole of Christianity has been corrupted and defiled by the Jewish apostles who were unable to permit their ties with nature to be severed by the clear light of Christ. This condemnation was made not only of the Jewish conception of God, but also of Jewish legalism and the idea that man should seek justification through works. The true God, says Marcion, never judges and never punishes; he only saves those who can be saved. The God of the Old Testament who creates, sustains, and offers rules for action is ultimately the source of evil rather than good.

As the logical consequence of this line of reasoning, Marcion recommended that the entire Old Testament be eliminated from Christian use. The New Testament should be substituted for it and considered to be the sole authority for Christianity. All references to the historic existence of Christ should be understood to indicate an appearance; they should never be confused with actual flesh-and-blood existence and certainly never with the outrageous Messianic tales of Jewish folklore. Beyond these considerations, Marcion advocated a life of strict fasting and absolute celibacy. This denial of bodily hungers was the only consistent ethical implication of his theology.

When Marcion presented these ideas to the Church at Rome, a schism resulted. He was one of the few men with Gnostic tendencies who took the trouble to organize a special church and establish a counter movement claiming to be the "true" Christianity. Because of his organizational abilities and the real strength of the Marcionite Church, Marcion was long thought to be the most subversive of all heretics. However, although the main body of Christianity rejected him and feared his power, the actual establishment of a counterdogma waited upon later events.

THE MONTANISTS

THE Gnostic movement was characterized by intellectual concerns and an ascetic ethic. There was little of the enthusiasm which had given so much impetus in the early days of the church. A much more popular heresy was begun by Montanus, a former priest of Cybele, who had been converted to Christianity in Phrygia about the middle of the second century. Montanus believed that the interpretation of the Age of the Spirit found in the Gospel of John was essentially correct. He went beyond John to assert that he, Montanus, was the new agent of the *Logos,* appointed to preach an immediate establishment of the heavenly Jerusalem on earth. At first this New Jerusalem was to descend from heaven at Pepuza, a town in Phrygia, rather than the more traditional site in Palestine. Montanus, and those who followed him, claimed to have received special revelations regarding the preparations necessary for entrance into the earthly paradise. From the beginning, the Montanist movement was concerned with practical rather than theoretical problems.

Special revelation rather than spirit-body dualism formed the basis of the Montanist emphasis upon asceticism. All Christians were supposed to relieve themselves of their worldly possessions and obligations and travel to Pepuza to await the return of Christ. With the arrival of the New Jerusalem, there was to be no concern for anything other than the glorious salvation. Clothing was to be of the simplest sort, fasting was to be so rigorous as to permit only sufficient food to keep the body alive, and chastity, modesty and abstention from amusements were to be necessary prerequisites for the full enjoyment of the fruits of Christianity.

The most distinctive characteristic of the Montanist sect was their attitude toward the indwelling Spirit. Like the primitive Christians before them, they believed that the Spirit communicated directly with living prophets who, in turn, uttered these revelations while in an ecstatic state of suspended animation. As the Spirit took possession of one of these men, he seemed to lose all volition and become a speaking automaton. Since the wisdom of God was obviously beyond the logical language categories of man, much that was said under conditions of prophecy made little sense to those not so possessed. The esoteric phrases in which such "truth" was clothed often required interpretation at a later point; their main burden could be immediately apprehended only by those who saw and heard. This emphasis upon Spirit possession was a reversion to the earliest days of Christianity, and it represented a kind of enthusiasm which was rapidly dying within the main body of the church.

As Christianity aged and mellowed, the Golden Age became less and less an imminent reality. The Montanists, by reviving the old hope and requiring a strict asceticism for salvation, drew to their ranks the confirmed ascetics and the emotionally excitable. The main body of the church, however, settled to a more sober and less fanatic understanding of the Christian message. They argued strenuously against the Montanist tendency toward exclusiveness—the feeling that the church was against the world. The primary duty of these more moderate Christians was to conquer the world by conversion and thereby insure the success of Christ's second arrival. This Second Coming, however, was far in the future. The Montanists, they thought, were diverting the energies of missions and undercutting the basis upon which a substantial number of conversions could be made.

22

PHYSICAL AND INTELLECTUAL CONSOLIDATION

CHURCH ORGANIZATION

LAW and dogma had been a part of the Christian community from the beginning of its organized activity. Nevertheless, neither found much expression in churchly organization until the various heretical movements of the second century forced a consideration of the problem of authority. The presence of Gnostic and Montanist heresy prompted the leaders of the church to make a sharp distinction between clergy and laity and finally to create a hierarchy of authority within the clergy itself. The head of an important church congregation came to be known as a Bishop, and his assistants, who preached and ministered to the smaller groups, were Presbyters and Deacons. Below these (the higher clergy), there were Readers, who were charged with the responsibility of reading the Scripture at divine service; Exorcists, who specialized in healing the parishioners and freeing them from demons; Acolytes, who were general handy men for the Bishop, attending especially to his personal needs; and finally the Deaconesses, who were charged with ministering to the needs of women.

The authority of any one person within the congregational hierarchy was derived from the bishop. The bishop was nominally elected by the community over which he presided, but in actual practice the presbyters and deacons had the decisive voice in the selection. Moreover, it was usual for the bishop to be selected from the ranks of presbyters, but it was not un-known for lesser clergy or even a layman to achieve such a position. In theory the congregation had control of all ap-pointments below the level of bishop, but again practice finally settled that responsibility upon the bishop. As the church grew, the rank of bishop increased in importance until he became the final authority for all matters of faith and prac-tice. Cyprian, bishop of Carthage, and one of the greatest churchmen of the early third century, furnished a theological basis for the bishop's assumption of power. The bishop, he said, the visible head of a community of believers, is the direct agent of the Holy Spirit. Through him his congregation shares in the blessings of the Spirit, and he is to be considered the Vicar of Christ and the only successor of the Apostles. Cyprian further maintained, and the other bishops did not dispute him, that true membership in the Church of Christ could be obtained only by complete submission to the bishop and his appointed assistants.

Two primary factors contributing to the bishops' power were the accumulation of property by the church and the ex-panding missionary enterprise. Buildings were being acquired, and if some of the anti-Christian writings of the time can be believed, a considerable degree of wealth was being amassed by church groups. Adherence to the ancient Mosaic practice of giving a tithe (ten percent) of yearly income to God meant the improvement of the church's financial position with each new convert. The philanthropic enterprises common to all the early communities were continued and even expanded. It was therefore requisite that the business functions of the church be given some centralized control in the hands of a single responsible agent. As the congregations in the centers of population became larger and more wealthy, they sent mis-sionaries to neighboring communities to establish churches. At first the bishop of the home church remained as head of the rural development. After a time the outlying parishes were organized according to the provincial divisions of the Empire, and finally the provinces were grouped into larger territories called dioceses.

An organization of such size could not be controlled adequately without periodic meetings at which representatives from the various churches could gather and deliberate. As a result there were constituted near the end of the second century provincial synods, first in Asia Minor and later in North Africa, Rome, Spain and Gaul. These meetings were attended by deacons, presbyters and bishops, but the bishops always held the final vote and therefore made all ultimate decisions. The natural importance of such centers of ecclesiastical and political power as Jerusalem, Antioch, Alexandria and Rome soon led to the assumption of even greater authority by the resident bishops in these cities. They became known as archbishops, exarchates and patriarchs, and their spiritual influence increased accordingly. Since Rome was the capital of the Empire, the bishop of Rome was accorded a respect higher than the rest. In controlling the synods these bishops were responsible for the establishment of a system of discipline and church law.

One of the principal functions of the bishop and the synods was to develop a common worship practice throughout the various congregations. From the beginning of the movement each group of Christians had taken over whatever order of service seemed most fitting to their background. As the heresies gained power and threatened the unity of the church, a more detailed and authoritative plan of worship was necessary. The ordinary service usually consisted of Scripture reading, prayers, hymns and a sermon. In places where Montanist influence was felt, this order was likely to be interrupted by ecstatic utterances and emotional outbursts of Spirit possession. In so far as it was possible, the church authorities discouraged all but the most sober type of worship. The *Agape*, or love feast, fell into disuse, and the Lord's Supper, a service commemorating Jesus' last meal with his disciples, became increasingly sacred. The part containing the actual Eucharist (Lord's Supper) was held on Sunday following the regular open service and was limited to Christians in good standing in the church.

As time passed, the bishops and other church leaders instituted more rigorous requirements for membership. The baptismal ceremony, which had been used from the very beginning to symbolize acceptance and admission, was now performed only after a period of intensive instruction. Those who presented themselves as candidates were called "catechumens." After a study of the Scripture and guided lessons in theology, a catechumen presented himself to declare his faith and to proclaim his renunciation of the Devil and all worldliness. Water blessed by the bishop was then placed upon the candidate's head, and after the appropriate words had been said, full membership in the sacred fellowship was granted. But it was not only these initial requirements that were made more rigid. The discipline of members also felt the tightening of ecclesiastical control. Those whom the bishop felt to be out of accord with the true faith and practice were subject to excommunication and exclusion from divine service. If the recalcitrant one proved through confession and acts of humiliation that he was sincerely repentant, the bishop could order his reinstatement. Both excommunication and reinstatement were surrounded with appropriately solemn and lengthy ceremonies.

The growing numbers and wealth of the church soon made it necessary for new buildings to be constructed in which divine worship, philanthropic activities and administration could be centered. The consolidation of administration in strategically located buildings greatly increased the efficiency of the Church's operation.

THE ALEXANDRIAN SCHOOL

BY THE third century the basic organizational pattern of the Christian Church was well established and it constituted a powerful instrument for advancing the faith. But the church still required a consistent theology which would appeal to the more sophisticated minds of the Mediterranean culture. The work of the Apologists and some of the New Testament writers was essentially an attack on paganism and an assertion of the primacy of the Christian faith. The thinkers of the great Catechetical School in Alexandria transformed the apologetic task. Out of the old rather haphazard rebuttal they constructed a positive and systematic theology. The most important scholars of this school, Clement (150?-220?) and Origen (185-256), built upon the foundations laid by earlier thinkers but went far beyond them.

Alexandria was a metropolitan center with cosmopolitan attitudes and a tremendous variety of intellectual concerns. The atmosphere of the city and the variegated crosscurrents of philosophic thought made it possible for teachers to produce a body of writing which was satisfying to the Greek intellectual and meaningful to the Christian believer. The subsoil of Alexandrian thought is found in Neo-Platonism. Although Neo-Platonism was not developed into a school until Ammonius Saccas (c. 160-242) and Plotinus (c. 205-270), all the ideas and attitudes which were later grouped under that name were current in Alexandria in Clement's day. In both its unorganized and organized form, Neo-Platonism was a skillful rival of Christianity. It claimed to meet both the religious and the intellectual demands of all men.

CLEMENT

CLEMENT followed Pontaenus, a converted Stoic philosopher, as the chief teacher in Alexandria. He attempted to develop an introduction to Christianity that would contain all the essential elements of true religion. Like Justin Martyr and Philo before him, Clement was sure that there are but two sources of divine knowledge: Scripture and reason. The Scripture describes in concrete historical images what the pure light of reason can discern if it is handled in the proper way. The connecting link between the philosophic wisdom of the Greeks and the revelation of Scripture is the *Logos*, which stands between man and the utterly incomprehensible God. The *Logos* first reveals God by creating a world with plan, design and order; then, through special knowledge given to the prophets and Scripture writers; and finally, by becoming incarnate in the person of Jesus. The universal character of the *Logos* makes truth, no matter where found or by whom, inherent in Christianity. The unlettered simple believer in Christ Jesus and the most profound of all Greek philosophers are both capable of possessing the divine knowledge from which salvation springs.

The uniqueness of Christ as the incarnate *Logos* results from the fact that in his person the *Logos* is not only the teacher of men's minds but also the high priest of their spirits. It is thus through Christ that religion and philosophy are unified and made into one divine whole. Education in the wisdom of philosophy and participation in the holy rites of the church are complementary rather than antagonistic. In this conjunction of free intellectual inquiry and the tradition of the church, Clement makes Christianity the natural outgrowth of both Hebrew and Greek civilizations, each of which had a specific mission. Both were developing according to a divinely appointed plan which was to be completed in the rapidly growing Christian Church. By this growth, theological speculation is raised to a level of high piety, and consequently all church traditions are placed under the protection of thought. Free inquiry, on the other hand, is now given ecclesiastical guarantees. Thinker and saint, churchman and philosopher are all in search of the same ideal: the eternal love and knowledge of God.

But Clement was too much the Greek philosopher not to consider the life of knowledge to be on a higher level than the life of simple acceptance. The deeper truths of Christianity must be found, he felt, by penetrating the surface of both Scripture and science. Like Philo, he spent considerable time developing allegorical interpretations of Scripture which would furnish Biblical authority for his theology and at the same time prove that there were esoteric meanings to Scripture clear only to those who could use rational analysis. From this point of view, the mature Christian was the one who looked beyond the obvious, while the immature Christian was satisfied with literal meanings. Both were acceptable to God, but surely the philosophical theologian stood upon higher ground. The anti-intellectual aspects of the primitive tradition should be discarded in favor of developing to its highest possible point the divine image in man, thought by Clement to be his rational nature.

In keeping with his emphasis upon knowledge, Clement's conception of salvation by faith differed from Paul's. The Alexandrian teacher thought that faith was the conviction that certain propositions were true, rather than a "mystical bond of union with Christ." Together with Socrates and Plato, Clement felt that moral convictions were derived from correct understanding, and correct understanding from certain knowledge. If man knows the difference between right and wrong, if he knows what he must do to be saved, he will act righteously and fulfill the conditions for salvation. The *Logos* is sent by God to instruct men, to enlighten their minds and dispel the ignorance which breeds sin and makes salvation impossible. The ancient Hebrew notion of original sin which played such an important role in Paul's thought is foreign to Clement, who believes that man is free to choose sin or salvation, but that in order to make the proper choice he must be receptive to divine truth and possessed of a loving trust in the goodness of God.

ORIGEN

CLEMENT's major contribution to the developing Christian theology was largely one of attitude and spirit rather than systematic presentation. His interests, though partially speculative, were always centered in the practical matters of ethics and the attainment of salvation. His theological ideas were largely borrowed from Philo, Plato and the Stoics, and he probably created more theological problems than he solved. Origen, who was a student of Clement's, took up the work where his master left it and produced the first real systematic theology to be inspired by the new movement. In the history of Christian doctrine, Origen is ranked with such giants as Augustine and Thomas Aquinas.

Origen's motivations were much the same as those of Clement: he wished to construct a Christian system of thought which would be as intellectually respectable as the systems of the Greek philosophers and as full of piety and moral fervor as the writings of the Gnostics and primitive Christians. Like his predecessors in the Hellenization of Christianity, Origen had an avid appreciation of all forms of knowledge and a special interest in the close interconnection between philosophy and the Christian Gospel. But with all his emphasis upon philosophy, Origen remained a scriptural theologian. The Bible, he felt—both Testaments—comprises the essential revelation of God to man and consequently should hold the position of primary authority. Clement had been content to consider faith as a kind of openmindedness toward all truth. Origen, on the other hand, defined faith as the complete acceptance of specific dogmas and facts which were to be found by searching the Scripture for its hidden meanings.

These meanings are actually in three levels which correspond to the three parts of man: body, soul and spirit. The first part is represented in the Scripture by historical narratives and stories regarding the method of creation. When the real meaning of these passages is sought, the inquiring intellect is pushed on to discover allegories which do not appear at the first reading. Indeed, on first sight many of these stories are downright offensive to the Christian conscience and spirituality. The second level of Biblical meaning is found in those passages which concern themselves with the nature of the individual soul in its ethical and religious relations with men and God. The moral truths expressed in these sections are difficult to grasp, much more difficult than those in historical narration, but once seen, they are clear and distinct. The third and last level is reserved for the mature Christian. This level of Scriptural understanding does not refer to any specific group of passages, but to the divine intent of the Scripture as a whole. Such insight as this results in a penetration into the ultimate mystery of God and the final sanctification of the believer. Those who are capable of only the first two levels are never permitted to see the great spiritual purpose and the unutterable majesty of God. Truth is thus supplied to men as they are able to grasp it.

God, although incomprehensible in normal categories, is revealed by the *Logos* in creation (nature) and in the Christ. As in previous *Logos* theologies, the *Logos* is here the first creation of God, existing from the beginning and responsible for creation, knowledge, and all mediation between God and man. Thus the incarnate *Logos*, Christ, becomes the sole object of knowledge for any wise man. In him all things which appear to be separate and diverse are unified, and in him all mysteries are solved. The entire Scripture builds to the climax of the incarnate *Logos*, and it therefore contains the fundamental truths of God. Whereas the Greek philosophers may have arrived at a species of truth, the Scripture offers the only final authority and the only norm for determining truth and falsity.

From the beginning of the Christian movement, the principal intellectual problem was the reconciliation of Christ with monotheism. Were there really two gods instead of one? Or was Christ an inferior divine creation—at least inferior to the One God? The writer of the Fourth Gospel and the later Apologists had utilized the *Logos* doctrine in their solutions of this question. But was there a time when the *Logos* did not exist? If so, the *Logos* would have the stature of an inferior divine being. If not, how is the *Logos* related to God? Origen recognized this problem and attempted to solve it by stating that God and the *Logos* are both divine, that the *Logos* is *begotten* of God rather than a creation. As such, the *Logos* is not self-existent as God is, but still there was never a time when the *Logos* did not exist. Both are eternal and ultimately embraced in a transcendental unity. The *Logos* of God is most closely analogous to the will or, to use a synonym employed by Origen, the wisdom of God. The will is separate from the person who generates it, and it is a unique entity in its own right. Both God and his *Logos* are personal, the proof being found everywhere in the Scriptures; they are not to be confused with the various types of impersonal absolutes to be found in Greek philosophy. Therefore, Origen's answer to the question of two gods is that there is one God, but his will (*Logos*) may be worshiped as an inferior divine being so long as this worship finally brings into view the One God.

The Christian speculation which was current when Origen was writing in the early third century mentioned a third divine being called the Holy Spirit. The Holy Spirit is inferior to the *Logos* in the same way that the *Logos* is inferior to God. As a being, the Spirit is not immediately related to God but belongs directly to the Christ. The existence of the church as a body of sanctified believers proves the existence of the Holy Spirit. Indeed, it is within this group that the Spirit operates. Only Christians, said Origen, can know of the Spirit, although all men can understand God as incomprehensible being, and the *Logos*. The Spirit, like the *Logos*, is an object of worship, but again, it must not be confused with the One God.

Origen's Doctrine of the Trinity can be summarized in the following fashion: God as Father is the ultimate source of all existence: rational existence is derived from the "Son of God" or the *Logos;* and the sanctified holiness of the Christian is the gift of the Holy Spirit. In his terms, "nothing in the Trinity can be called greater or less"; the three are of equal honor and dignity and possess eternal existence.

According to Origen's theology the universe is divided into two separate spheres, the eternal and the temporal. The eternal, or spiritual, part is filled with free rational spirits who were originally created so that they could enjoy blissful communion with God. Since they were endowed with freedom, it was for them to decide whether they wished to follow the path of goodness and maintain uninterrupted union with God, or whether they would choose evil and rebellion. Those who chose goodness became angels; their rebellious brothers became demons and associates of the Devil. The in-between group, less virtuous than angels but not so evil as demons, became human beings. For them was created the earth, or temporal sphere, as a place for good works and a training ground for salvation. Their souls are as eternal as those of the angels or demons, for all souls have existed from the time of the first creation.

With this interpretation of the world, Origen sees the whole of man's physical existence as being filled with spiritual significance. While on earth, the once-free spirits are subject to the discipline, pain and torment of material substance. These must be borne until good is preferred to evil and man is willing to reconstitute his original relationship with God. Hence, it is clear that the fall of man did not occur after the creation, as the Genesis story is usually interpreted to say, but physical creation came as a result of the fall. This new interpretation explains the universality of sin while at the same time vindicating the justice and righteousness of God. All of man's life on earth is a struggle between the forces of light and the forces of darkness. The good angels and the evil demons fight for possession of each single soul; which group will triumph is the decision every individual must make. God's eternal love is evident in the fact that he sent the *Logos* for instruction and the Holy Spirit for sanctification. Thus the physical universe, the *Logos* manifest in prophetic utterances, the *Logos* incarnate in Jesus, and the holiness achieved through Christian fellowship all conspire to lead men back from disobedience and ignorance to the perfection which was originally theirs.

Origen's eschatological hope was a refined and spiritualized version of that held by the earliest church. He looked forward to the day when all rational creatures, demons and men alike, would finally be restored to a oneness with God. The body would be resurrected, but not in its material form, for in the redeemed state there would be no material characteristics and consequently no sensuousness. The popular conceptions of heaven as a place of sensuous delight and hell as a place of physical torment were untenable for Origen. Rather, he maintained that the Biblical allusions to such places were symbolic representations of the essentially spiritual state of a conscience in torment or bliss. Those who died in sin would go to hell, but by this he meant that they would have another chance to reject evil and recognize their kinship with God, for even in hell the soul retained its freedom. Some day all souls would return to God, but until that time the discipline of earth and hell was required. However, universal salvation would not necessarily be a permanent state since the purified souls would always have freedom to choose good or evil. Thus Origen was prompted to insist that there have been many worlds before this one and that there may be more after this is ended. Salvation can never be conceived as being absolutely guaranteed.

In Origen's hands Christianity becomes not only a moral philosophy, but an ontology and a cosmology as well. Where man comes from, why he is here, and what his destiny is, is related to and correlated with a theory of the physical universe. At the center of the total structure is the *Logos*, who became incarnate in Jesus of Nazareth that men might have just this knowledge. Origen, like many of his successors in the history of Christianity, found in the words of the Bible and the person of Jesus the keys to all understanding, all truth and, indeed, all existence.

POPULAR RELIGION

THE speculations of the philosophic theologians were relatively unimportant to the great majority of believers. The average Christian had no time to pursue the intricate logic of such system-builders as Origen, and further, he was able to find little meaning in philosophic abstractions. The main body of Christendom looked to the Lord Jesus Christ as a divine being and their savior. As such, Jesus was an object of religious worship rather than an anchor for a philosophic world-view. The whole of the *Logos* theology implied a Neo-Platonic metaphysic and, for the most part, Stoic ethics. The average man was concerned to find within Christianity the answers to his religious problems, and in this respect the intellectually sophisticated Neo-Platonist and Stoic had little to offer. The intellectualization of the faith seemed to imply that theologians and philosophers were the only ones capable of penetrating the mystery of divine action within the world. Most Christian believers considered their faith and their personal experience of Christ to be adequate; they could see little reason why they should be dependent upon an intellectual elite.

The scholars who developed the *Logos* theology were primarily concerned to show how Christ was related to a monotheistic conception of deity. From the very earliest days, Christian thinkers had maintained that one of Christianity's greatest superiorities over the disorganized polytheisms of paganism was its affirmation of one God. In popular practice, however, Jesus was considered to be God and was accorded divine worship. Most people felt that the theologians were demoting Jesus by subordinating him to an incomprehensible, abstract, unreachable God. The immediate Christian experience was the important thing, they believed; theological speculations were inconsequential. For the Christian cultus, then, Jesus was God incarnate, and there was no other God before him.

To say that Christ was really the Father in heaven, that *also* he had been born of the Virgin Mary, that *also* he had suffered death on the cross, was to the philosophically trained mind an absurd blasphemy; yet this was the formulation of Christ's nature which most appealed to the pious church-goer for whom the philosophic problem never arose. But he had few who would take up his battle with the *Logos* theologians.

MONARCHIANISM

IN THE early part of the third century Sabellius (c. 215), an important scholar of the church at Rome, worked out an intellectual defense of the commonly accepted view of Jesus Christ. Sabellius' position, which was called Modalistic Monarchianism, attempted to reassert primary monotheism as the first principle of Christianity. Sabellius and his followers saw in Christ the total incarnation of deity—God in human form. It was the contention of this school that the *Logos* theology was ditheistic, and that, moreover, it was untrue to the Scripture.

God, said Sabellius, is not the incomprehensible deity of Neo-Platonic philosophy; he is a warm, loving personality who appears to the pious in three different forms. One of his forms, or "energies," is Father-creator, another is Son-redeemer, and the last is Holy Spirit-sanctifier. These are actually all the same person since God is ultimately an indestructible unity. The differences are seen first in terms of the time of appearance and secondly in terms of function. As Father, God created the world and all things in it; as Son, he appeared on earth in the guise of a man, historically known as Jesus; and finally he lives in the church as the Spirit of holiness.

Another so-called Monarchian position maintained that Jesus had been a mere man who was "adopted" at the time of his baptism. Like Modalism, this position was popularly held in the nonphilosophic segments of the church. The earliest exponent of this "dynamic" Monarchianism was Theodotus, a leather worker who came to Rome from Byzantium about the year 200. Theodotus appears to have been motivated by a feeling that both the *Logos* theologians and the Modalists were losing sight of the essential humanity of Jesus. The *Logos* teachers held Christ to be a pre-existent divine being who became incarnate but who could never actually have participated in human life the way mere mortals do. The same could be said for the Modalist theory that Jesus Christ was really God in his fullness. Theodotus and his followers represented that segment of Christian piety which has always found the exalted humanness of Jesus to be of great religious value. To offset the extreme emphasis upon divinity, the Theodotians maintained that Jesus was a real man who, through leading a pious life, had received the Holy Spirit at baptism. Although it seems rather inconsistent with this premise, the Theodotians further insisted that Jesus was born of the Virgin Mary by a special decree of God.

Neither the Modalists nor the "dynamic" Monarchians were particularly concerned with logic. Each group was trying to save what seemed to be the most essential parts of the faith by expressing the common Christian experience of Christ as savior in some meaningful way. In so doing, they combated the tendencies of both the *Logos* theologians to make of Christ an abstract philosophical principle, and the Gnostics to make of the historical Jesus a mystical blur.

23

TRIUMPHANT CHRISTIANITY

THE movement which began with the immediate followers of Jesus of Nazareth was finally officially recognized as a permissible religion when Emperor Constantine issued the Edict of Milan in 313. An ancient story records that Constantine, who was fighting Maxentius for control of the Empire, saw on the eve of his victory a cross in the sky with the accompanying motto, *"In hoc signo vinces."* Later that same evening God visited Constantine in a dream and told him that his troops would be unharmed and victory would be assured provided he adopted emblems in the form of a cross. On the following day Maxentius was defeated, thus insuring Constantine's conversion to Christianity. Having had his trust vindicated, the Emperor set about to restore the razed church buildings and stop the persecutions of Christians. What actually happened is, of course, in doubt; nevertheless, this was the end of the age of persecution and the beginning of a new period of power for the church.

REASONS FOR SUCCESS

THE reasons for the success of the Christian movement are varied and permit of no conclusive generalizations. Certainly the conversion of Constantine can be considered an important factor. From him the church received the imperial blessing which enabled it to assume an impregnable position in the center of world power. Constantine's tenure of office was sufficiently long and his personality sufficiently strong to vest the religion of his choice with considerable authority. However, since the persecution in the long years prior to 313 had proved impotent against the rising numbers of Christians, perhaps the conversion of Constantine merely crystallized an already powerful religious organization.

One important factor in the success of Christianity was the highly effective organizational structure developed by the church. No other religious sect of the time had anything like it. Its system of derived authority beginning with the bishop and pushing down through the clergy to the lay worshipers was without parallel except in the Roman state. It was a kind of constitutional monarchy with definite rights, privileges and duties accorded to all members. The church was not only a place of worship but also a school, a philanthropic society and a mutual benefit association. Each function played a definite role in the lives of its members, and the entire enterprise had an aura of sacredness lacking in the various secular associations. Whatever the doctrinal and theological differences among congregations, they all seemed to be imbued with a loyalty and a consciousness of divine fellowship. In many instances the persecutions intensified rather than lessened this feeling, and the church drew strength from its opponents.

This closely knit Christian fellowship fed upon the social disintegration of the first three centuries after Christ. Trade and commerce had increased urban populations to such an extent that the more ancient social bonds were being broken with nothing to take their place. The presence within this changing scene of a unified group providing a spiritual home in life and a heaven after death must certainly have been welcome to many. The cultural, religious and ethical traditions were all being questioned; the authority of the past was losing its power. Help and succor seemed to be offered by the Christian Church and its message, which claimed to be both old and new.

Christianity was also the most universal and inclusive of all the competing faiths. There was room within its fellowship for the mystic, the rationalist, the poet, and the simple uneducated believer. As we have seen, Christ could be looked upon as a holy man, as the incarnate *Logos,* or as God in human flesh. He was commonly believed to be unique, but the definition of "unique" was never positively formulated, so that it was quite possible for the convert to reinterpret and maintain after conversion many things that had been of importance to him as a pagan. The Christian movement was inclusive not only in an intellectual but also in a social sense. Its members could come from any level of society, from either sex, and from any race. The rich worshiped with the poor, women could be saved as easily as men, and there were no distinctions between Jew, Greek, Roman or barbarian. In such fashion the Christians exploited the intellectual and social cosmopolitanism of the age. The idea of a single Catholic Church with one faith and one organization took root in Christianity a short time after the crucifixion, and its development provided a most important tool of conquest.

Many scholars have insisted that one of the basic factors contributing to the success of Christianity is its origin in Judaism. The Greek and Persian cults lacked that sense of historical continuity which the Jews considered essential to true religion. No matter to what extent philosophers and mystics reinterpreted Christian concepts and experience, the God of Christianity was always the Jewish God of history. All the events of everyday life had cosmic significance. The creator and redeemer of the world was interested in political, economic and social affairs, as well as in the yearnings of the human heart. This earth, set in motion with a purpose, was slowly yet surely working out its ordained pattern. The righteousness or evilness of individual men was not related simply to their own salvation, but also to the pleasure and displeasure of the cosmic Father. The evangelistic activities of the Hellenistic Jews had prepared the way for such a conception of deity, and the Christians reaped the harvest. The Jewish Scriptures furnished a history, a whole body of ethical prophecy, and a promise; Christianity claimed to fulfill the history and promise while at the same time generalizing and expanding the Jewish ethical consciousness. To an age which was searching for moral improvement, cultural roots and ultimate salvation, the Jewish elements in the new faith must have been important indeed.

Though the reasons for the success of the Christian movement were varied, underlying them all was the fact that the Christian movement satisfied the basic needs of a vast number of people in the Greco-Roman world. The energies released by various visions made possible the creation of a new culture and a new civilization. The conversion of Constantine marks the climax of a rapid three-hundred-year development and the beginning of a Christian culture destined for unparalleled achievements.

CHURCH AND STATE

THE immediate effect of Constantine's conversion was to set in motion a series of events which led to the adoption of Christianity as the official state religion. In 313 Constantine and Licinius had divided the Empire, Licinius ruling the East and Constantine the West. The Edict of Milan had actually been issued as a joint declaration. Licinius, however, was much less convinced of the merits of Christianity, and some years after the Edict he became an avowed enemy of the church. This situation, plus certain political differences, finally led to Constantine's victorious march against Licinius in 323. There was now no question about the religion of the Empire. Constantine's specific measures included laws and proclamations providing the following: Christians were to be protected from Jews; the clergy was exempted from taxation; wills could be made in favor of the church; Sunday, the day Christians commemorated the resurrection, was made a legal holiday; state money was granted for the building of churches and the publication of editions of the Scripture; and state lands were donated for Christian burial grounds. Many of these laws and gifts were also applicable to non-Christian religious bodies, but Constantine's obvious favoritism endowed the Christian Church with a dignity and status far exceeding that of its competitors.

When Diocletian (284-305), Constantine's predecessor as Emperor, took over the control of the Roman Empire, it was in a state of rapid decay. The borders of the Empire were so far-flung that efficient administration under the old provincial system was impossible. The army had achieved such exorbitant power that individual generals were constantly being hailed as emperors by their troops. The result of this military and political chaos was a long series of civil wars which both hampered trade and left much of the land in waste. Moreover, there was a constant threat of invasion from the outside. Various barbarian bands, mostly Franks and Goths, penetrated the border provinces of the Empire. The Emperor's principal problem, then, was the development of a strong central government which could control its army and defend the borders. Diocletian began a program of reorganization which Constantine continued and elaborated.

Both Emperors abandoned any idea that Rome was a republic. In order to strengthen imperial control, the West borrowed its new organizational principles from Persia and established the Emperor as an absolute autocrat with godlike powers. Diocletian, for example, claimed to be Jupiter, the high god of the Roman pantheon, while Constantine asserted that his authority was divinely given by the Christian God. When this divine authority was passed down to the lesser magistrates, the result was a gigantic bureaucracy under the Emperor. Obviously it was necessary to revise the military system: the rebelling provincial governors were relieved of their control and replaced by the Emperor's own commanders. A strongly centralized government thus met the crisis of the third century. In part at least, peace and unity were restored.

The Christian Church played an important role in this last desperate attempt to unify the Empire. The movement toward centralization seemed to require not only a concentration of political and military power, but also a common belief to be expressed through an organizational form essentially subordinate to the state. The hierarchical structure of the church was ideally fitted to control by a centralized religious authority in the hands of a relatively small number of people. There is little question that Constantine used Christianity as a basis for consolidating his own political power. In the years following his death his sons, who succeeded to the throne, used it more and more until, in the reign of Emperor Theodosius (d. 395), paganism was completely outlawed and Christianity became the only recognized religion. The one interruption in this development came during the reign of Emperor Julian (361-363), when a pagan reaction was instituted. This movement, however, was short-lived and of little importance.

THE "NEW" CHURCH

THE official recognition and support accorded the Christians produced a number of important internal changes. As the Diocletian persecutions spent their force with no appreciable effect, and when his successor, Constantine, became a Christian, the average man of the Greco-Roman world must have come to the conclusion that the old religions were without power and that the future belonged to Christianity. The result of this realization was a tremendous influx of new members. Many were undoubtedly attracted by sincere conviction, but by far the greater number of the converts saw the "wave of the future" in the new relation between church and state. Those who had been committed to Neo-Platonism, the Roman pantheon or the mystery cults brought to Christianity influences which wrought many changes in the character of primitive tradition. As an arm of the state, the church became an effective proving-ground for men seeking careers and power in government. It is no wonder that out of this situation a "new" church was born. Whether the original church was more conquered than conquering is a matter of historical debate.

The civil relations into which the church was now thrown demanded new offices and a general expansion of episcopal administration. Professional men were added to the ecclesiastical structure to handle the increased wealth, to act as legal advisors, to represent the church in the imperial court, and for a host of other business and legal details. The number of new converts was another imperative reason for increasing the professional personnel who would call on the sick, bury the dead and administer charity and relief. For the most part, the church tried to draw these new professionals from the ranks of pre-Constantine Christians, but the necessities of expansion forced the selection of an increasing number of ambitious converts.

From the first, these semisecular and legal positions were radically distinguished from the religious offices held by the clergy. New converts were generally denied ordination, as were slaves, actors, dancers and military men. The schools which had been established in Alexandria, Caesarea, Edessa, Nisibis and Antioch tried to impose educational standards on the clergy, but the church was expanding too rapidly for any effective long-term educational requirement. Many bishops tried to hold to a minimal standard, but the press of necessity allowed a large segment of the clergy to go unlettered. Although the ignorance exhibited by some of them was compensated for by intense evangelical zeal and administrative fervor, this sort of unlettered leadership was bound to result in a complex variety of beliefs, since no single bishop could oversee all the sermons and worship services in his diocese. Such confusion was the exact opposite of what the emperors intended, and there was a time when it looked as though the "new" church might break up into warring antagonistic sects.

THE GREAT CONTROVERSIES

PRIOR to the official recognition of Christianity, its major theological battles were waged against Judaism and paganism. When in the fourth century the whole Empire became nominally Christian, the controversies were within the church. Nevertheless, the central theological problems remained the same. Who was Christ? Was he God? *Logos?* the adopted Son of God? or a divinely inspired prophet? Where was the seat of authority? In Scripture alone? in personal experience of Christ? in man's reason? in the church's three-hundred-year tradition? or in the absolute dictates of the bishop? These problems were not confined to the theologians; people of all classes and professions engaged in the debates. Gregory of Nyssa describes the public interest in Constantinople during the Arian Controversy in the following terms:

Every corner and nook of the city is full of men who discuss incomprehensible subjects; the streets, the markets, the people who sell old clothes, those who sit at the tables of the money-changers, those who deal in provisions. Ask a man how many oboli it comes to, he gives you a specimen of dogmatizing on generated and unregenerated being. Inquire the price of bread, you are answered, "the Father is greater than the Son and the Son subordinate to the Father." Ask if the bath is ready, and you are answered, "the Son of God was created from nothing." [1]

ARIANISM

THE most serious theological controversy that Constantine had to face sprang up over the views of a presbyter named Arius (280?-336). Preaching in Alexandria, which was the center of the *Logos* Christology, Arius claimed that Christ could not be called God, and further that he was a creature whom God had brought into existence. Indeed, he insisted, the Father and Son of the Trinity were totally unlike and could never be said to have "identical natures and substance." Christ was the first creature of God's hand, and should always be considered the highest, but this did not make Christ deity, or even an aspect of deity. The only permissible conception of God was as an eternal, self-existent and utterly indivisible being who was never created, but who created all else. In Arius' view those who made Christ God, however they formulated their belief, were blaspheming against God's true nature. If the Son of God is to be called *Logos*, then *Logos* must be carefully distinguished from the reason which is God's by his nature.

The incarnation of the Son in the person of Jesus was not a union of the human and the divine. When Jesus was born into the world, the soul encased in his physical body was the soul of God's first-born. Therefore only the body was human; the soul was not. Arius was further interested to show that whereas God is unchangeable, the Son is constantly growing in knowledge and wisdom. Although this growth is analogous to human growth, the Son operates on a considerably higher

[1] Quoted in George Park Fisher, *History of Christian Doctrine* (New York: Charles Scribner's Sons, 1899), p. 129. By permission.

level. His glory and honor are hard won, and his selection by God to become the incarnate revelation is a tribute to his success.

By this theory, Arius hoped to meet the arguments advanced by Sabellius while at the same time maintaining a conception of Christ that would inspire both religious worship and intellectual acceptance. The bishop of Alexandria strongly condemned Arius for degrading Christ and introducing a second lesser deity, or demi-god. Many in the Alexandrian synod, feeling that the Arian Christology was really polytheism, consistently called it "heathenism introduced to Christianity." Actually Arianism was not a very new doctrine. Lucian, an Antioch presbyter, had taught it before Arius, and certainly some of it can be traced to Justin Martyr and Origen. But it was Arius' personal dynamism and effective oratory that made the idea popular with a larger number of people. It so happened that the bishop of Alexandria, absolutely convinced of the deity of Christ, had sufficient political strength to make a real issue of the matter. The conflict stirred up by the two parties eventually reached Constantine who, though he considered the whole affair petty, was forced to call an ecumenical council to solve the difficulty. The council was held at Nicea in 325.

THE NICENE SOLUTION

THE Nicene Council was the largest assembly of bishops, presbyters and laymen ever to gather in the early church. The approximately three hundred bishops present represented the whole of Christendom, but the largest delegation came from the Eastern sections, especially Asia Minor, Syria and Egypt. The Roman West seemed less disturbed and had only a few attending delegates. It was clear when the Emperor opened the session that his concern was for peace rather than theological niceties.

The Council sustained the bishop of Alexandria. Arius and his followers were excommunicated and anathematized. Having disposed of this first order of business, the Council went on to attempt a formulation of the essential conviction of the church regarding the nature of Christ. Many conflicting creeds were advanced by various parties, and finally a compromise statement was issued. The new creed was entirely anti-Arian, yet sufficiently general to be capable of a number of interpretations. The statement was couched in the following terms:

We believe in one God, Father Almighty, maker of all things visible and invisible; and in one Lord Jesus Christ the Son of God, begotten of the Father, only-begotten, that is from the substance of the Father, God from God, Light from Light, true God from true God, begotten, not made, of one substance with the Father, through whom all things were made, both the things in heaven and the things on earth; who for us men and for our salvation came down and was made flesh, was made man, suffered, and rose again on the third day, ascended into heaven, and cometh to judge quick and dead; and in the Holy Spirit. But those who say "There was once when he was not," and "Before this generation he was not," and "He was made out of nothing"; or pretend that the Son of God is of another subsistence or substance, or created or alterable or mutable, the Catholic church anathematizes.

The Nicene formulation proclaimed the full divinity and the full humanity of Jesus Christ. As is readily apparent, it did not solve the question of how two such diametrically opposed natures could be contained in one man. Nor did the Nicene Creed end the controversy. Soon after the Council disbanded, efforts were made to achieve some kind of compromise with the semi-Arians who had signed the document. The unity desired by Constantine was repeatedly shattered, and new councils were called in an effort to heal the wounds. Political considerations based in the geographical locations of opposing groups helped to cloud the real issues. Personal antagonisms made their contribution to the confusion. In general, the Latin West held to the Nicene formulation and declared all who denied that Christ was both God and man heretics. The Eastern sections of the church, however, were much less enthusiastic about the Nicene Creed and consequently set out to write a more moderate statement of faith.

AUGUSTINE

PRIOR to Augustine (354-430), the one great theological problem of the Christian Church was the nature of Christ. The character of the controversy was largely dictated by Greek metaphysical ideas and a concern for rational cosmology. In the thought of Augustine, however, Christological speculations are subordinated to questions of goodness, sin, freedom and grace. The shift of emphasis resulting from Augustine's thought gave Latin Christianity a chance to consolidate various aspects of the primitive church tradition and build the synthesis of Greek and Hebrew ideas which came to be known as medieval theology.

Augustine's personal life had led him through many varieties of Neo-Platonism and the non-Christian religious cults which had gained adherents in the Greco-Roman world. His spiritual autobiography, *The Confessions*, describes his search for some rational understanding of the world, and his discouragement because the problems of evil and authority, particularly, resisted logical solution. His deeply religious nature would not permit him to become a philosopher, yet his powerful mind always saw difficulties and logical incongruities in the competing religions of the time. For a while he found hope in the radical dualism of Manichaeanism, a religious fusion of Gnostic Christianity and Zoroastrianism, but the logical difficulties inherent in dualism finally made him reject it in favor of Neo-Platonism. Here Augustine was able to avoid both dualism and intellectual skepticism, but he could find neither peace nor spiritual rest within this semireligious philosophy. He finally had to reject the solution offered by Neo-Platonism, but it and its categories contributed a great deal to his understanding of Christianity.

Augustine's theology makes everything, including knowledge, dependent upon faith. Man's reason searches after understanding and attempts to distinguish between true and false knowledge. However, the very activity of reason, says Augustine, implies that there is some norm or standard of judgment higher than man and more stable than sense perception. This highest of all realities is the eternal God, the basis upon which all rational knowledge is founded. Since God is the rational ground of all being, it is impossible to know God through the use of reason. Faith, not reason, is the avenue to God and the foundation upon which all knowledge must rest. After faith is achieved, knowledge and the rigorous exercise of thought can produce legitimate results in discovering truth. Indeed, Augustine goes so far as to say that "knowledge is the reward of faith."

With faith exalted above reason, it then becomes necessary to define the nature of faith and its object. For Augustine, faith "works by love and possesses hope." God, the object of faith, speaks to man through the Scriptures and the tradition of the church. He who is united with God in love recognizes that the canonical Scriptures are the product of divine inspiration and represent the wisdom of God; without faith they seem to be little more than superficial stories and silly tales. The same can be said of the Catholic Church. Those lacking a love union with God see the church as a far from blameless social institution engaging in a struggle with other institutions for power and dominion; the eyes of faith, however, endow the church with divine authority and a spiritual mission. Augustine is so convinced of the divine nature of the church that in one place he says that even belief in the Scriptures is dependent upon the church's authority. "I should not believe the Gospel, did not the authority of the Catholic Church move me thereto."

Although Augustine's speculative structure was built upon faith, his conversion to Christianity had ethical rather than intellectual roots. Augustine, like Paul before him, felt the weight of sin and the burden of a guilty conscience. The principal allure of the Manichaean doctrine had been its assertion that evil can be explained by equating it with matter. Because man is cursed with a body (matter), he is therefore sure to sin and disobey the will of God. In this fatalistic doctrine, however, there is one alternative: the repudiation of body and all things material. Manichaeanism held Augustine for eight years, but finally he concluded that it was merely an escape rather than a solution of the problem of evil. Christianity, he felt, was finally the real answer.

The Christian God was kind, benevolent, righteous, merciful and in all ways good. Since he was also the creator and sustainer of the world, certainly he could not be responsible for the existence of evil. When God created angels, man and matter, he made them perfect. As a part of their perfection, both men and angels were given freedom to exercise choice. Of his own free will, Adam, the first man, abused his freedom and thus converted the perfection of the original creation into sinful human nature. "Man [seen in Adam] chose to be under his own dominion rather than under the dominion of God." By this action the whole human race was condemned to sin and "ordained to punishment." In following the Scripture, Augustine found part of the punishment to be physical (hard work, suffering and death), and part spiritual (loss of the knowledge of God and an inability to perform truly good actions).

By such reasoning was God relieved of the responsibility for evil and man forced to shoulder the entire blame. But God, whose mercy is as infinite as his righteousness, could not leave man to eternal torment and pain, and therefore the Christian drama was a saga of salvation rather than damnation. In Christ Augustine saw the burden of guilt lifted and the enormous debt paid, for he, the only perfect man since Adam, was crucified as a sacrifice to God for the sins of mankind. This ransom offered man the opportunity for a new life in the spirit which, however, was not earned by any human action but was the free gift of God. The new life was symbolized by the rite of baptism. After baptism it was possible for the Christian to say that he had truly been "born again," not in flesh, but in spirit.

Augustine accepted the prevalent Christian concept of the Devil, one of the fallen angels who had rebelled against God and now exercised tremendous power on earth. Although he was never consistent regarding the atoning work of Christ, Augustine often maintained that the reason Christ had to die on the cross was that he had to break the power of the Devil. By killing one sinless person, the Devil would irrevocably lose his dominion on earth, so Christ tricked him into thinking that he was an ordinary mortal, born of sinful parents and destined to live a sinful life. After the Devil discovered his mistake it was too late and his power was forever broken. Whatever the theory of atonement preferred, Augustine was sure that redemption was a free gift of God, and that Christ in his life and death was somehow the means of this grace.

Whether Augustine speaks of fallen angels or fallen men, pride always remains the root of sin. It is through pride that man rejects God's dominion; therefore only by unquestioning obedience can he once again be restored to full communion with his Lord. The grace which leads to union with God is unbreakable and irresistible. The union itself is neither ecstasy nor mystical absorption, but rather obedience and submission to his will. After man's pride has been broken, the world in which he lives still calls for action and resistance against evil. Augustine followed the Hebrew prophets in their conception of a divine, universal ordering of events in which the redeemed man cooperates with God to achieve ultimate triumph.

There are two cities or kingdoms in the world: the City of God and the City of Earth. The one begins with Abel and continues as the church; the other originates with Cain and moves through time as empire. The City of Earth lacks any true knowledge of God and does not have the power of redemption. It expresses self-love, will to power, and even contempt for God. The City of God, however, condemns self, power, and all forms of earthly love. It is comprised of the redeemed and those to whom God has given the grace to see and believe. The City of God is expanding and moving forward toward ultimate triumph. The City of Earth becomes more evil and corrupt each day, inevitably moving nearer and nearer final damnation. Although the church is the *Civitas Dei* (City of God), all church members are not thereby citizens of the heavenly city. Some may be in the church for fraudulent reasons, others may never have been given the grace necessary for salvation. On the other hand, membership in the visible church is necessary for all who are actually members of the *Civitas Dei*, since the church has been designated by God as the administrator of his grace. From within the church man must work with God for the eventual triumph of the Kingdom of Heaven.

This conception of the primacy of the church gave the ecclesiastical institution a solid foundation for absolute claims. Salvation, it said, which is possible through Christ alone, can be achieved only through the church which dispenses his mystical body through the sacraments. Because the church is the only agency which can administer the sacraments, it must be accorded complete authority over all men. The truth of God is a unity just as God himself is a unity, and this fact permits of no schisms or separatist movements. Thus Augustine answered the vexing problem of authority which had worried him during his Manichaean and Neo-Platonic days. His declaration also allowed the Catholic Church to establish itself as the single and primary spiritual authority in Western Christianity.

Augustine's fundamental contribution to Latin Christianity was to enunciate a doctrine which gave absolute authority to the Catholic ecclesiastical institution, and at the same time to redirect religious thought to the saving work of Christ. He, like the other great Western writers, held to the Nicean Creed and its formulations regarding the nature of Christ. Jesus Christ was both God and man, it said; and Augustine left the statement undisputed. Cosmological problems regarding God or Christ had little meaning for him. He was more concerned with religious salvation. The question of redemption took precedence over any discussion of Christ's nature or even proofs for the existence of God, for God was known to Augustine by direct experience, and religious communion was always more important than intellectual discussion.

AUGUSTINE AND PELAGIUS

Augustine's view of human nature was pessimistic in the extreme. Human beings were totally incapable of performing good actions without the redemption of Christ. In order to be saved, man had to have the proper faith, or trust, and give himself wholly to God's will. Although this faith was a free gift, there were always some men without it. Augustine explained this fact by Paul's doctrine of predestination. From the beginning God elected certain of his creatures to salvation.

They are given faith, and upon them depends the ultimate success of the divine plan. The rest of mankind is doomed to perish in darkness. On the surface this concept seems to deny God's justice, making him appear arbitrary and compassionless. Actually, Augustine said, predestination is proof of the fact that God's justice is tempered by mercy. The just fate of all mankind is death through sin and guilt. Therefore any salvation at all must be considered an undeserved bounty, true evidence of God's goodness; in no way does it indicate a lack of justice toward the damned.

Against this austere doctrine Pelagius, a British monk who flourished around 400, asserted the intrinsic goodness of God and all creation. God did create man with freedom of choice, he said, but it does not necessarily follow that one decision made by Adam corrupts the whole of the human race. Each person is free to choose good or evil; if he chooses evil he does so on his own responsibility and not because the entire race is lost. At birth we have only what God has given us, and he has given all men an equal chance for salvation. To conceive of some as being elected while others are left to misery is to blaspheme the goodness of God. Already many men have chosen to live without sin, and it is the job of the Church of Christ to increase that number. The grace of God, which has revealed to man through the Law, the prophets, and the life of Christ the proper modes of action, is forever available to those who seek it. However, grace is not irresistible; each man has the power to accept or reject it.

Pelagius went so far in his attack upon Augustine as to maintain that "life eternal" can be achieved by a person who has never been baptized. No one is determined by accident of birth, historical circumstance or divine election to become a partisan of the Devil. However, Pelagius and his followers were sufficiently impressed with the authority of the church to believe that a "higher" state of blessedness would be the lot of the sinless who were baptized. The church, they felt, could also act as the dispenser of grace through the establishment of disciplines and the clarification of moral regulations. But the absolute authority with which Augustine endowed the ecclesiastical institution was undercut and at least partially destroyed by the Pelagian emphasis.

The chief difference between Augustine and Pelagius is seen in their estimates of human nature and their ideas of grace and freedom. Augustine saw man as being completely and utterly dependent upon God and his free gifts, for he is so low, so corrupt, and his soul so distorted that good actions and self-help are out of the question. Pelagius believed that man is created good, with the power of salvation in his own hands. The grace of God is apparent in the various revelations which have been given to guide men and keep them from possible sin.

The argument between the Augustinians and the Pelagians finally came to a head at the synod of Carthage in 418. Pope Innocent of Rome had approved the condemnation of Pelagius at two regional councils two years earlier. At the synod of Carthage in 418 Pelagius was again branded heretical and he, together with his chief disciple, Coelestius, was excommunicated. Although the Augustinian party defeated Pelagianism, the great majority of Latin Christians were by no means united in their acceptance of Augustine's theology. The totality of man's sin, the irresistibility of God's grace, and predestination could hardly be called the doctrines of the church at large. Nevertheless, the condemnation of Pelagius gave authority and at least tacit support to Augustine's views.

ASCETICISM AND MONASTICISM

IN ADDITION to theological speculation and the development of a strong ecclesiastical hierarchy, day-to-day Christian piety was finding expression in a variety of forms. Worship was di-

rected to God and Christ through the heavenly souls of saints
and martyrs. The Virgin Mary came to be regarded as the
"Mother of God," and her assistance was sought in petitions
sent to the throne of grace. Besides these historical figures,
there were all manner of angels with different heavenly functions who were honored in varying degrees. In all cases these
supernatural beings rendered aid and comfort to earthly souls
in their spiritual struggles. Their pictures and images adorned
the churches, and often prayers were directed to such representations in the belief that in this way God's ear could be
more easily reached. Although many of the newer forms of
worship were condemned by the theologians, they were destined to be consolidated into the general Christian tradition.

One of the most important practical expressions of piety is
seen in the growth of asceticism. From the very beginning of
the Christian movement various forms of self-denial had been
common. A number of its holiest men were noted for their disregard of bodily pleasures and their renunciation of the material world. During the persecutions, when at any time a Christian might be required to die for his faith, the ideal of self-
denial was generally regarded as an essential part of devotion.
Even that early there were Christians who took vows of complete sexual abstinence. These virgins, both male and female,
were often thought to be more perfect Christians than the
majority who contented themselves with a less rigid discipline.
The women who took a vow of chastity were looked upon as
brides of Christ, wholly consecrated to him. Although chastity
was considered the highest form of self-sacrifice, the denial to
oneself of comfortable clothing, decent food and drink, sleep
and cleanliness were important on the list of ascetic practices.
Indeed, anything that was physically pleasurable was an appropriate sacrifice to God.

In the early days of the church, asceticism did not entail
separation from friends and family. After Christianity became

the official religion of the Empire and the threat of martyrdom was removed, it was felt that retreat into the hills and deserts brought intensified danger to the sacrifice and therefore made it more complete. Moreover, companionship with others was both pleasurable and a distraction from the spiritual exercises essential to asceticism. Solitude came to be one of the primary conditions of this life, and most of the ascetics in the third and fourth centuries were hermits. This extreme individualism, however, did not last long. Not only were the hermits exposed to undue hardships from external dangers, but perhaps more importantly, they discovered a deep need for sympathetic understanding of their enterprise. The answer was found in the establishment of monastic villages, where ascetics came together to lead a common life.

The earliest of the known monasteries in the West was a nunnery in Rome dating from 353. Soon afterwards, various bishops organized monasteries for young men and used them as training schools for the priesthood. Although monasticism was approved and generally promoted by the church hierarchy, its major force in premedieval days was felt among the laity. As monks and nuns became more numerous, their lay status often bred conflict with the clergy. It was only natural that these ascetics should feel that they were embracing a more complete Christianity than those who enjoyed material comforts. The clergy, on the other hand, considered themselves mediators of divine grace, and therefore members of the highest of all professions. The official church finally had to take control of the monasteries and place monks and nuns under the rule of a bishop.

The reasons for Christians entering monasteries were varied. The idea of self-sacrifice already alluded to was certainly a strong motive, for in some way complete fellowship with God always seems to imply self-discipline and the acceptance of punishment. For others the world of matter was sinful; no true godliness was possible as long as an individual was tied to it. The only emancipation was through denial of all carnal desire and devotion to prayer and contemplation. Furthermore, the ascetic life provided an opportunity to test the sincerity of one's religious convictions. The Christian faith had always been difficult; the conversion of Constantine must have made it seem far too easy to many who were accustomed to a history of rigors. Finally, it must have appeared to a large group a sure way of proclaiming their essential goodness. Like Hinduism and Buddhism, ascetic Christianity afforded a rule-of-thumb measure by which the world could judge the religious quality of a given life. Whatever the motivations of its adherents, organized and unorganized asceticism flourished until it became one of the main pillars of the medieval Catholic Church.

Since monasticism grew out of essentially practical considerations of piety, it is not surprising to find most of the monks Pelagians or semi-Pelagians. Augustine insisted that man can achieve nothing by his own efforts; everything is dependent upon the free grace of God. If this theory were accepted, there was no merit gained by the monk who renounced worldly pleasures for sackcloth and ashes. He was making no progress toward holiness or salvation, for his cosmic destiny had been sealed at the beginning. Pelagius, however, recognized the importance of merit and the exercise of free choice in gaining redemption. Within his system it was possible for the monk to be rewarded for self-denial and achieve a status with God denied to those less strong in will and purpose. Monasticism was completely impossible unless God looked with pleasure upon a free soul struggling away from the sins of the flesh towards holiness of spirit.

The monastic movement was finally organized and reformed by Benedict of Nursia in 529. The Rule which he first applied to the monks at Monte Cassino established the ideal of seclusion but abolished excessive asceticism. Benedict's Rule made labor and obedience the cardinal virtues for monks, while at the same time regularizing worship practices. Although there is nothing in the Rule about monks working for the good of mankind, the Benedictine Orders became the centers of learning and of organizations interested in the distribution of charity. The cultivation of individual piety and holiness slowly came to include acceptance of social responsibility, a love of mankind as well as of God. As a consequence, monks became teachers, missionaries, scholars and unpaid laborers in the fields.

Benedict's regularizing of monasticism had a profound effect upon the priesthood. Bishops and priests began to form communities under ascetic discipline and thus to abstract themselves from the ordinary life of the city or village. The monastic ideal soon came to represent the higher Christian life, and laws were passed against clerical marriages and clerical ostentation.

FOUNDATIONS OF MEDIEVAL CHRISTENDOM

IN SPITE of internal struggles and controversies, the church became a powerful political and religious force. The Roman imperial system was weakening to the point of chaos. Not only was the military and political bureaucracy corrupt: there were also threats of invasion from the outside. Since the earliest days of the Empire, the borders had fluctuated with the strength and activity of large groups of barbarians. The northern border was subject to raids by the Germanic peoples who lived north of the Danube and east of the Rhine. During the third century they began to exert increasing pressure, and Rome was unable to offer effective resistance. By the end of the fourth century German infiltration had gone so far as to blur the lines of the old frontier. Meanwhile, the Huns invaded the Balkans and unsettled the relatively peaceful Goths. The early years of the fifth century saw a number of barbarian tribes moving across the Rhine into Gaul, Rome captured by the Goths, and the Vandals establishing a sort of outlaw kingdom in Spain and North Africa. Under Attila, the Huns were able to conquer most of the territory north of the Danube and demand tribute from the Roman emperor.

These various barbarian movements resulted in the complete breakdown of the Roman administrative system and the establishment of a number of small kingdoms under the rule of their conquerors. At first the barbarian kings considered themselves dependent upon the emperor in Rome, but after 476 even this courtesy nod to the emperor's authority was dropped. With the disestablishment of the emperor at Rome, the Eastern emperor in Constantinople declared himself ruler of the entire Empire. Constantinople had not suffered from the invasions except for the loss of certain areas in the Balkans, but there was actually little hope that the ancient Empire could be re-established. In the sixth century Justinian (527-565) attempted to reconquer the West but without much success. North Africa, Spain, Gaul and Italy were almost completely gone by the time of Justinian's defeat. Imperial authority remained in some scattered seacoast towns and a few small islands.

The first distinctly new and Western civilization developed in the Frankish kingdom after Justinian, with the subsequent aid of the Moslems, had destroyed the rule of the Ostrogoths and Visigoths. The two most important factors contributing to the unification of the West were the Frankish monarchy and the Roman papacy. Both these agencies had extended their influence over a considerable portion of northern Europe, especially in Gaul and Germany. In doing so they had fused Roman and Germanic elements of procedure, culture and ideology. Since the Arabs had taken over the Mediterranean, European trade and commerce had virtually ceased.

In place of the commercial enterprises of the ancient world, the new economy of Europe was largely agrarian, and both church and state reflected the change. No longer was the state merely an abstract administrative bureau with far-flung agents working through established channels of communication. The Frankish kings divided the land into patrimonies and estates, and law was dependent upon the local rulers. For the most part these princes were sons of the kings, and a strict law of inheritance was observed. As political power became decentralized in this way, however, the landed aristocracy tried to increase their holdings and declare themselves independent of the Frankish monarch. The resulting confusion laid the basis for medieval feudalism.

The church was certainly not immune to the generally unsettled conditions of the period. Whenever the emperor was strong, as in the case of Justinian, the papacy was required to submit to the exigencies of politics. When the emperor was weak the church had freedom, it is true, but little understanding of the direction it should take. The establishment of the church as a potent force came early in the eighth century with an alliance between the papacy and the Frankish kingdom. Bishops and priests were now temporal as well as spiritual lords, and many of the kings considered themselves rulers with divine rights. On Christmas Day of the year 800, Pope Leo III crowned Charlemagne "Emperor of the Romans" and officially instituted the Holy Roman Empire. From 800 to the Protestant Reformation, religious and political interests were indissolubly merged.

The two most important factors contributing to the almost unlimited power of the church were monasticism and Augustine's claims regarding the primacy of ecclesiastical authority. Monasteries flourished throughout the whole of northern Europe, England, Scotland, Ireland and Wales. They not only were centers of prayer and solitude, but had also become concerned with missionary activity. Monks, some of whom later became famous Roman Catholic saints, went from area to area converting and baptizing whole populations. Although the pope in Rome was unable to keep these distant missionary-monks under any kind of real surveillance, his authority was unquestioned and most of their conversions were made in his name. The power of the church increased with the number of new converts. These people were taught that the priests were mediators between God and men; without their aid, salvation was impossible. But they had only a derived authority. They could mediate grace only so long as they were in good standing with the bishops who, in turn, were dependent upon the supreme pontiff, the Vicar of Christ on earth. The church's assumption of absolute authority based upon the conception of its being the earthly City of God led to innumerable struggles with later emperors, but for the Frankish kings it was a heaven-sent vehicle for achieving unity.

THE CONVERSION OF EUROPE

IN THE early centuries Christianity had made a compromise with Greek philosophy and the mystery religions. By absorbing elements of both, Christianity was able to develop theological systems and establish a variety of worship practices. Then the organizational structure of the ancient Roman Empire was borrowed by the Christians as being the most effective method of expanding their faith. As Christianity made its way into the barbarian communities of northern Europe, further compromises became necessary.

The indigenous religions of this area were much like primitive religions all over the world. Principally concerned with demons and fate, they taught that the universe was filled with spirits, dreadful powers who usually worked in darkness, and innumerable special deities who, after proper propitiation, would guide and protect wandering men. For the most part there was little theological speculation, and what religious ideas there were found expression in epic tales and folklore. Teutonic mythology divided the various forces of nature and history among three mighty gods: Thor, ruler over the air, weather and fertility; Wodon, charged with the responsibility for wars and the maintenance of courage in the face of danger; and Fricco, the god of light and peace. Each of these gods had his own priests and his own particular type of worship. Slavic mythology possessed a larger number of gods, many of them also representing or controlling aspects of nature. The god Rodŭ, for example, was responsible for good harvests and a fertile earth, while Dažĭbogŭ, a powerful god of life, was identified with the sun.

Each of the many tribes had its own deities and demons, so a catalogue of names would serve no purpose. It is important to recognize, however, that most of the north and central European paganisms were disorganized, vague polytheisms. None of them had anything corresponding to a church organization, and their priests were usually either tribal officials or medicine men. There was nothing that even remotely resembled a theological orthodoxy. The jumble of ideas reflected in the folklore had to do with the existence of life after death in a kind of hazy spirit world, with the magical power of amulets and divine signs, with the personality of the gods and their concern for human life, and finally with the fact that many of the gods and demons had once been earthly chieftains.

The Christian missionaries who pushed into the far corners of Europe were armed with two virtually invincible weapons. The first was a relatively systematic statement of faith which offered an explanation and a promise. The indigenous religions were vague about immortality and the means of attaining it. The evangelists painted for these people a picture of paradise and all its glories, while at the same time they were able to map out a course of action which would culminate in heavenly citizenship. The missionaries further told the dramatic story of the way Christ had come to earth, conquered the forces of darkness, and how he was now a heavenly chieftain leading his armies of angels against whatever new aggressions the Devil planned. The disordered polytheisms were neither so dramatic nor so cogent. In addition to being ambassadors of a new religion, the missionaries were symbols of the ancient Greco-Roman culture. They used the Latin and Greek languages and told of the splendors of Rome and cities of the Mediterranean. Into what must have been uncomfortably rude civilizations, they brought a vision of life which was almost wholly new, and certainly more agreeable.

The tribal kings could see considerable political advantage in becoming Christians. The Roman papacy was benevolent in relations with its adherents, but it could also be violent in its drive to stamp out heathenism. The constant dangers which these small kings faced from the landed aristocracy and foreign aggression were generally minimized by attachment to the church. The clergy, especially the more politically-minded bishops, had it within their power to mediate disputes, and they could often prevent raids and wars. Obviously they were not inclined to use their good offices in behalf of those who denied Christ. Since religion among the barbarians had generally been a public matter, the king set the religious pattern of the people, and his conversion to Christianity meant the nominal conversion of all his subjects. By this sort of cooperation between the church and the various states, both were able to increase their power.

As the new religion was more widely adopted, many of the tribal hero-gods became angels and saints within the Christian system. The absence of any non-Christian theology made the acceptance of the church and its doctrines easy, while at the same time the breadth of the Christian structure allowed many of the pagan forms of worship to remain virtually unchanged. The magical potency which had once been ascribed to heathen idols and images was now transferred to the Christian sacraments, pictures of Christ, and relics of the early church. Miraculous cures, dramatic deliverances and a host of other feats were attributed to the new Christian symbolism. In many respects popular religion changed its verbiage and its forms, but its content remained the same. The result was European Christianity, an all-inclusive fusion of many traditions of both East and West.

24

THE EASTERN CHURCH

SUCH rapid increase in the power and influence of the Roman See was not favorably looked upon by the bishops of other large cities. Alexandria, Antioch, Jerusalem and Constantinople all contested the primacy of Rome. The most important rival to papal supremacy, however, was the patriarch of Constantinople, who considered himself the legitimate heir to the ancient church. When Constantine moved the seat of government from Italy to the East, the Eastern emperors claimed dominion over the whole of the Mediterranean world. The Byzantine Empire had not been subject to barbarian invasions; thus it had been able to maintain prosperity and, until the rise of Islam, peace. The emperors soon established the patriarch of Constantinople as the visible head of a glittering imperial church which functioned as the right arm of the state. Although relations between the Eastern and Western branches of the church were often strained, the idea of a single universal Catholic Church was sufficiently well embedded to prevent a complete break until 1054.

The rising power of Islam was the real force which broke the back of the Eastern Imperial Church. From the relatively small beginnings in Medina and Mecca, Mohammed and his followers had built Arabia into a first-rate military power. The Arabian expansion, at least in its first phases, should not be viewed, however, as a religious crusade. There was in this period no deliberate attempt to win converts among those conquered by arms. In the main, the seventh-century expansion was motivated more by a desire for land and political control than by religious fervor.

Whatever the motivations, Islam soon covered a vast area of the known world. By the early years of the eighth century, when the conquests were finally successfully resisted, the Arabs had complete control over Syria, Mesopotamia, Persia, Palestine, Egypt and Spain. Frankish power in Western Europe kept them south of the Pyrenees. Northwestern Europe was threatened only once when the Arabs tried to invade Gaul, but they were turned back at Tours by Charles Martel in 732. Their inability to pass beyond the Pyrenees and their failure in the battle of Constantinople (717-718) virtually ended Arabian land conquests for the time being.

Nevertheless the Eastern Imperial Church went into decline when the Moslem conquest of the seventh century reduced the size of the Empire and cut off its wealth. As a result, the patriarch at Constantinople lost much of his authority over outlying churches, and various national groups set up their own religious institutions without regard for external authority. As the Byzantine Empire declined, the Latin popes attempted to reassert their claims of supremacy, all the while consistently interfering with the internal affairs of the Eastern hierarchy. By so doing, they stirred up age-old controversies and made more apparent the differences between the two traditions. Many of the theological differences stemmed from the early councils which had attempted to define orthodoxy and establish standards of worship. The major antagonisms, however, arose out of practical considerations. For example, the East allowed clergy below episcopal rank to marry, while the West prohibited the marriage of all clergy; the West allowed and encouraged fasting on Saturday, the East forbade it; the East prohibited the use of the lamb as a symbol for Christ, while the

West allowed it; the West considered only fifty of the apostolic canons to be valid, whereas the East increased the number to eighty-five. In addition to such minor variations, the East refused to accept the theological idea that the Holy Spirit proceeds directly from both the Father and the Son, insisting that the Spirit could stem only from the Father. In all probability these differences of faith and practice were used as public justification for an essentially political schism: the break caused by the formation of the Frankish kingdom, and which the church was unable to mend.

JOHN OF DAMASCUS

THE orthodox theology of the Eastern Church was formulated by John of Damascus in the eighth century. Although his work bore few signs of originality, he accurately expressed the fundamental faith of the Eastern Christians. His rise to prominence came during the iconoclastic controversy. Emperor Leo the Isaurian had proclaimed the worship of images and statues to be unscriptural and blasphemous in the sight of God. John of Damascus attacked this conception. He maintained that material representation of the divine is not only necessary for devotion but also consistent with God's own action in materially embodying himself in Jesus Christ. The main point of John's attack was his assertion that the concerns of worship are for "synods and not for emperors." The church, he felt, should be free of secular political control, especially when the emperor was really degrading the incarnation and promoting heresy.

From Augustine on, Western theology was primarily concerned with a theory of salvation. The sinful character of man's will, his inability to recognize truth without the aid of an authoritatively established revelation, and the conviction that salvation was final only after death, all led the Western

Church to a theology of authority rather than a theology of experience. Eastern orthodoxy, on the other hand, made the cultus and the experience of devotion and worship the bases of faith. John's defense of the use of ikons (images and pictures) is a case in point. Their fundamental purpose was to enhance the devotional life and to serve as a means of communication between the earthly and the divine. Christianity was to prove its validity in the experience of God rather than in an authoritative structure of beliefs and a churchly hierarchy; and this experience was open to all men who would submit to the ritual and practice of the church.

Eastern orthodoxy maintains that although God is above and beyond all knowledge and therefore all human comprehension, he has not left man without some light. By nature all men have the conviction that God exists, and through his revelations in Scripture and the person of Jesus, he has given as much knowledge of himself as is wise. Beyond these limits the human intellect should never go since God knows what is best for man and what he should be given. The excessive speculations of philosophic theologians who would penetrate the mystery of divine nature are blasphemous and indicate a lack of faith in God's justice and wisdom. In his formulation of Eastern orthodoxy, John of Damascus was asserting the primacy of devotional simplicity and the ultimate futility of philosophic speculation. Truth is a conviction of the "inward parts," he felt—a conviction inborn and purified by Christian experience.

This emphasis upon direct experience did not, however, preclude the possibility of an orthodox structure of creeds and dogmas. John held to the Doctrine of the Trinity, the Incarnation, the Virgin Birth, the Resurrection, the Second Coming of Christ, immortality, the existence of angels, and the Christian idea of creation. But these beliefs did not possess the character of scientific truth which they acquired in the West;

instead they were considered to be symbols and aids to worship. Whenever theological ideas such as predestination and the pre-existence of the soul seemed to offer no incentive for devotion, they were rejected as being heretical. John and the Eastern Church always believed in free will and the responsibility of man, maintaining that every individual has it within his power to be virtuous and, with the aid of creedal and material symbols, to communicate in love and devotion with God.

Theology, in losing its independent validity, became a part of ritual. Its function was not to aid people in understanding their faith, but rather to supply them with another instrument of devotion. John of Damascus held that theological and creedal writing "is to the literate as the image is to the illiterate"—and nothing more. As one might expect, this sort of attitude led to the decay of creative theological writing and the preservation of creedal statements in their original forms. The rituals of the Eastern Church came to embody long recitations of various creeds with primary emphasis placed upon correct repetition and the proper musical cadence. Although there were theologians who followed John of Damascus, the Eastern Church always maintained a deep veneration for the past and rarely broke new ground in man's attempt to understand the mysteries of nature and God. The West, on the other hand, never subordinated intellectual activity to cultic experience and was thereby able to produce a vast and impressive literature in philosophy, science and theology.

THE END OF BYZANTINE UNITY

THE final breakup of the Byzantine Empire came at the hands of the Ottoman Turks in the fifteenth century. After the decline of Arabian power, the center of Islamic power shifted to the Turks of Asia Minor. About the year 1300, Othman, a brilliant military strategist and a gifted statesman, began the unification of the Turkish tribes. He and his successors soon extended their control over all Moslem peoples in Asia Minor. As the Ottoman Turks became more powerful, the Greco-Roman emperors in Constantinople saw their lands taken and their Christian subjects converted to Islam. In the second half of the fourteenth century, the Turks moved up into south-eastern Europe, and by the end of the century, they had conquered the entire Balkan peninsula except Constantinople and a few remote cities on the Aegean. In 1453, Mohammed II, one of the most brilliant of the Ottoman sultans, captured Constantinople and ended the Christian empire in the Near East. Christians and Jews were considered second-class citizens, and many of their churches and synagogues were converted into Moslem mosques.

As the Byzantine Empire was dying, frantic calls for help were rushed to the Christian West. Some popes and Christian princes raised armies for crusades against the "infidels," but the aid was too little and too late to be of much use. The help given by the West at this time nevertheless marks the beginning of a long series of crusades and wars against the Turks which culminated in the dissolution of the Ottoman Empire after World War I. It is in the environment of this constant political and religious warfare that for centuries the Eastern Church has had to live.

The extreme emphasis upon the cultus, the victories of the Moslems, the destruction of the Empire in 1453 by the Turks, and the rising brilliance of the West—all conspired to destroy the unity of the Eastern Church. As late as the nineteenth century, the patriarch of Constantinople claimed spiritual supremacy over the entire Eastern Church, but actually he has exercised little power since the time of Justinian. Each of the various national branches of the Eastern Church has attained autonomous status, and in many cases has been established by national law. From time to time there have been jurisdictional disputes which have led to mutual excommunication, but for the most part each national unit has been content to operate within the borders of its own state. Today the major Eastern Orthodox Churches are to be found in Russia, Greece, Yugoslavia, Rumania, Poland, Bulgaria, Albania, Finland, Esthonia, Latvia, Lithuania and Czechoslovakia. Since early modern times the Russian patriarchate has exerted the greatest influence and has been largely responsible for the establishment of archbishoprics in North America and the Orient.

25

THE MEDIEVAL LATIN CHURCH

THE comparative peace and orderly progress brought about by cooperation between the Frankish kingdom and the papacy were shattered in the tenth and eleventh centuries by new invasions and internal corruption. Feudalism, which took the place of the disintegrated Empire founded by Charlemagne, was based upon a noncommercial, agrarian economic system, thus causing a reorganization of both political and religious institutions. Landowners rather than those in high political office held the power in this new social structure. The state, either in the old Roman or in the modern sense, ceased to exist. As government broke up into smaller and smaller units, it ultimately reached the relatively self-sufficient village community. With extremely primitive methods of communication, the erstwhile central governments could not perform even the most elementary police functions, so each little hamlet was almost entirely dependent upon its own resources for the protection of life and property. In such circumstances it was inevitable for the small landowners to look to those who were more powerful. In return for protection, the small landholder usually had to forfeit ownership and pay the larger landlord in goods and services.

Under this system the property and power of a few of the landowners greatly increased, but so did their responsibilities. Each new piece of land acquired carried with it a duty to protect and guard the previous owner. The lord was thus obli-

A fourteenth-century French wooden madonna. (*Edouard Corrayer Collection, Paris.*)

A Greek terra-cotta figurine (madonna) by a Greek artist, about 500 A.D.

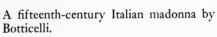

A fifteenth-century Italian madonna by Botticelli.

A sixteenth-century picturization of the crucifixion by Mathias Grünewald. The figures other than Jesus are Mary, John, Longinus, and an unidentified woman weeping at the foot of the cross.

An Italian fresco by Perugino, 1481. It pictures the charge to Peter. Jesus is giving Peter the Keys to the Kingdom with the Apostles grouped on each side. The background indicates the future glory of the Roman Catholic Church.

gated to raise an army and generally see to it that his tenants had freedom to work. Further, he took over the supervision of the farming, the administration of justice, and the responsibility for order. Each person within the community had his own particular function and certain accompanying rights. For example, the small owners were dependent upon the lord, but they had the right to his protection; in like manner the lords of given manor communities were dependent upon more powerful lords or barons who had either conquered the village or purchased it with a guarantee of protection. The most characteristic feature of the feudal system was this chain of dependence and vested interests which ran from top to bottom. The entire structure could be symbolized by a pyramid, the broad base representing the small owners and the apex the king. The king, however, could not rule his subjects directly; he too was bound by contractual relations which required him to channel his orders and commands through the various barons and so on down the pyramid. The personal loyalty of a given individual was to his immediate lord and not to the king. His lord, on the other hand, might be dependent upon a more powerful lord above him; if so, the first lord owed no personal loyalty to the king. Finally, however, there would be some baron of high station whose loyalty belonged exclusively to the king.

THE FEUDAL CHURCH

THIS network of dependence and right included the church. The turmoil and chaos of the time required that the church look to kings and barons for the protection of its property. Over a period of three centuries the bishoprics and monasteries had come into possession of vast holdings. Most of this land was worked exactly like that belonging to the secular lords. Since, under the feudal system, military service at least was required of landowners, the church was forced either to

[399]

raise armies or to be in sufficiently good standing with the kings to draw upon their protection. As the church accumulated increasingly greater land holdings, the bishops who presided over the various dioceses became more concerned with political and military matters than with religion. Indeed, many of them were appointed by secular rulers from the families of the landed aristocracy. This growth of the church's temporal power resulted in religious offices' being bought and sold and passed on from father to son. The old laws concerning clerical marriage and discipline fell into disuse, and the princes of the church became indistinguishable from the princes of the realm.

Had the papacy been sufficiently strong, many of these abuses could have been corrected. But the headquarters in Rome was a beehive of political intrigue. Various aristocratic factions vied with one another for control of the Holy See, and popes were made and deposed in the space of weeks and months. Some men, Sergius III (904-911), for example, used armed force to gain the papal throne. But by far the largest number assumed office under the watchful eyes of whatever political faction happened to be dominant. The situation became so chaotic that finally Emperor Otto I (936-973) was forced to interfere and restore some kind of order, if not purity, to the papacy.

With the hierarchy primarily concerned in empire and local politics, the spiritual message of the church was left to the local parishes and monasteries. Both these institutions had also felt the corrupting influence of temporal power, but by virtue of their isolation they were able to do a certain amount of real religious work. For the most part the village priests were unlettered and ill trained in the history and faith of the church. As a result they allowed many unorthodox and often superstitious practices to creep into the services of worship. The outward forms of Christianity were maintained, but magical formulae often superseded what earlier theologians had called

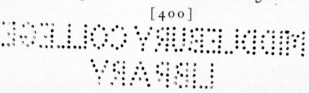

"true piety." On the popular level, religion and morality were virtually divorced. Early Christianity had conceived of God as a stern judge who demanded righteous action. In the tenth century many nominal Christians thought of God as an object of fear for whom one must perform rites and offer propitiating sacrifices. With a weakened hierarchy and an ignorant clergy for guides, most people felt such an attitude to be the essence of Christianity; there was little conception of the necessity for a moral code.

THE PENITENTIAL SYSTEM

RUNNING counter to this divorce of religion and morals was the development of a new form of penitential discipline modeled on monastic practices, particularly those in Ireland. A monk who had been guilty of some infraction of ascetic rules was bound to make public confession and seek help from others in his petition for pardon. In addition, the abbot would probably impose some especially difficult penance which would "make good the fault to God." As the monasteries became stronger they extended this discipline to laymen. At regular intervals a church member was required to confess his sins to the priest, who would prescribe penance. The most usual forms of penance were fasting, recitation of psalms and prayers, and in some cases banishment to a monastery for a given period of time.

As the penitential system spread, it became increasingly elaborate. For example, books to guide the priests in classifying sins and administering penance were written and circulated. The number of crimes against God was multiplied, and in many cases the list included civil as well as religious offenses. The most severe penance, however, was that demanded for heresy and for questioning the authority of the church. The universal conviction of the Middle Ages that the life after death was more important than earthly existence gave the church a power unrivaled by any secular sovereign, for as the mediator of God's grace, it could consign people to heaven or hell. Moreover, any person who left the church and refused to do penance was sure that his soul was doomed to everlasting torment and misery.

Through the instruments of confession and penance, the local priests were able to establish a nearly absolute control over the members of their parishes. They became arbiters of good conduct and administered the most effective punishments in the name of God. In terms of church theory, the priest had no power to punish; but in actual practice his sentences were penalties rather than fatherly advice. By refusing to allow a person to partake of the Eucharist he made it impossible for him to become mystically united with the divine; by withholding absolution he consigned one of the faithful to hell; and by publicly declaring a man to be an unrepentant sinner he effectively ostracized him from decent society. On the other hand, the priest's *"Absolvo te"* assured the penitent of God's forgiveness and reunited him in the mystical fellowship of Christ's body. But most important, the penitent was reinstated as a candidate for heavenly bliss in the life after death.

Closely associated with the penitential system was the use of indulgences. In certain circumstances, especially when some extraordinary work had been performed in behalf of the church, a person or a whole parish might be granted a "remission of penance," or an indulgence. These indulgences could only be granted by popes or bishops, and the Fourth Lateran Council (1215) set definite limits on their duration. For example, at the consecration of a new church building, the presiding bishop could grant the builders (i.e., the whole congregation) an indulgence for a fraction of the penance they would be required to make for their sins in the ensuing year.

Popes were permitted to grant plenary indulgences which remitted the entire penalty, and in some cases even anticipated whatever sins might be committed during the remainder of an individual's life. Plenary indulgences were often received by military men and wealthy landowners who made extensive gifts of services and land to the church. By such devices the papacy and the episcopal hierarchy increased their control over the peoples of Western Europe.

POPULAR RELIGIOUS EXPRESSION

BUT popular religious activity went far beyond the bounds of worship and penance. Beautiful new cathedrals were constructed in most of the major cities of Europe even though the economic situation of the time hardly warranted such tremendous ventures. The hierarchy contributed money and leadership to the enterprise, but the real basis of the building program lay in a mass revival of religious enthusiasm. Vast numbers of workers gave their time and effort, with no reward other than the feeling of having glorified God and in some sense having assumed a more direct part in the great drama of salvation. Another important means of expressing religious enthusiasm was the crusading movement which began in the eleventh century. Thousands of peasants and noblemen from all over Europe engaged in holy wars to free Jerusalem of Moslem control. There were certainly economic and political reasons for these wars, but the records of the crusades indicate a strong religious motivation. At times the popes attempted to discourage these mass marches to Jerusalem, but more often they gave them their blessings. Pope Urban II granted the following plenary indulgence to the crusaders of 1095: "Whoever out of pure devotion, and not for the purpose of gaining honor or wealth, shall go to Jerusalem to liberate the church of God, may reckon that journey in lieu of all penance." In time the official church took over the direction of the crusading spirit and used the mass armies against heretics of all sorts.

The religion of medieval Europe was hopelessly confused and inextricably bound up with political, economic and social desires. All of life seemed to be permeated by supernatural sanctions and controls. Kings ruled their subjects by the grace of God and divine right; God was concerned in the most minute details of everyday life, including the price one could charge for the produce of his land; temporal power for the church, which was, after all, Christ's earthly body, was looked upon as wholly necessary and completely justifiable; cathedrals, parish churches and religious schools formed the center of social life; and the fact that Palestine, which was to be liberated by the crusaders, was not only the scene of Christ's life but also the key to commercial empire made the cause no less holy. Soldiers of the Cross were religious fanatics, calculating power politicians, and merchants in search of markets; they built and destroyed, conquered and freed, killed and healed, all in the name of the carpenter of Nazareth.

The most outstanding characteristic of the nonpolitical religious life of medieval Christendom was the common fusion of superstition and piety. For the most part the service of worship conducted by the priest before the altar had little intellectual meaning for his parishioners. The mysterious words spoken over the bread and wine in the Eucharist were unintelligible, but the laity generally understood that a miracle was taking place. It was supposed that the bread turned into the actual body of Christ and that the wine became his blood. Thus the few words of consecration repeated by the priest had an effect which allowed the worshiper to take into himself the material embodiments of God's own Son. In addition to the wonderful properties of the Eucharistic elements, the relics of the ancient church also possessed a potency which guarded and protected believers. Although there was undoubtedly much genuine Christian piety in medieval Europe, the unseen world of good and evil spirits dominated the mind of the average unlettered layman, who was quite convinced that the only effective method for coping with it was by magical formulae and supernaturally empowered relics.

THE MENDICANT FRIARS

THE far-flung empire of the Church was necessarily a loose federation rather than a closely knit structure. Many areas received only occasional visits from papal representatives, and much of the popular local practice was but vaguely known to the Vatican. In the latter centuries of the Middle Ages, both towns and monasteries exhibited a marked spirit of independence with regard to episcopal and lay princes. New monastic orders were founded in protest against the corruption of the Church hierarchy and the insinuation of secular controls. Some of these received official recognition and blessing, but by far the larger number were merely tolerated, and in some extreme instances they even became objects of persecution. The older monasteries had been incorporated into the general Church structure, and from them bishops and popes had been selected. The creation of new orders was an attempt to re-establish the monastic ideal in its pure form and once again to provide the proper conditions for spiritual exercise and devotion.

The increasing number of these orders led Innocent III to request the Fourth Lateran Council (1215) to outlaw and forbid the organization of any new ones. Not long after the decree was issued, two new orders came into existence. They not only forced Innocent to make an exception to his ban, but they also laid the foundation for a new type of monasticism. Previous orders had emphasized the necessity for withdrawing from society for the purpose of prayer and acts of self-mortification. Individual salvation was their end, and whatever they did for others, whether in Church or in society, was more or less incidental. The new orders, established by Francis Bernardone of Assisi (1182-1226) and Dominic Guzman (1170-1221), were, however, based upon the opposite idea. These mendicant orders set out to save others through self-denying labors. Both Francis and Dominic wished to establish among the laity the kind of pure spiritual life which they felt had either never been known or had been allowed to languish. Both movements began as preaching missions to convert Christian Europe to a higher level of Christianity.

Francis Bernardone began life as the son of a wealthy Italian merchant. His early years were filled with luxury, and because of his father's great property, he seemed destined to become one of the more influential thirteenth-century commercial princes. After a severe illness he was suddenly converted to a kind of Christianity which in his day had few adherents. He sold his possessions, gave everything to the poor, and presented himself to the bishop of Assisi for complete dedication to God. His enthusiasm was fired by his conception of Christ as a beautiful but materially poor soul who devoted his life to the underprivileged and socially outcast. With no thought of starting a new order, thousands of like-minded people renounced their former patterns of life and gave themselves wholly to the service of man. These Franciscans, as they came to be called, paid little attention to conventional notions of monkish conduct. Although they took vows of celibacy, poverty and obedience, their natural simplicity and obvious good humor always marked them off from the austere and rather morose monks of other orders. They had but one goal: the conversion of mankind to the "simple Gospel of Christ"— absolute trust in God and service to man.

Whereas the Franciscans worked with the lower economic

groups, the Dominicans preached to the wealthy. Dominic Guzman was a Spanish priest of good family and sound education. He established his order to aid in the stamping out of heresy, especially one known as Albigensianism which was rampant in southern France. Dominic was impressed with the ineffectiveness of the crusades, inquisitions and the various other forms of coercion which had been employed by the Church against heretics. In contrast to these official methods, the Dominicans set out to persuade the heretics to return by showing them the rational basis of the Church's doctrine. They proposed to win heretics' minds through preaching and argument, and their hearts through the example of their own pure lives. To facilitate this mode of procedure, the Dominicans encouraged the establishment of schools, the education of the clergy, and the development of learning and scholarship.

By the middle of the thirteenth century the mendicant orders had grown to considerable strength. They had both received recognition from the papal throne, and their monks and nuns were in evidence in all the major cities of Europe. Their emphasis upon preaching gradually led certain of their number to chairs in the universities, where began the development of theological systems. As Franciscans and Dominicans came to positions of influence in these centers of learning, their power in Church Councils increased. The great formulators of Roman Catholic orthodoxy who labored in the latter years of the thirteenth century were all members of either one or the other mendicant order.

THE SCHOOLMEN

FROM the time of Augustine to the eleventh century, the Church, and indeed all of western Christendom, was primarily concerned with the establishment of temporal control and order. Although the major efforts of the Church went into organizational development, the resultant intellectual darkness was occasionally relieved by some first-rate philosophic minds. Boethius and Pseudo-Dionysius, both of the fifth century, produced writings which combined Neo-Platonic philosophy with Christian devotional piety. Neither of these writers was particularly original in approach or content, but both did reflect accurately the important ideas of the age. In general, the thought of the period was characterized by a low estimate of man's ability to discern rationally the will of God. Human reason, an instrument clearly distrusted by Augustine, was subordinated to divinely authored faith. With such a point of view, it is little wonder that the cathedral schools were more concerned with the cultivation of piety than with the development of a critical philosophy or theology. They had, however, preserved the documents from which the schoolmen of the later Middle Ages drew the materials for the construction of scholastic theology.

The intellectual stirrings of the eleventh century brought about the development of universities from the foundations provided by the ancient cathedral schools. At the same time the way was opened for a re-examination of the fundamentals of the Christian faith. The movement toward an intellectual clarification of the truths of faith was begun by Anselm of Canterbury (1033-1109). Anselm maintained that the basic propositions of Christianity—the existence of God, the incarnation, the doctrine of the trinity, and the authority of the Church—could all be demonstrated without recourse to revelation or the tradition of the Church. From the beginning made by Anselm, the work was carried forward by that much more brilliant dialectician, Abelard (1079-1142), who taught at the cathedral school in Paris. With a ceaselessly inquiring mind, Abelard went through the statements of the tradition and found them confused and contradictory. In the last analysis, he insisted, the truth or falsity of any theological proposition must be determined by critical investigation. The authority of the past can be considered at best only a "provisional substitute for reason." God is not pleased by ignorant worship; he implanted natural reason in men so that these children of his hand could know what and why they believed. Contrary to the prevailing notion, Abelard felt doubt to be both honorable and necessary: "Through doubt we come to investigation, and through investigation to the truth."

The new spirit of rational inquiry revealed the confused and chaotic condition of the medieval Christian's mind. The loosely formulated articles of faith and practice which had been assimilated through the ages from Jewish, Greek, Roman, Slavic, Teutonic and Saxon sources were neither consistent nor particularly understandable. The preoccupation of the Church with organizational and political matters had allowed beliefs to multiply with no guiding principle. As the light of reason pointed up the contradictions, schoolmen all over Europe demanded a new synthesis which would structure the faith and endow it with intellectual respectability.

The most serious attacks on the traditional beliefs of the Church came from mysticism and from the assertion of the primacy of rational knowledge over faith. The mystics placed major emphasis upon immediate personal experience of the divine, and by so doing minimized both the authority of the Church and its historic creeds. Church authority had been founded on the idea that the Church was the only agency through which man could obtain the grace needed for salvation. By emphasizing the importance of direct unmediated experience, the mystic challenged the whole basis of medieval Catholicism. The conflict between faith and reason posed the major intellectual problem, especially when, in the twelfth century, all the Aristotelian writings became known. Christian scholars were forced to defend their statements against such Mohammedan and Jewish Aristotelians as Avicenna, Averroës and Maimonides. Averroës (1126-1198), the greatest of the Mohammedan philosophers, set the problem by formulating the relation of knowledge to faith in a way that was wholly unacceptable to the Christians. Knowledge, he said, has no relation to religion; it is attained by the use of man's rational powers and by his sense perception. Faith comes without any mediation, and its revelation must be completely accepted. It is possible, therefore, that the truths of faith might contradict the truths of rational investigation and inquiry. Such contradictions must stand since the two spheres are utterly separate.

Such a position made the apologetic mission of the scholars impossible, for within it there could be no rational argument which all men of intelligence could be expected to accept. And if the Christian scholars were to prove the primacy of Christianity, it was necessary for them to show that its claims were reasonable for all right-thinking men. By separating natural knowledge from faith, the Aristotelians set religion off in a private area which allowed little if any communication with the rest of life. The Church hierarchy recognized that the new doctrine was sufficiently dangerous to warrant a ban on the teaching of Aristotle in the University of Paris. But the wealth of material and the obvious merit of Aristotelian methodology made the works of the ancient philosopher impossible to ignore. The conflict was finally resolved by a systematization of Catholic theology and the development of a Christian Aristotelianism.

The movement toward the development of a unified critical theology which was begun by Anselm and Abelard culminated in the work of Thomas Aquinas (1227-1274). Thomas, the son of an Italian nobleman, began his work at Cologne under Albert the Great, one of the most prominent scholastic teachers. His closely reasoned summary of the Christian faith fills thirty-two quarto-size volumes. It purports to answer the basic questions put to Christians by Jews and Mohammedans, while at the same time reconciling the natural life of man with his position as a child of God. The *Summa Theologica* of Thomas is not especially original, but it does bring into one system all that was then known about nature, society, man and God. The doctrines set forth were worked out in the various academies of Europe from a reconciliation of the traditions of the Church with the newly discovered writings of Aristotle and other ancient Greek philosophers. Thomas' codification of them has remained to this day the basis for Roman Catholic orthodoxy.

SCHOLASTIC DOCTRINE: PHILOSOPHY

WITH the introduction of Aristotelian philosophy into theological discussion, it became necessary to distinguish between the functions of reason and the functions of revelation. Averroës' formulation resulted in an unbridgeable gap since it seemed to leave religious propositions in the realm of subjectivity without means of public verification. Thomas and most of the other schoolmen were sure that man, unaided by revelation, could have at least a minimal knowledge of the divine. Indeed, there appeared to be no reason why all men could not agree that there is a God and that this God has certain definable characteristics. One need not be a Christian or even a student of the Bible to understand that the world of common experience is unexplainable without reference to a supernatural agency. It is therefore philosophy's function to prove God's existence and establish it as an incontestable fact. Thomas selected five proofs which he felt to be beyond attack:

The first and more manifest way is the argument from motion. It is certain and evident to our senses that some things are in motion. Whatever is in motion is moved by another, for nothing can be in motion except it have a potentiality for that towards which it is being moved; whereas a thing moves inasmuch as it is in act. By "motion" we mean nothing else than the reduction of something from a state of potentiality into a state of actuality. Nothing, however, can be reduced from a state of potentiality into a state of actuality, unless by something already in a state of actuality. Thus that which is actually hot, as fire, makes wood, which is potentially hot, to be actually hot, and thereby moves and changes it. It is not possible that the same thing should be at once in a state of actuality and potentiality from the same point of view, but only from different points of view. What is actually hot cannot simultaneously be only potentially hot; still, it is simultaneously potentially cold. It is therefore impossible that from the same point of view and in the same way anything should be both moved and mover, or that it should move itself. Therefore, whatever is in motion must be put in motion by another. If that by which it is put in motion be itself put in motion, then this also must needs be put in motion by another, and that by another again. This cannot go on to infinity, because then there would be no first mover, and consequently, no other mover—seeing that subsequent movers only move inasmuch as they are put in motion by the first mover; as the staff only moves because it is put in motion by the hand. Therefore it is necessary to arrive at a First Mover, put in motion by no other; and this everyone understands to be God.

The second way is from the formality of efficient causation. In the world of sense we find there is an order of efficient causation. There is no case known (neither is it, indeed, possible) in which a thing is found to be the efficient cause of itself; for so it would be prior to itself, which is impossible. In efficient causes it is not possible to go on to infinity, because in all efficient causes following in order, the first is the cause of the intermediate cause, and the intermediate is the cause of the ultimate cause, whether the intermediate cause be several, or one only. To take away the cause is to take away the effect. Therefore, if there be no first cause among efficient causes, there will be no ultimate cause, nor any intermediate. If in efficient causes it is possible to go on to infinity, there will be no first efficient cause, neither will there be an ultimate effect, nor any intermediate causes; all of which is plainly false. Therefore it is necessary to put forward a First Efficient Cause, to which everyone gives the name of God.

The third way is taken from possibility and necessity, and runs thus. We find in nature things that could exist or not exist, since they are found to be generated, and then to corrupt; and, consequently, they can exist, and then not exist. It is impossible for these always to exist, for that which can one day cease to exist must at some time have not existed. Therefore, if everything could cease to exist, then at one time there could have been nothing in existence. If this were true, even now there would be nothing in existence, because that which does not exist only begins to exist by something already existing. Therefore, if at one time nothing was in existence, it would have been impossible for anything to have begun to exist; and thus even now nothing would be in existence—which is absurd. Therefore, not all beings are merely possible, but there must exist something the existence of which is necessary. Every necessary thing either has its necessity caused by another or not. It is impossible to go on to infinity in necessary things which have their necessity caused by another, as has been already proved in regard to efficient causes. Therefore we cannot but postulate the existence of some being having of itself its own necessity, and not receiving it from another, but rather causing in others their necessity. This all men speak of as God.

The fourth way is taken from the gradation to be found in things. Among beings there are some more and some less good, true, noble, and the like. But "more" and "less" are predicated of different things, according as they resemble in their different ways something which is in the degree of "most," as a thing is said to be hotter according as it more nearly resembles that which is hottest; so that there is something which is truest, something best, something noblest, and, consequently, something which is uttermost being; for the truer things are, the more truly they exist. What is most complete in any genus is the cause of all in that genus; as fire, which is the most complete form of heat, is the cause whereby all things are made hot. Therefore there must also be something which is to all beings the cause of their being, goodness, and every other perfection; and this we call God.

The fifth way is taken from the governance of the world; for we see that things which lack intelligence, such as natural bodies, act for some purpose, which fact is evident from their acting always, or nearly always, in the same way, so as to obtain the best result. Hence it is plain that not fortuitously, but designedly, do they achieve their purpose. Whatever lacks intelligence cannot fulfil some purpose, unless it be directed by some being endowed with intelligence and knowledge; as the arrow is shot to its mark by the archer. Therefore some intelligent being exists by whom all natural things are ordained towards a definite purpose; and this being we call God.[1]

Thomas maintained that all the above arguments are derived from the common experience of men, regardless of their cultural or religious traditions. Atheism is therefore the result of inaccurate thinking; true philosophy will always give unerring testimony to the existence of God. But philosophy can go even further. If these arguments are closely examined, it will be found that they say something definite about God's character. First of all, God is obviously the creator (efficient cause) of the world. Since the world is intelligible, and God created it, he must be looked upon as an intelligent being with purpose and will. The fourth argument attests to God's perfection, while the first indicates his primary and unchangeable nature. Without the aid of revelation, philosophy is thus able to assert that God is perfect, an active creator, an intelligent cause, the primary being, and utterly unchangeable. So much for those who thought religion to be founded upon nonrational illusion.

[1] *Summa Theologica,* translated by the English Dominican Fathers, 2 vols. (London: Burns, Oates, and Washburne, Ltd., 1916-38), I, Qu. 2, Art. 3. By permission of Benziger Brothers, Inc., New York.

Although scholastic philosophy's prime function is to prove the existence of God, it is also used to establish belief in moral freedom and immortality. In these, as in the arguments for God, the scholastics utilized the tools and materials derived from Aristotle. Many centuries earlier Aristotle had purported to demonstrate that man could attain his fulfillment only after his soul had been separated from material existence and was allowed to return to God. The rational soul of man is always tending toward the highest good (God), so final satisfaction is achieved only when the soul is reunited with God. Such a tendency toward God is meaningful only if the will of man is morally free. All human experience seems to indicate that each individual is free to choose good or evil. If the will were not free, such experience would be without meaning and beyond understanding. Thus, the soul must be both immortal and free if it is to complete itself.

As is readily apparent, one of the fundamental bases of scholastic philosophy is teleology. In so far as both Aristotle and the schoolmen could see, all things are created for a specific purpose and move directly toward a given fulfillment. All man's natural desires are found to be capable of adequate satisfaction, and at no time does the world produce either desires or beings which have no purpose or function. Indeed, the clue to understanding nature is found in the fact that the entire world is ruled by ends, or "life-wholes," which perfect themselves through organic processes. Nature is a single harmonious whole composed of a multitude of processes, each with its appointed end and each with its own means of fulfillment. The fact that none of these processes appears to intersect another indicates design and the ultimate rationality of nature.

SCHOLASTIC DOCTRINE: REVELATION

PHILOSOPHERS can show the existence of God, the purposive character of nature, the immortality of the soul and the freedom of the will, but such ideas as the Trinity and the incarnation lie outside their province. The proof of these latter rests upon the specific revelation which has been given to the Christian Church.

An analysis of human nature indicates that man can complete himself only by obtaining a "love union" with the divine. What can be said for man as a totality can therefore certainly be asserted for that limited part of him called *natural intelligence*. Natural intelligence recognizes that the ultimate good is transcendent and supernatural, but it also understands itself as being limited and imperfect. It therefore becomes obvious that the full vision of God is to be seen only if God reveals his own nature to man. Natural intelligence leads toward God, and is in no way contrary to God, but its ultimate success is dependent upon divine self-disclosure.

The revelations of God fall outside the areas which can legitimately be considered by philosophers. Through religious faith God opens the eyes of Christians and causes them to see his truth expressed in Scripture and the tradition of the Church. Human writers could not possibly have achieved the purity, foreknowledge, nobility and power which men find expressed in the Scriptures. Its authors must have been guided by divine illumination. And indeed, they never claimed to be speaking their own minds; they always made it clear that they were under the command and absolute guidance of God. Since they were not speaking for themselves, much of their material is beyond the understanding of men outside the Christian faith. If one has eyes to see and ears to hear, he will understand; but the eyes and ears for ultimate truth are given only to committed Christians.

SCHOLASTIC DOCTRINE: MIRACLES

THE supernatural illumination embodied in the Scriptures and the Church tradition is impressed upon a disbelieving world by miracles. Each Biblical miracle—and there are many—is part of some important occurrence designed to indicate a necessary part of God's character. The most notable in the Old Testament, the exodus story, shows God as a savior of men. Moreover, it testifies to the fact that his people, the children of Israel, were chosen to perform specific functions for the divine. This single miraculous event offers a vindication for the prominent place of the Old Testament in Christian thought and practice. The major miracles of the New Testament attest to the divinity of Jesus and to the beginning of a new dispensation. Here the Virgin Birth and the Resurrection are most important, but in addition to these are such wonders as the fulfillment of Old Testament prophecy, instantaneous healings, feeding large numbers from a small supply of food, and a multitude of others. Within the tradition of the Church, miraculous happenings have continued as an ever-present reminder of its supernatural origin and divine mission.

According to scholastic doctrine it would be both philosophically and empirically unsound to deny miracles. Since it is already clear that man must have something beyond natural knowledge to be fulfilled, it is inconceivable that God would not authenticate his truth by concrete and readily understandable means. As creator and sustainer of the world, God can do anything he chooses. He can set aside natural laws, and he can certainly interfere in the cause-and-effect relationships which guide ordinary affairs. In one sense a denial of miracles is tantamount to denying the efficacy and necessity of prayer. Further than this, it would deny God's complete mastery over his own creation. Such denials would make all the activity and thought of the Church meaningless.

But man does not have to be philosophically trained to recognize the existence of supernatural intervention. Indeed, the very fact that such a large number of people swear with sincere conviction to miraculous happenings should be overpowering. Individuals have been supernaturally healed before the eyes of thousands, prayers have been answered by an obvious change in the normal course of events, and nations have emerged victorious when all the odds of the battlefield were against them. Such events have no natural causes, say the scholastics. They must be ascribed to supernatural intervention.

However, men must learn to read the great moral purpose behind miraculous events. God does not change the course of his creation without reason. Each miracle is performed to bring man closer to God and to show him once again that the moral ends of life are the most exalted. Thus all miracles must be studied closely and their lessons carefully learned by the observers.

SCHOLASTIC DOCTRINE: AUTHORITY

SCHOLASTIC doctrine considered the historic institution of the Church, presided over by the Roman Pontiff, to be absolute in all matters of faith and morals. Following the earlier tradition, they held to the belief that the Holy Roman Church is the continuation of Christ's body on earth. According to Scripture, Jesus singled out the disciple Peter as the one he commissioned to establish the divine Church on earth.

And I also say unto thee, that thou art Peter, and upon this rock I will build my church; and the gates of Hades shall not prevail against it. I will give unto thee the keys of the kingdom of heaven: and whatsoever thou shalt bind on earth shall be bound in heaven; and whatsoever thou shalt loose on earth shall be loosed in heaven.

(Matthew 16:18-19)

By virtue of these words, Peter, who according to the scholastics was the first pope, was given power to direct with complete authority the religious affairs of mankind. He was given the "keys of the kingdom," and through him men could be granted salvation or sent to hell.

But Jesus also made provision for the future when Peter would become aged and ultimately leave this earth to enter heaven. The earthly body of Christ was to be a continuing organization, carrying out the dictates of Christ and dispensing the grace of God. Jesus' words as recorded in the Gospel of John guarantee the continuation of the Church and provide that later popes will succeed directly from Peter, keeping all his powers intact.

So when they had broken their fast, Jesus said to Simon Peter, Simon, son of John, lovest thou me more than these? He saith unto him, Yea, Lord; thou knowest that I love thee. He saith unto him, Feed my lambs. He saith to him again a second time, Simon, son of John, lovest thou me? He saith unto him, Yea, Lord; thou knowest that I love thee. He saith unto him, Tend my sheep. He saith unto him the third time, Simon, son of John, lovest thou me? Peter was grieved because he said unto him the third time, Lovest thou me? And he said unto him, Lord, thou knowest that I love thee. Jesus saith unto him, Feed my sheep. Verily, verily, I say unto thee, When thou wast young, thou girdedst thyself, and walkedst whither thou wouldest: but when thou shalt be old, thou shalt stretch forth thy hands, and another shall gird thee, and carry thee whither thou wouldest not.

(John 21:15-18)

With the Scriptures established as authentic records of supernatural revelation, the words of Matthew and John must

[419]

be taken as final truth. The hierarchy of the Church, having derived its authority from the pope, could therefore be considered absolute spiritual masters, operating on the authority of Christ himself. For the greatest number of scholastic thinkers, the Church's control over life was complete and final in all areas. The state and its rulers derived authority for their functions from the Church and its hierarchy, the ceremony in which the pope crowned the emperor being the visible symbol of the supremacy of the Holy See. The priestly control of medieval guilds and the Church's definitions of just prices and fair trade practices gave further evidence of the extent to which churchly authority penetrated into everyday existence. In the last analysis, the scholastics maintained, there is no valid distinction between the sacred and the profane. All of life should be looked upon as a divine activity under the explicit guidance of God and his representatives. Pope Innocent III well expressed the absoluteness of churchly authority when defending himself after taking land from England and giving it to France:

It belongs to our office to correct all Christian men for every mortal sin, and if they despise correction, to coerce them by ecclesiastical censure. And if any shall say, that kings must be treated in one way, and other men in another, we appeal in answer to the law of God, wherein it is written, "Ye shall judge the great as the small, and there shall be no acceptance of persons among you." But if it is ours to proceed against criminal sin, we are especially bound so to do when we find a sin against peace.[2]

THE SCHOLASTIC IDEAL

THE scholastic thinkers were bent upon making theology a science, a science which would bring all of man's experience

[2] Innocent III, quoted in A. J. Carlyle, *Medieval Political Theory in the West*, 2 vols. (New York: Putnam, 1903-36), Vol. II, p. 219.

into a harmonious whole. Neither the Dominicans, who generally followed Aristotle, nor the Franciscans, who promoted the Platonic-Augustinian tradition, thought they were simply building a defense for the authority of the historic Roman Church. Rather, they all felt themselves to be seeking after that eternal and immutable truth which is knowledge of God. The absolute authority of the scripturally based Church, they believed, was the conclusion rather than the premise of their thought. The intellectual ideal of the scholastics is admirably expressed by Thomas in the following words:

The prime author and mover of the universe is intelligence. Therefore the final cause of the universe must be the good of the intelligence, and that is truth. Truth then must be the final end of the whole universe; and about the consideration of that end wisdom must primarily be concerned. . . . Of all human pursuits, the pursuit of wisdom is the most perfect, the most sublime, the most useful, and the most agreeable. The most perfect, because in so far as a man gives himself up to the pursuit of wisdom, to that extent he enjoys already some portion of true happiness. "Blessed is the man that shall dwell in wisdom" (Eccles. XIV, 22). The most sublime, because thereby man comes closest to the likeness of God, "who hath made all things in wisdom" (Ps. ciii, 24). The most useful, because by this same wisdom we arrive at the realm of immortality. "The desire of wisdom shall lead to an everlasting life" (Wisdom, VI, 21). The most agreeable, because "her conversation hath no bitterness, nor her company any weariness, but gladness and joy" (Wisdom VIII, 16).[3]

If, then, the final happiness of man does not consist in those exterior advantages which are called goods of fortune, nor in goods of the body, nor in goods of the soul in its sentient part, nor in the intellectual part in respect of the moral virtues, nor in the virtues of the practical intellect, called art and prudence, it

[3] Thomas Aquinas, *Summa Contra Gentiles* (London: Burns and Oates, 1905), Bk. I, chs. 1 and 2; tr. by Joseph Rickaby as *Of God and His Creatures*. By permission.

remains that the final happiness of man consists in the contemplation of truth. This act alone in man is proper to him, and is in no way shared by any other being in this world. This is sought for its own sake, and is directed to no other end beyond itself. By this act man is united in likeness with pure spirits, and even comes to know them in a certain way. For this act also man is more self-sufficient, having less need of external things. Likewise to this act all other human activities seem to be directed as toward their end. For to the perfection of contemplation there is requisite health of body, and all artificial necessaries of life are means to health. Another requisite is rest from the disturbing forces or passion: that is attained by means of the moral virtues and prudence. Likewise rest from exterior troubles, which is the whole aim of civil life and government. Thus, if we look at things rightly, we may see that all human occupations seem to be ministerial to the service of the contemplators of truth.[4]

This emphasis upon the power and glory of intelligence was not meant to indicate that only philosophers were capable of attaining truth or blessedness. The pious mystic who disclaimed all intellectual pretensions could rise to the full vision of God through prayer and devotion. The long road of rational deduction was but one way for man to reach his goal; other ways, such as intuition, vision and mystical insight, were also valid and, in some senses, less dangerous and perilous. The intellectualism of the scholastic theologians and the visions of the mystics were not so much contradictory as complementary. They both began with Augustine:

I asked the earth, and it answered me, "I am not He"; and whatsoever are in it confessed the same. I asked the sea and the deeps, and the living creeping things, and they answered, "We are not thy God, seek above us." I asked the moving air; and the whole air with his inhabitants answered, "Anaximines was deceived, I am not God." I asked the heavens, sun, moon, stars, "Nor," say

4 *Ibid.*, ch. 37.

they, "are we the God whom thou seekest." And I replied unto all the things which encompass the door of my flesh, "Ye have told me of my God, that ye are not He; tell me something of Him." [5]

They ended by viewing with Dante the "Light eternal who only in thyself abidest, only thyself dost understand, and to thyself, self-understood, self-understanding, turnest love and smiling" (Dante, *The Paradiso*, Canto XXXIII).

The ultimate ideal of the scholastics and, indeed, all the thinkers of the Middle Ages was an all-embracing unity—unity in belief, unity in spirit, unity in church, unity in government and unity in thought. Dante expressed both the ideal and the reason for it when he said: "The human race . . . is ordered well, nay, is ordered best, when according to the utmost of its power it becomes like unto God . . . [and] the human race is most like unto God when it is most one, for the principle of unity dwells in him alone" (Dante, *De Monarchia*, Bk. I, Ch. 8).

MEDIEVAL DISUNITY

THOUGH ideally unity of thought and practice was the goal, actually it was almost nonexistent. Among the formulators of scholastic doctrine there was constant warring and very little real understanding. St. Bernard, for example, accused Peter Abelard of "trying to make void the merit of Christian faith, when he deems himself able by human reason to comprehend God altogether." The Platonists, who called themselves realists, argued that the Aristotelians, or nominalists, were undermining the Christian faith and leaving nothing but doubt and uncertainty in the minds of Christians. No matter how much each side protested its respect for the other, their fundamental

---

[5] Augustine, *Confessions*, Everyman ed., 208, 209.

differences caused antagonisms and revolts. The intellectual unity so fervently sought after could hardly flourish when the basic premises of each group were so divergent.

This lack of unity among the schoolmen was not an isolated phenomenon. The pope was constantly struggling with the emperor, and the minor kings and princes fought running battles among themselves and against the clergy. Religious offices were sold to gain economic and political advantage, while the diplomatic duplicity of both Church and State increased mistrust among the rulers. The religious and political aristocracy tended more and more to lose interest in the common people and to deal with all government as an instrument for personal power and gain. The proclaimed ideal of unity required a common goal which would transcend personal interests and desires. But neither hierarchy, secular or religious, appeared to have such a commitment.

Moreover, although every class of society received instruction from the Church, there was unbelievable disunity in religious thought and expression. Coexisting with the mighty scholastic structures was always the practice of non-Biblical magic and belief in what the theologians considered superstition. Although the possibility of miracles was defended by the leading theologians, they were usually chary about admitting that special new events were the result of supernatural intervention. Local communities and their unlettered priests had no such compunctions. For them, any occurrence which had no immediate natural explanation was an instance of God's special action. Fantastic stories relating to the bread and wine of the Eucharist were spread through medieval communities. In Bolsena a disbelieving priest saw the bread of the sacrament bleed and discolor the altar cloth, and in Brussels the consecrated bread was stolen by a Jew on Good Friday and bled until it was returned to the church. Few churches of any size were without the relic of some such supernatural happening, and these relics became attestations to God's interest in the local church and vehicles for the working of future wonders.

However, the most important manifestations of disunity were not the theological differences or even the superstitious or magical practices of local communities since these were, after all, tolerated by the Church leadership. The major lack of unity was evident in the rise of sects which in one way or another opposed the authority of Rome. The Waldensian Movement, for example, was started (about 1179) by a wealthy resident of Lyons, Peter Valdes, as a protest against the corruption of the official Church. Valdes, in much the same fashion as Francis of Assisi, gave his possessions to the poor and set out to preach the Sermon on the Mount as a simple gospel of love and charity. He gathered together a group of like-minded people, mostly from the lower economic levels, and wandered from town to town preaching and teaching. The pope refused to sanction this evangelism for a number of reasons, not the least of which was the Waldensians' insistence upon their right to read Scripture and interpret it for themselves. The sect thrived on persecution and soon extended far over southern France and Italy.

Whereas the Waldensians had no idea of leaving the Church when they founded their movement, the other great medieval sect, the Albigensians, was started in the eleventh century as a group frankly competing with Rome. The Albigensians resurrected the ancient Manichaean heresy and asserted that there was a God of light who made the invisible universe and a God of darkness who was responsible for physical nature. They rejected all the practices and institutions of the Roman Church, and attempted to achieve their salvation through ascetic devotional exercises. The Albigensians were never great in number, but their influence was sufficient for the official Church to launch a successful crusade against them in 1209.

The Roman hierarchy indicated its awareness of divergent

beliefs and practices by giving increased power to the inquisition. By 1235 the Dominicans were given control of this agency, and it was soon extended all over Europe. Its primary concern was to abolish heresy and to see that proper punishment was meted out to the offenders. As the disunity of Christendom became more and more apparent, the inquisitors doubled their efficiency and zeal. But the seeds of conflict were so deeply embedded that such coercive measures ultimately proved ineffective. The external shell of unity was finally broken in the sixteenth century by the Protestant Reformation.

26

THE REFORMATION AND ITS
CHURCHES

THE sixteenth-century schism which produced the
Protestant churches was as much political and economic as it was religious. The hegemony which the
uneasy Church-State alliance exercised over Europe was based
upon feudalism in both economics and politics. Nationalism,
with the support it would need in local patriotism, could not
be tolerated. What money either pope or emperor desired
from a specific area was taken on the grounds that it was theirs
by absolute right; and it was necessary that local areas accept
even their own financial destruction if it so pleased the Roman
control. After the quickening of trade and commerce in the
late Middle Ages, such a situation proved intolerable for a
large number of central and northern Europeans. Industries
were being developed, surplus capital was accumulating in the
hands of merchants, and new centers of economic power were
coming into existence. To protect themselves against Church
and Empire taxation, the merchant princes contributed to the
development of local pride and to the rise of ambitious local
politicians. Inevitably these new states, absolute in their own
right, came into conflict with the privileged Roman Church
which, under feudal conditions, had been granted its own
courts and taxing powers and had effectively been removed
from any secular control.

THE CHRISTIAN HUMANISTS

THE social revolution which laid the basis for Protestantism was greatly aided by the critical scholarship which characterized the Renaissance. The influence of the humanist writers, who developed and perpetuated a cult of classical learning, spread from Italy into the northern sections of Europe. In northern Europe especially, humanism became interested in a study of early Christian literature. The method of study was the same as that employed on pagan classics, and the consequence revolutionized man's thinking about religion. The traditional Roman Catholic attitude had been to ascribe primary authority to Scripture, but it was only to Scripture as interpreted by the official Church. As a consequence, the ever-increasing commentaries written by accepted theologians came to take the place of the original texts. The humanist scholars made new philological discoveries which rendered older translations invalid, and thus began anew to search out the true meaning of Scripture and ancient Church documents. In bypassing the established commentaries they produced a new and critical attitude toward religion and especially toward the Church.

The northern humanists were principally concerned with the ethical teachings of Christianity. Inevitably these thinkers drew comparisons among the ethical ideas found in Scripture, the existing attitudes of the official Church, and the prevailing popular practices. In so doing, they brought to light much of the superstition which was passing for Christianity. But more important for them was recognition of the extent to which the Church had departed from the comparatively simple gospel of love taught by Jesus. The Sermon on the Mount, which in the opinion of the humanists embodied the basic Christian ethical teaching, was used in devotional exercises, but few took it seriously as a foundation for action. The Christian Church had become a formal institution interested in stereotyped expressions which wholly lacked the power of the Christian spirit. Desiderius Erasmus, the outstanding Renaissance humanist, expressed the attitude of the whole movement in the following words:

How many are there, who put more trust in the safeguard of the Virgin Mary, or St. Christopher, than Christ Himself? They worship (!) the mother with images, candles, and songs; and offend Christ heinously by their impious living. A mariner when in a storm is more ready to invoke the mother of Christ or St. Christopher, or some one or other of the saints, than Christ Himself. And they think they have made the Virgin their friend by singing her in the evening the little song *Salve Regina*, though they don't know what it is they do sing; when they have more reason to be afraid, that the Virgin should think they jeer her by their so singing, when the whole day, and great part of the night is spent in obscene discourse, drunkenness, and such doings as are not fit to be mentioned.[1]

Again I both hear and see many who place religion in places, garments, meats, fasts, gestures, and songs, and for the sake of these things judge their neighbor contrary to the precept of the Gospel. From whence it comes to pass, that whereas faith and charity constitute the Christian religion, they are both extinguished by those superstitions. For he is far from the faith of the Gospel who depends upon these acts; and he is far from Christian charity, who for the sake of meat or drink, which a person may lawfully use, exasperates his brother, for whose liberty Christ died.[2]

Although most of the humanists maintained their allegiance to the Roman Church, their criticisms and attitudes tended to

[1] *The Colloquies of Desiderius Erasmus Concerning Men, Manners, and Things* (London: Cribbings and Co., 1900), Vol. ii, pp. 309-310.
[2] *Enchiridion Militis Christiani, ibid.*, p. 114.

undermine an already tottering ecclesiastical structure. The social and intellectual revolutions which capitalism, nationalism and humanism represent prepared the ground for the specifically religious reformers and the ultimate success of their venture.

MARTIN LUTHER

THE unrest of the sixteenth century lacked both organization and leadership. The situation called for an individual who could be made into a symbol of revolt and an event which would focus attention upon the conflict between the absolute authority assumed by the Roman hierarchy and the claims of local groups and interests. Such a symbol came in the person of a young, pious, and highly explosive professor of theology at Wittenberg, Martin Luther. The event which touched off the successful revolt was the crisis of 1517, which was partly economic, partly political and partly centered around religious indulgences.

Luther was born into a family which lived on the borderline between the old and the new. Its tradition lay in the pattern of medieval peasantry, but Hans Luther, Martin's father, left the land and became a partner in a firm of copper miners. As the business flourished, he and his family moved out of the peasant class into the expanding new bourgeoisie. Thus Martin Luther partook of two traditions, both of which were reflected in his religious actions and attitudes. Luther accepted, largely without criticism, belief in the efficacy of witchcraft and the magical practices so characteristic of medieval peasant communities. Throughout his life he maintained a strong belief in the good and evil spirits which the peasants assumed to reside in forests and fields. The Devil, for example, was no abstract theological construction; rather, he was the concrete and personal source of all evil at whom Luther is supposed

A Byzantine icon representing the Trinity by means of a man with three faces merged into one. This form of representation was popular in both the East and West for some time. The Western Church outlawed such pictures in 1628 through an edict issued by Pope Urban VIII. (*Photo by Giraudon. Athens, Soverdo Museum.*)

St. Dominic receiving heavenly authority for his order from St. Peter and St. Paul. The symbols of authority are a scepter and book. (*Louvre.*)

The interior of a Catholic Church in Rome noted for its ornateness and the splendor of its paintings and decoration

The interior of a Protestant Presbyterian Church in New Jersey. Its simplicity is in striking contrast to the traditional Roman Catholic form of church architecture.

once to have thrown an inkpot when he saw him sitting in the corner of his room.

But if he was a child of peasant traditions, Luther was also strongly influenced by the bourgeois spirit of freedom and enterprise. He did not fit well into the conventional pattern expected of monks and theological professors, and this was primarily due to his uneasy feeling that his personal salvation was not as certain as the Church would have him believe. The more he studied, especially in the writings of Paul and Augustine, the more he became convinced that the Church's claim to being the sole means of salvation was either false, or at best completely misunderstood. He was moving toward the idea that salvation was dependent upon an individual's faith rather than upon the sacraments and other "good works" prescribed by the Church. Luther's emphasis upon the individualistic nature of salvation and the very fact that he felt free to challenge one of the Church's most cherished and established claims indicate the extent to which he was a product of a bourgeois rather than a peasant environment.

As Luther was developing his theological understanding, he had no idea of leading a revolt against the Church. Many of his professorial predecessors had argued against one or another of the Church's positions without causing a revolution. Some, and probably Luther considered himself to be of this group, had succeeded in changing official doctrine and in bringing the Church into more direct alignment with their interpretation of Scripture. The indulgence scandal of 1517, however, brought Luther's views to the attention of the public, and from that time on there was little chance of preventing an open break.

Pope Leo X had sent a number of agents throughout Europe in an attempt to get sufficient money to rebuild the basilica of St. Peter's Cathedral in Rome. The method employed was to sell indulgences to those who wished their punishment after death to be remitted. The Church's practice regarding the dispensation of indulgences had not been changed, but some of the pope's emissaries made little effort to find out whether or not the sinner in question was sincerely penitent before the indulgence was granted. One such overzealous salesman, Tetzel, was working the territory around Wittenberg and came to the attention of Luther. Luther protested that the pope, through such agents as Tetzel, was corrupting Christian doctrine, and that poor and ignorant people were being defrauded. As was the usual custom in university towns, the young theology professor wrote out his protest in the form of theses (or assertions) and posted them on the cathedral door. They were a challenge to public debate for anyone interested in defending either the pope or Tetzel.

The ninety-five theses which Luther posted criticized not only the selling of indulgences but also the very basis upon which the pope built his claims. Although it was certainly not clear to many, the official Church maintained that an indulgence had no efficacy if the sinner were not truly repentant. Luther argued that "the Christian who has true repentance has already received pardon from God altogether apart from an indulgence, and does not need one." Such a position not only attacked the use of indulgences, but went further to strike at the very heart of the whole "good-works" theory. The official doctrine had always made a separation between guilt (*culpa*) and penalty (*poena*). It held that a contrite heart moves God to remove guilt freely, but that this removal did not reduce or affect in any way the penalty which must be paid either on earth or in purgatory for the committed sin. It was to this penalty that the indulgence applied, not to the act of forgiveness. As holder of the "keys of the kingdom of heaven," the pope could grant penalty remission for works which promoted God's plan on earth, and thereby shorten the time to be spent in purgatory. Luther refused to make any such distinction between guilt and penalty, and by so doing challenged the foundation of the pope's power. For if Luther's view were accepted it would have to be admitted that there was no "treasury of merit" upon which the Church could draw; and without the "treasury of merit" the pope would have no bargaining power in his efforts to advance the cause of the Church against expanding secular institutions.

The posted theses attracted little attention, and at first no one came forward to debate the issues. However, a copy finally fell into the hands of a printer who translated it into German and caused it to be distributed over Germany. Many of the German people, especially the petty princes, immediately recognized the implications inherent in Luther's propositions. The income from indulgence sales dropped, and nationalist agitators began using Luther as an authority for their attacks on Church and Empire. The issues were clarified when spokesmen for the pope answered Luther's charges and pointed out that "whoever says that the Roman Church has not the power to do what in fact it does with regard to indulgences is a heretic." Public debates were held throughout Germany, especially in ducal Saxony, and people were forced to take sides. All the pent-up resentment against the centralized Roman authority was brought out and in many cases given public expression for the first time. The new bourgeoisie resented the taxing power of both Church and Empire; the local princes and noblemen resented the extralegal power of the clergy and the coercive authority of the emperor; and the common man resented the methods of extortion which the Church had used. At this point in history, to be a heretic did not seem too heinous a crime.

While the debate raged, Luther continued to write about the corruption of the Church and its scriptural infidelity. In each sermon or pamphlet he moved further and further away from the Church's position until finally, on January 3, 1521, he was officially excommunicated. The papal bull, *Exsurge Domine*, which was issued some months earlier, warned all peoples that Luther was a heretic and further ordered them, under pain of excommunication, to denounce his views and shun those who accepted them. By this time, however, papal authority had been weakened beyond the capacity to quell a revolt.

LUTHER AND NATIONALISM

WITH the excommunication of Luther, the defection became at once more bitter, more widespread and more self-conscious. In the early stages neither the revolting secular princes nor the clergy knew exactly where they were going or what kind of religious expression they would substitute for the uprooted Roman tradition. Thousands of the German people, however, were severing their relations with Rome and looking toward Luther for guidance. In a series of pamphlets published in 1520, Luther outlined his basic criticisms of the Roman Church and issued a call to the people of Germany for the establishment of a true Christian Church.

Let us, therefore, awake, dear Germans, and fear God rather than men, that we may not share the fate of all the poor souls who are so lamentably lost through the shameful and devilish rule of the Romans, in which the devil daily takes a larger and larger place,—if, indeed, it were possible that such a hellish rule could grow worse, a thing I can neither conceive nor believe.[3]

In the first of the pamphlets, *An Open Letter to the Christian Nobility of the German Nation Concerning the Reform of the Christian State*, Luther charged that the Roman hierarchy maintained its insidious control over Christian peoples through three great false ideas. These ideas had been built

[3] *Works of Martin Luther*, 2 vols. (Philadelphia: A. J. Holman Co., 1915-32), Vol. ii, p. 80.

into walls behind which all manner of evil could be masked. The first wall was the declaration that spiritual authority, represented by the clergy, was absolute, and totally above all secular authority. Thus the representatives of the Church were a class apart—a spiritual aristocracy with rights, privileges and immunities denied other Christians. Their presumption of spiritual superiority was based solely upon a declaration made by power-mad popes and bishops. Luther insisted that this hoax, which had long defrauded Christian men, be recognized and stopped. The second wall concerned the pope's claim to be the only person who could correctly interpret Scripture. God, said Luther, left his holy record for every man to read and for every man to understand. He is revealed through the Bible, and not through commentaries written under the guidance of papal authority. In effect, each man is his own priest, since God speaks to his condition through the "living word" of Scripture. To vest interpretive power in one person or his agents is to give up the "living" power of the word and accept form without content. "If we are all priests . . . and all have one faith, one gospel, one sacrament, why should we not also have the power to test and judge what is correct or incorrect in matters of faith?" The third wall, which declares that only the pope has the power to convene councils of the Church, has no foundation if the first two are razed. Councils can be called by any group of sincere Christians who desire the aid of their brothers in understanding Scripture.

The other two pamphlets, *The Babylonian Captivity of the Church* and *On Christian Liberty*, attacked the sacramental system of the Church and reiterated Luther's concept of all believers being their own priests. The net effect of these three documents was to undermine the authority of the Roman hierarchy and appeal to the German people for the establishment of a national church under local leadership.

Luther's nationalist appeal brought an increasing number of local princes into his camp, and it also provided the basis upon which a substitute religious organization could be reared. To some, the ideas that every man is his own priest and that justification is by faith alone implied that there should be only democratically operated religious associations rather than an episcopally organized church. For Luther the issue became clear when in 1524 a group of peasants from around Stükingen who desired redress for obvious economic inequities began a revolt against their prince. Their spokesmen leaned heavily upon Luther's arguments against authority, and asserted that their reading of the Scripture informed them of their right to Christian justice. Many of the princes felt that Luther was responsible for the revolt; they appealed to him to clarify his position and to declare that their authority was absolute. At the same time the peasants appealed for Luther's aid in their cause. Luther sided with the princes and issued a burning denunciation of the peasants in a pamphlet called *Against Robbing and Murdering Peasant Bands*. The tract was written in May of 1525 and the revolt was quelled by the fall of that year.

Out of Luther's reaction to the peasants' revolt came the basic Lutheran principles of church organization. The Church, he said, was dependent upon the divinely instituted secular government. Its ministers and bishops, possessed of no special privileges or sanctity, were to be paid by the state to perform the sacraments and preach the Gospel. In other words, the Church was to become a supported branch of secular government without independent power. As such, it did not have the power to criticize state actions except in cases where the purity of faith was at issue, and it certainly could never be put in the position of fomenting revolutionary activity. In effect, Luther's attitude took the Church out of politics and asserted the right of the secular state to absolute control. It is small wonder that such a position had strong appeal for the politically and economically ambitious princes and merchants of northern Europe.

THE LUTHERAN CHURCHES

ALTHOUGH Luther's criticism of the Catholic system was sufficiently devastating to cause revolt, his constructive suggestions did not immediately cohere into a binding creed. The basis of his criticism lay in a deep sense of sin and a belief in the total corruption of natural man. He had little use for philosophy, and, indeed, felt that both Plato and Aristotle were dangerous perverters of truth. Whatever salvation there is, he said, must come from God alone, and it is certainly not mediated through philosophico-theological writings or priests. Such a low estimate of human ability could not but find expression in a distrust of words and ritual. The only words Luther could really have faith in were to be found in the divinely authored Scripture; the only rituals were those expressly sanctioned in the Holy Writ—baptism and the Eucharist. The meaning of Christianity was not shown to Luther through outward forms, creeds and dogmas, but through the direct experience of faith in a living and loving God. When man goes beyond this immediate personal experience, said Luther, his apprehension of the divine becomes hazy and distorted.

Had Luther been entirely consistent, there could have been no Lutheran Church. Yet, for the revolt against Rome to be successful, there was need of some common understanding which could be verbally expressed. This need was met by a fellow Wittenberg professor, Philip Melanchthon, who, in 1530, wrote the Augsburg Confession. This Confession was intended as a conciliatory statement of the Lutheran position regarding the abuses which they felt were corrupting the Catholic Church. It expressly stated that there was no basic disagreement about essential articles of faith, but that the Roman Church had become apostate in matters of its own conduct. The Mass, Confession and "good works" had been given unchristian superstitious meanings, and prohibitions such as those against clerical marriage were clear cases of presumptuous meddling. The Confession went further to define the true nature of ecclesiastical power and to describe how the Roman system had misused and perverted it.

Naturally the Augsburg Confession was not accepted by the Catholic leadership. But it formed a document around which the protesters could rally. If a prince declared himself to be in accord with the Confession, he thereby severed all relations with Rome. In the new Protestant churches the basic structure of faith remained unchanged, but a different organizational pattern, together with a revised system of interpretation, was soon adopted. The Confession did not so much restrict as it granted permission to vary forms of worship to suit differing groups of people. At a later date the Schmalkald Articles and the Formula of Concord modified and expanded the Augsburg Confession. These documents, in addition to the Apostles' Creed, the Nicene Creed, the Athanasian Creed and Luther's Catechism, form the basis of Lutheran theology. From the very beginning there was no attempt to make all Lutherans believe alike, and the various local churches always maintained considerable freedom.

As this freedom has been exercised down through the years, Lutherans of divers nations have been unified by an attitude rather than an orthodoxy. This attitude remains one largely dictated by Luther himself, and it is perpetuated through constant reference to his writings and the use of his music and liturgy. In late years there have been attempts to make Lutheranism international, but churches in general remain tied to the ethos of given states. In some countries, Lutheranism is still the official church, either in whole or in part supported by national treasuries.

HULDREICH ZWINGLI

ALTHOUGH the German revolt represents the most important and conspicuous beginning of Protestantism, Germany was not by any means the only area that was removing itself from the Catholic system. The Scandinavian countries, Denmark, Norway and Sweden, took over the Lutheran form as early as 1520, and by 1537 the churches in this section of Europe were all reorganized. Switzerland entered the Protestant movement under the guidance and leadership of Huldreich Zwingli (1484-1531). Zwingli was influenced by Luther, but the Swiss revolt was a parallel to rather than an extension of the German movement. Switzerland had for a number of years exercised a certain degree of independence from Rome. Her cantons were only loosely federated, and each section governed itself without much regard for either the empire or ecclesiastical dignitaries. The Swiss reformation, therefore, was the culmination of a long tradition rather than a violent revolt.

Whereas Luther hated philosophy and humanistic learning, Zwingli loved them and consequently set Swiss Protestantism on a divergent course. Along with the other Biblical humanists of his time, Zwingli maintained that the Scripture was the only religious authority, and that accordingly the practices of the Roman Church which were not firmly founded in the Holy Writ should be discarded. In 1522 he and other prominent citizens of Zürich refused to observe the usual abstinence required during Lent. They argued at the Town Council meeting that such a practice had no Biblical authority and that it, together with certain other deviations, should be eliminated from Swiss church custom. Although the Council decided that Lenten abstinence should be retained for the sake of public order, this challenge to Roman authority was generally well received. Soon there were public debates on all religious subjects ranging from such topics as the nature of the mass and Eucharist to the form of church organization. As these critical debates spread, it became increasingly apparent that the Catholic system was founded upon a number of stated propositions rather than upon the written word of Scripture. Such Roman customs as the celibate clergy, the worship of saints, papal infallibility regarding the interpretation of Scripture, and the use of pictures, images, statues and music in divine worship were all found lacking in Biblical authority.

Discussion increased until it became imperative for the civil officers of the Swiss cantons to declare themselves either for or against the Catholic system. Since the majority of the people agreed with Zwingli, it was most fortunate for the peace of the country that release from Rome was in accord with the political and economic ambitions of the officials. As a consequence, in 1525 the break with Rome was completed and the Swiss church underwent a radical reorganization. The congregational system of government, which was much more in line with Swiss political practice, was instituted; public processions dedicated to saints were stopped; pictures and organs disappeared from church buildings; clergymen abandoned celibacy; the mass was declared to have no sacrificial meaning; the Eucharist became simply a rite of commemoration in which there was no physical presence of Christ; and a host of other changes were made which brought the Swiss Protestants closer to what they felt was the true meaning of Scripture.

JOHN CALVIN

THE fruits of the Swiss reformation were gathered and consolidated into a system by John Calvin, a French theologian (1509-1564). It was his job to build a theological structure which would not only answer the objections raised by Catholics, but also provide a common basis for Protestant thought and practice. Calvin achieved his purpose, but the achievement was limited to the non-Lutheran branch of the Reformation.

Reformed Protestantism, which is rooted in Zwingli and Calvin, has always been more impressed with the absolute sovereignty of God's will than with the inner joyous experience of salvation which forms the basis of Lutheran theology. The idea that a Christian was somehow freed of external obligations once he was convinced that Christ dwelt within him was for Calvin a misinterpretation of Scripture. Man is never free from God's will, said Calvin, and this will is expressed once and for all in the Holy Writ. The Bible is not merely the vehicle of the Gospel, of the promise of salvation; it is a blueprint for life and an utterly infallible "rule for faith and practice." Although Luther never worked out a doctrine of Scripture, Calvin's position was as far from expressing the Lutheran attitude as one could imagine. In place of the spontaneous freedom which Luther considered the hallmark of a true Christian, Calvin offered rigorous subjection to the Biblically expressed will of God.

Luther's major objection to Catholicism concerned the corruption of the Church and its coercive exploitation of Christians. There was no essential difference in matters of faith, as the Augsburg Confession admitted. For Calvin, however, Catholicism erred because it misconstrued Scripture and substituted a doctrine of Church infallibility for Biblical authority. Catholicism was not wrong because it was corrupt; rather, it was corrupt because it had long since deserted God's will for man's. There was no hope for Christians, he felt, until they reorganized themselves according to the pattern ordained in Scripture and rigidly adhered to all of its dictates, no matter how minor they might appear. As a consequence of this position, Calvin interested himself in church organization, and the form he developed, built largely along the lines of the Republican-Congregational system adopted by the Swiss reformation, has continued to this day as a distinguishing mark of Reformed Protestantism.

Calvin's *Institutio Christianae Religionis*, first published in 1536 and then issued in its final form in 1559, contains the outline of Reformed Protestant theology. Its original purpose was to show Francis I, then King of France, that Protestantism was not an anarchistic movement intent upon destroying law and order. Indeed, Calvin asserted, it was a movement dedicated to the establishment of divine order on earth, and through its good offices peace and justice would finally be operative in the affairs of men. After a careful study of Scripture, especially the Old Testament, Calvin concluded that a theocratic form of government was the only kind directly dictated by God. Although he was unable to convince Francis, his ideas were accepted by the leaders of the Swiss reformation. On the invitation of Zwingli's religious and political heir, William Farel, John Calvin began in August of 1536 to organize a scripturally based theocratic commonwealth. From this time on, Geneva became the center of Calvin's work and the wellspring from which Reformed Protestantism spread throughout Europe.

Calvin's government in Geneva was more repressive than most of those which had been established under Roman auspices. Although the Calvinist clergy had none of the sacramental character which distinguished the medieval priests, they did claim the power and authority to instruct the state and all its people in matters of morals and faith. In Calvin's terms, they were the educated interpreters of Scripture who could teach and guide the congregation, but could neither punish nor coerce. At least in theory, final authority rested in the congregation as they were possessed of the Holy Spirit.

In actual practice, however, the clergy exercised a power which could regulate the smallest detail of a communicant's life. Their knowledge of Scripture far exceeded that of the layman, and their social status within the community was more exalted than that of anyone else. As a consequence, the Geneva theocracy was actually a clerical state.

Calvin and his fellow ministers were determined to see that their people lived in complete accord with the moral precepts of the Bible. This meant that all of the so-called private activities of men and women became matters of public concern. Since ornaments on clothing were decried by certain Old Testament prophets, women were prohibited from wearing jewelry; comedy entertainment was forbidden because it allowed man to forget the seriousness of life; following an ancient Deuteronomic law, adultery was proclaimed punishable by death; Sunday was made a compulsory day of rest; and so on through the whole range of human activity. Most important of all was the attempt to regulate the thoughts and opinions of people regarding religious questions. Heresy, that is, anything which differed from the Calvinistic interpretation of Scripture, was a crime against God and was made punishable by the civil branch of government. When the heretic was recalcitrant, Calvinistic theology required that the state exact a death penalty so that the faithful would suffer no corruption.

If such control was to be actually exercised, an extensive organization was necessary. In the *Ordonnances Ecclésiastiques* which were adopted in 1541, Calvin divided control along four functional lines. The top group was to be known as the *Vénérable Compagnie des Pasteurs*. This council of ministers was given final authority in recommending punishments to be effected by the civil office holders. Another group, chosen because of the purity of their doctrine and their ability to give a clear Calvinistic interpretation of Scripture, were given absolute authority over instruction; all educational matters were placed under their control and direction. Twelve elders composed the *Consistory*, the third group. The *Consistory* was charged with the responsibility of overseeing conduct and general lay opinion. Each of the twelve elders was responsible for a given section of Geneva, and he was equipped with assistants to aid in the necessarily detailed investigations. The *Consistory* was probably the most feared segment of the entire clerical organization. The fourth council was composed of deacons who were responsible for visiting the sick, maintaining hospitals, and generally providing for those in need of charitable aid. According to Calvin, these were the only functions expressly dictated by Scripture.

As one might expect, such an all-inclusive organization, empowered to investigate any and all affairs, turned up many heretics. In so far as the records show, at least fifty-eight persons were executed and seventy-six were exiled in the four years between 1542 and 1546. The most famous execution, that of a Spanish theologian named Servetus, came in 1553 after he had attacked the doctrine of the Trinity. Calvin held not only that such punishment was necessary to preserve public order, but that anyone who denied the Trinity was belittling God's majesty and therefore relinquished his right to life. Most theological differences, however, were not settled by execution; banishment from the city or prison was the more usual punishment. Sebastian Castellio, a teacher in Geneva, was driven from the city for suggesting that the Old Testament book "Song of Songs" was actually a collection of love poems rather than a revelation of Jesus' relations with the Christian Church, as it was usually considered to be. A few years later Jerome Bolsec, a French Protestant refugee, openly declared that Calvin's doctrine of predestination was wrong. Moreover he said that it committed a scandalous error in ascribing the origin and maintenance of sin to God's hand.

As a result, Calvin reasserted the idea of predestination, which he found in both Paul and Augustine, and banished Bolsec from Geneva. The number of such cases could be multiplied many times, but these should be sufficient to indicate the absoluteness and efficiency of Calvin's organization.

THE CALVINIST CHURCHES

THE moral austerity of Calvin's Geneva and the form of government he devised became the dominant characteristics of the expanding Calvinist churches. Theoretical control of the church lay in the hands of the congregation, and the congregation, guided by the Holy Spirit, elected "ruling elders" who were always laymen, and "teaching elders" who were always ministers. The emphasis upon correct theology which characterized the Geneva system was also taken over by the Reformed churches. The Calvinist clergy were more able and better educated than the ministry of any other Christian group, including Roman Catholics. Universities and theological seminaries patterned on Calvin's school in Geneva were immediately established wherever the Reformed faith spread. Although the Geneva theocracy disintegrated shortly after Calvin's death, its inspiration and experience have remained alive in Reformed churches throughout the world.

Theologically, the Calvinist side of the Reformation was much more unified than the Lutheran. Together with the Lutherans, Calvinists maintained a firm belief in justification by faith rather than works, and in the idea that man was predestined to salvation. Calvin's thought, however, was much clearer than Luther's, and consequently, Calvinist orthodoxy was capable of more definite creedal expression. In Lutheran theology, justification was always an inner experience of salvation, whereas the Calvinists felt it to be an objective legal act in which "God receives us into grace, (and) counts us as righteous." The subjective assurance of God's love which the Lutheran considered decisive was of little or no consequence for the Calvinist. The same difference in approach held for the idea of God's sovereignty. Both Luther and Calvin agreed that God reigned in majesty over all creation. Luther's preoccupation with personal salvation interpreted this as an assurance that man would ultimately find his spiritual rest in God. Calvinists, on the other hand, conceived of the sovereignty of God as indicating complete predestination in which some men were elected to salvation while others were allowed to go their natural way to damnation. Moreover, this conception further indicated the absolute rightness of the rules of conduct found in Scripture. As a result, Calvinists could translate Scripture into creeds and doctrines with the utter assurance of final correctness.

Accordingly, distinctly Calvinist churches became both moralistic and legalistic. Because of this objective and legalistic character of doctrine, each of the several national groups which embraced the Reformed faith was able to draw up independently its own confession and have it agree with the others in all important particulars. Thus, the Gallican Confession, composed by an assembly of French Reformed ministers in 1559, was in accord with the Belgic Confession of 1561 and the Heidelberg Catechism which appeared in 1563. Although the Scottish Confession of Faith, adopted in 1560, was in a different form, it was in substantial agreement with the others.

In establishing the Bible as the only authority for "faith and practice," Calvinist churches became centers of revolt against established institutions. Lutherans had a theoretical basis for revolt against religious tyranny, but the Calvinists could make no such separation between Church and State. If God was to be sovereign over all creation, then no institution, sacred or secular, could have the power to dictate non-Biblical conduct. Using this logic, Calvinist churches argued against the local absolute monarchs who had replaced the medieval overlords. Moreover, they took upon themselves the task of defining such concepts as "laws of nature," "rights of man" and "toleration." As a result they encouraged the development of a political theory which enthroned representative government and democratic forms. In spirit the Calvinists were just as absolutistic as those they attacked, but the net result of their efforts was to help break the power of national monarchs.

This aspect of Calvinism brought large numbers of the recently emerging middle class into the Reformed churches. In Holland, France, England and Scotland, the commercial bourgeoisie left the older faith, eschewed Lutheranism, and established Reformed churches. The virtues of industry and thrift which Calvin found in the Bible were in exact accord with the necessities of an expanding commercial age. Indeed, business success was looked upon as an obvious indication of a life lived in the pattern set by God. In many instances, worship became less important than the struggle to make over individuals and society in the light of Scripture. Although Reformed church members spent considerable time in prayer, by far the greater portion of their energies was devoted to a study of the Bible and an attempt to put its precepts into practice. The English Presbyterians (so named after the Calvinist form of government) were largely responsible for the Puritan rebellion and the establishment of Scotland. Their influence, far greater than their numbers, did much toward the development of American constitutionalism.

The very fact that all Reformed churches looked to Scripture as the one final authority caused the communion to be split into many dissident groups. For as Christians of all ages have discovered, the Bible can be used to support a wide variety of opinion, much of it contradictory. With their progressively intense study of the Bible, Reformed scholars began to see that Calvin's interpretation of certain passages was not by any means the only one possible. Resulting from this discovery, a large number of splinter churches came into existence, each claiming the authority of Scripture and each accusing the other of error. In Holland, for example, a theologian called Cocceius reread the Scripture and found that the whole of God's word could be grouped under three covenant headings, each of which covered a historical era. The first was called the pre-Mosaic, the second, the Mosaic law, and the third, the Covenant of Grace which was ushered in by Christ. Thus, he said, Christianity teaches that there exists a contractual relationship between man and God. If man lives up to his side of the bargain, salvation is assured; if he does not, he is damned. Any such idea cut athwart Calvin's rigid predestinarian doctrine and therefore placed the Cocceians outside the Calvinist circle. As a consequence, the Covenant Presbyterian Church was formed. In much the same fashion well over a hundred different schisms have occurred in the Presbyterian and Reformed churches since Calvin established his theocracy.

THE ANGLICAN REVOLT

THE revolt of the English Church from Rome was founded on purely political and personal reasons. The Catholic Church in England had not been immune from the religious unrest which was disturbing the continent, yet during the early part of Henry VIII's reign (1509-1547), England remained a strong Catholic country, bound by faith and practice to Rome. As late as 1521 Henry wrote a stern denunciation of the Lutheran position on the sacraments and defended the position of the Catholic system. Wherever he found Lutheran ideas in English churches and universities, the heretics were either imprisoned or executed. His early zeal for the Roman cause was so great that the pope conferred the title *Fidei Defensor* (Defender of the Faith) upon his person and his office. Religiously, Henry and his followers never seemed to question the rightness and authority of the Roman hierarchy.

At the same time, however, England was beginning to feel her power and position in European politics. A spirit of national patriotism was rapidly rising among the commercial groups, while the ancient feudal attitudes and institutions were giving way. The Catholic Church was the major defender of the older regime, and her political maneuvers were no less abundant and complicated in England than on the continent. As in other sections of Europe, it was to the economic interest of the new English middle class to stamp out the independent power of the Roman Church and establish all power in the hands of an absolute national monarch. The sentiment for revolt, however, was unorganized and, until Henry's defection, without leadership.

The Anglican Church officially declared itself free of Rome when the pope refused to grant Henry a divorce from Catherine of Aragon. Pope Clement VII's refusal was not made in terms of principle, such favors to monarchs having been granted many times, but rather it came as a result of extreme pressure from Emperor Charles V, Queen Catherine's nephew. As the controversy wore on, Henry, by this time in love with Anne Boleyn, a court lady-in-waiting, became convinced that such papal action was an affront to England's sovereignty. This incident, irrespective of the merits of Henry's divorce, was the event necessary to crystallize the already existing opposition to Rome. Henry had little difficulty in getting Parliament to pass the "Act of Supremacy" in 1534 which declared: "Be it enacted by authority of this present Parliament that the king our sovereign lord, his heirs and successors, kings of this realm, shall be taken, accepted, and reputed the only supreme head on earth of the Church of

England." In short order Henry married Anne Boleyn and was promptly excommunicated.

The "Act of Supremacy" was an attack upon the power of the pope; it was not a doctrinal revolt against Catholic orthodoxy. Henry still adhered to the main articles of the Catholic faith, such as the sacrifice of the mass, the veneration of saints, treasury of merit and the seven sacraments, and had no intention of putting England in the Protestant camp. The few Lutheran Protestants in England who denied the Catholic doctrine of transubstantiation were punished just as severely as the Catholics who continued to recognize papal supremacy. But the hold of Rome had been broken, and in spite of Henry's efforts the new religious ideas from the continent could not be kept from the English people. Under Henry's successor, Edward VI (1547-1553), England became effectually a Protestant country. Both Lutherans and Calvinists were free to preach their doctrines, and the *Book of Common Prayer*, published in 1552, made it clear that a new order was being instituted.

The Anglican Church became definitely Protestant during the reign of Queen Elizabeth (1558-1603). Once again the English Church asserted both its independence of Rome and the supreme authority of the monarch. The *Book of Common Prayer* underwent further Protestant revision and the official Anglican doctrine was given expression in thirty-nine articles of faith which were passed by Parliament. The thirty-nine articles not only proclaimed the Scripture to be the final religious authority, but they also declared that justification could be achieved by faith alone. The articles further denied the doctrine of transubstantiation; instead they asserted that Christ is present in the bread and wine, but in a "spiritual manner." The *Book of Common Prayer* retained a more liturgical service than either the Lutheran or the Reformed churches, but the liturgy no longer had the sacramental meaning ascribed to it by Catholic theory. Like the Reformed type of Protestant church, the Anglicans used liturgy and worship in general as prayer which both glorified God and asked for guidance.

THE EPISCOPAL CHURCHES

THE Anglican Church has retained the episcopal form of organization together with the idea that all its clergy are in direct succession from the original Apostles. As a consequence, they have consistently refused to recognize the ministries of non-Episcopal churches as being valid spokesmen for God. Their theory of apostolic succession has prevented the Episcopal churches from uniting with other Protestant groups while at the same time tending to keep them closely bound to the culture of English-speaking peoples. The most important expression of Episcopalianism outside England has been in the eastern part of the United States where the British cultural tradition has been particularly strong.

In general, the Episcopal churches have thought of themselves as the bridge between Catholicism and Protestantism. Their form of organization and theory of the ministry are Catholic, whereas their basic doctrine of salvation is Protestant. The Archbishop of Canterbury, titular head of the Anglican Church since Queen Elizabeth renounced religious control in 1571, holds a unique position which is a mixture of papal authority and Protestant ministerial teacher. The very fact that the Anglicans and their sister churches in the United States have assumed this bridge position has led to conflicting internal movements. One group, composed of both clergy and laymen, has argued that everything except the doctrine of papal supremacy should derive from the Catholic system. These so-called Anglo-Catholics have been a strong and ever-present minority. By far the greatest number of Anglicans and Episcopalians have belonged to the "low church," which in general has been influenced by Calvinistic Protestantism. It is to the efforts of this group that Episcopal churches as a whole owe their liberal theology and much of their emphasis upon social welfare. Although the two groups live together in the established Anglican and the disestablished Episcopal churches, their union is uneasy and their struggle for ecclesiastical control is constant.

27

POST-REFORMATION CHANGES

THE breakup of medieval Christendom, accompanied
as it was by a denial of earthly religious authority, was
bound to set the stage for the development of a number of churches and sects. The three traditions, Lutheranism,
Calvinism and Anglicanism, were by no means the only fruits
of the Reformation.

THE ANABAPTISTS

ONE of the most heterogeneous of the sectarian movements
was begun about 1523 under the leadership of Conrad Grebel
and Felix Manz as a reaction to the Swiss reformation. The
Anabaptists, as they were called by the opposition, spread
throughout Germany and to a lesser extent into France, England, Sweden and Denmark. They were never organized into
a single church or even into a single tradition; rather, the
group was broken up into innumerable sects usually named
for specific leaders.

The Anabaptists were given their name from their insistence
upon adult baptism. According to their views, the church
should have nothing to do with any secular power; indeed, the
only real meaning of "church" came in its consideration as an
assembly of regenerate souls. Since according to their reading
of Scripture baptism could be administered only after conversion, it could not be administered to infants. People had to be-

[453]

come members of the church; certainly they could not be born into it, as Catholics, Lutherans, Calvinists and Anglicans believed. Considering themselves a select group of regenerate believers, the Anabaptists had little regard for any civil authority. Some of the sects within this movement refused to pay taxes, and most of them looked upon war as a sinful enterprise in which no Christian could engage. It was usual for groups of Anabaptists to gather together in small communities, make their own laws, and regulate their common life in terms of their individual interpretation of Scripture. These communities often outlawed private property and, moreover, established their own rules for marriage and sexual behavior. As a result they were usually on the periphery of national social life.

For the most part, the Anabaptist sects joined a strict legalistic interpretation of the Bible with mysticism. All areas of the Christian tradition were subject to the possibility of special revelation, but people who claimed to have received such illumination were usually looked upon with suspicion unless their revelation agreed with the established dogma. On the other hand, the Anabaptists took the view that God was constantly guiding the destiny of each individual and could therefore speak to him at any time and under any condition. When God was not speaking, however, the literal meaning of the Holy Writ was to be followed. The net result of this mixed conception was the development of a multitude of Anabaptist sects based either upon a special revelation to some particular prophet or upon a previously slighted passage of the Bible.

Whereas the Protestant Church tradition drew heavily upon the middle class for support, the sectarians were predominantly members of the lower economic levels. For the most part they stood outside the tradition in which theological scholarship was important and contented themselves with developing the devotional and pietistic aspects of Christianity. Denying as they did any concern for theology—an attitude dictated in part at least by their extremely rude educational backgrounds—the sectarians propounded a plethora of radical and bizarre beliefs. Some were quite convinced that the second coming of Christ was only a few months or years away; others worked out prophecies from the numerical computations of the Book of Revelation; and still others believed that the spirit of Christ was resident only in the bodies of those belonging to a particular sect. Aside from their stated beliefs, the general effort of the sectarians was toward living that kind of godly and pious life which the Gospels said Jesus lived. This particular emphasis is probably the most important single quality common to all the sects.

As the Anabaptist movement spread, it was finally encompassed by a more general devotional revival which sprang up in Germany in the Seventeenth Century. Since the time of Luther, the German people had been exposed to the highly subjective and individualistic Lutheran theology. The Pietist movement, which ultimately incorporated the Anabaptists, was based firmly in Lutheranism. Largely derived from the politically and economically oppressed classes, the Pietists turned to a devotional Christianity in hope of salvation. For them Christianity was a life, an inner assurance of redemption, rather than a church or a creed. Although Pietism was responsible for the growth of a number of sects such as the Mennonites, Moravians, Dunkers, Inspirationists, Schwenkfelders and Swedenborgians, it also captured segments of both the Lutheran and Reformed clergy. As a result, the Pietist movement tended to soften the rather harsh orthodoxies of the Reformation churches and turn attention toward the development of a Christian devotional life.

THE CONGREGATIONALISTS

ENGLISH Christians were no more free of Pietist influence than were Christians on the Continent. Many Englishmen saw in the Anglican compromise a threat to true New Testament religion and a dangerous tendency toward arid formalization. The English Church, like the orthodox Reformed churches of the Continent, was developing a rigid theological structure which offered its communicants little in the way of emotional satisfaction. Robert Browne (1550-1633), a young Anglican clergyman who felt this lack strongly, left the established Church to organize a religiously radical sect called the *Congregationalists*. The members of this group, also called *Independents* or *Separatists*, held the conviction that each congregation of regenerate believers should hire its own minister and control its own actions. They were to have no intercourse with other churches; they were simply members of the invisible universal Church of Christ. Since the "covenant" between God and the congregation was drawn up in a democratic meeting of all members, each of the assemblies could be as exclusive or inclusive as it desired. In the beginning the various Congregational churches held to a Calvinistic form of Biblical interpretation. As time went on, however, this semblance of creedal unity vanished, and the only unifying factor remaining was the congregational polity.

THE BAPTISTS

THE congregational form of government was popular with other sectarian groups. The Baptist Church, organized in England through the influence of the Mennonites, a major continental Anabaptist sect, took over the congregational form and applied it even more rigorously than the followers of Browne had. The Baptists were influenced very little by Calvinism, principally because Calvin had advocated both infant baptism and theocracy, which were anathema to this new group. They preached complete religious toleration and the absolute separation of church and state. In so far as they were concerned, their church was independent of the world and responsible only to God. Baptist communions attracted to their number the most radical of the English Protestants. Like many of the other sectarians, however, the Baptists achieved their most notable success in the United States.

THE METHODISTS

THE Church of England received its greatest shock from pietistically inspired enthusiasm when, in the eighteenth century, the Methodist Church was established. Its founders, John and Charles Wesley and George Whitefield, were impressed with the lack of emotional warmth in the official church. For them as for the earlier sectarians, Christianity was a system of devotion which would change men's hearts and issue in godly action. In committing one's soul to Christ, salvation could be achieved without all the intellectualization and formalism which characterized the major Christian denominations. At the start of the Wesleyan movement there was no intent to revolt against the Anglicans; rather there was hope that the established Church could be reformed along Pietist lines. But the formalism which the Wesleys were fighting was too firmly entrenched, and separation became necessary.

The Methodist movement, like the other pietistic sects, drew its membership from the lower economic levels. The early Methodist preachers went into the newly settled industrial communities of England, where they held camp meetings and revival services in the open air. Wherever they went they urged their hearers to live a "Christlike life" and achieve for themselves that sense of inner peace which would be their assurance of ultimate salvation. The type of service used, both in its preaching and its forms of worship, was designed to appeal to the emotions rather than the intellect. The scholarly exercises of the Anglican sermon, surrounded by stately and highly refined music, gave way to enthusiastic shouting and less formal hymns. For the uneducated and religiously forgotten workers of industrial England, the Methodist revival met and filled an emotional and spiritual need. Before long large Methodist groups organized themselves into definite churches and spread throughout the world.

The Methodists retained a denationalized version of the Anglican form of organization. Bishops were assigned areas within which they controlled the ecclesiastical activities of individual congregations. The local church groups were required to pay the salaries of their ministers, but the bishop was empowered to install or remove a pastor at his own discretion. Although some compromises were made with the congregational form, the Methodists were originally and have remained episcopalian in government.

In the Wesleyan movement, sectarian influence was felt principally in the area of theological understanding. The use of the episcopal form of government was not based upon any idea of Apostolic succession, or any idea that the clergy should be considered members of a special "holy order." Rather, the episcopal organization was deemed more efficient and less subject to confusion and conflict. In line with his nonsacerdotal conception of the church, Wesley's followers held that theological formulations were of little importance when compared to the quality of a Christian life. The hallmark of a Christian was not to be found in what he thought, but in the fact that he had "faith working by love" in his attempt to make the world and himself more Christian and Christlike. This faith was not foreordained by God; it was achieved by the proper use of human freedom. Wesley and his followers, in particular agreement with the Moravian pietists, denounced predestination and the absoluteness of human sin. Methodist theologians have always been convinced that man has both the freedom and the opportunity to attain Christian perfection here on earth.

In addition to their doctrines regarding freedom and perfection, Methodists show their sectarian roots in emphasizing the importance of direct religious experience. Religion without experience of the divine is an empty form which has no relevance to salvation or to man's ultimate destiny. People who attend church and recite theological propositions without experiencing the assurance of faith are not religious, they are simply conventional. Like many of the other pietists, Methodists conceive of God as a warm and loving personality who issues few orders but lives in the hearts of true Christians. Without the experience of God man is lost; with it, he is saved.

RATIONALISTIC SECTARIANISM

IN GENERAL, sectarian Protestantism derived its force from a highly emotional desire to recapture the religious life of Jesus and the primitive church. However, there was an opposite tendency operating in post-Reformation Protestantism which produced rationalistic rather than evangelical sects. The rationalists were suspicious not only of religious experience, but also of any kind of literal reading of Scripture. As devotees of reason they considered the miraculous occurrences recorded in the Bible offensive. At the same time they mistrusted anyone who claimed to have had a mystical or nonrational religious experience. Above all else, Christianity, in order to be pure, had to be reasonable; everything in the tradition which could not be fitted into rational categories was to be discarded as invalid superstition. Such requirements ultimately forced these sectarians to deny such doctrines as the Trinity, the Virgin Birth and a host of others which Catholic and Protestant churches considered essential. The most significant rationalistic sect became known as *Unitarians,* a group which has inhabited a dimly defined region between secularism and Christianity.

THE CATHOLIC REFORMATION

WHILE Protestantism was splitting and spreading throughout the world, the Roman Church was consolidating its position and reforming its structure. In spite of what might be said by Catholics about Protestant heresy, there were a large number of adherents to the old faith who recognized the clerical corruption of Rome. There was general truth in the Protestant charge that the Catholic priesthood was filled with people ignorant of the Gospel, lax in their morals and utterly self-seeking in their churchly activities. Since many of the popes partook of this same corruption, the disciplinary system inherent within the Church was not effectively put into practice. As a result, reforming parties sprang up within Catholicism and ultimately forced a housecleaning and a stricter discipline. The reform movement culminated in the famous Council of Trent (which met 1545-47, 1551-52, 1562-63), where the practices and doctrines of Catholicism received fresh definition.

One of the most important Catholic organizations working for reform was called the Oratory of the Divine Love. This Oratory was originally composed of about sixty devout Catholics who banded together in order to cultivate further their own personal piety. Although they held widely divergent theological opinions, some even adhering to the Protestant doctrine of justification by faith, they were all agreed that the Roman Church could fulfill its mission only if it were morally

purified. They were convinced that the Protestants were totally wrong in seceding from Rome even though they might
conceivably be right in some of their criticisms and theological views. As time went on, the Oratory became more powerful until finally two of its leaders, Contarini and Caraffa,
were given cardinal's hats and made advisers to the pope.
Through their influence and the constant insistence of the
Emperor, Pope Paul III called the Council of Trent in 1545.

Of the various conflicting parties represented at the Council, the pope's delegates were by far the strongest. The pope's
plan, largely formulated by the Oratory of the Divine Love,
was to draw a definite line between Protestants and Catholics
in terms of specific doctrines. Whereas the Protestants made
so much of scriptural authority, the Council, under the leadership of the papal party, declared "that unwritten traditions,
which have been received either from the lips of Christ himself, or transmitted in the Church, are all to be accepted with
respect and veneration equal to that which is due to the Scriptures." The Council went further: it asserted that all the Protestant translations of the Bible were in error and that the
"books of Holy Scripture, including the Old Testament
Apocrypha, should be used only in the Vulgate version and
interpreted not by individuals, but by the Church." From this
time forward there could be no question about where the
Catholics stood with regard to Holy Writ.

On other points such as the Eucharist and Penance, the
Council reaffirmed the established Roman doctrines. The only
theory of the Eucharist possible, they declared, is transubstantiation, in which it is believed that the bread and wine
actually change into the body and blood of Christ. The documents of the Council assured Catholics that in spite of Protestant denials the Treasury of Merit actually exists, and that
absolution can only be given by a Roman priest. In short, it

was made clear that Protestants were lost souls with little if any chance for salvation.

Although the Council claimed that the Roman Church was the exclusive agency of the divine on earth, it did urge a reformation in the Church's moral standards. The pope was directed to exercise a rigid discipline and to make sure that all of the clergy lived "holy and pious lives." Priests and others were required to curtail their extrareligious business activities, spend a greater amount of time in meeting the spiritual needs of their parishes, and learn the fundamentals of Christianity from the established theological writings. After the Council concluded, a succession of reforming popes set about to renovate the entire Catholic structure. By the end of the sixteenth century the Roman Church was reorganized, cleansed and aggressively seeking the destruction of Protestantism for the greater glory of God.

The Catholic revival caused the Church to lose some of the accommodating breadth which had characterized its early years. Aside from defining dogma more explicitly, the central authority took upon itself responsibility for protecting good Catholics from heretical books which might lead them to Protestantism or make them renounce Christianity altogether. The *Index Expurgatorius*, or list of condemned books, was published throughout the Catholic parishes, and specific punishments were prescribed for those who transgressed its prohibitions. In addition, the medieval Court of the Inquisition was revived and reorganized as a means for coping with heresy. The Inquisition was especially strong and brutal in Italy and Spain where the Roman Church exerted its greatest efforts to maintain supremacy. When such methods were coupled with the force of the established military and political powers of the southern European countries, Catholicism was able to effect a decisive turn in the rising Protestant tide.

One of the most potent instruments for the preservation and

extension of Catholicism developed out of the formation of new monastic orders. The most significant of these orders, the Society of Jesus, was founded by Ignatius Loyola (1499-1566) soon after the German Reformation got under way. The Jesuits, as its members were called, took an oath of absolute allegiance to the pope in addition to the usual vows of poverty, chastity and obedience. They were sent into the areas that were tottering on the brink of Protestantism, and it was largely through their efforts that Poland was reclaimed from Calvinism and Ireland saved from the Anglican Church. Throughout their various activities the Jesuits never hesitated to use whatever instruments were at hand to achieve a papal victory. All possible means were justified as long as the end was a return to the Mother Church and the authority of the Bishop of Rome.

The Jesuits early recognized the necessity of education in Catholic doctrine, particularly for the young. If children could be taught to think in Catholic terms and interpret their experience from Catholic presuppositions, the Jesuits felt that the chances of losing them later in life were materially reduced. Consequently they organized elementary and secondary schools all over Europe. They became versed in the secular sciences as well as theology, thus winning back the respect of those who had considered the Catholic clergy to be ignorant and lacking in culture. In addition to their tremendous educational and political undertakings on the Continent, the Jesuits sent representatives to North and South America, India, China and other parts of the expanding world. Their missions immediately set about to convert the natives to Catholicism and teach them obedience to Christ's vicar in Rome. Although hated, feared and persecuted by groups both inside and outside the Roman Church, the Jesuits have become the most powerful single force in the far-flung Catholic system.

Notwithstanding its claim of being the only true faith,

Catholicism soon had to learn to live with Protestantism. No amount of coercion, political intrigue, education or preaching could heal the sixteenth-century breach. Albeit unwillingly, the Roman Church was reduced to the status of one Christian denomination among other denominations. It was no longer necessary for Europe to look to the Eternal City for either political support or spiritual guidance. As a result of an expanding capitalism, the center of European civilization shifted to the northern countries where Protestantism was strong and Catholicism weak. Although the Holy See has since remained a potent political power, especially in southern Europe, South America and Ireland, the modern period of Western culture has been a Protestant rather than a Catholic era.

SECTION SUMMARY

As is readily apparent from this survey, the name *Christianity* implies a highly diversified religious phenomenon. From small and, at the time, insignificant beginnings, it has developed into a world-wide movement encompassing over 2000 different denominations. It has been largely responsible for what we call Western Civilization, and the officials of its churches have made and deposed kings. It has numbered among its adherents some of the greatest men of politics, science and philosophy, together with some of the worst criminals and extortionists in history. It has been part and parcel of Western man's life from birth to death since Constantine found that joining the movement was more economical than fighting it.

The basic world-view which Christianity gave to Western man is comparatively simple in spite of the various elaborations that have been made on it. The earth was created by God. Originally, all things were perfect. But man, of his own free will, rebelled against God and was consequently pushed out into a hard, strange and alien world to earn his bread by the sweat of his brow and to seek eternally his creator's forgiveness. God, being merciful and kind as well as just, also sought to regain his children. The Holy Scriptures are a record of the dealings between him and them. Time and again he sent prophets, and time and again man, in his stiffnecked obtuseness, rejected God's ways for his own. Finally God made the ultimate sacrifice for man's sake and sent his only begotten son, Jesus Christ, to teach the way of salvation. But again God was rejected, and Christ was put to death on the Cross. This time, however, a small group of Christians, as they came to be called, were convinced; and they committed themselves to the task of convincing the whole of mankind. Through the organization which they left, the True God has been preached and the road to salvation made clear. The history of power and influence which Christian institutions have had points to the successful outcome of man's struggle. Although he will never return to the Garden of Eden, an even greater glory will be his at the end of time in the Kingdom of Heaven.

The Christian faith has supplied its believers with answers to life's basic questions. Where does man come from?—he was created by God in the image of his perfection. Why is man on earth?—to be God's companion in holiness. How should man act?—he should act in such a way as to fulfill the purpose for which he was put on earth; he should act in accordance with the dictates of God as he has revealed them. Where is man going?—his ultimate destiny is a spiritual oneness with God: citizenship in the Kingdom of Heaven. Most important, the Christian faith asserts that life has meaning and purpose, and that its creator cares about the thoughts and actions of each individual. No one walks alone; everyone is watched over and sometimes cared for by a great cosmic father who wishes each soul to return home. Thus all of life, even in its minutest detail, is freighted with meaning and cosmic purpose.

The central core of the Christian tradition has always conceived of man as a poor weak sinner who is strengthened and sustained through grace. This grace of God is apparent in the fact that man was created, that he is preserved in the face of the dangerous exigencies of life, and beyond all else, that he has been redeemed through the life, death and resurrection of Jesus Christ. It is only through grace that life is made tolerable, and only through grace that death is a doorway to heaven rather than a crushing defeat.

The whole structure of Christian doctrine would have little meaning were it not for a distinctive attitude toward man. Man is by nature a fallen being, fallen in the sense that he was once good but is now a sinner. To be a sinner in the Christian sense means that there has been a serious rupture, caused by man's rebellion, between God and man. It is this alienation from God that makes salvation necessary, and it is this same alienation that results in the evils of history and the imperfection of man's will and mind. In essence Christian sin is the denial of the sovereignty of God and the affirmation of man's pretensions to self-mastery. This original sin, scripturally expressed in the Adam and Eve narrative, infects all man's deeds and thoughts. The early church felt it could be overcome by a mystical identification of the believing soul with Christ; Roman Catholicism sees obedience restored by subjection to Christ's vicar and the eating of the sacramental elements in the Eucharist; Protestantism generally believes that the contrariness of man is obliterated by a faith which includes both intellectual acceptance of revelation and wholehearted commitment and trust in God and his promises. When Christians have achieved whatever goals their particular group has defined, they are saved from both moral evil and meaninglessness. The hold of sin is broken, the natural, or fallen, man is dead, and they are "born again into the richness of God's glory."

The vitality of the Christian tradition is most evident in the reformations it has undergone. No church has ever rested content in the knowledge that it has achieved the perfection preached in the Gospel. Theological and organizational controversies, although often mixed with political and economic motivations, have usually been based in a desire to serve God more completely through Christ. In each new age there are powerful individuals who initiate revolts from the established institutions and proclaim what seem to them to be a purer doctrine and a more complete understanding. This protesting attitude, this inability to find complete satisfaction in any historical institution, began with the Old Testament prophets, continued through Christ and his followers, and is today well represented in both Catholic and Protestant traditions.

Although this permanent revolution is an evidence of vitality, it is also the cause of schisms which destroy Christian unity and tend to weaken the total impact of Christian ideas upon the secular world. But in spite of this cost, Christianity can be no other way. The God of the Christians is so far removed from the world and so unlike all things within the world that his communication with man must be necessarily difficult and his ways obscure. He sits in constant judgment upon sinful man's attempts to know him and live with him. As this judgment is felt, man is forever forced to revise his opinions and his ways of action. If the revision leads to disunity, with some men clinging to the old ways and others taking the new, it cannot be helped, since Christians must serve God rather than history.

VI

RELIGION IN THE MODERN WORLD

28

RELIGION IN THE MODERN WORLD

THE religions we have discussed have been part and parcel of the world's major cultural traditions. The Hindus were largely responsible for present-day India; the Buddhists laid the basis for modern China and Japan; Judaism still lives in the Western world, but more significantly, it was the parent of both Mohammedanism and Christianity; and Christianity gave to Western civilization both its ethical standards and its fundamental world-view. It would be difficult to exaggerate the decisive importance of religious traditions in the formation of our contemporary cultures.

Beyond this historical consideration, however, is the question regarding the meaning and function of religion in the modern world. What does it mean to be religious in the twentieth century? Are the ancient ideas and creeds which contributed so much to the past now obsolete? Has the development of the scientific method made religion, with all its theories of revelation and ritualistic practice, merely a remnant of superstition and primitive magic? In other words, what is the relation between present-day religion and the development of mankind's religious heritage? To answer such questions as these, the contemporary student must examine carefully not only modern religious institutions, but the nature of twentieth-century culture as well. Such a task is enormously difficult and can only be sketchily described in these concluding pages.

RISE OF THE PHYSICAL SCIENCES

THE major religious creeds were well established long before the systematic beginnings of modern science. The preceding periods of man's history certainly had science; indeed, anthropologists assert that no culture about which we have any knowledge whatsoever has lacked some activity or mode of thought which could be called scientific. In the broadest use of the term, any systematic search for truth can be called *science;* and in this sense some of the theologies produced by Hindus, Buddhists, Jews and Christians could be grouped under this heading. In the Western tradition, such theologians as Origen, Aquinas and Calvin considered their labors to be scientific and looked upon their systems as the ultimate codification of all true knowledge.

But when the phrase "modern science" is used, something entirely different is indicated. Modern science also means the systematic search for truth, but it limits the area within which truth can be found. To be scientific in the modern sense is to utilize a method which combines experimentation with mathematical analysis. From the time of the Renaissance, Western man has been investigating nature, not as a creation which is tending toward perfection, but as a physical mass upon which experiments can be made and which contains within itself relationships expressible in mathematical terms. The desire to know nature has sprung from varying motives, but in each case the mathematico-experimental methodology has remained constant. The increasing dominance of this modern scientific method has led to a revaluation of the "truth value" of religion and, indeed, of the whole function of religion in the life of man.

Probably the original motivation for modern science came from a desire to increase man's knowledge of God. Francis

Bacon, who was among the earliest of the modern scientific thinkers, looked upon the pursuit of truth as the highest ambition any man could have: "The inquiry of truth, which is the wooing of it; the knowledge of truth, which is the praise of it; and the belief of truth, which is the enjoying of it, is the sovereign good of human natures." Moreover, Bacon was convinced that the old methods for gaining truth were wrong; if man was ever to realize his ambition, he had to be freed of every philosophical and theological preconception while he went about his task of investigating all the particular aspects of nature. Truth is never found, he asserted, by descending from revealed principles to the facts of experience; it can be obtained only by beginning with particulars and *inducing from them* whatever general principles possible. The facts turned up by experimental investigation must never be referred to philosophers or theologians for validation; they must validate themselves in concrete experience. From Bacon's viewpoint, such an activity was more religious than theological speculation since it gave a more sturdy and dependable knowledge of God. In short, he felt, the way to know God most accurately is through his creation, not through a supposed revelation in some ancient book. The restless and inquiring "mind of man looketh upon scattered causes (in nature), it may sometimes rest in them and go no further; but when it beholdeth the chain of them, confederate and linked together, it must needs fly to Providence and Deity."

Although Bacon was certainly saying nothing new, his *Novum Organum* was published at a time (1620) when Western intellectuals were acutely dissatisfied with the older systematic philosophical and theological systems. Medieval feudalism was cracking under the pressure of capitalism and nationalism, the authority of the Roman hierarchy was being successfully challenged, and a new spirit of freedom was sweeping Europe. With changes taking place in all areas of

[473]

life, the emerging modern world needed a new orientation toward nature, man and God.

René Descartes, who closely followed Bacon, took over the task of building a philosophy based firmly in the method of the new science. Descartes, like Bacon, had no real doubts about God's existence, but he wanted complete proof which would be independent of all ancient authorities. The serious questions are, "What can I call truth? How can I know that I am not being deluded? Why should I believe the Bible, the Church, Plato, Aristotle, Aquinas or any other message from the past?"

To meet these questions Descartes set out to construct an independent methodology which would be an unerring guide to truth. The first step would have to be a doubt of everything, even his own existence. There could be no concern for the consequences to Christian theology. The earlier theologians might have reached right conclusions by wrong methods. If their conclusions could be substantiated by an inquiry beginning with critical doubt, all would be well; if they could not be, mankind would be better off for having purged itself of superstitious error. In any case, natural science and philosophy should be indifferent regarding the fate of theological propositions and churchly pronouncements; they should be concerned with the truth alone. But nothing should be assumed to be true regarding which "the least ground for uncertainty" can be imagined. Complete doubt, therefore, must be the beginning of wisdom.

Since Descartes set out to doubt everything, it was necessary that he first establish, beyond all question, the fact of his own existence. This he did by means of his famous phrase, *Cogito ergo sum:* I think, therefore I am. The very act of doubting indicates a subject who is doing the doubting; doubt could not exist without a doubter. Descartes went on from this point to prove, at least to his own satisfaction, that the material world and God have an existence which is just as clear and just as distinct as his own being. The particular arguments which Descartes used are of little importance for our study, but the weight of the spirit and direction of his thought can hardly be exaggerated. From his day forward, Western philosophy and science took a new road, independent of the religious tradition, and helped to create what we now call secular culture.

The new road of science led to a completely revised understanding of nature and what is commonly called "reality." The Christian world-view which formed the basis for interpretation during the Middle Ages was essentially an economy of redemption. The physical universe was created by God as a home for man. All its parts were striving, as man strives, for perfection and final rest in the unity of God. The natural world was chaotic in appearance, but it was assumed to be a harmonious whole from God's perspective. In any event, the only really important thing was man's salvation; for man was the center of the universe, and the earth upon which he dwelt was the footstool of God. However, independent critical inquiry soon radically altered this conception of the world and its status. Some years before Descartes, the Church's conception of the universe had been successfully attacked by Copernicus, Tycho Brahe, Kepler, Galileo and Giordano Bruno. Ptolemaic astronomy, upon which it was based, was slowly replaced by a new astronomy founded upon observation and mathematical analysis. As the new science progressed, it became increasingly clear that physical nature was like a giant machine, operating according to its own laws which were quite independent of the moral laws Christian theology held to be primary.

The Newtonian world-view which was built out of the mathematical and physical investigations of the new science finally supplanted the ancient system. In the Newtonian

[475]

scheme it was not necessary to assume that in some mysterious way the apparent confusion of the world was, in God's eyes, order. Rather, nature was seen to be both orderly and rational in its own right, and if man would but view it correctly, he would understand. Everything belongs to the proper functioning of the cosmic machine; nothing is out of place; and most important of all, no single earthly event requires a supernatural cause. The whole machine can be thought of as the creation of an omnipotent God, but the individual parts are explainable in terms of their relations to the whole.

To say that the entire universe was originally constructed by God but now functions according to its own inherent laws was small comfort for those who wished to preserve the old Christian "economy of redemption." Truth was no longer to be sought in the Bible, in miracles, or in churchly pronouncements, but rather in reading the rational and logically organized book of nature. And for this reading, supernatural aid was neither necessary nor permissible.

THE SPREAD OF THE SCIENTIFIC SPIRIT

THE radical changes which modern science produced in man's conception of the universe soon made themselves felt in all areas of life. Man himself was obviously just as much a part of nature as the sticks and stones of his environment. His history, his morals, his rights and his duties came to be looked upon as subjects for independent critical inquiry. Both the Bible and religious experience soon fell under the microscope of scientific scrutiny. As a result, the authority of science supplanted the authority of ancient religious documents and established religious institutions.

At first, science was important only for the comparative few who dealt with intellectual issues, and particularly with the problem of knowledge. However, through a series of dramatic scientific discoveries and the increasing dependence of modern society upon newly invented mechanical wonders, the general population came to trust the scientist's word above that of the priest or theologian. The marriage of science and industry produced a continuous stream of labor-saving devices, and the economy shifted from an agrarian to an industrial base. The fundamental conflict between a naturalistic and a supernaturalistic world-view became, in one form or another, the common property of a large proportion of the population of the West. Slowly but surely the absolute claims upon which the Western religious tradition had been built were critically examined. Many of them could not meet a naturalistic test. The resulting confusion has led to important changes in religious doctrine as well as to a new conception of religion's function.

The most dramatic innovation came in terms of an assertion of man's power, with the consequent loss of that sense of dependency which religion considered to be primary. The Western religious tradition had interpreted man as a creature of God's hand, fallen from perfection and dependent upon God's grace for salvation. The new science, on the other hand, made knowledge and—which was more important—salvation dependent upon man's own efforts. Truth was now sought through reason and investigation rather than revelation. And, according to this theory, the more man knew about himself and his world, the greater would be his chance for health, happiness and the "good life." The creeds, dogmas, church pronouncements, and even the Scriptures became objects of investigation rather than sacred and therefore incontrovertible writings. The tools of science, which required that man believe only in his own ability, dissected the records of the religious past just as impartially as they dealt with nature and secular history. The general result was simply a loss of interest in religion rather than a direct frontal assault upon it. As the religious world shrank in importance, it was outstripped and finally engulfed by an optimistic, aggressive secular culture.

THE "NEW" SOCIETY

JUST as a "new" culture was born out of the fusion of the ancient Greco-Roman Empire and Christianity, so a "new" culture came into being with modern science. Philosophy changed its base from theology to physics; literature became concerned with the "natural" man rather than the "child of God"; morals were no longer founded in an ideal of other-worldly asceticism; politics lost its former concept of religious unity and embraced secular nationalism; and Western man's economic life moved from the "just price" to the market price. Institutions were developed which embodied the positive meaning of the new secular life. The center of community activity, which had previously been in the church, now divided itself among such secular concerns as motion pictures, radio programs, newspapers and rides in the family car. Such atomization forced religious institutions into a competitive position. The privilege once accorded representatives of the divine on earth was no longer accepted as axiomatic. The world-view taught from the pulpit was forced to argue its case before the independent citizen just as naturalism and materialism were. Nor could any recalcitrant who refused to accept the church's view be subjected to business or personal reprisals. All over the Western world more and more churches became disestablished; and the states concerned refused to take responsibility either for enforcing correct belief or for financing the institutions. Thus the "new" society developed into a secular society.

Although shrunken in importance, the traditional religious institutions absorbed much of the new secularism. Slowly but surely theological seminaries took over secular and scientific instruments of Biblical criticism. Candidates for the ministry were taught the relationship between religious and profane history as well as the latest secular economic and political philosophies. The churches, in turn, placed less and less emphasis upon doctrinal and dogmatic teaching while increasing the attention they paid to problems of social welfare. Often the "Christian view" became simply the "moral view," and the virtues of love, faith and charity were preached as the essence of the Gospel. Churches and religious thinkers now became champions of democracy and capitalism, whereas in the past they had upheld feudalism and the divine right of monarchs. Science was accepted in all but the most rigid circles of both Catholic and Protestant orthodoxy. Indeed, the critical philosophies created by nonreligious thinkers and based upon science were slightly changed but then generally accepted by the churches—laymen, ministers and theologians.

This absorption of secularism into religion was both rapid and chaotic. Much that was embraced was wholly incompatible with the tradition, and a great deal of the philosophic and scientific material was never adequately understood. As a consequence, Western religious institutions achieved a surface reconciliation with secularism at the cost of consistency and uniqueness. The minds of laymen became confused as to the true nature of Christianity, and indeed, the special functions of both church and religion seemed to have disappeared. The traditional Christian values now found expression in all manner of secular groups. Labor unions emphasized brotherhood and solidarity; secular novels defined and praised love and devotion; secular poetry gave expression to naturalistic piety; and political parties offered programs for social justice. It soon appeared that religion was not so much wrong as simply irrelevant. Everything an individual needed could be found under other guise than the ancient trappings of traditional religion. At least this is the way it seemed to a large number of people.

[479]

One of the most striking departures from religious culture toward secularism came in the field of education. The religious spirit operating through organized churches had long been responsible for all levels of education. In Europe the parochial school system was employed by both Protestant and Catholic groups. Much of the curriculum was concerned with establishing right belief and providing specific training in church dogma. The first schools and colleges in the United States were founded along the same lines. As the study of science gained prominence, the study of religion went into decline. At the same time, the various nations of the West came to recognize education as a civic responsibility. For example, trained men and women were required for the operation of the increasingly technical and highly complex machines of production. The result of these and other factors was the establishment of public education, financed by the state and adjusted to secular demands.

Virtually the first requirement placed upon public education was that it remain free of both ecclesiastical control and religious indoctrination. Since the Reformation, however, there had been no unified doctrine, and few of the leaders of the organized churches could agree on a common faith. Therefore, in order to be fair to all religious groups, Catholic, Protestant and Jewish, public education from its very beginning has had little or nothing to say about religious issues. The result of this conscious neutrality has been to push religion farther and farther toward the periphery of common concern. Moreover, since adults have found their positive values in secular institutions, little religious instruction has been carried on in the home. With both school and home maintaining silence, the growing child has inevitably looked upon religious institutions as ancillary to the main business of living. The churches of the West have tried to counter this secularization of education by establishing Sunday Schools and by keeping some parochial secondary schools and colleges under their control. However, by far the greater number of students have gone to public schools. Further, Sunday Schools meet but an hour or two each week, and attendance is compulsory only for those who live in disciplined religious families. And finally, the church-controlled colleges are forced to compete with publicly financed universities whose equipment and resources are, in comparison, unlimited.

The secularization of education reflects rather faithfully the general condition of modern society. The state is no longer religious in any meaningful sense, marriages are increasingly performed by civil rather than religious agencies, and the economy generates its own values and rules rather than looking to religion for help and guidance. Certainly modern secular society has put religion and religious living on the defensive. But even though some militant secularists would undoubtedly like to see the end of organized religion, the tradition has shown evidence of real vitality and considerable strength.

CHRISTIAN MISSIONS

ONE of the most important evidences of this vitality is the enthusiastic expansion of Christian missions. Since the earliest days of Christianity, numbers of committed believers have felt themselves called to preach the Gospel of Jesus to all peoples of the earth. Much of the first exploration of unknown lands was conducted by missionaries in search of converts. Dominicans, Franciscans and Jesuits traversed the vast continents of North and South America. At the same time, other members of these orders were establishing mission outposts in Africa and the Orient. Both European Christianity and European culture were brought to millions through the efforts of such devoted sons of the Church. The importance of organized mission activity was recognized by Roman Catholicism in the seventeenth century when the Sacred Congregation for Propaganda was established at Rome. Although Protestantism came into the field at a later date, its activity was ultimately no less extensive. During the eighteenth century, small-scale missions were put under way by the German Pietists, the British sectarians and the Anglican Church. The most extensive Protestant efforts, however, began in the late years of the eighteenth century and the first fifty years of the nineteenth century. By the opening of the twentieth century, more Protestant money was going into missions than into any other single church concern.

The motives underlying missionary enthusiasm are varied and often vague. Many of the churches considered this expansion to be the opening of new worlds which had never heard of Christ or his saving love. The problems raised by secularism at home seemed not only less glamorous, but also provided much less challenge. Among the heathen the church saw a chance to convert to pure doctrine, to establish specifically religious schools, and possibly to construct a Christian nation without having to come to terms with the confusing problems of a secularized West. To the religious people of the West, thoroughly steeped in Christianity, the religious practices of the non-Christian world seemed completely barbarous and primitive. The opportunity to save these lost souls from their false gods fired their imaginations much more than local difficulties were able to do. Thus, in a sense, the mission enterprise was both a challenge and an escape.

Other religious people looked upon missionary activity as an opportunity to express the spirit of brotherhood which Christianity had always considered primary. The newly opened areas of the world lacked the labor-saving devices, the scientific medicine and the knowledge of agriculture which were part and parcel of Western culture. If the Christian ethic was to be put into effect and if there was to be a fully practical Christianity, this new opportunity must be met. For one thing, it was discovered that the life expectancy of people in India and China was far below that of Western man; nor did anyone seem to care. As a result, churches raised funds to establish medical centers and various types of educational institutions. Trained doctors went into disease-infested areas to supplement the work of the evangelists. Experts on agriculture served under the banner of Christ to help increase crop production and reclaim worn-out land. As a practical expression of Christian love and charity, it would be hard to find any activity more dramatic or more fruitful than that possible to the missionary. For many, this practical Christianity offered the best possible answer to the secular charge that the religion of Jesus was irrelevant. After all, neither governments nor business agencies cared about raising the standards of health and decency; such a concern seemed to belong to those who were not in search of either power or profit. The mission field offered Christians a chance to prove the practical worth of their religion.

Missionary expansion was intimately connected with a general religious revival in the Western world. This revival, from which sprang Wesleyanism and countless other sects, was directed toward a more social interpretation of Christianity. The industrial revolution was reducing large numbers of small owners to the position of being dependent wage-earners, thus creating a new and more complicated social problem. The tendency toward considering man a factor of production rather than a child of God was given impetus as factories became larger and more impersonal. The religious criticism leveled at this dehumanization of man was a local expression of the same spirit which financed and dispatched evangelistic, medical and agricultural missionaries throughout the world. At first there was little or no theological foundation for this domestic and foreign protest, only the strong conviction that men are children of God and not mere cogs in economic and political machines. It was not long, however, before Christian theologians turned their energies toward the construction of a theoretical basis for this outpouring of good will.

LIBERAL CHRISTIANITY

LIBERAL theology took its cue from the ethical side of the Jewish-Christian tradition. The primary message of the Scripture and the life of Christ is the revelation of how man should deal with man; how he should act as a member of a community; how he should recognize his responsibilities; and how he should discharge them. The true basis of religion lies not in the acceptance or rejection of metaphysical beliefs, but in the consciousness of moral responsibility. For after all, beliefs concerning the nature of the cosmos change from age to age. New scientific discoveries make the older statements, built upon an earlier science, seem ridiculous. Clearly one could never base one's ultimate faith upon them. Liberal Christianity, on the other hand, recognized the eternal primacy of moral experience.

The Christian theologians who renounced all dependence upon metaphysical belief were, for the most part, Protestants. Roman Catholicism consistently maintained its historic position regarding the absolute correctness of its dogma and the unholy error of any changes suggested by modern scientific thought. As we have seen, the faith of Roman Catholic orthodoxy always includes statements regarding the nature of metaphysical reality. Protestant theologians, on the other hand, were bound only to the Scripture and whatever interpretation they wished to place upon it. As a consequence, they were at liberty to interpret it as moral rather than metaphysical revelation. And that is precisely what they did.

The philosophic orientation of liberal Christianity springs

[484]

primarily from Immanuel Kant, a great eighteenth-century German philosopher. Kant's critical philosophy endeavors to show that such ideas as human beings might have of God, freedom and immortality are intrinsically beyond the scope of human knowledge. Science, which is founded upon empirical data, can solve physical, but not metaphysical, problems. Consequently, all statements which claim to give metaphysical knowledge can only lead to futile argument and irreconcilable conflict. The real foundation of religious doctrine, says Kant, is seen in the practical rather than the theoretical life of man. Religious convictions are rooted in a moral faith which cannot be theoretically demonstrated. There is no way to prove or disprove religious doctrines; they can only be accepted or rejected as moral postulates. For Kant, the ones he considered primary—God, freedom and immortality—are eminently qualified for practical acceptance.

The chief exponent of the Kantian position among liberal Protestants was the German theologian, Albert Ritschl. The real job of religion, said Ritschl, is to win a moral victory over the evil of the world. Although God is unknowable, man's moral experience teaches him that the great moral reality is brotherhood. To work for brotherhood is the first and final religious expression. In so far as the dogmas, creeds, and practices of the churches aid in this enterprise, they are good and necessary; in so far as they do not, they are without religious meaning. Social work, whether at home or abroad, is not the practical expression of a theoretical belief; it is rather the Christian faith, its essence and its existence. The Kingdom of God is not a far-off heavenly city to be enjoyed after death; it is the social ideal which religious living must realize in the present world.

Like other liberal Protestants, Ritschl looked upon Christ as the supreme expression of moral goodness. Religious health depended upon all men's being motivated by the same spirit which motivated his actions. If everyone could be like Jesus, the "Reign of God" on earth would begin and never end. The controlling idea would be the Kingdom of God; the controlling passion would be the love of man for man. According to liberals, Christianity went completely wrong when it tried to make salvation metaphysical rather than social. In this process, the church denied Jesus, promoted asceticism and allowed the world to go unhappily to hell. The future, they said, lay not with pessimistic despair and dialectical argument, but with practicing Christians living the "simple Gospel of Jesus."

Although this theology furnished a basis for Christian welfare activity, it also tended to undercut the authority of the church. Within liberal circles it became possible to be a "good" Christian without either worship or systematic belief. As a consequence, such ancient Christian concepts as sin, salvation, God and redemption were radically changed in meaning. The words and dogmas were retained, but reinterpreted to fit modern conditions and the scientific temper. The church defended its existence on the grounds of social utility rather than cosmic sanction. This new wine being poured into old bottles had little of the absoluteness that made the medieval Church the powerful force it was in the life of Western man. For many it meant the loss of any distinctions in Christianity and the final and disastrous capitulation to secularism; for others it was the beginning of a new and wonderful age.

COMPARATIVE RELIGIONS

THE intensive study of non-Christian religions by Western scholars further tended to weaken the authority of the Western church. Christian theologians had always been aware that other religions than theirs existed, but by and large there was little attempt either to know them or to understand them. The march of mankind was interpreted in terms of the Jewish-Christian drama of salvation, and Western history was viewed as *the* history of the human race. Under such conditions the non-Christian religions were looked upon as degenerate systems of idolatry which forever debarred their votaries from ultimate salvation. This provincialism permeated not only theological literature, but the general consciousness of all Christian communicants as well.

Then came the new scientific interest in human culture. Part of this was the rapid accumulation of relatively objective data pertinent to non-Christian traditions. It soon became apparent that Christian scholars would have to spend a greater portion of their time than formerly in explaining why Christianity should be considered true and other religions false. The scientific spirit demanded a kind of dispassionate objectivity which made impartiality necessary. Obviously the more orthodox Protestants and Catholics could never agree to such impartiality. Liberal Christians, however, found that the results of comparative study were in essential accord with their general outlook.

Liberal Christianity came to look upon all religions as examples of man's striving for knowledge of God. The cultural variations one sees throughout the world in matters of government and social organization would necessarily be evident in religious expression too. Worship practices, dogmatic formulations, creedal statements and the like all belong to particular ways of expressing the one universal divine nature. Most of these liberals assumed that religions could be graded philosophically by their attainment of monotheism, and ethically by their understanding and appreciation of love, charity and justice. Under this system polytheistic religions were "primitive." Therefore it was incumbent upon monotheistic religions to engage in active missionary work. The moral goodness which liberal Christians considered the foundation of "true" Christianity was in like manner thought to be the highest form of ethical religion. Moreover, it was usually assumed that the highest in religious morality could not be achieved except as it was correlated with the highest monotheistic understanding of the divine. In this fashion liberal Protestantism preserved the supremacy of Christianity while at the same time giving positive religious importance to the other religions of the world.

However, this view of Christian supremacy did not take into consideration most of the beliefs which orthodox Protestants and Catholics felt to be essential. There seemed to be no room for supernaturally inspired Scriptures, miracles such as the Virgin Birth and the bodily resurrection, the supernatural efficacy of the bread and wine of the Eucharist, or any special story of creation such as that found in Genesis. For after all, each of the several religions of the world make absolute claims in these respects, and make them quite differently. The historical evidence for all of them has the same tenuous quality, and the deeper scientific study penetrated, the more implausible such claims became. Finally, as study progressed, the sciences of religion could look upon such beliefs only as expressions of man's religious yearning, not as statements of truth. For the modern liberal, religion became a natural rather than a supernatural phenomenon.

NATURAL RELIGION

THE consideration of religion as a fact of nature rather than a supernaturally instituted ordinance placed religious feeling above religious beliefs. To seek the divine is natural, just as it is natural to seek food. Further, it is natural that religious hunger should attain some kind of satisfaction. The fact that man hungers for the divine is no reason to assume that God exists in any ontological sense. All that can reasonably be said is that religion is an expression of a psychological need. Therefore, religion may be looked upon as a creation of man's psyche rather than as something of cosmological significance. With many people, mostly those who have left the literal Catholic tradition, this natural religion is the poetic expression of man's relation to the cosmos. The practice of worship and the writing of religious literature lie outside the realm of truth and falsity but within the realm of esthetic imagination. Bible stories and theological creeds are myths with poetic and moral meanings. They are nothing more. To consider them as science or philosophy is to make a grievous social and intellectual error.

George Santayana, the best known representative of this kind of theological reconstruction, has put the case for esthetic natural religion in this fashion:

The conditions and the aims of life are both represented in religion poetically, but this poetry tends to arrogate to itself literal truth and moral authority, neither of which it possesses. Hence the depth and importance of religion become intelligible no less than its contradictions and practical disasters. Its object is the same as that of reason, but its method is to proceed by intuition and by unchecked poetical conceits. These are repeated and vulgarised in proportion to their original fineness and significance, till they pass for reports of objective truth and come to constitute a world of faith, superposed upon the world of experience and regarded as materially enveloping it, if not in space at least in time and in existence. The only truth of religion comes from its interpretation of life, from its symbolic rendering of that moral experience which it springs out of and which it seeks to elucidate. Its falsehood comes from the insidious misunderstanding which clings to it, to the effect that these poetic conceptions are not merely representations of experience as it is or should be, but are rather information about experience or reality elsewhere—an experience and reality which, strangely enough, supply just the defects betrayed by reality and experience here.

Thus religion has the same original relation to life that poetry has; only poetry, which never pretends to literal validity, adds a pure value to existence, the value of a liberal imaginative exercise. The poetic value of religion would initially be greater than that of poetry itself, because religion deals with higher and more practical themes, with sides of life which are in greater need of some imaginative touch and ideal interpretation than are those pleasant or pompous things which ordinary poetry dwells upon. But this initial advantage is neutralised in part by the abuse to which religion is subject, whenever its symbolic rightness is taken for scientific truth. Like poetry, it improves the world only by imagining it improved, but not content with making this addition to the mind's furniture—an addition which might be useful and ennobling—it thinks to confer a more radical benefit by persuading mankind that, in spite of appearances, the world is really such as that rather arbitrary idealisation has painted it. This spurious satisfaction is naturally the prelude to many a disappointment, and the soul has infinite trouble to emerge again from the artificial problems and sentiments into which it is thus plunged. The value of religion becomes equivocal. Religion remains an imaginative achievement, a symbolic representation of moral reality which may have a most important function in vitalising the mind and in transmitting, by way of parables, the lessons of experience. But it becomes at the same time a continuous incidental deception; and this deception, in proportion as it is strenuously denied to be such, can work indefinite harm in the world and in the conscience.[1]

The social and moral emphasis is well expressed by another advocate of natural religion, A. Eustace Haydon:

The gods are on this side of the mystery that enshrouds the universe. Like man, they are earth-born. The roots of their lives are in the rich soil of human hopes and hungerings. If man had

[1] George Santayana, *The Life of Reason* (New York: Charles Scribner's Sons, 1913), pp. 10-12. By permission.

been perfect in joy and mastery, the familiar folk gods of history would never have been. They were born and grew to grandeur because of man's desperate need. Through the ages they have walked with him, beloved companions of the way, powerful helpers in the age-long quest for knowledge, beauty and the joy of living.

The gods move across the stage of history in forms innumerable: one note of pathos dominates the drama, man's longing for support, security, companionship and help from the environing universe. The biography of every god is an epic into which are written the dreams and sorrows, tragedies and achievements of some human group. The names and characters of the gods are numberless but from the beginning even until now, faith in God is the daring confidence of man that the universe in its deepest meaning does allow and give support to our human hopes and ideals. The history of the gods is the fascinating story of human adventures in co-operation with what seemed helpful and trustworthy amid the dearth and danger of the changing centuries.

The divine figures of our human story are, therefore, rooted in the social needs and aspirations of men. They grow and change with their peoples. To define God is labor lost, for the meaning of God is a definite and specific meaning in a localized phase of the life of humanity in a definite span of time.[2]

Only one more word remains to be said. More important than faith in God is devotion to the human ideals of which he has become the symbol. Too long the strong gods have been made to bear the burden. Wistfully man has watched for the day of divine action to dawn and ever healed the hurt of disappointment with more passionate faith. Hopes hung in the heavens are of no avail. What the gods have been expected to do and have failed to do through the ages, man must find the courage and intelligence to do for himself. More needful than faith in God is faith that man can give love, justice, peace and all his beloved moral values embodiment in human relations. Denial of this faith is the only

[2] A. Eustace Haydon, *Biography of the Gods,* p. vii. Copyright 1941 by The Macmillan Company and used with their permission.

real atheism. Without it, belief in all the galaxies of gods is mere futility. With it, and the practice that flows from it, man need not mourn the passing of the gods.[3]

Very few who accept either of these two positions find a spiritual home in the established churches of the West. Whether orthodox or liberal, the vast body of churchmen refuse to give up a literal belief in God's existence and the scientific truth of at least some of the traditional dogmas. The extreme forms of natural religion find expression in comparatively small humanistic organizations like the Ethical Culture Society, and in the writings of academic philosophers. Although the religious liberal rejects the finality of specific traditions, he usually maintains a firm belief in the existence of a God, no matter how imperfectly known, who guarantees the ultimate validity of moral values.

Those who hold religion to be of natural origin but still align themselves with established churches usually claim that belief in God is validated by philosophical reasoning. To be sure, this reasoning does not establish the finality of Christianity, but it does, they claim, indicate the objective existence of that which the religious man worships. Many of this group reject Kant's analysis of the ancient arguments for God and cling tenaciously to the arguments from design and purpose. The existence of a purposive nature implies some entity which does the purposing; the design of nature indicates a designer. When such contentions are joined with Kant's moral argument, a structure of philosophical theology can be reared. Within such theistic systems there is no room for revelation, and the religious traditions are looked upon as nonrational means for attaining the truths which can also be achieved by natural reason. Knowingly or not, these theists follow the idea and attitude of the final scholium of Newton's *Principia*:

[3] *Ibid.*, p. 329.

This most elegant system of suns, planets and comets could only arise from the purpose and sovereignty of an intelligent and mighty being. . . . He rules them all not as a soul of the world, but a sovereign lord of all things, and because of His sovereignty, He is commonly called "Lord God Almighty."

WORLD-WIDE SECULARISM

ALTHOUGH the most fundamental change in religion and man's attitude toward it has occurred in the West, Eastern traditions have also felt the impact of modern secularism. The last two hundred years have seen the rise of Europe and America to world-wide dominance. India, China and Japan have all felt both the political and economic imperialism of the West. Large portions of Asia have become colonies of Western powers, supplying the conquering countries with markets and raw materials. The industrial system, Western education, clothing, motion pictures, bathtubs, military weapons and books have all been introduced to the East. Inevitably the secular values which surround these objects and processes have gone with them. The result has been a general Westernization of the established social institutions; and this Westernization has been more secular than religious. The nationalist movement, inspired largely by the West, is attempting to establish secular states and free the peoples of the East from bondage to both the traditional past and their Western conquerors.

Many of its young political leaders find the main cause of the East's backwardness in the ancient religions. In India one such leader wrote, "Of all the people in the world it is we Indians who require more and more materialism. We have had too much of religion. That accounts for our position today as a bankrupt nation." A Chinese writer argues that China can never advance without "throwing off the yoke of religion," and closes by saying, "Religion is other-worldly and ignores the material welfare of human beings. It teaches sacrifice of the known for the unknown and undervalues the importance of physical existence." Although such sentiments are largely confined to the intellectual and economic aristocracies, they nevertheless indicate the spread of antireligious feeling and the attempt to substitute secular values for those of the indigenous religious traditions. The advance of secularism in the Orient is characterized in the following fashion by a Chinese scholar:

Everything is being questioned, even the holiest sanctions of the old faiths are now sneered at as foolish superstitions. Science is overthrowing geomancy. The idols of the temple and of the mind, shaken and undermined by the New Thought, are tottering to their fall. The cake of custom is being hopelessly smashed. The process once begun cannot be stopped until every doctrine and every institution is thrown into the crucible out of which most will never emerge at all, and only a few will stand the ordeal of fire.[4]

TENDENCIES IN HINDUISM

JUST as in the Western world, the secular attack upon established Hindu religion produced an attempt at compromise. The new truths unearthed by science had to be reconciled with the ancient truths handed down by tradition. In some ways Hindu liberals had an easier job than their Western brothers. Hinduism had never produced dogmas which claimed to be absolute and final scientific fact. As we have seen, many brands of religious faith and practice were accorded equal status by the pious of India. There was no single church which demanded the right to exclusive authority. The exclusiveness which formed such an integral part of Western religion was almost completely absent from Indian religions. The Hindu liberal was therefore relatively free from the pow-

[4] R. Y. Lo, *China's Revolution from the Inside* (New York: Abingdon Press, 1930), p. 52.

erful institutional pressures which have long bedeviled the Christian liberal.

The liberal movement in Hinduism really began in the early part of the nineteenth century with the formation of the Brahmā Samaj. This "Brahman society," or "society of God," was the first religious reaction to the Western invasion. In part it was an attempt to correlate the Christian New Testament with Upanishadic philosophy, but it went further in declaring that its belief and practices represented the true essence of all religion. No single scripture of any historic religion could be accepted as infallible, since historical scholarship had long since shown them all to be of dubious origin. The fact that God exists is thoroughly attested to both by nature and by man's intuition. As a result, all religion should be considered natural, free of any special supernatural sanctions. Out of the wide variety of human experience it is possible, said Ram Mohan Roy, the founder of Brahmā Samaj, to discern certain fundamental truths. First, God is to be understood as a unified personal being, so majestic that he could never demean himself by becoming incarnate in human flesh. The incarnation of deity is foolishness to science and utterly incomprehensible to philosophy. A personal God who maintains his majesty is consistent with both. Human experience further indicates that man is forgiven and saved by God when worship and repentance are real. By the very fact that they continue to exist from generation to generation, all religions testify to the reality of forgiveness. If God did not forgive, mankind would long since have ceased expecting and receiving it. Therefore, the forgiveness of God is not a matter of faith but an empirically verified fact consistent with the canons of truth established by experimental science. Finally, all religions indicate that worship must be a matter of spiritual achievement. The spiritual commitment which God demands means the end of egotism and its material concerns, and the beginning of a godly life lived in justice and peace.

Although the theology of the Brahmā Samaj maintains a definite monotheism, its central concern is for the development of a pious ethical life. The actual members of the society have never been large in number, but their influence in social reform has been tremendous. They were, for example, largely responsible for the Marriage Act of 1872, which forbade child marriage, made polygamy a crime, sanctioned intercaste marriage and permitted widows to remarry. The Brahmā Samaj and its various offshoots were consistently critical of the caste system, not only in matters of marriage but in all of its social ramifications. Their meetings were open to everyone, and they advocated free public education for men and women of all levels. This emphasis upon the reorganization of society earned the Brahmā Samajists the enmity of their orthodox countrymen and the tag of "Westernizers."

During the latter part of the nineteenth century when the Brahmā Samaj, under Keshab Chander Sen, Ram Mohan Roy's successor, was at the height of its power, Ramakrishna of Bengal became an important religious figure. In many ways Ramakrishna represented a conservative reaction to the liberal Western influences that were making themselves felt in India. He was much more at home in the traditional doctrines and attitudes of Hinduism than was either Ram Mohan Roy or Keshab Chander Sen, yet it was the Brahmā Samaj which introduced Ramakrishna to the world.

Ramakrishna's most important contribution to Indian religion is found in his insistence upon the validity of all religious traditions. By family tradition Ramakrishna was a Vishnuite, and early in his life he had an ecstatic experience of Rama, Vishnu's ethical incarnation. Soon afterward, by a method which he called "dramatic imitation" he attained to the highest

Vishnuite experience when he saw a vision of Lord Krishna and so knew truly the love of God.

Ramakrishna then employed his method of dramatic imitation in testing the other religions which had found a home in India. At one time he temporarily became a Mohammedan and soon found that he had visions of Mohammed. He became a Christian, and before long he saw the risen Jesus sitting in all his glory on the right hand of God. The same was true of every brand of Hinduism. He could see Kali, the consort of Siva, just as easily as he could see Krishna or Rama. He could feel self-identification and union with the impersonal Brahma as completely as he could experience Jesus Christ and the prophet Mohammed. For Ramakrishna the conclusion was obvious. All religions are true since all religions offer exactly the same result. Therefore, they must all be looked upon as different paths leading to the same God.

In method, Ramakrishna certainly belongs to the general liberal movement. His final test for truth is the experience of the divine, and his attitude is decidedly experimental. However, his interpretation of his experience is actually a ringing defense of traditional Hinduism. Since all religions are true, he said, there is no reason to leave one for another. Indeed, there is every reason for a person to maintain allegiance to the religion into which he is born. The Brahmā Samaj is wrong in trying to determine the essence of true religion by taking snippets of doctrine from all religions. This can only serve to confuse the paths to God, and in the midst of such confusion the soul of the seeker may be lost. Ramakrishna's experience indicated that the paths to God are exclusive, even though each ends in the same divine goal. The Ramakrishna movement was therefore a counteroffensive against all foreign religions while at the same time liberally granting the validity of their paths to God.

Ramakrishna's chief disciple, Swami Vivekananda, set out

to preach his master's gospel to the world. In addition to founding missions in India, he was instrumental in establishing the Vedanta Society in America and Europe. The burden of Vivekananda's teaching was his emphasis upon the love of God and the unity of all things in God's nature. If philosophers find peace in thinking of God as an impersonal absolute, they are no worse and no better than those who find God in the worship of Christ or Krishna. Distinctions among atheists, agnostics, monotheists, polytheists and the like are just as fruitless as distinctions among Jews, Christians and Buddhists. "Be brave and sincere, then follow any path with devotion, and you must reach the whole."

The Ramakrishna missions of India propagated their gospel with evangelical zeal. The essence of religion is experience, they said, and the experience of the eternal absolute, God, will issue in a pious feeling of love and brotherhood. Often the Ramakrishna missions did little to differentiate simple sentimentality from religious love, but whatever one's judgment of them, the end product was interpreted as a "god-infused" man. The Vedanta societies which Vivekananda established in the West are less evangelical and more philosophical. Their primary purpose is to show that Ramakrishna's philosophy of religion is the one true way of understanding man and his relations to the universe. The ethical content of both the missions and the Vedanta societies is the primacy of love. This emphasis upon love has led to a general popularization of the *Bhagavad Gita* and its central doctrine of bhakti.

The intense religious enthusiasm which the Ramakrishna movement touched off was countered somewhat by the establishment of the Dev Samaj. The Dev Samaj was founded by Shiv Narayan Agnihorti as an offshoot of the Brahmā Samaj. In his early days Agnihorti was a determined theist who associated goodness with the life and power of God. As he became increasingly aware of Western science, especially British empiricism and evolution, his conviction grew that theism is both false and dangerous.

Neither does God exist nor is He of any use, but on the contrary His belief has made men blind followers of a wrong and most imperious belief and led them to commit many kinds of evils which would not be so if this harmful belief in God were removed and fact, reason, experiment, and higher senses of highly evolved masters would guide humanity.[5]

Agnihorti set about to write a new religion which he claimed to be grounded in science. Based in large part upon Herbert Spencer's *First Principles*, the new religion looked at the world in terms of the impersonal law of evolution. Man is the highest product of the evolutionary process, and therefore the whole world must be understood in terms of man. Having once achieved such understanding, a concern for the promotion of a healthy happy life rather than absorption into some mythical metaphysical absolute becomes man's chief end. The ancient religions, which are "fiction-grounded" rather than "science-grounded," divert man's energies from the achievement of happiness to misery and denial. True religion should concern itself with ethics, the ethics of happiness. As a consequence the Dev Samaj actively engaged in breaking the caste system together with the provisions it carried for child marriage and other forms of vice and exploitation. If man needs something to bow before and worship, let him worship the fullness of human personality rather than some unknown metaphysical being. Unfortunately for the movement, Shiv Narayan Agnihorti came to look upon himself as the ultimate fulfillment of the evolutionary process, and before his death in 1929, he actually demanded that his followers worship him. At this point the influence of the Dev Samaj began to decline.

[5] S. N. Agnihorti, *Why Do We Not Believe in God?* (Lahore: Dev Samaj Book Depot, n.d.), p. 9.

The new liberal and semiliberal religious movements produced opposition in the form of "back-to-the-Vedas" sects. One of the most important of these groups was organized in 1875 by Swami Dayanand as the Arya Samaj. Much like the fundamentalists of the West, the Arya Samajists felt that science had nothing to say about religion, and that true doctrine had been revealed in its finality in ancient scripture. The followers of Dayanand held to the absolute infallibility of the Vedas and to the literal truth of its many doctrines. In its enthusiasm for the completeness and purity of the Vedas, the Arya Samaj claimed that within these ancient writings could be found all the real germs of the new practical science. By correctly interpreting them, one could find virtual blueprints for electric and steam engines, machines of war, and electrical communication. In short, everything important and true is right there; all else is either a corruption of the Vedas, or false.

Swami Dayanand's interpretation of the Vedas produced a fifty-one-point theological system. Contrary to ancient belief, Dayanand's system claimed that the many gods of the Rig-Veda are really diverse names for the one eternal God. In this manner the Arya Samaj was able to recruit members from late theistic Hinduism as well as the staunch traditionalists. The remaining fifty teachings are modern statements of Upanishadic philosophy regarding matter, soul, ways of salvation, transmigration, Karma, and rules pertaining to the organization and arrangement of the caste system. All fifty-one are taught and interpreted by the preachers of the Arya Samaj in terms of present problems confronting modern minds. Services of worship which mingle ancient Vedic fire rituals with modern hymn singing and preaching are conducted each Sunday. In line with this general attempt to modernize, the Arya Samajists have created the Young Men's Arya Association, Women's Arya Samaj, Arya Tract Society, and the Vedic Salvation Army. In both preaching and teaching, the Arya

Samajists have put the content of Vedic learning into Christian propaganda forms.

The success of this "back-to-the-Vedas" movement has been phenomenal. Today there are well over a million active members of the society who participate in its many religious and philanthropic activities. Most of this membership is fairly well educated and strongly nationalistic. They have established one of the largest Indian universities, the Dayanand Anglo-Vedic College at Lahore, while at the same time providing leadership for the movement toward national independence. Throughout India the Arya Samaj is recognized as the most important indigenous religious reform movement of the present century. Its primary purpose is to purify India of both invading religions and invading armies.

Modern India is not without its contemporary counterparts for the spiritual heroes of old. Men such as Mohandas Karamchand Gandhi and Rabindranath Tagore have led the Indian masses in a way very similar to that of the great sages of the past. Gandhi, who could best be described as a syncretistic Hindu, lived and died as the prophet of national independence and the saint of nonviolence. He believed firmly in the essential integrity of the Hindu tradition and was willing to see all material gain lost in an effort to prove the final validity of a way of life based upon love and passivity. As the spiritual father of millions, he identified religion with a quality of life rather than with a group of theological opinions. Tagore, much in the spirit of Gandhi, wrote new poetic words to the traditional Indian theme of the "Eternal Spirit which is Endlessly Further." Gandhi, the practical politician, strove for the freedom of a nation; Tagore saw freedom in the love and unity of mankind. Both were mystical in some senses of the word, and both were practical. Their greatest contribution was the offering of themselves as symbols of India's ceaseless striving.

The modern-day saints of Hinduism together with the country's masses worked long and hard for Indian independence. Commonwealth status was finally granted in the summer of 1947, and India today is divided between Hindustan and Pakistan. Pakistan is the province of the Mohammedans, while Hindustan maintains the traditions of ancient Aryan Hinduism. The struggle between these two faiths is far from decided. When Gandhi was killed in 1948, many foresaw a running fight, lasting at least a hundred years, which would decide the religious future of India. No one can now predict which side will triumph. In any case both religious groups will have to meet and answer the persistent problems raised by an imported Western secularism.

MODERN TENDENCIES IN CHINA

The Western secularism which moved Gandhi to say, "Europe today is only nominally Christian. In reality it is worshiping Mammon," produced the opposite effect in China. Religious and cultural conservatism is hardly a force among the Chinese. For the most part they recognize that the West, with its machines and its science, has the power to overcome poverty and establish China on an economically secure foundation. Few Chinese want to return to the days of the Manchu Dynasty which was overthrown in the tumultuous revolution of 1911. The Chinese are not looking back, they are looking forward. And looking forward means looking to an age of science and industry.

The ancient traditions still live in China, but their strength is rapidly decreasing. Western philosophy is taught on the same level as the historic indigenous wisdom, but more often than not the Western learning is given prominence. Writers have forsaken the classic literary language; they write for the masses who now are taught on the basis of a large-scale general-education program. Relations between the sexes as well as the traditional family structure have seen great changes; today they possess at least the external characteristics of Western culture. Corresponding innovations have occurred in the Chinese attitude toward religion and its institutions.

At the time of the Revolution, China's three religions were decadent and, in general, disregarded by their nominal adherents. Confucianism, which had always been the religion of the State, was a party to the corruption and exploitation which characterized the Manchu Dynasty. With the rise of the Republic the State shrines were closed, public Confucianist ceremonies ceased, and the national officials were no longer considered priests. Even the time-honored ethical teachings of the Sage were demoted by constitutional law to a position which put them in competition with other wisdoms. Although this brought strong objections from the remaining enthusiastic Confucianists, the law has remained in effect. Taoism, with its complex systems of magic and superstition, has lost ground with the advance of education and public enlightenment. Few Chinese authorities see anything but its eventual disappearance.

Contrary to the tendencies in both Confucianism and Taoism, Buddhism has experienced a revival under the government of the Republic. It was the first religion of China to make peace with science and it has further been undergoing a rapid process of socialization. Monks who once retired from the world are today founding charities and establishing seminaries to "train men to benefit the world, not self." Preaching services are now conducted in the temples and on street corners; sutras are published and distributed in railway coaches and hotels; Buddhist colleges, Young Men's Buddhist Associations, and homes for orphans have been organized. All this has been done with the studied opposition of both of the principal political parties.

The majority of Buddhist scholars see no inherent contradiction between Western science and Buddhism. Rather, they are inclined to look upon modern science as a confirmation of much that Buddhism has always taught. For example, Buddhist theology has claimed that matter has no real permanence and that ultimately it must be considered nonmaterial force. This teaching, Buddhist thinkers say, is confirmed by present-day physics. They also point to the acceptance of cause and effect as Universal Law and maintain that such a position was first enunciated by Gotama six centuries before Christ. A modern Buddhist writer speaks of Western science and Buddhism in the following fashion:

There is in the West a growing body of knowledge about each aspect of the physical Universe which is in entire accord with Buddhist principles, for it must be realised that the oft-mentioned breach between "Science" and "Religion" is really that between Science and, not true Religion, but the dogmas of the Christian Church.[6]

This attitude is expressed primarily for the Western student. The greater number of Buddhists look upon the investigations of natural science as unimportant or, at most, of secondary concern. Nothing that science discovers has any real meaning since it can deal with nothing but the transitory world of sense impression. The scientific method can never penetrate to the spiritual core of the universe, it can never truly know that the "Buddha nature *is* all things," and it can never get away from the relativities and confusions inherent in its assumption that the scientific method is the only method for arriving at truth. Writing to his coreligionists, T'ai Hsu, an eminent Chinese Buddhist, stated the case most clearly: "The central core of Buddhism science can not reach, for Buddhism has to do with

[6] *What is Buddhism?* (compiled by the Buddhist Lodge, London, 1929), p. 191.

inward illumination, the direct insight into the reality of the universe, an intuitive experience only acquired by one himself, where all logic, analogy, or scientific method or hypothesis are of no avail."

Although this position preserves the theoretical integrity of Buddhist theology, it has scant appeal for the young men and women of Buddhist countries who see the political and economic advantages of a working science. For them the Buddhist inner experience has less validity and less meaning than the powerful armies and physical comforts made possible by science. The new vistas of material prosperity opened by the formation of political parties have little place for the inwardness of traditional Buddhism. The faint gestures in the direction of social orientation have been able to do little toward stemming the tide of communism and the various alternatives offered by the Nationalist Party. To be a sincere and devout Buddhist in twentieth-century China is an enormously difficult task. In the area of religion the Chinese people have always been syncretists. When Buddhism was first introduced, it was cut and tailored to fit traditional Confucianism. For many long years it has lived with Confucianism and Taoism with little or no strife. All three traditions have borrowed extensively from each other, and neither has tried to develop an attitude of popular exclusiveness. This age-old syncretism continues in the present day. Five religions, Confucianism, Buddhism, Taoism, Christianity and Islam comprise a group calling themselves "The Apprehension of Goodness Society" and the "Tao Yuan." Other groups, not as important but nevertheless numerous, embrace Judaism and Hinduism as well. Most of these syncretistic groups claim to have found the universal solvent which will make all religions meaningful while at the same time destroying none of their distinctive characteristics. The underlying philosophy of these groups is much the same as Indian syncretism, but without the foundation of Upanishadic literature.

All in all, it is improper to consider any religious movement in contemporary China as a significant revival. Confucianism still lives as a kind of vague collective moral code, but it has no real power. Taoism is certainly discredited for those who accept even part of the Western scientific attitude. And Buddhism's major emphasis is still on monastic contemplation. The forces which work for revolution are primarily secular, and the values which they seek are not those of the traditional religions. Chinese Buddhism may very well be of little importance in the future life of the nation.

MODERN TENDENCIES IN JAPAN

THE influence of the expanding secular West has been more profoundly felt in Japan than in any other Eastern nation. The results of modern science have been eagerly assimilated, and within the last fifty years Japan has changed from a country with a local agrarian economy to a highly industrialized world power. Immediately following the First World War, when Japan was on the side of the United States and her allies, industrialization was begun in earnest. In the early 1930's she was able to equip and supply a modern army which captured Manchuria and penetrated deep into Chinese territory. By 1941 Japan felt herself ready to wage war on the United States and establish Japanese hegemony over all of Asia. This amazingly rapid growth in material power was made possible by an enthusiastic absorption of Western thought and practice.

Whereas Chinese Buddhists tended to play down science and assert the independence of their doctrine, Japanese Buddhists developed new confidence by showing their complete agreement with all the conclusions of Western science. Nor did they limit their treatment to technical physical science.

They usually went further and proclaimed a unity between their doctrine and Western philosophic systems. Professor Anesaki, a distinguished Buddhist scholar, reports that

to their surprise and delight, the young Buddhists found the Buddhist conception of the world as a perpetually flowing process and the continuity of Karma had anticipated the Darwinian theory of evolution; that the dialectical method of Buddhist philosophy in analysing all conceptions and dispelling the idea of permanent entity was quite congenial to Spencerian agnosticism; that the Hegelian logic of reaching a higher synthesis over the concepts of being and non-being was exactly the kernel of the Tendai doctrine of the Middle Path. Whether correct or not, these ideas provided a strong incentive to a conviction that Buddhism was not a mere relic of the past but had a mission for the future.[7]

The Buddhists of Japan also took over Western methods for propagating their faith and teaching their young. Most of these techniques were borrowed directly from the Christian Church. Very soon after industrialization began, Buddhist scriptures appeared in compact printed form designed for mass circulation. Many sects established their own presses and flooded the countryside with mottoes and tracts for the times. The ancient beliefs were translated into modern language and made applicable to modern problems. Preaching missions were organized to hold services on street corners, in factories and in the small rural communities. In each case the emphasis was the same: Buddhism was not a faith of the past, but the dynamic hope of the future. Sunday Schools taught children to live by the "Buddha ideal," while Christian hymns which emphasized the future were slightly changed and incorporated into the worship services. One well-known Christian Sunday

[7] Masaharu Anesaki, *History of Japanese Religion* (London: Kegan Paul, Trench, 1930), pp. 261-62. By permission.

School hymn with "Amida" substituted for "Jesus" became popular.

> What's the use of weeping
> What's the use to sigh
> With Amida guiding
> We'll reach there by and by.
>
> Trust to dear Amida
> With his loving care
> Shall find its garden path
> And all these pleasures share.

Even the Christian festivals, Christmas and Easter, were taken over and given Buddhist significance. The Christmas tree, traditional in Christian countries, was assimilated by the Japanese in commemoration of Gotama's vigil beneath the Bo-tree at the time of his enlightenment. Easter, the Christian celebration of resurrection, was changed into a festival emphasizing the grace and merit of Amida. In this fashion the Japanese Buddhist took over the Western calendar and gave it meaning within his own historic tradition.

The social service activities in Japan have followed much the same course they took in America. Just as the Christian churches established welfare centers, orphanages, settlement houses and the like, so the Japanese Buddhists did in Japan. Most of these social service institutions grew out of sectarian interests, but they nevertheless claimed to be inspired by the ideals of Buddhism. Many hospitals, schools for the blind, employment centers and even universities owe their existence to Buddhism's new emphasis upon the future and to its borrowings from the Western world.

In general, the sharp lines which previously marked the differences among various Buddhist sects have been softened by an increasing sense of national unity. The United Buddhist Organization, which has sponsored a large number of the social service activities, represents almost all the Buddhist sects. The Nichiren, however, clings to its traditional exclusiveness and continues to excoriate all who do not recognize it as the only group possessing complete and final truth. The Kakaishu Rengokai, an interdenominational association corresponding to the Protestant Federal Council of Churches in the United States, issues pronouncements on matters of common concern and also represents the various sects (again excepting Nichiren) in their relations with the government. For the most part this unity is only in the field of social service and public questions. Theological differences are still as clearly defined as in the past.

The extreme nationalism which was a dominant factor in producing both the war in China and the role of Japan in the Second World War has had an important effect upon the nation's religions. At least part of the revival of Buddhism has been nullified by governmental emphasis upon the national cult of Shinto. Before leaving for either Manchuria or the islands of the South Pacific, the soldiers of Japan stopped before Shinto shrines to receive blessings and encouragement from official priests. All during the long years of war the government consistently maintained that Shinto worship was a matter of patriotism, and therefore need not interfere with either Buddhist or Christian religious duties. Although such a position was unacceptable to Japanese Christians, the Buddhists never found it difficult. Consequently there was and is a strong tendency to fuse Buddhism with Shinto, worship with patriotism. A separation may be in progress today since the United States military government has disestablished Shinto. But it is now too early to be sure.

Buddhism may be, as some Japanese scholars fervently maintain, the religion with a future in Japan. Certainly it has shown a greater degree of independence and more evangelical zeal than either its Chinese counterpart or its local rival Shinto.

It does not, however, offer an alternative to nationalism, nor does it effectively counter tendencies toward economic and political injustice. Throughout its long history in Japan it has made no headway in the job of systematizing and articulating a comprehensive social ethic. If the future belongs to those who oppose the traditional morality of Japanese feudalism, Buddhism must change its ethical orientation radically or be discarded. And in the Japan of today either can happen.

BUDDHIST MISSIONARY MOVEMENT

FROM the days of Gotama the real strength of Buddhism has lain in its desire and its ability to make converts. As soon as any group of Buddhists forgot Gotama's command to "fare forth on the mission that is for the good of the many," the distinctive elements of the original doctrine were lost in a welter of superstition, magic and strange religions. Such was certainly the case in Tibet and China. Tibetan Buddhism and the indigenous Pön are today one and the same. The monks who control the government are the same soothsayers and magicians who roamed the countryside two thousand years ago. If the term Buddhism is to be reserved for the followers of Gotama, the Tibetan Buddhists are such in name but not in fact. Chinese Buddhism has met a similar, if not exactly parallel, fate. Since the days when the faith was introduced to Japan, the Chinese Buddhists have been content to say nothing and do nothing about winning new converts. It has thus been over a thousand years since they have made any missionary effort at all. Confucianism, Taoism and Buddhism have so completely penetrated each other that the once important lines of distinction are hopelessly blurred.

The Buddhist missionary enterprise is now dead in all countries except Ceylon and Japan. The Ceylonese missions, which propagate the Southern or Hinayana type of Buddhism, have directed their efforts toward India, Europe and the United States. Through the Maha Bodhi Society, centers of Buddhist evangelical activity have been established in Calcutta, Bombay, New York City, London, Berlin, Paris and other centers of population. In general they still preach the cosmic agnosticism enunciated by Gotama, and the hope of a final annihilation in Nirvana. Although the enthusiasm of the Maha Bodhi Society is high, it has received little support from the Buddhists of Ceylon. The austere doctrine of Hinayana Buddhism is probably a contributing factor to the relatively ineffective work of the Southern missionaries.

The most progressive and active Buddhist missionaries have been sent by the Japanese to China and the Pacific islands. For the most part these missionaries have directed their attention toward those of Japanese or Chinese origin who now inhabit foreign lands. There has been no real attempt to proselytize among Europeans or Americans of European stock. California, Hawaii, the East Indies, Formosa, Saghalien and the Malay Peninsula are the chief centers of activity. Aside from the purely religious motivation, these missionaries have been convinced that "Asia is for the Asiatics," and that Buddhism is the one unifying religion for the entire area. Since Japan has been the effective leader of the movement to expel Europeans from Asia, it is not unusual that its missionaries should be the most active.

Since Buddhist sects on the home islands are responsible for financing and training the missionaries, the work in the field is on a fairly consistent basis. They all teach the universal love of Amida and the doctrine of unselfish devotion to duty. There is little of the original pessimism regarding man's earthly estate. The major emphasis is upon the future, and particularly the future unity and progress of Asia. As is true with many Christian missionaries, it is impossible to separate the diverse strands of religious and national motivation. The story of how the recent war has affected Buddhist missions will have to await more accurate information.

RELIGION AND THE FUTURE

WHATEVER else might be said of present-day religions, they are certainly not dying. All the traditions we have studied show evidence of real vitality, and they all have eloquent and persuasive spokesmen. Protestantism is showing signs of unification through its various interdenominational councils. Roman Catholicism is gaining new members every day, and the political power of its hierarchy is on the increase in both western Europe and America. Judaism has at long last achieved one of its two-thousand-year aims in the re-establishment of the nation of Israel on Palestinian soil. Hinduism and Buddhism continue to serve their adherents in the East and both are showing renewed signs of life. Although we do not live in what historians call a religious age, we nevertheless live in an age of important religious activity.

The battle between science and religion which seemed so important just a few short years ago is rapidly subsiding. The contest has been won by neither side, but the issues have seemed less important than our present political and social problems. The bitter controversy which raged only twenty-five years ago over the Darwinian hypothesis now seems to most American Christians like a bad dream which they feel they had best forget. Few Sunday-morning sermons deal with the blasphemy of science; most of them try as best they can to give a religious answer to the problems of individual and social living. The great depression of the thirties and the horrible war of the forties have together presented a more than effective challenge for our day. Whether theological systems agree with scientific theories seems to many to be of small importance when life itself is at stake.

Today's groping for adequate programs of action and well-founded principles of interpretation has turned many thoughtful people to a re-examination of religious traditions. In general, this renewed interest in religion is not in terms of technical philosophy; rather it springs out of a deep-seated need for a workable orientation toward life. The nineteenth-century and early-twentieth-century faith in Progress, which encouraged men to feel that the past must be wrong simply because it is the past, has suffered a spectacular defeat. Hope for the future is not dead, but many are coming to realize that not yet, if ever, is modern man ready to cut himself off from his history.

The serious question for the future is not whether it will be religious, for it most surely will be; what we must ask most carefully is what kind of religion it will have. The various forms of political and economic totalitarianism which threaten the present world have some of the characteristics of the religions we have studied. Although most of them deny any supernatural deity, they certainly make the state function as God. They have their incontrovertible doctrines, they have their public rituals; in the case of communism there is even a succession of prophets—Marx, Engels, Lenin and Stalin. Most important of all, these systems require absolute obedience and loyalty to the cause. To be disloyal or to live apart from spiritual communion with the state is the greatest sin of all. In effect, the state is God and its bureaucracy is the church.

Within totalitarian states there is no room for an independent religion demanding complete and independent loyalty. Sooner or later the two centers of loyalty would conflict and one or the other would be the victor. Unless the church controls the state, its only chance for independent life is within a free society where government is founded upon the moral sense of the community. History is full of examples, and our contemporary experience is one more chapter in the book.

The future of free religion is inextricably bound to the future of free society.

Whatever the future may hold in the way of social organization, we can be sure that man will find some way of expressing his awe and wonder at the mystery of the universe. If history is any guide at all, he will always feel the necessity for worshiping a power above himself "that makes for righteousness." The religious experience is a primary experience, and the need for salvation seems to be a primary need. There are some who maintain that the tragedy of present-day churches lies in their inability to recognize that new conditions of life require new ways for the expression of religious experience. In an age of momentous scientific discovery, it is not possible to formulate articles of faith in antique molds. But if the creeds and dogmas of the past were soundly based in human experience, they can be reformulated to appeal to any era. The basic stuff of human nature does not change as readily as do ideas or social institutions. The vision of a triumphant Christ on the Cross, the loving comfort of a watchful Amida, the fervent moral response to a divine Torah, and the helpful companionship of a heavenly Vishnu all express basic religious reactions to the universe. Our ways of reacting and understanding will change from age to age; consequently we should be less concerned with the words we use and more concerned with the understanding itself.

If a study of the religious record of the past means anything, it means that we should be able to recognize the inevitability of change. Religion is bound to be conservative in that its documents and past experiences become normative for the present and future. But the traditional past should not become a dead hand restraining the future. Vital religious traditions conserve the past without retreating into it. If they do retreat, mankind soon discards them in favor of a new form of religious expression. The adventure of spiritual discovery is still man's most meaningful quest. This adventure is over when the letter of it is taken instead of the spirit, for the spirit is its cause and its reality. The great lesson of our religious past is that by studying the Bible, the Vedas, the Buddhist Sutras, the Torah, and the lives of saints and seers we can discover new spiritual truth. But these are source books for a beginning, a beginning which will lead us into an uncharted world which is the future. Those who have been religiously great, Jesus and Gotama to name only two, were great because they had wisdom enough to read the past and courage enough to face the future.

GLOSSARY

WORDS and concepts which are adequately explained in the text are not included in this glossary. The following words are those which beginners in the study of religion have found to be most easily confused or forgotten. When the special meanings of words used in discussions of religion are adequately defined in standard nontechnical dictionaries, these words too have been omitted.

Readers should be reminded that all short definitions are to be held suspect, especially in religion. Long detailed articles on all of the words given here are to be found in the general reference works listed in the bibliography.

Absolution. Used in Christian theology to indicate an act of the Church which frees a person from his sins and their consequences. It is now used mostly as a term designating an act of the priest in confession. Absolution is dependent upon the theory that the Church is the channel through which God's grace is given to men.

Aditi. The term means "boundless." As used in Vedic Hinduism it indicates the goddess who is mother of the Adityas. She is identified with a variety of objects, usually the sky and earth.

Adityas. A group of Vedic gods which originally included Varuna, Mitra, Aryaman, Bhaga, Daksa and Amsa. In later times the list was expanded to twelve with the addition of Dhator, Indra, Vivasvant, Surya, Vishnu and Martanda.

Agnosticism. The position which neither affirms nor denies the existence of God, but claims that further evidence is needed before a positive decision can be made about his existence or nonexistence.

[517]

Anathema. A thing or person rejected by God and those who count themselves as God's representatives. The term is most commonly used in the announcement of excommunication.

Animism. A belief which ascribes souls, or consciousness, to natural objects such as stones, the sky, mountains, rivers, etc. Animistic belief may be limited to a few objects, or it may be expanded to include the whole of physical nature.

Anthropomorphism. The belief which ascribes human traits and activities to nonhuman objects. The term is used most often in religion to describe those who understand God through an analogy with man.

Apocalyptic writings. A distinctive type of literature produced by both Jews and Christians when they were under severe persecution. The authors intentionally hide their meanings under a cloak of fantasy and esoteric symbolism. It is assumed that only the faithful will be able to understand the true meanings. The book of Daniel in the Old Testament and Revelation in the New Testament are outstanding examples of this kind of writing.

Apocrypha. That body of Jewish and Christian sacred writing which was composed in Biblical style and used for instructional purposes, but which for one reason or another was excluded from the canon.

Apologetics. The study of the defenses of basic Christian propositions against non-Christian attacks. Positively, it is an attempt to formulate the Christian faith in such a way as to attract the intellects of non-Christians. In late years the term has been used to designate the same activity in other religions.

Arhat. The Sanskrit word designating one "who has removed worldly attachments." It is most often used to indicate a saint in Hinayana Buddhism. An Arhat is one who has attained salvation for himself without the aid of gods.

Asceticism. A belief which requires its adherents to renounce those activities and thoughts which are normally considered pleasurable in order to reach a higher degree of spirituality.

Atheism. A denial of theism. It technically means a denial of god, no matter how the term is defined.

Avatār. The Hindu word for incarnation when it refers specifically to the divine.

Bhakti. The Hindu way of salvation which is most closely parallel to the Western method of faith. Devotion, love and faith are all indicated by this term.

Bodhisattva. The "enlightened one" of Mahayana Buddhism who has gained the right to enter Nirvana and become a Buddha, but who elects to remain outside to work for the salvation of others. All Mahayana traditions have many bodhisattvas, some of whom were originally non-Buddhist deities. Bodhisattvas are regularly worshiped in Mahayana temples, and are often revered as family and vocational patrons.

Brahma. A personal manifestation of Brahman. Brahma is the Hindu creator god and one of the great triumvirate, Brahma, Vishnu and Siva.

Brahman. In the Rig Veda Brahman means prayer; in the Brāhmanas it indicates the power behind the prayer; and in the Upanishads Brahman becomes the ultimate reality which is absolute, impersonal and indescribable.

Buddha. The word literally means "awakened" or "enlightened." It is a title applied to one who knows all mysteries. Most especially it refers to Gotama, the founder of Buddhism.

Canon. Canon has many meanings, most of which are used in religious discussions. Some of the meanings are: (1) a body of established ecclesiastical law; (2) that part of the Roman Catholic Mass which follows the Sanctus and precedes the Lord's Prayer; (3) certain special litanies in the Greek and Russian Orthodox Mass; (4) a title given to certain clergymen on a cathedral staff or in special churchly orders; (5) the authoritatively established list of sacred books or writings, such as the Old and New Testaments in Christianity.

Caste. A type of social system which divides according to heredity. It was most extensively worked out in India, and consequently it is that country which is usually referred to when the term "caste system" is used.

Cosmogonies. Theories regarding the origin of the world, including all heavens, hells, sensible and nonsensible beings.

Cosmos. The universe conceived as an orderly whole with all of its parts operating harmoniously. The word is often used to indicate the totality of all things.

Daimon. In early Greek religion, "daimon" was a common name applied to any and all of the gods. In the fifth century B.C. and after, "daimon" came to mean the psyches, characters and reasons in men. Often the daimon was thought to be the divine in man.

Demons. Superhuman beings who are below the rank of gods. They can be either friendly or hostile. In Christian usage demons were distinguished from angels, the former being considered evil and the latter good. In non-Christian literature, however, the term indicates nothing regarding moral character.

Dharma. A Hindu word meaning "law" or "justice." It is sometimes used so generally as to mean "religion."

Diaspora. The spread of the Jews outside Palestine. The term is technically applied to the dispersions which took place after the Babylonian Exile.

Empirical. That type of thought which draws its propositions directly from experience, and accepts them because they are required by experience.

Episcopal. A form of church government in which bishops rule over priests and deacons.

Epistemology. The study of the problem of knowledge. Epistemology concerns itself with such questions as: "What is truth?" "How do I know?" and "What are the limits of my capacity to know?"

Eschatology. The doctrine or the study of the end of history or "last things."

Essence. That which is permanent and unchanging in things or Being. Essence is usually distinguished from existence (i.e., that which places an object in a definite species). In many theologies God is thought to be the only being in which Essence and existence are identical. In other words, there is no accident in God.

Eucharist. The Greek word meaning "thanksgiving." In New Testament usage it means any form of prayer; later the word is restricted to designate the Lord's Supper and its celebration. The Lord's Supper is one of the sacraments of the Christian Church.

Evangelical. Literally the word means "gospel" or "good news." Since the Reformation it has been used to designate that type of Christianity which holds the individually interpreted Bible to be the only rule for faith and practice, in contrast with Roman Catholicism.

Faith. A devotional trust in the absolute rightness of a given doctrine, institution, scripture or divinity.

Gnosticism. A mixture of Oriental and Greek mysticism which had no clear limitations. It did, however, have a plan of salvation, and in most cases a number of myths telling of the world's origin, the reasons for its present state, and the possibilities for the future. Gnosticism also placed heavy emphasis upon the necessity for esoteric, revealed knowledge.

Grace. An act showing favor, kindliness and mercy. The Grace of God is the deity's disposition to grant salvation and aid. One of the central themes in most theologies concerns the conditions under which God's grace is obtained.

Henotheism. The stage between polytheism and monotheism in which a worshiper is committed to one god but does not deny existence to others.

Idol (Ikon). An image of a deity which is worshiped as a physical embodiment of the divine.

Image. A representation of a sacred person or deity which may be accorded veneration, but not worship.

Incantation. A verbal phrase which has sufficient power to coerce deity. Its primary use is in magical rites. It should be carefully distinguished from prayer, which is a religious exercise.

Incarnation. The term used when a deity assumes earthly existence (in man, animals, plants or minerals).

Inquisition (the). An ecclesiastical tribunal set up in the Middle Ages to combat heresy. It was specifically empowered to punish all Roman Catholics who were found to hold unauthorized beliefs.

Kabbala. The tradition of mysterious, esoteric lore of Judaism which has been handed down from generation to generation. It contains much speculative theosophy, magic and general superstition. It was particularly important in sixteenth- and seventeenth-century Europe.

Liturgy. Organized public worship usually directed by an ordained priest or minister. Present usage often limits the word to inherited traditional orders of service.

Mana. A name derived from the Melanesian Islanders which signifies a mysterious power in nonhuman objects of nature. Mana is often used when referring to the potency of the dead.

Manichaeanism. A religious movement begun by a southern Babylonian named Manichaeus (or Mani) about 240 A.D. His doctrine was a kind of dualistic gnosticism growing out of Zoroastrianism. Manichaeanism held that: (1) there were two original kingdoms, one of light (good) and another of darkness (evil); (2) the Kingdom of Evil attacked the good and robbed it of some of its beauty, peace and order; (3) since the Kingdom of Good could not resort to violence, it had to develop subtle means of purifying itself; (4) this method was the development of an elect group on earth who would slow down the Kingdom of Evil through gaining spiritual perfection. The ethical attitude of Manichaeanism was found primarily in quietism and asceticism. For a time Augustine was a most ardent Manichaean. Manichaeus claimed that he had come to complete the unfinished work of Zoroaster, Gotama Buddha and Jesus Christ. It is today almost extinct as an independent religious system.

Mantra. A Hindu term which covers many different kinds of religious and magical writings. It was used in the Vedic period to indicate hymns and prayers; it later came to be understood as a spell or charm.

Mass. Since the Reformation this term has been most often applied to the Roman Catholic Eucharistic service. In general, however, it means any liturgical service of worship which employs ecclesiastical officials and music.

Mendicant orders. Religious societies which have renounced all property and live by mendicancy (begging). The most important medieval mendicant orders were the Franciscans, Dominicans, Augustinians and Carmelites. Mendicant orders are also found in Hinduism and Buddhism.

Messiah. The technical meaning of the term is "anointed" or "chosen of God." In the Old Testament the word is applied to priests, prophets and kings who were anointed with oil in a ceremony which symbolized their sacred status. The Apocalyptic literature speaks of a Messiah who is to be sent by Yahweh to re-establish and purify Israel. Christians look upon Jesus of Nazareth as the Messiah. The Greek term *Christos* is often used instead of Messiah.

Metaphysics. The term is variously defined by different philosophical writers. In general it is that branch of philosophy which includes noumetology, ontology and cosmology. These three areas are combined to give an inclusive theory of reality. In Aristotle, metaphysics is the science of being as being, the study of first principles and causes. The term should not be used (as it often is) to indicate anything that is supersensuous, occult or mysterious.

Miracle. Miracle usually refers to an event in which supernatural causes set aside those that are commonly called "natural." It is sometimes loosely used to indicate an event which is incomprehensible. The first meaning is the more common in religious literature.

Moksa. The Hindu word for salvation. Its meaning, of course, varies with different authors and among the different sects. It is sometimes spelled "Moksha."

Monism. When used in metaphysics, monism refers to the theory that there is one reality. It is, therefore, to be distinguished from metaphysical dualism (two realities, such as Mind and Matter) and metaphysical pluralism (many realities).

Monotheism. The belief that there is only one God who has actual existence.

Moral Law. The ultimate principles, inherent within the universe and independent of human desires, which should form the basis of man's conduct.

Mystery Plays. Religious dramas, usually given in church buildings, which portrayed a series of events in sacred history. They were particularly important in medieval Europe, where they were given in cycles by the various guilds. By the early seventeenth century they had lost most of their religious significance and were prohibited from being given in church buildings.

Mysticism. A much abused word which has several meanings. The most general usage defines mysticism as a nonintellectual emotional apprehension of spiritual reality. The more restricted use of the term indicates only that experience where subject and object become one. Since the first usage confuses mysticism with intuition, the second is preferable.

Myth. A story or a fiction used to indicate a truth which either cannot or will not be put into scientific language. Although a myth is not true, it may be meaningful.

Naturalism. In metaphysics naturalism is a monistic theory that all reality must be defined as nature. In other words, naturalists see a continuity of being, whereas supernaturalists recognize discontinuity, as between God and man. Methodological naturalism holds that the only way to truth is through a scientific method which is based upon experience in the exact sciences.

Neo-Platonism. An amorphous blend of many philosophical and religious ideas which was given a semisystematic statement by Ammonius Saccas and Plotinus in the third century A.D. In general, Neo-Platonism asserts that: (1) the center of all reality is the One, or God, or the Good, which is an undifferentiated Unity; (2) from this single source, through a succession of emanations, a hierarchical world is formed; (3) the highest emanation is Mind or Spirit, which corresponds to Plato's world of Ideas, the next level is the Over-soul which is the principle of life and process, and this Over-soul over-

flows to become the concrete world; (4) matter is in itself
unreal, but the human mind understands it as the outer limit
against which the soul is broken into many parts; (5) the soul
of man must remove itself from sensuous desires and move
up through contemplation to its ultimate rest in the oneness
of God. Neo-Platonic conceptions were of prime importance
in the formulation of much early Christian doctrine.

Omnipotence. Power in its most perfect and absolute form which
is above, beyond and over all things.

Omnipresence. The power, usually ascribed to deity, of being in
all places at all times. It is often used to distinguish God from
other beings, since all but God must be localized in a given
space and time.

Omniscience. The power, usually ascribed to God, to know all
things at one time. In omniscience there is no past, present
and future; there is only an unmediated timeless knowledge.

Ontology. That part of metaphysics which concerns itself with
the study of being as such. Being in this instance is to be distinguished from particular beings. The study of particular
beings is the duty of the various sciences. An ontological
statement is a statement about the nature of existence and
not a description of an object.

Pagan. The term originally meant "countryman" and was applied
in early Christianity to those who held to Greek and Roman
religions and refused to accept Christianity. It is now popularly used to designate anyone who has no interest in and
does not adhere to one of the monotheistic faiths.

Pantheism. That form of theism which considers all reality to be
God. This does not mean that all things are *within* God (this
view is called "panentheism"), but rather that the sum total
of all that is real *is* God.

Pantheon. Pantheon is used in two senses: (1) a building consecrated to the gods; (2) a group of gods belonging to a given
group of people. The latter meaning is used in this book.

Phenomenology. In modern philosophical literature the term
means "the science of that which displays itself." In this book

it is used in this sense, to indicate the study of things that are observable.

Polytheism. The belief that there are many gods, each of whom is important in a specific area.

Positivism. Originally the philosophy of Auguste Comte and his followers. In general the term now covers all philosophies which reject the search for final causes, or a First Cause, and limit knowledge to mathematics and the physical sciences. The term also designates an antitheistic religion of small importance which was founded by Auguste Comte.

Prayer. A form of worship. Prayer is an attempt to communicate with God, or the gods, in order to (1) give praise, or (2) ask for a particular blessing. Worship may take place without prayer if there is no attempt to communicate with the divine.

Predestination. A religious doctrine used to express the feeling that man is completely dependent upon God's grace for his salvation. Since God is thought to be omnipotent and timeless, the ultimate destiny of each soul must be determined prior to any action on man's part. Predestination is not identical with the philosophical doctrine of determinism since it has no reference to physical nature or a cause-and-effect series.

Pythagoreanism. A religio-philosophic movement reputedly founded by Pythagoras of Samos in the sixth century B.C. Pythagoreanism held belief in: (1) a self-existing soul which went through a number of incarnations; (2) an eternal memory which the soul possessed throughout its incarnations; (3) all things as eternal cyclical repetitions; (4) the sacred and mysterious reality of number. Pythagoreanism was particularly influential in Plato's thought and the development of numerologies.

Revelation. The acquisition of knowledge or understanding through the activity of some one or thing other than yourself. The term is most intimately connected with those theologies which have an active personal God who shows himself to man in his own time and in circumstances of his own choosing.

Sabbath. The seventh day of the week, which was set aside by the Hebrews as a day of rest to commemorate creation and the escape from Egypt. According to Genesis, Yahweh created the world in six days and on the seventh, "He rested." The holy day for the Christians became the first day of the week, Sunday, which commemorates the resurrection of Jesus. After Constantine, Sunday took on many of the characteristics which originally belonged to the Jewish Sabbath. Seventeenth-century Protestantism further developed the idea that Sunday is the Christian Sabbath.

Sacrament. A part of religious worship which indicates the presence of divine favor, or of the divine itself. Many primitive traditions have sacramental meals in which the divine is present in the food that is eaten. Roman Catholic Christianity recognizes seven sacraments: baptism, the Lord's Supper, confirmation, marriage, penance, holy orders, and unction. Protestantism recognizes two: baptism and the Lord's Supper.

Savior. One who brings salvation. The savior-gods are those who actively work to help men fulfill their spiritual destinies. An aloof god who is not active in bringing salvation cannot claim the title of savior.

Secularism. A term first used by G. J. Holyoake (1817-1906) to designate the belief that man is well advised to avoid the traditional religions and place his trust in science and human reason. Through the rational use of the social and physical sciences, man can, according to secularism, gain the good life and live in peace and harmony.

Sin. Sin is a specifically religious offense. It is to be distinguished from crime (an offense against state law) and vice (a violation of society's ethical standards). Sin is meaningful only within the context of a particular religious tradition which defines its content.

Skepticism. The belief that certain knowledge is impossible. Skepticism may be general or particular. When general it is applied to all knowledge; when particular it refers to a special type of knowledge. The term is usually used to indicate man's inability to determine metaphysical truth.

Substance. A philosophical concept usually used to signify the real being of the world which underlies all things. Philosophers have never agreed to its exact character or to its knowability. Some have called it matter, others mind; some have said it is knowable, others that it is not knowable; and some have said it is one, others that there are two fundamental substances, and still others that there are many independent substances.

Supernaturalism. This term is used in two senses: (1) to indicate that form of religious or philosophical conviction which places God above and beyond nature—a metaphysical dualism; (2) to designate the belief that man is incapable of finding God through reason, and therefore must be dependent upon divine self-disclosure.

Superstition. The survival of a religious practice or belief which has been discarded by the majority of a given tradition. The word is sometimes more generally used to indicate any religious or magical belief which is not held by a particular writer or speaker.

Symbol. A religious symbol is a physical object or a word formation which is designed to lead the believer from ignorance to knowledge of the divine. Symbols do not attempt to capture the reality of the divine, nor are they scientific descriptions; rather, they point toward that which is incapable of concrete description.

Taboo (*Tabu*). An object or an act which is inherently dangerous and therefore prohibited. The term is usually applied in the study of religions to those objects which have a mysterious power to do evil.

Teleology. The philosophical study of final ends and causes.

Temple. Strictly speaking a temple is any place that is set aside for and dedicated to the worship of deity. In some traditions the deity is thought to actually live in the temple. Temple worship is usually more individual than corporate, so a temple is thereby distinguished from other places of worship.

Theocracy. A form of government which gives the control of human organization to the representatives of the divine.

[5 2 8]

Totem. A non-human object, especially an animal or plant, which is regarded by a tribe or family as a regular member. Emile Durkheim built his theory of religion around the existence of totems. He maintained that society is the true object of worship, but it is too abstract to be conceived by the primitive mind. As a result, society is represented by a totem which is then used as a symbol in worship.

Transmigration. The rebirth of a soul in another form—plant, animal, human, divine or demonic—after death. It is to be distinguished from reincarnation, which means rebirth in another body of the same kind.

Vulgate Bible (the). A translation into Latin of the Christian Bible made by Jerome near the end of the fourth century. It was the commonly accepted version of the Middle Ages, and remains as standard for Roman Catholicism.

Zoroastrianism. A religion which grew out of the work begun by Zoroaster (Zarathustra) in Iran about 1000 B.C. Zoroastrianism holds: (1) a dualism of Light (represented as coming from the good god Ahura Mazda) and Dark (coming from an evil spirit called Angra Mainya); (2) that all living things are involved in the constant warfare which goes on between Light and Dark; (3) that Ahura Mazda needs help from man if he is to win over Angra Mainya. It lives today in small communities, such as the Indian Parsis, and in certain ideas which were borrowed from it by Judaism, Christianity and Islam.

SELECTED BIBLIOGRAPHY

THE FOLLOWING BOOKS have been selected by two criteria: (1) their general availability in public and college libraries in the United States; (2) their authority in specific areas of religious study. The latest standard edition is listed.

This list is offered to the reader as a guide for further investigation, but is not intended to be of use to the research scholar.

GENERAL WORKS OF REFERENCE

Encyclopoedia of Religion and Ethics, edited by James Hastings, 12 vols. New York, 1908-27.

The New Schaff-Herzog Encyclopedia of Religious Knowledge, 13 vols. New York, 1908-14.

Mythology of All Races, edited by G. F. Moore and L. H. Gray, 12 vols. Boston, 1916-31.

Encyclopedia of Religion, edited by M. A. Canney, 1 vol. London, 1921.

An Encyclopedia of Religion, edited by Vergilius Ferm, 1 vol. New York, 1945.

A Dictionary of Religion and Ethics, S. Mathews and G. B. Smith, 1 vol. New York, 1921.

VARIOUS SACRED SCRIPTURES

Sacred Books of the East, edited by Max Müller, 50 vols. Oxford, 1823-1900. All major Eastern religions. 22 vols. on India.

The Bible of the World, edited by Robert O. Ballou (1 vol. of Selections from Hinduism, Buddhism, Confucianism, Taoism,

Zoroastrianism, Judaism, Christianity and Mohammedanism). New York, 1939.

The Thirteen Principal Upanishads, translated by Ernest Robert Hume. London, 1934.

The Upanishads, translated by Swami Nikhilananda. New York, 1949.

The Chinese Classics, translated by James Legge. London, 1871.

Buddhism in Translations, translated by Henry Clarke Warren. Cambridge, 1915.

The Hymns of the Rig-Veda, translated by Ralph T. H. Griffith, 2 vols. Benares, 1896-97.

The Bhagavad-Gita, translated by Annie Besant, Wheaton, Ill., 1929. (Many other editions.)

Tao Te Ching, translated by Ch'u Ta Kao. London: Buddhist Lodge, 1937.

The Judeo-Christian Scriptures:

The Holy Bible: The Latin Vulgate Version, a revision of the Old Latin by Jerome (after 380 A.D.).

King James Translation (1611).

The Holy Scripture according to the Massoretic Text; Jewish edition (1917).

American Standard Version, 1901.

A New Translation, James Moffatt, 1926.

An American Translation, Smith and Goodspeed, 1935.

BOOKS ON RELIGIONS OF THE WORLD

Archer, John C., *Faiths Men Live By*. New York, 1934.

Barton, G. A., *The Religions of the World*. Chicago, 1917.

Braden, Charles S., *Modern Tendencies in World Religions*. New York, 1933.

Clemen, Carl, Ed., *Religions of the World*. New York, 1931.

Friess, H. L., and Schneider, H. W., *Religion in Various Cultures*. New York, 1932.

Hume, Robert Ernest, *The World's Living Religions*. New York, 1924.

Jurji, Edward J., Ed., *The Great Religions of the Modern World.* Princeton, 1946.
Moore, George Foote, *History of Religions,* 2 vols. New York, 1920.
Noss, John B., *Man's Religions.* New York, 1949.

HINDUISM

Cambridge History of India, Vol. I. Cambridge, 1922.
Barnett, L. D., *Hinduism.* London, 1906.
Bloomfield, M., *The Religion of the Veda.* New York, 1908.
Coomaraswamy, A. K., *The Dance of Siva.* New York, 1924.
Dasgupta, S., *A History of Indian Philosophy,* 2 vols. Cambridge, 1922-32.
Deussen, Paul, *The Philosophy of the Upanishads.* Edinburgh, 1906.
Eliot, Sir Charles, *Hinduism and Buddhism.* London, 1921.
Farquhar, J. N., *An Outline of the Religious Literature of India.* Oxford, 1920.
——, *A Primer of Hinduism.* Oxford, 1912.
Griswold, H. D., *The Religion of the Rigveda.* London, 1923.
Hopkins, E. W., *The Religions of India.* Boston, 1895.
Macfie, J. M., *Myths and Legends of India.* Edinburgh, 1924.
Pratt, J. B., *India and its Faiths.* Boston, 1915.
Radhakrishnan, S., *Indian Philosophy,* 2 vols. London, 1923-27.
——, *The Philosophy of the Upanishads.* London, 1924.
Rolland, Romain, *Prophets of the New India.* New York, 1930.
Stevenson, Mrs. Sinclair, *The Heart of Jainism.* Oxford, 1915.
Zimmer, Heinrich, *Myths and Symbols in Indian Art and Civilization.* New York, 1946.

BUDDHISM

Anesaki, M., *A History of Japanese Religion.* London, 1930.
Beck, L. Adam, *The Story of Oriental Philosophy.* New York, 1931.

Bell, Sir Charles, *The Religion of Tibet*. Oxford, 1931.

Eliot, Sir Charles, *Japanese Buddhism*. London, 1935.

Evans Wentz, W. Y., *Tibetan Yoga and Secret Doctrines*. London, 1935.

Giles, Herbert A., *Confucianism and Its Rivals*. London, 1915.

Gung-hsing Wang, *The Chinese Mind*. New York, 1946.

Hamilton, C. H., *Buddhism in India, Ceylon, China and Japan: A Guide to Reading*. Chicago, 1931.

Pratt, J. B., *The Pilgrimage of Buddhism*. New York, 1928.

Reichelt, K., *Truth and Tradition in Chinese Buddhism*. Shanghai, 1934.

Reischauer, A. K., *Studies in Japanese Buddhism*. New York, 1917.

Smith, Vincent A., *Asoka, The Buddhist Emperor of India*. Oxford, 1920.

Suzuki, D. T., *Essays in Zen Buddhism*. London, 1934.

Thomas, E. J., *The Life of Buddha as Legend and History*. New York, 1927.

Tsaichi, *A Short History of Chinese Civilization*. New York, 1943.

Yang, Y. C., *China's Religious Heritage*. Nashville, Tenn., 1943.

THE HEBREW TRADITION

The Jewish Encyclopedia, 12 vols. New York, 1901.

Albright, W. F., *From the Stone Age to Christianity*. Baltimore, 1940.

Baron, S. W., *A Social and Religious History of the Jews*, 3 vols. New York, 1937.

Bertholet, A., *A History of Hebrew Civilization*. London, 1926.

Cohen, Israel, *Jewish Life in Modern Times*. New York, 1929.

Finegan, Jack, *Light from the Ancient Past*. Princeton, 1946.

Freehof, S. B., *Reform Jewish Practice and Its Rabbinic Background*. Cincinnati, 1944.

Graetz, H., *History of the Jews From the Earliest Period to 1870*, 6 vols. Philadelphia, 1891-98.

Grayzel, Solomon, *Through the Ages: The Story of the Jewish People*. Philadelphia, 1947.

James, Fleming, *Personalities of the Old Testament*. New York, 1939.

Kaplan, M. M., *Judaism as a Civilization*. New York, 1934.

Kittle, R., *The Religion of the People of Israel*. New York, 1925.

Kohler, K., *Jewish Theology*. New York, 1917.

Lazarus, M., *Ethics of Judaism*, 2 vols. Philadelphia, 1900.

Loehn, Max, *A History of Religion in the Old Testament*. New York, 1936.

Margolis, M. A., and Marx, A., *A History of the Jewish People*. Philadelphia, 1927.

Meek, T. J., *Hebrew Origins*. New York, 1936.

Moore, G. F., *Judaism in the First Centuries of the Christian Era: The Age of the Tannaim*, 3 vols. Cambridge, 1927.

Pederson, J., *Israel, Its Life and Culture*. London, 1926.

Philipson, David, *The Reform Movement in Judaism*. New York, 1931.

Scholem, G. G., *Major Trends in Jewish Mysticism*. New York, 1946.

Smith, Henry Preserved, *The Religion of Israel*. New York, 1914.

Wallis, L., *The Bible is Human*. New York, 1943.

CHRISTIANITY

The Catholic Encyclopedia. New York, 1928.

The Catholic Catechism (Cardinal Gasparri). New York, 1932.

Adam, Karl, *The Spirit of Catholicism*. New York, 1931.

Angus, S., *The Environment of Early Christianity*. New York, 1928.

Atkins, G. G., *The Making of the Christian Mind*. Garden City, 1928.

Ayer, J. C., *A Source Book for Ancient Church History*. New York, 1913.

Bettenson, Henry, editor, *Documents of the Christian Church*. Oxford, 1947.

Bevan, E. R., *Hellenism and Christianity*. London, 1921.

Briggs, C. A., *History of the Study of Theology*, 2 vols. New York, 1916.

Case, S. J., *The Social Origins of Christianity*. Chicago, 1923.

Edman, Irwin, *The Mind of Paul*. New York, 1933.

Enslin, M. S., *The Ethics of Paul*. New York, 1930.

Foakes-Jackson, F. J., *An Introduction to the History of Christianity*, A.D. *590-1314*. New York, 1921.

Goodspeed, Edgar J., *Paul*. Philadelphia, 1947.

Grant, F. C., *The Gospel of the Kingdom*. New York, 1940.

Harnack, Adolf von, *History of Dogma*, 7 vols. Boston, 1896-1900.

Inge, W. R., *Protestantism*. London, 1928.

Kidd, B. J., *A History of the Church to 461*, 3 vols. Oxford, 1922.

——, *The Churches of Eastern Christendom, from* A.D. *451 to the Present*. London, 1925.

Klausner, Joseph, *Jesus of Nazareth*. New York, 1925.

Latourette, K. S., *History of the Expansion of Christianity*, 7 vols. New York, 1937-45.

McGiffert, A. C., *A History of Christian Thought*, 2 vols. New York, 1932-33.

——, *Protestant Thought Before Kant*. New York, 1911.

MacKinnon, J., *Luther and the Reformation*, 4 vols. London, 1925-30.

Moehlman, C. H., *The Story of Christianity in Outline*. Rochester, 1930.

Niebuhr, H. R., *The Social Sources of Denominationalism*. New York, 1929.

Ricciotti, G., *The Life of Christ*. New York, 1945.

Schaff, P., *History of the Christian Church*, 7 vols. New York, 1882-1900.

——, *The Creeds of Christendom*, 3 vols. New York, 1890.

Scott, E. F., *The Ethical Teachings of Jesus*. New York, 1925.

Stuber, S. I., *How We Got Our Denominations*. New York, 1927.

Sullivan, John F., *The Visible Church*. New York, 1920.

Troeltsch, E., *The Social Teaching of the Christian Churches*. New York, 1931.

Walker, Williston, *A History of the Christian Church*. New York, 1918.

CONTEMPORARY PROBLEMS

Atkins, G. G., *Modern Religious Cults and Movements*. New York, 1923.

Aubrey, E. E., *Present Theological Tendencies*. New York, 1936.

Baillie, John, *The Interpretation of Religion*. New York, 1933.

Barth, Karl, *The Word of God and the Word of Man*. Boston, 1928.

Brightman, E. S., *A Philosophy of Religion*. New York, 1940.

Dewey, John, *A Common Faith*. New Haven, 1921.

Fanfani, A., *Catholicism, Protestantism, Capitalism*. London, 1935.

Haydon, A. E., *Biography of the Gods*. New York, 1942.

Hegel, G. W. F., *Lectures on the Philosophy of Religion*. London, 1895.

Hickman, F. S., *Introduction to the Psychology of Religion*. New York, 1926.

Hocking, E. W., *The Meaning of God in Human Experience*. New Haven, 1912.

Horton, W. M., *Theism and the Modern Mood*. New York, 1930.

James, William, *Varieties of Religious Experience*. New York, 1929. (Many editions.)

Macintosh, D. C., *Social Religion*. New York, 1939.

MacMurry, John, *The Structure of Religious Experience*. New Haven, 1936.

Maritain, J., *Religion and Culture*. London, 1912.

Marrett, R. R., *The Threshold of Religion*. London, 1914.

Mathews, S., *The Growth of the Idea of God*. New York, 1931.

Moore, J. M., *Theories of Religious Experience*. New York, 1938.

Morris, Charles, *Paths of Life: Preface to a World Religion*. New York, 1942.

Niebuhr, Reinhold, *The Nature and Destiny of Man*, 2 vols. New York, 1941-43.

Otto, Rudolf, *Mysticism East and West*. New York, 1932.

——, *The Idea of the Holy*. London, 1925.

Santayana, George, *Reason in Religion* (Vol. II of *The Life of Reason*). New York, 1906-16.

Sturzo, Luigi, *Church and State*. London, 1939.

Turner, J. E., *Religion in Essence and Manifestation*. London, 1938.

Underhill, Evelyn, *Mysticism*. New York, 1919.

——, *Worship*. New York, 1937.

Wach, Joachim, *Sociology of Religion*. Chicago, 1944.

White, A. D., *A History of the Warfare of Science and Theology*, 2 vols. New York, 1896.

Whitehead, A. N., *Religion in the Making*. New York, 1930.

Wieman, Henry and Regina, *Normative Psychology of Religion*. New York, 1935.

INDEX

Solomon, 225
Soma, 64 f.
Song of Songs, Book of, 444
Sophirim, 277
Sophists, 249
Soul, Primitive religions, 35 f.; Upanishads, 81 ff.; early Buddhism, 114 ff.; see also Mass for the Dead, Paul, St. Augustine, Scholasticism
Southern Kingdom (Judah), 231
Spencer, Herbert, 499, 507
Spirit, indwelling, 344, 348
Spirits, 20 f.
"Spiritual Israel," 330
Stalin, Joseph, 513
Stephen, 272
Stoicism, 18, 268, 271, 315 ff., 324, 328, 337, 353, 359
Suiko Tenno, 182
Sukkot, see Tabernacles, Feast of
Summa Theologica, 411 ff.
Sunday, 366
Sunday Schools, 480 f., 507
Sun Gods, Vedic, 57 ff.; Canaanite, 215
Supernaturalism, 113, 477; see also Nonnatural
Sūrya, 57 f., 70, 105
Susa-no-wo, 184 f.
Sutta Pitaka, 143
Swedenborgians, 455
Synagogue, 238, 258, 264 f., 276, 281, 286, 292, 298, 330
Syncretism, 328, 340, 501, 505

Synods, 348
Syria, 227

Tabernacles, Feast of, 286
Taboo, 10
Tagore, Rabindranath, 501
T'ai Hsu, 504
Talmud, 275 ff., 292 ff., 296, 299 f., 302, 305, 306
Tannaim, 277
Tantras, 148, 174, 176, 178, 181, 188 f., 191, 205
Tantrism, 150
Tao, 156 ff.
Tao Hsüan, 169
Taoism, 158 ff., 163, 168, 170, 172, 205, 503, 505, 510
Tao-Te-King, 158 ff.
Tao Yuan, 505
Tārā, 105
Tekoa, 428
Teleology, 415
Temple, 29 f.; Jerusalem, 258, 266 f., 275, 277, 281, 292, 298, 303, 332
Temporal, Upanishads, 78 ff.
Ten Commandments, see Decalogue
Tendai Sect, 171, 507
Tenno, Jummu, see Jummu Tenno
Tetzel, 432
Teutons, 388
Thales, 248
Theism, 5, 492 f.
Theocracy, Geneva, 442 ff.
Theodosius, 367